For

Christ and Country

RADIO MESSAGES BROADCAST IN

THE NINTH LUTHERAN HOUR

By

WALTER A. MAIER, PH. D.

Professor of the Old Testament
Concordia Theological Seminary
Saint Louis, Missouri

"Hear the Word of the Lord,
O ye nations, and declare it in
the isles afar off."
—*Jeremiah 31:10*

St. Louis, Mo.
CONCORDIA PUBLISHING HOUSE
1942

FOREWORD

AFTER the December 7 attack on Pearl Harbor, religious broadcasting was put to a new test. Would the radioed Gospel of Jesus Christ continue to find the ready response with which it had been blessed during peace times? Would the hearts of the hearers be too distracted by news reports from battle fronts to heed the message of redemption? Would there be an outspoken protest against the appeal for repentance and return to God which Christian churches — even when using the channels of the air and during the stress of war — must proclaim unwaveringly? — These questions called for answer after the Japanese planes had swooped down on our Hawaiian naval base. For, contrary to widespread opinion, years of international strife generally do not advance the cause of Christ's kingdom. War does not lead the masses to their Savior.

Praised be our heavenly Father, all these problems were solved in a marvelous way! During its ninth season our mission of the air experienced the widest and richest blessings since the beginning of this radio endeavor. The results were far beyond human understanding, exceeding even our highest expectations, and to the gracious God who alone can achieve such marvels be all glory, every word of honor, each tribute of recognition!

The Lutheran Hour broadcasting chain last season was the largest we have ever employed. No fewer than 223 stations in the United States featured our message. These were affiliates of the Mutual Broadcasting System or supplementary independent outlets carrying the live program or using transcriptions. The Gospel message of the crucified Savior was also proclaimed over 123 stations in

the following twenty-five countries outside the United
States and Alaska:

Argentina	Cuba	Nicaragua
Bolivia	Dominican Republic	Panama
Brazil	Dutch Guiana	Paraguay
British Guiana	Ecuador	Peru
Canada	Haiti	Philippine Islands
Chile	Hawaii	Puerto Rico
China	Honduras	Uruguay
Colombia	Mexico	Venezuela
Costa Rica		

The restrictions and ravages of war were disastrous
to some of our foreign work. In China, the Lutheran
Hour, which continued for some weeks even after the
United States entered hostilities, was finally discontinued.
The most serious setback sustained, however, was the loss
of KZRM in Manila. This 50,000-watt superpower station
had previously covered the entire Far East from inland
China to Australia and New Zealand. Shortly before the
Japanese seized Manila, the management of KZRM dis-
mantled its equipment.

With the outbreak of war Lutheran Hour short-wave
programs for the Orient were also interrupted. We regret
especially the loss of Station KGEI in San Francisco, which
was heard in India and a thousand miles up the Yangtze
River in China. Most serious of the reverses sustained
in consequence of the world conflict was our inability to
add stations which had promised their participation but
which were prevented from joining the Bringing-Christ-
to-the-Nations system because of military restrictions,
Japanese occupation, or transportation difficulties. For
example, we had the invitation to submit Dutch programs
for an East Indies network. We were assured of an outlet
in North India. Two cities in Africa had requested our

broadcast. Negotiations were under way for Australian stations. These and other opportunities for extending the Kingdom's call were denied us. We pray God, however, that with the cessation of hostilities — and may we soon be granted an honorable, righteous peace! — we will not only regain these outlets, but also add many more countries to the nation-roster in this radio mission. It is our constant hope that the Lutheran Hour will be an all-through-the-year, all-around-the-world glorification of the Savior.

Even the war brought compensations, however. Notable among these were the invitation to broadcast in British Guiana, in Dutch Guiana, and particularly in Iceland. As these lines are printed, transcriptions are on their way to the superpower, 100,000-watt station in Reykjavik. The first programs will go out in English and, under divine blessing, should be heard not only by American soldiers in Iceland but also by masses throughout England, Scotland, and Ireland. It is hoped that we may soon use also the Icelandic language.

Particularly gratifying were the Spanish broadcasts in Latin America. Here, despite predictions to the contrary and repeated efforts to nullify our work, the preaching of the full Gospel was warmly received. A number of striking recollections like these stand out in our memory: The letter from a missionary at Tegucigalpa, Honduras, who wrote us that on the Epiphany festival only eighty women and children, besides two men, worshiped in the cathedral, while across the plaza a crowd heard the Lutheran Hour. — Five hundred and eighty-two letters in a single mail from Stations CX16 and CX24 in Montevideo, Uruguay! — The owner of Station CC133 in Chillan, Chile, who wrote us that he would consider our program but could not promise to use it, yet who, after hearing the transcriptions, not only accepted them but also secured two additional outlets in Chile for us. — The group of non-Lutheran pastors in Cuba who use our transcriptions in their churches after the stations have finished with them. — The Aztec Indians at Milpa Alta, D. F., Mexico, who regularly listen to the Lutheran Hour and have difficult Spanish terms explained to them by an Aztec student at the National Polytechnical Institute in Mexico City. — The "intellectuals" of Ciudad Trujillo, Dominican Republic, who week after week hear our broadcast over Station HIT and who have written that their country needs this truth more than anything else in the world. — The large and progressive Spanish newspapers in metropolitan centers — *El Pueblo,* Banes; *Luz* and *El Pais,* Havana, Cuba; *La Nacion,* Ciudad Trujillo, Dominican Republic; *La Tribuna,* Tampico, Mexico; *El Tiempo,* Caracas, Venezuela; *El Cronista,* Tegucigalpa, Honduras, which have generously given our broadcast prominent, even front-page publicity. — The burdened listener in Port au Prince, Haiti, who wrote: "Your broadcast proved a great blessing. It was like an oasis in this desert." — Friends in Cali, Colombia, who pleaded that the Lutheran Hour be heard even more frequently. — A Protestant leader in Puerto Rico, who has repeatedly expressed the desire to have the congregations affiliated with his group, the Council of Christian Churches, become associated with our Church, to send theological students to our seminaries, use our Spanish literature, and in other ways work closely with us. — These and similar happy experiences in Latin America, too numerous for recording, have brought much joy during the ninth broadcasting season.

Those who have worked, prayed, and given financial support for this radio mission will rejoice to know that the mail response has been larger than ever before. No fewer than 260,000 letters were received at Lutheran Hour

headquarters and at our office. Naturally most of these came from the United States, but many were received from listeners in thirty-five countries. Correspondence was addressed to us in Norwegian, Swedish, Danish, Dutch, German, French, Spanish, Portuguese, Hungarian, Slovak, Polish, and Chinese. Letters from the blind were written in Braille, New York Point, and Moon type.

A new department in this mission of the air was directed to help the men called to the nation's colors. We sought to bring Gospel appeals systematically to the Army, Navy, Air, Marine camps and bases throughout the country. Here, too, divine favor rested unmistakably on our efforts. Military men in hundreds of camps throughout this country and some abroad wrote us that they were strengthened. Letters from Pearl Harbor were unusually interesting. There, on that fateful Sunday, sailors on a battleship sunk within a few hours, were listening to the Lutheran Hour, heard in Hawaii at 7:30 on Sunday morning. The broadcast was hardly finished when the Japanese bombs began their destruction. A pastor writes for one of these young men:

Our sailor friend, by the grace of God, came through unscathed. He cannot help but feel that the Lutheran Hour which he had just heard gave him strength in those dangerous moments when life was hanging by a thin thread and that his Savior's guarding hand alone kept him safe through that ordeal.

A soldier from Fort Benning, Georgia, sent his entire month's pay of twenty-one dollars to support the radio mission. Notable as the first coast-to-coast religious broadcast in history to originate in a United States Army Camp was the Lutheran Hour which emanated from the Headquarters' Chapel, Fort Leonard Wood, Missouri, on November 30, 1941.

One of the special services extended the nation's military

men was the offer of Christian literature, tracts, periodicals, particularly the Lutheran Hour prayer book, *My Daily Prayer Guide,* and the Army and Navy Commission *Service Prayer Book.* How this material was appreciated may be seen in this letter from a sailor aboard a fighting ship:

The prayer book you sent me is one of the nicest presents I have ever received, and I have enjoyed its use very much. I would also like to report that it has been instrumental in arousing the interest of at least one of my shipmates. I have spoken to him various times, but never could seem to make the way of justification by faith clear to him. So, on receipt of the book, after having looked through the first few pages, which show it so clearly, I immediately asked him to read it. He seemed very much impressed and said, "Now I see what you mean by justification by faith." He has borrowed my Bible, and I pray that he may soon be saved. We have listened regularly to the Lutheran Hour for over a year whenever regulations would permit use of radios. It is a grand feeling to hear "the old, old story" go out in such power to so many.

Encouraging, too, were the letters received from those enlisted in the Canadian forces. An Ontario father wrote:

Recently I received from my oldest son, who is with the Royal Air Force in the Canadian West, five dollars with the request that I forward the amount to you in support of the broadcasts. Though my son is now away from home and cannot tune in regularly, he does so when opportunity affords and derives spiritual enjoyment therefrom. We have another son in training for the Air Force in Toronto. Last week he was home and told us of a young habitual gambler with whom he remonstrated, knowing that he listens to the Lutheran Hour. The reply to the remonstrance was to the effect that there is an irresistible force about the broadcast that compels him to tune in and listen. The Holy Spirit evidently is working! We pray for the conversion of that young man.

To a more astonishing degree than ever previously this Bringing-Christ-to-the-Nations mission has demonstrated the remarkable penetration which has made the radio the

most potent agency for the far-reaching spread of the Gospel. A young aviator, ferrying a bomber to Europe, wrote: "I have heard the Lutheran Hour 20,000 feet above the Brazilian jungle." Another letter tells of our message being received aboard the submarine *Sailfish*. And between these heights and depths the Gospel of our crucified Lord has been proclaimed over wide areas as never before. From remote Alaskan districts; isolated Canadian settlements near Hudson Bay or Fisherman's Cove, Newfoundland; through Nova Scotia, our own country, to Gulf of Mexico islands off Panama, where missionaries, away from civilization for months at a time, work among the San Blas Indians; throughout thousands of Spanish-speaking communities in South America, the Lutheran Hour has testified to the only hope that men can ever have — faith in Jesus Christ. A Christian worker among the western Indians writes:

All last year when I was away back in the river country, inland, I used to listen with a little battery set. No one knows how much it means when you are out alone in the places of gross darkness. Many of the Indians who have found the Lord as their personal Savior listen, too, and are blessed. They, of course, could not write and tell you their feelings about the hour; so you see many are helped that you will never know about.

A woman who had heard the Lutheran Hour in China testifies:

We found little spiritual life here; so when we were able to hear your program, we felt that we had discovered an oasis in the desert of Shanghai life.

No other agency is able to penetrate into homes closed to the Christian message or into religious institutions which would exclude our message; yet letters like this, written by a distracted Tennessee father, often come to us:

My great sorrow lies in the fact that my older daughter has been for nearly six years a Dominican sister. She has even taken the final vow. I know now with greater certainty each passing day that my child cannot be saved by indulgences, her own self-denial or anything except faith in the substitutionary offering of God's Son, who "bore our sins in His own body on the cross." I try, as I write to her week by week, to bring this fact to her understanding and acceptance, but until recently got no response from her. Then on my pastor's advice I asked her to tune in the Lutheran Hour. She replied that one of the older sisters has her own radio. In a letter received today she declared: "Sister B—— got Dr. Maier on her radio yesterday. She said he is on the Lutheran Hour, but she enjoyed hearing him and asked me to tell you." The "but" was something to smile at; but who knows what may have begun?

Year after year the mail from people outside our Church has steadily increased.

We have frequently commented on the service which the radio renders those confined to hospitals, old folks' homes, asylums, and public institutions, including prisons and schools of correction. During the past season this work was intensified. Many touching stories show that if the Lutheran Hour did nothing else than bring Jesus' comfort to these multitudes, it would more than justify the expense it entails.

The missionary task in Bringing Christ to the Nations starts with introducing the Savior's message to American hearts and homes ruled by unbelief. In this endeavor, we thank God, the broadcast has proved itself a valuable asset to our pastors. Expressing sentiments frequently voiced by Lutheran clergymen, a young missionary in North Carolina writes:

When I recently accepted the call as pastor to our newest mission in the Southeastern District, it was with pleasure that I learned that Raleigh and vicinity were covered by the Lutheran Hour through WRAL. In my brief ministry here I have received some of the most encouraging results from the Bringing-Christ-to-the-Nations program. Although I have been here only a little more than a month, I already have begun instructing my second group of adults for membership. When the first class was only half through the course, others had requested instruction. I take no credit for this sudden harvest of souls; the Lutheran Hour deserves and received the credit. I cannot express the great help the radio mission has been in paving the way for our future and successful work, under God, in this part of our country.

Through the Spirit's power the broadcast has similarly helped open the door for many brethren; it has removed from masses an entirely erroneous opinion of our Church; it has strengthened Gospel preaching in other religious circles. Especially has it served Christians in remote districts who have no access to a true, Biblical congregation. For all this, once more, all glory to God!

We cannot adequately thank our heavenly Father for the actual conversions and definite reconsecrations which the Holy Spirit has wrought through the ninth season's broadcasting. It would take a volume much larger than this to recount the stories of those who attribute their conversion to God's grace as proclaimed in the Lutheran Hour; yet from their correspondence we present snatch sentences like these to show what marvels God, and He alone, has wrought:

California: Thanks to your broadcast, my husband, under God, is now a Lutheran. . . . I rejoice that the Lutheran Hour has made our family all of one faith.

Ohio: Before the throne of God on the great Judgment Day, I shall be one of those who say, "You helped get me to heaven."

District of Columbia: I am sincerely grateful that you sent your pastor to help me. I have decided to be baptized soon in his church.

Michigan: A lady recently approached me, saying that her parents had belonged to another denomination, but when the Lutheran Hour came on the air and brought the pure doctrine of Scripture to them, they soon decided to join the Lutheran Church. Never having been a Christian up to that time, she also learned from her parents the joy of true faith in Christ, listened to your broadcast, joined the Lutheran Church and has been a devout member ever since.

Illinois: Mrs. C—— found the truth in the message of the Lutheran Hour and expressed her joy over the fact by tithing to this radio program. She soon began to take instructions and has now become a very zealous church worker.

Oklahoma: On March 1 we had the unusual and happy experience of accepting twenty-nine adults into membership through conversion and on April 12 another class of thirteen adults. Naturally, their decision is due entirely to the miracle-working power of the Holy Spirit, through the Word, and glory for their coming to the faith belongs to God; but humanly speaking, they were interested in listening to the Word after they had heard the Lutheran Hour.

Missouri: Your broadcast played an important part in my husband's conversion and baptism.

Missouri: Your letter came just before the school term opened. I went to the minister and joined the church and enrolled my daughter in the Lutheran day school.

Massachusetts: After your broadcast a Jewish person, who was listening with me, accepted Jesus as her personal Savior. May the Lord bless you!

Wyoming: I am so happy that I found the Church that preaches the truth! I am going to be baptized soon. I have just a few more lessons in my Catechism, and then I shall be ready. I was saved by listening to the Lutheran Hour.

Illinois: My husband joined the Church after we were married. He heard several broadcasts, then had a talk with our minister, and secured instruction immediately. That is why I feel such gratitude toward your broadcasts.

Oregon: It is my desire, after reading and studying the literature which you sent, to unite with the Lutheran Church.

Hawaii: I do not belong to the Lutheran Church but would like to become a member. My husband is a member of the Missouri Synod; so I would like to have some information about it.

Missouri: Last fall you wrote me about Mrs. M——. She and her brother subsequently joined our adult class and have been received into membership.

Massachusetts: It was only by accident that I discovered how two of my members, converts from Roman Catholicism, were led into our midst. Through the Lutheran Hour they were prompted to search for a Lutheran church, and so they came to us.

Ohio: It was through your radio ministry that I accepted Christ, and I am sure there are thousands of others who have done the same.

Illinois: Your program has helped me to join the Church.

Oklahoma: Your sermons have been a great blessing to my wife and me. She was almost an unbeliever up to the time that she heard your sermons. Now our humble little home is sunshine.

Indiana: The Lutheran Hour did some great work here. I baptized a man of eighty-one who had been a scoffer all of his life and never before had any use for the Church. He is now a changed man.

Pennsylvania: I was a backslider but found Christ again through your broadcasts.

Wyoming: We have recently talked with a Lutheran minister and have arranged to take instructions. The decision of the three of us for the Lutheran Church was made because of your broadcast.

Missouri: I want to tell you how much your Gospel broadcasts have meant to me. After listening to your programs I resolved to join Saint Stephen's Lutheran Church, because the pastor preaches the Gospel in the same way you preach it, basing all on the Word of God. I want this testimony to encourage the broadcasting of Christ's Gospel.

For these, as countless other records of conversion and reconsecration, we praise and bless God's holy name, as we also thank those who have helped sustain and continue the broadcast. First of all, we are grateful to our own pastors who have endorsed the Lutheran Hour, calling their members' attention to its work, visiting prospects, and sending us lines of personal encouragement. Likewise, we are indebted to many Christian day-school teachers, whose vital work we have constantly tried to emphasize, and to the many eager, consecrated workers in the laity.

The co-operation of Christians outside our circles has been especially welcome. Although this is a Lutheran broadcast in title and in spirit, they have recognized that we have but one chief purpose — to exalt the Scriptural teachings concerning the Lord Jesus, the only but complete Savior of mankind. They have found in the Lutheran Hour emphasis on the Bible as the literally inspired Word of God and in its constant stress on repentance and personal faith in Christ's atonement, the Gospel message required for this distracted age. By their prayers, gifts, and personal testimony they have courageously leaped over denominational lines to promote our cause. Oh, that God would give all who love His Son as their Redeemer and acknowledge His Word as infallible, a complete doctrinal unity and the privileges of unlimited fellowship!

The loyalty to the Lutheran Hour which these letters expressed was proved by the most generous financial support our radio mission has ever received. It will not be difficult for the reader to understand how much encouragement the Lutheran Hour staff received from incidents like these: A Wisconsin nurse (whose fiancé died) had the linens of her trousseau sold and the proceeds sent to our treasury. — A New Jersey woman, hearing the broadcast for the first time, immediately mailed a check for $300. — A Hawaiian listener has given us, almost every two weeks over a ten-week period, two United States money orders totaling $150. — A Michigan friend forwarded $1,000 through a relative. — An eight-year-old Kansas lad wrote, "I am sending one dollar, which I earned at my Dad's barber shop shining shoes to help the cause of the Lutheran Hour on the air." — Philippine listeners mailed gifts in pesos. — A Pennsylvania man created a thirty-dollar Lutheran Hour annuity in his will. — An Illinois housewife saved a five-cent contribution every day out of her grocery budget and said, "We never feel it." — A Kansan sent $112.40, the amount of money received from an oil well that had been abandoned. — An Illinois husband and wife gave their Christmas gifts to the Lutheran Hour instead of to each other. — In few branches of our Church's work has stewardship been as generous and spontaneous as in the support of this mission. People appreciate the fact that the radio is the most inexpensive means of broadcasting the plan of salvation. It is estimated that one dollar invested in the Lutheran Hour will bring the Gospel to at least 1,500 individuals.

Publicity for our cause came from many circles outside the Church. Once again Mr. Edward C. Donnelly, Jr., of Boston, helped display large numbers of Lutheran Hour posters throughout New England, an example followed to a smaller degree by many other outdoor advertising companies. Newspapers were co-operative in calling the attention of their readers to the Lutheran Hour. It is with a sense of indebtedness to their wholehearted work that we mention particularly the following papers and commend their interest in this vast Christian enterprise: The Saint Louis *Globe-Democrat,* with its rotogravure and feature articles; the Milwaukee *Journal;* the Fort Wayne *News Sentinel;* the Fort Wayne *Journal Gazette;* the Boston *Globe* and *Herald,* for their rotogravure pictures; the Memphis *Press Scimitar* and *Commercial Appeal;* the Jackson (Tennessee) *Sun;* the Cleveland *Press;* the Rock Island *Daily Argus.*

We thank the Lutheran Laymen's League, its officials, members, keymen, and committees, for their sponsorship of this mighty missionary enterprise. How encouraging that laymen, recognizing their duty of spreading the Gospel, have supervised this widespread radio program!

Serving on the Lutheran Hour program and deserving the public acknowledgment of our thanks was the announcer, Mr. Reinhold W. Janetzke, and the Lutheran

Hour Students' Chorus, under the direction of Mr. Arthur Werfelmann. The Orion Quartet (Mr. Paul Lessmann, director) furnished the musical background for the Spanish programs, for which Mr. Manuel Morales delivered the messages. For these broadcasts, which were to be directed to Brazil, Portugal, and West African colonies, we were fortunate to have had the services of Professor Albert Lehenbauer, President of Colegio Concordia, Crespo, E. R., Argentina. While on a furlough to this country, he assumed the arduous duty of translating and delivering the Portuguese sermons. He also helped train the Portuguese Lutheran Hour Quartet (Mr. Lloyd Behnken, director). To all these and to the volunteer clerical workers of the Lutheran Business and Professional Woman's League, who regularly gave their assistance without any compensation, we say, "Thank you, and God bless you!" It may be helpful to add that no one who appears on the Lutheran Hour — the announcer, the singers, the speaker — receives a salary for these services.

This recognition would not be complete if I were not to mention especially the outstanding work of Dr. E. R. Bertermann, who has now stood at my side for five years. No task that this arduous mission could place on his shoulders has ever proved too difficult and no obstacle in its progress insurmountable.

It is also appropriate that we express our appreciation for the co-operation of the Mutual Broadcasting System. As a matter of principle this chain has refused to discriminate against independent religious programs. — While these lines are written, news is flashed that the petition of the Federal Council of the Churches of Christ in America, addressed to the annual convention of the National Broadcasters Association and of the Mutual Broadcasting System, requesting that paid religious programs be barred from the air and virtually asking that Protestant broadcasting be placed under its direction, was emphatically refused by both bodies. A subsequent appeal before the Federal Communications Commission in Washington was rejected with the same emphasis. Christians of America have every reason to thank God that such totalitarian tendencies suffered this double rebuke.

It is an additional privilege to issue these messages in printed form, enlarged to cover the various subjects more adequately than the nineteen-minute maximum on the air permits. We are indebted to Concordia Publishing House; to Miss Harriet E. Schwenk, who again read the manuscript and the proof, offering valued assistance in expediting the issuance of this volume; to Miss Lucille Biehl, who generously gave each Saturday to type the messages into their final form; and to Miss Bertha Wernsing, who by her unselfish disregard of Friday and Saturday working hours also offered much practical help. For the ninth time Professor William Arndt, D. D., Ph. D., Professor of New Testament at Concordia Seminary, read these sermons in their original form and in proof. His counsel is always Scriptural, constructive, and helpful. For this service, offered without any compensation, we extend our deep gratitude. Finally, this annual expression of thanks includes especially my wife, who has been a patient, efficient helper and counselor, not only in the production of the present volume, but throughout the discussion and solution of the many problems which the last season brought.

We have given these printed messages the title *For Christ and Country,* since no four words could more aptly summarize the double duty which imposes itself on us in these critical days. May God Almighty, with whom *"nothing shall be impossible,"* soon intervene in human affairs, so that we may have a true, blessed peace, with the promise that this mission of the air, as all Kingdom-spreading work, may be increased for the spiritual strengthening and the comfort of the masses! This book goes out into a world torn by conflict, into a country embattled in a struggle far more crucial than many anticipated. May the testimony these pages offer to the full, free, and final salvation in Jesus Christ be abundantly blessed by the Holy Spirit and used as God sees fit for the defense of His Church and our nation! May all readers find within these covers the faith and the incentive for loyalty to Christ and country!

WALTER ARTHUR MAIER

Concordia Seminary
Saint Louis, Missouri
The Festival of Pentecost, 1942

He commanded us to preach unto the people
and to testify that it is He which was ordained
of God to be the Judge of quick and dead.

The Acts 10:42

To

Mr. and Mrs. Harry J. W. Niehaus

"My helpers in Christ Jesus"

Romans 16:3

CONTENTS

XXI

NEVER NEGLECT JESUS!

"How shall we escape if we neglect so great salvation?" — Hebrews 2:3

God, the Father of Our Lord Jesus Christ:

In this world-wide distress, when millions are blindly pushed into disaster and death, teach us, above all else, to approach Thee, trusting in the full salvation, blood-bought for us on the cross, by Thy Son, our only Savior! Let Thy Spirit fill us with a contrite sense of our own unworthiness and make us realize, personally and forcefully, that if we neglect Jesus, we can never escape Thy Judgment! Turn many to Christ! Use this broadcast to convert sinners, recall the unfaithful, strengthen the weak in heart, and save many from despair over their transgressions! Bless our country in this critical hour! We plead: O Father Almighty, if it be Thy will, restore to the world peace; yes, O God of grace, help our bleeding world! But more than all else, give us inner peace with Thee and pardon for our sins through Thy Son! We ask this according to His promise. Amen.

THE deepest danger for America today is the sin of neglect. I do not mean our country's past carelessness in providing adequate defense; not the shameful waste of our natural resources that has helped turn fertile farm lands into desert dust-bowls; not the disregard of the underprivileged, underpaid, underfed millions within our borders. Incomparably more grievous is our continued ignoring of the Lord Jesus Christ, the world's Savior, the only Hope for our bewildered, bleeding age.

America should learn the fatal folly of this neglect from the horror which has gripped Europe, the continent that forgot God. Germany, mightily blessed as the land of the Reformation, produced the world's most scornful Bible critics, evil leaders of millions who rejected the glorious Gospel. And the result? Dictatorship, race hatred, militarism, appalling wars and suffering! In Russia worldly, power-seeking churches neglected Christ and helped keep the masses poor, ignorant, superstitious. The consequence? An atheistic revolution filled with crime, horror, murder! Despite frequent statements to the contrary, freedom of worship was ruthlessly restricted under the Red regime as churches were closed, their property confiscated by the government, religious papers banned, Christian schools locked, the clergy persecuted, exiled, even martyred.

France is broken, prostrate. Why? Let those who best know the reason answer! When the first Parisian newspaper appeared after the fall of that city, its editor printed this confession across the top of the front page: "Citizens of France, we are going to pay for sixty years of de-Christianization. . . . We have worn out the patience of Providence! We have disgusted the good God Himself!"

Great Britain also has suffered by neglecting Jesus. Earnest Christians in England, valiantly fighting for their country's victory, acknowledge the widespread indifference to our Lord, bemoan the unbelief that admittedly marks some of their leading clerics. Listen to a British churchman, Dr. W. Percy Hicks, who recently wrote: "As a nation we have not turned to God. We have desecrated His day, forsaken His house and neglected His Word. We have shown that we are lovers of pleasure more than lovers of God."

Can you not see, therefore, what our course must be in this crisis, when millions in the nation tremble with dread of the disasters each new day may bring? We should tirelessly warn against shelving Christ's Gospel in a day when our own sins cry to the high heavens. Crime increases. (The city of St. Louis has recorded a 50 per-cent annual upswing.) As American atheism spreads, American education becomes saturated with the denial of the Savior, and many American churches, denominations, theological seminaries, close their doors on Him. The plea and warning that would speak directly into our hearts since you, I, and 130,000,000 others like us make this nation, must be:

Never Neglect Jesus!

This is the lesson of our text for the season's first broadcast, the question of Hebrews, chapter two, verse three, *"How shall we escape if we neglect so great salvation?"*

I

FAITH IN CHRIST OFFERS *"GREAT SALVATION"*

The salvation mentioned in these words is the rescue from sin, the deliverance from eternal death, the triumph over hell and the pledge of heaven which is yours and mine, since Jesus Christ, the only Savior of mankind, suffered on the cross for our transgressions, bore their full guilt in His own battered body, died the death of all men, and then — Praise be His love and power! — rising from the grave, broke death's cold grip on our lives, to give us a blessed eternity, face to face with Him, the King of kings, the Lord of lords, the "very God of very God." All this and nothing less Christ pledges whenever you hear this word *"salvation."*

All this and nothing less our broadcasts, which today begin their ninth season, would bring straight to your soul. As I speak from the campus of one of the country's largest divinity schools — and during the 102 years of its history not a single Christ-denier, skeptic, or Bible critic has served on its faculties or boards — I promise you, with one hand raised toward the cross placed high on our radio tower and the other hand resting on the Bible, that each message will offer you the surety of salvation in Jesus. Repeatedly I am urged to use our Gospel network for the support of partisan politics, racial hatred, and war projects; but, *"My kingdom is not of this world,"* our Lord Himself declares;

time is short, men's souls are dying, and my Savior's mercy is so marvelous that no substitute "gospel" will ever push the blessing of His cleansing blood to the background of this radio mission. The world may hate Christ; diplomats may ignore Him; unbelieving preachers betray Him; dictators dethrone Him; atheists blaspheme Him, — yet this Bringing-Christ-to-the-Nations broadcast, God helping us, your support strengthening us, will proclaim Jesus, first, last, forever uppermost, as the great God, the Redeemer of the entire race. If during the coming months with their uncertainty and the increasing probability of war this exaltation of our Savior should be barred from the air — Pray God it will not be removed! — our almighty Father who can make the stones cry in witness to His truth will bring us back in His time with stronger power and increased blessing.

This *"salvation"* is called *"great"* in our text; and it is *"great"* beyond words because it comes from the Lord of heaven Himself. Think of it, God, who scattered the stars across the measureless expanse of the universe, the Creator to whom the highest mountains are but as specks of dust, the deepest oceans merely dwindling water drops, the largest armies only powerless shadows — that holy, omnipotent God took time to love *you, you* especially, *you* individually, *you,* despite your sins and sorrows. You may be lonely, pushed to the side, hated in your own home; but may the Spirit help me to show that through Christ you have a heavenly Father who has mercy, help, and heaven for you!

His *"salvation"* is *"great,"* immeasurably *"great,"* because of the price it demanded. We are accustomed to the mention of multiplied billions in this age of easy money (though I shudder to picture the day of reckoning and the hardships then to be placed on the churches); yet the staggering totals spent throughout the world, hundreds of millions of dollars every day for the purpose of destroying men, would not be enough to pay your way into heaven. You were *"bought with a price,"* the supreme price of all history, the highest the great God Himself could offer. The Father gave His Son, Jesus gave His loving, sinless Self to atone for your iniquities, to bring you back to God, to give you a sure title to a prepared place in the many mansions. Never have heaven and earth witnessed a costlier payment than Christ's crimson blood by which we were ransomed from death.

Your salvation is *"great,"* indescribably *"great,"* also because it is offered freely, without payment, by the most magnificent mercy sinners can ever receive. Your redemption cost Jesus a fearful price; but it costs you nothing. You can come to the Savior just as you are, without fee or price. You need only say: "O Christ, my sins crush me. I hardly dare draw near You. There is nothing good or praiseworthy in me. But I am sorry for my transgressions and, O Jesus, I believe with my whole heart that on the cross You became my Substitute and Atonement. Forgive me, bless me, help me!" And the Savior whose arms are outstretched to the weary and heavy laden will reply: *"Be of good cheer, thy sins be forgiven thee." "Thy faith hath saved thee."*

This blood-bought salvation is *"great,"* altogether too *"great"* for sinful, selfish men because of its world-wide, all-inclusive extent. No one hearing these words now broadcast across the country or later to reach South America, Asia, Africa, the islands of the sea, should ever doubt that the full blessing of Christ's Gospel can be his. Man's cruelty may deprive you of many earthly advantages, and your own transgressions may destroy happiness, peace, even freedom; but when you read this summary of divine grace, *"God so loved the world, that He gave His only-begotten Son, that whosoever believeth in Him should not perish but have everlasting life,"* remember that you have never sinned too grievously to be received, if penitent and believing, by the Savior of whom it is written, *"He died for all"!* Not long ago, a prisoner serving a life sentence in a Wisconsin penitentiary for murdering his wife, wrote us for help. In the depth of his misery, thinking that he had fallen too far from grace ever to be forgiven, he heard of Christ through our broadcasts and asked whether the Savior would have mercy for him. We sent a pastor to bring him peace in Jesus. He was instructed in the faith; the same Savior who says: *"Him that cometh to Me I will in no wise cast out,"* has pardoned, cleansed, and now received him as His own.

Once more this *"salvation"* is *"great"* because of its absolute truth and certainty. Blessed by the full Christian faith, you never need be torn by doubt as to whether you are saved. Looking to Jesus, you know with unwavering conviction that *"salvation"* is assured, since you are His and He says of His own, *"Neither shall any man pluck them out of My hand."* — Is not this the positive, immovable confidence for which you yearn in these grim, forbidding days? Come what may, extended war or — God grant it! — constructive peace, depression or prosperity, sickness or health, home life for better or for worse, if Christ is yours, you have an inner joy that no blasts of bombs, blood of conflict, suffering and destruction, can remove. Every sorrow you may endure, as a redeemed child of God, will finally work for your good.

II

NEGLECT OF CHRIST BRINGS INESCAPABLE JUDGMENT

Now, with its immeasurable greatness, matchless mercy, love beyond compare, God's promise of *"salvation"* should be the most highly prized of all benedictions. If we stop to realize what shame and agony Jesus endured for us when

He bore our sins; if we survey the endless blessings with which He enriches us for life and death, we must wonder why the doors of our Christian churches are not stormed by masses determined to claim the Savior their own, why Jesus is not revered throughout the world, the Bible exalted in every home, the Gospel treasured in each heart, its power proved in every life. Instead, too many neglect the Son of God. They hear that Jesus died for them, that as their God He offers the solution to every problem, the lightening for every burden; but they shrug their shoulders indifferently.

Some of you are too busy with the entangling affairs of your business, your profession, your work, your pleasure, your social life, to find time for Jesus, who devoted His lifetime to you. People stand in line all night to secure front row seats for baseball series; they travel hundreds of miles to attend football games; but it is expecting too much, we are told, to think that they should set aside an hour on Sunday for worshiping their God and Savior.

Others turn a deaf ear to Christ because they love sin. They do not wish to be disturbed in their secret affairs or favorite vices. But they know that if they come to Christ, these must be renounced. They are making money in sinful occupation, finding pleasure in breaking God's law of purity. They derive too much sensual satisfaction from following their own lusts to heed the Savior's call for repentance and faith. So they pass Jesus and heedlessly turn their faces from the only Savior they can ever have.

Still others spurn their salvation because Jesus seems to offer little of practical value, dollars-and-cents profit, everyday comfort. They like soft religions with all the alleged answers to questions concerning the ease of life. They prefer the new sects that have mushroomed over the land (more than fifty new creeds sprang up within the last ten years) to take the place of the old Gospel, to supplant the old cross, to push aside the old, unchanging atonement of grace.

Many of you, however, are discarding Jesus against better knowledge. You grew up in a Christian home. God-fearing parents brought you to the Savior, taught you to pray. You were baptized and accepted as church members. Some of you became leaders in youth groups, officials in your congregations. You were happy to sing in the choir, attend Bible class, work actively for the spread of the Gospel. — Now you have turned away from Jesus, lost the faith and for years have not seen the inside of a church.

And how many there are among you who trifle with Christ, wavering between accepting or rejecting His grace! You see the benefits of the Gospel. Your conscience tells you to accept the Savior. But you reject every plea that would make you decide for Jesus, saying: "What is the hurry? Let me think this over again! Tomorrow, not today." During this delay and postponement you may be summoned to eternity, too suddenly even for the death-bed repentance on which many build their hopes.

Whatever the reason for this negligence may be, more than half the people in this country, blessed by the Almighty as no other nation since the beginning of history, are so utterly indifferent to the Lord Jesus that they have never acclaimed Him the Redeemer of their souls, the Guardian of their lives. American homes disregard the Christ. How many families are there throughout this radio assembly in which our Lord's presence is exalted as the highest benediction on the home or in which His help is invoked daily by Scripture reading, prayer, and sacred song? American schools sometimes oppose Christ, and I mean our tax-supported higher educational systems, often outspokenly anti-Christian, as well as the large colleges and universities not under State control. Here the young people of 1941, the leaders in 1951 and 1961, are being trained for their responsibilities without Jesus, often against Him and everything for which He stands. Even many American churches are pushing Jesus aside. A few years ago Calvin Coolidge declared: "I think most of the clergy today are preaching socialism. . . . The Church must preach a new birth." And in the eight years since his death the number of pulpits featuring economics, politics, ethics or seeking to enflame the passions of hatred, but omitting Christ as God and Savior, has increased enormously. — Consequently the American way of life often completely discards Jesus. True, men speak of God vaguely and mystically; but the only God who can ever save us and besides whom there can be none other is the everblessed Trinity: Father, Son, and Holy Spirit. Our age has much to say about religion; it herds all creeds together as though no differences separated them; yet only one religion can sustain us in this crisis — faith in the atoning, sin-removing death and resurrection of Jesus Christ. Men have much praise for the Bible, although somehow public speakers generally avoid passages mentioning the Lord Jesus, His cross, His blood, His death; but the only faith that can ever help a man or a nation is the acceptance of God's errorless truth centering in Christ's redemption.

How timely, personal, forceful, then, is the question of our text, *"How shall we escape if we neglect so great salvation?"* There is a sure retribution for disregarding Christ, and its penalty is often executed during this life. Many of you suffer because you have turned from Jesus. You have been defeated by continued sorrow and adversity, money trouble and home trouble, worry about your work and business, fear concerning the health of your body or mind; for while the Savior, ready to share your burdens, pleaded, *"Come unto Me!"* you spurned Him and deliberately invited these sorrows as God's punishment. Even if you shout back that you have escaped all this and now earn twice as much as a year ago, that you have never been sick or sorry, I still say the time is coming when, boastful, self-confident, neglectful of Christ, you must stand before the divine judgment. You will not always have inflation salaries. You cannot keep your health, your haughty pride, your sinful life forever. Disaster may even now be knocking at your door. Tomorrow death may reach out for you. What then? The Bible answers, *"We must all appear before the judgment seat of Christ."* Will you be able to stand before the all-holy God with your unforgiven sins, brazen rebellion, slavery to your passions, when His truth insists, *"The soul that sinneth, it shall die"?* Here is the hardest sentence for human lips to speak: Without Jesus to take away your sins and restore you to the Father, you are doomed to eternal death, forever banished from God, self-sentenced to the hell that fearful men try to deny, although it is as real as heaven itself.

When I thus repeat what God's infallible Word proclaims in a hundred places, "Without Christ you are lost," I must add the crushing word, "forever." When Scripture today asks, *"How shall we escape?"* it answers pointedly, "There is no escape." Prisoners have managed to find their way out of the Bastille of Paris. They have escaped from Siberia's exile or Devil's Island's torture. They have dug through the strongest penitentiary walls or built long tunnels beneath war-prison barricades, but no one who neglects Christ can outrun God's avenging retribution. A few spots remain on the face of the earth whither criminals may flee beyond the long reach of justice, but if you should try to elude the Almighty in flight to darkest Africa, the lonely South Sea Islands, or the uninhabited vastness of the Arctic, His all-seeing eye would still discover you.

If even Federal authorities can bring draft dodgers back across the ocean, how can you expect to be a successful fugitive from the all-knowing God?

Those who break man's law often avoid punishment through bribery and corruption; the records of American courts reveal repeated instances of graft; but you cannot buy your way out of God's court. You will never have enough money to purchase release from His judgment. Master minds use legal tricks and perjured testimony in cheating the law; but you will never be smart enough to deceive God and argue yourself out of paying the full penalty for every unforgiven sin. No college course or university degree will enable you to avoid standing face to face with the divine Judge.

You are not able to escape yourself, and neither is anyone else able to help you outrun holy justice. If two mighty nations had to cancel their plans for the release of wounded war prisoners, how, do you suppose, can any human influence free the prisoners of sin? Don't build false hopes on the thought that a friend or relative can take your place! When a woman was recently sentenced to meet death in the lethal gas chamber, the convicts at San Quentin Prison, California, wrote the governor proposing that lots be cast to find a substitute who would die in the place of the murderess. Their petition was refused since the law makes no provision for one man dying in the place of another. Similarly, according to God's Law men can never substitute for their fellow-sinners. Heavenly truth has decreed that *"none of them can by any means redeem his brother, nor give to God a ransom for him."* If you have been relying on the faith of your parents, the prayers of a God-fearing husband or wife, the intercession of a saint or martyr, this will never save you.

Above all, don't send your soul to hell by believing that

you can live without God, blaspheme Christ, reject His Gospel and then, after death, have someone pay or pray your way into heaven! There can be no reprieve after death, no second chance beyond the grave, no intermediary stage between heaven and hell; for the record of eternal truth testifies: *"It is appointed unto men once to die, but after this the judgment."*

I have been trying to impress on your souls that when the Scriptures ask, *"How shall we escape if we neglect so great salvation?"* there will not be, either here or hereafter, any escape whatever for those who have neglected their Christ. Yet I cannot close this first message without stressing the glorious truth that full pardon for every sin and for every sinner is granted by our merciful Savior Jesus Christ. Through the simple, penitent, trusting faith which acclaims Him the God of all grace, you and I, my fellow-redeemed, can find the escape from God's wrath and the pledge of His peace, the liberation from sin and the promise of full forgiveness, the deliverance from hell and the gift of heaven. Once more let me warn you, "Never neglect Jesus!" Never, even for money, pleasure, fame, power, or for the avoidance of pain and suffering, never neglect your Savior! But let me also plead fervently with everyone of you: Give Christ your penitent and contrite heart! Approach Him in personal, sin-convicted, pardon-promising faith! Find in Him the Rock of Ages where you can break away from the treacherous tides of sin, the swirling conflict of hatred, war, bleeding anguish, to receive never-ending peace and protection! Accept Jesus now! Come to Him quickly, contritely, yet confidently; and as we rededicate these broadcasts to that Savior, we promise that He will come to you with heavenly grace, guidance, and glory! Our heavenly Father grant all of you that escape through Jesus, eternal Refuge of our souls! Amen.

THE BEAUTIFUL SAVIOR

"Thou art fairer than the children of men:
grace is poured into Thy lips." — Psalm 45:2

God of All Grace and Glory:

Gladden our hearts with the divine assurance that in the Lord Jesus
Christ everyone of us can find pardon despite our sins; peace with
Thee, though war surround us; courage even if the sorrows of
affliction threaten to overwhelm us! Mercifully look down on all
troubled souls throughout the land! Answer their prayers! Supply
their needs! Turn them to Christ! Recall them to Thy love!
Father, as we ask Thy Son's guidance for our own souls and bodies,
we entreat Thee with our whole hearts to direct our beloved nation
along the paths of truth and righteousness, to bless all in authority
with the deep desire to follow and please Thee. We have not
deserved Thy consideration, for we have too confidently leaned on
the arm of flesh, instead of putting our trust in Thy grace. Penitently we pray: Forgive us our transgressions for Jesus' sake and
help us in every hour of need! We ask it in the Savior's glorious
name. Amen.

ON a fatal September day in 1939 a weary man stood
before the House of Commons to explain why England had declared war. In a halting voice he protested
desperately, "Everything that I have worked for, everything
that I have hoped for, everything that I have believed during my public life has been crashed into ruins this morning."
This pale speaker was Neville Chamberlain, Prime Minister
of Great Britain, marked for death even as he spoke, for
he lived scarcely a year longer. Yet his song of sorrows
still goes on, intoned by millions who today cry — and some
of your voices swell this lament — "Everything that we
have worked for, everything that we have hoped for, everything that we have believed in has crashed into ruins."

How different the haughty self-assurance a quarter century ago! Then "evolution" was the watchword; "We are
on the way up!" the slogan; "On to the golden age!" the

marching cry; "No more war!" the rosy pledge. But at the height of this overconfidence the earth was ripped by the explosion of international hatred; and when the smoke of four years' struggle lifted, 8,500,000 corpses were counted on the field of battle.

If men without God were not stark mad, the prohibitive price paid for World War I would have stifled the lust for blood. But just as jungle beasts slink back into their lairs to lick their wounds and regain strength, so men waited for a new generation; and then, only twenty-one years after the "war to end all wars," World Conflict II began.

We ought now be honest enough to admit that the boasting catch-phrases exalting human advance are cruel lies. Whatever progress this generation sees, is largely scientific or mechanical, not spiritual or moral. We boast of stratosphere flights streaking across the continent in less than twelve hours; but the airplane also helps a criminal commit forgery in Los Angeles before breakfast, bigamy in Chicago before lunch, murder in New York before dinner, all on the same day! The radio is marvelous; yet how dangerous it can become when used by unscrupulous interests to teach children crime-tactics, to introduce young people to temptations, and to stupefy nations with poisoned propaganda!

As the scope of war increases, taking its toll on civilians — their homes blasted away before their eyes; on sailors, their ships torpedoed at high sea; on women and children, barely existing on starvation rations; on innocent hostages, fifty shot to avenge an assassinated Nazi general; — where in all this hideous hatred and sin can we find beauty for the soul, peace for the mind, happiness for the heart? Certainly not in modern education! If culture were the key to peace and progress, would ours be the

only generation which has witnessed two world conflicts —
at a time when we have more learning and laboratories,
more culture and colleges than ever before? Not Zulus,
Hottentots, Congo pygmies or Australian bushmen are
leaders in this aggression, but highly civilized people.
Neither can we discover the radiance of a better day in
legislation (if larger law books meant increased happiness,
our statute-burdened age would be the most joyous), nor
in any religious creed that sets the full Gospel aside. As we
thank you for the remarkable response to last Sunday's
message, the largest for any opening broadcast in these nine
years, let me point, high above the ugliness of sin, the
squalor of human vice, the specter of increasing bloodshed,
the scarecrows of human fears, to our "fairest Lord Jesus,"

THE BEAUTIFUL SAVIOR

concerning whom we read this ancient record in Psalm
Forty-five, verse two, *"Thou art fairer than the children
of men: grace is poured into Thy lips."*

I

JESUS HAS THE BEAUTY OF GRACE

Right at the outset some may ask why we believe that
this psalm speaks of Christ, when He lived long centuries
after these lines were written. We should recall, however,
that the forty-fifth psalm is a prophecy centering in the
Lord Jesus because it is so quoted by the New Testament,
in the first chapter of Hebrews. The Bible does what no
other volume has ever achieved — prophesy future events
with accurate truth. If you yourself need a convincing
demonstration of the Scriptures' power; if you want to
persuade some skeptic that the Sacred Volume is the errorless truth, take recourse to the proof furnished by fulfilled
prophecy. The Bible must come from God, for only He

knows the future; He alone could reveal, centuries in advance, the startling course of our Savior's life, death, resurrection, as well as scores of other events in the histories of individuals and nations. While I appeal to you, my fellow-clergymen, to preach with increasing force this unanswerable argument from fulfilment, I also plead with you not to mislead your people by predicting that after the war a golden age of peace and plenty will reign. On the contrary, we ought to be prepared, at the conclusion of hostilities, for heavy hardship. Do not deceive yourself or your hearers by promising that the struggle will bring our country closer to God! History clearly teaches that international strife has never built the Church or produced a widespread acceptance of the Lord Jesus. War tears churches down. The worldliness, vice, irreligion that every conflict, no matter how completely justified, provokes, creates unspeakable damage for Christ's cause.

When the Hebrew psalmist in prophetic vision sees Christ and says, *"Thou art fairer than the children of men,"* he plainly implies that Jesus is more than a man. Hold fast to this cornerstone truth! If Jesus were merely a human being, as you and I, though He were the best, truest, noblest man ever to walk the face of the earth; if He came into this world as we did and left it as we shall, He could not be the Savior, and our reliance on Him would be misplaced. *"Put not your trust in man,"* the infallible Scriptures warn. The deep-rooted trouble with these tangled, twisted years is this, that our age has placed its confidence in mortal guides who, with their broken promises and frightful failures, have become blind leaders of the blind. For help in trouble, for the lightening of burdens, for the removal of sin, for life after death, you need a Helper, a Burden-bearer, a Redeemer, a Victor over the grave who is almighty, unlimited in power. Eternal praise be to His holy name, our Jesus is God in the full, unrestricted sense of that glorious term. He taught that He was God and proved that He was. Do not argue, question, or object! Instead, accept, believe, trust! Take Christ in faith as your God, and He will manifest His divine power in your life!

I know, of course, that thousands of churches once built on this Foundation have shifted to the quicksand denial of His deity. But no matter how prominent or persuasive the teachers who seek to pull Jesus from the throne of His Godhead, I ask you who are His to uphold this truth with prayer, testimony, action. A man who denies that Jesus is his God is not a Christian and has no place in the Savior's Church.

Now, what does the text mean when it declares, *"Thou art fairer than the children of men"*? Was our Lord, as He walked the pathways of Palestine, handsome, commanding, godlike in form? Today millions of pictures of political candidates are scattered throughout the land before elections. Men in public office are honored, even during their lifetime, when their portraits are hung in conspicuous places. Admittedly, however, we know little about Christ's appearance, for we have no drawings, paintings, statues or detailed descriptions of His person left by those who were blessed in beholding Him. On occasion there may have been about Jesus something kingly and commanding. He was faced by a mob of murderous enemies with rocks in their hands, ready to stone Him to death; yet displaying His divine power, He could stride safely through their midst. Even when Jesus permitted Himself to be captured, one glance from Him was enough to cast heavily armed soldiers helpless to the ground. Usually, however, Christ went about as an ordinary traveler, a typical working man. The Son of God and the Redeemer of the race was often unnoticed during His life and despised, disgraced even during the anguish of His death. In that suffering we must discover the real, saving Christ, the only Redeemer who can ever assure us of heaven. When we follow Pilate's direction *"Behold the man"* and see our thorn-crowned Savior; when — oh, my fellow-redeemed, drop everything now to concentrate your thoughts on this crucified Christ — we find Him on the cross, His wounded countenance marked by the blood and sweat and tears, not of a statesman, but of the world's most agonized Sufferer, we must confess with the prophet Isaiah, *"He hath no form nor comeliness; and when we shall see Him, there is no beauty that we should desire Him."*

How, then, can the text say of Jesus, *"Thou art fairer than the children of men"?* To discern Christ's true radiance, we must fall on our knees in penitent faith before Him. A scholar once entered the Lutheran Church in Copenhagen to view Thorwaldsen's world-famous statue of Christ. At first he seemed critical, dissatisfied. Then a child, aware of his disappointment, explained, "You must kneel down and look up into His face." The visitor followed the child's direction, and, kneeling, he saw the marble masterpiece in a new, glorious light. He found a countenance of heavenly beauty directed toward him. Similarly, when we humble ourselves before the Lord Jesus as our only Redeemer from sin, when we become as nothing and He looms before us as everything, He becomes *"fairer than the children of men."* Christ's beauty, then, as our Scripture testifies when it continues, *"grace is poured into Thy lips,"* is His grace — and what inexhaustible treasure, what unlimited mercy, what endless love are contained in that short five-letter word, *grace!*

Consult your dictionaries to find its exact meaning, and

you will discover that it is widely used in law, royalty, music, sports, in a dozen other ways! But take your Bible, stand beneath Calvary's cross, and *"grace"* has only one ever-blessed assurance. It is the mercy of God in Jesus; it is Christ's compassion, the love that brought Him from heaven's highest glories to be born of a virgin on this earth of evil and sorrow, to live as a man among men, yet without sin, and then, as the *"Lamb of God that taketh away the sin of the world,"* to bear in His own holy body the transgressions of every man, woman, child during the past, present, and future of all history. Forcefully does Scripture teach — and nothing else is the Bible truth concerning our Lord's grace — that His death on the cross was the one perfect, all-sufficient, all-embracing sacrifice for human iniquity. He left nothing undone, unpaid, unfinished. His mercy cannot be bought, earned, or received as a reward. It is not restricted to a few or reserved for those classified as the most unselfish or most virtuous among men. Your eternity in heaven or in hell, joy indescribable, face to face forever with Jesus, or banishment never ending, in darkness and death, this is the "either-or" that always comes with the acceptance or rejection of divine grace.

Therefore, my fellow-redeemed, think prayerfully, contritely, trustingly of this indescribable gift and its full, free salvation. Certain great church bodies today officially teach that it is not enough to believe in Christ's compassion. They insist that you must live so worthily that by charitable acts, repeated prayers, prescribed acts of penance you literally pay your way to heaven. But that is a man-made creed, not the Savior's Gospel of grace. Jesus wants hearts crushed in contrite confession of their sins. He welcomes the sinner who cries out, "I am less than nothing in God's sight, for I am false, unclean, impure, full of transgression;

but Jesus is more than everything to me, since on the cross my sins have become His; my punishment, the penalty He bore; my condemnation, the nails that riveted Him to the accursed tree."

That merciful promise of salvation through faith is the heart of our Christian creed. This week, as the Reformation anniversary approaches, we recall gratefully the epochal work of Martin Luther, who, as no prophet since the apostolic days, led believers in all lands and subsequent ages to the cross with the cry "Only by grace, only through faith!" As few men, Luther had tried to earn the redemption which Jesus has fully won for everyone; he sought to pay the tremendous debt the Savior's suffering and death have canceled altogether. He employed every available means of putting himself into God's favor, dedicating his life to the Church and entering the holy orders. He took his monastic duties so seriously, mortified his body so systematically, practiced the rites of penance so relentlessly, that often he collapsed under this self-inflicted torture. But all his pilgrimages and prayers, his devotion to holy relics and miracles, his fasting days and sleepless nights drove him into deeper despair. Only when he learned the meaning of "mercy" and beheld in Christ not an angry Master, but the fairest Lord Jesus, with words of grace for him; when with Saint Paul he could *"conclude that a man is justified by faith without the deeds of the Law"*; when he could exult, *"By grace are ye saved through faith; and that not of yourselves: it is the gift of God,"* only then did the peace of pardon completely take possession of his soul as he became the great Reformer of Christendom.

May you have a personal knowledge of this complete compassion! Every radiant Gospel promise which fell from Christ's grace-filled lips can be yours. *"Be of good cheer,"* He says, *"thy sins be forgiven thee!"* Take this assurance at its full value and let the joy of salvation reign in your heart! *"Learn of Me,"* says Jesus, *"and ye shall find rest unto your souls!"* Believe this! Build your hope on that truth, you, the restless and distressed! Go all the way with Christ! Keep nothing back from Him! Trust Him entirely, and you will find a calm, confident rest, even in these terror-filled days! *"Be not afraid,"* Jesus repeatedly declares. *"Let not your heart be troubled,"* He adds. If only you of small faith could catch the overflowing pledge of these words! With the Savior you can throw off worry, assured that life's hardships and sorrows come to you as God's child from His grace, to help keep you safe and sure in Christ. *"I am the Resurrection and the Life,"* Jesus, the Easter Victor over death, proclaims in triumph, and no matter how blasphemously godless men contradict this promise, you who have been bereaved of a dear one, fallen asleep in faith, unshrinkingly believe that, by His grace there is a resurrection of the body and a life everlasting.

In this heightless, depthless, endless grace of our Lord, we find the beautiful Savior. No human loveliness, earthly brilliance, or radiance of natural splendor can be compared with Him who is *"fairer than the children of men."* Well do we sing:

> Fair are the meadows,
> Fair are the woodlands,
> Robed in flow'rs of blooming spring;
> Jesus is fairer,
> Jesus is purer;
> He makes our sorr'wing spirit sing.

But if it is impossible to describe His compassion, we dare not overlook this warning: With all its limitless mercy, His grace is not irresistible. God will not force His forgiveness on anyone. A hundred years ago in Pennsylvania, George Wilson, a murderer, sentenced to be hanged, was pardoned by President Andrew Jackson; but the hardened criminal rejected the pardon, insisting that it could never be legal and valid until he accepted it. President Jackson consulted the Supreme Court of the United States, and Chief Justice John Marshall read this verdict: "It is hardly to be supposed that one under sentence of death would refuse to accept a pardon, but if it is refused, it is no pardon. George Wilson must be hanged." And George Wilson was hanged. We shake our heads at such stubbornness, but some of you are even more perverse. I have been broadcasting for nine seasons. How much longer must I plead before some of you find in Christ the fairest Lord Jesus, with full grace for you? How many more years will elapse before those living under God's wrath repent and return to the heavenly Father? If you value the eternal welfare of your immortal soul, crystallize that inner urge and approach Christ now, weighed down by sins yet supported by His assurance *"My grace is sufficient for thee!"* While the Spirit stirs your heart, write us at once! Every letter will be treated with confidence, sympathy, prayer. Thousands of pastors who preach this same Gospel are eager to bring you the Savior's message. Grasp the blessing and strength of Christ-centered faith now, and He, fairest Lord Jesus, removing hideous sins, will make you pure, radiant, glorious in God's sight!

II

WE, TOO, CAN SHOW THE BEAUTY OF HIS GRACE

For the Savior's grace not only assures us of forgiven sin, defeated death, sealed salvation, opened heaven: it also pledges us a new birth in the beauty of holiness. His merciful words bring purity, joy and loveliness to life, for He Himself assures those who are His, *"Now ye are clean through the Word which I have spoken unto you."* Again, it is the promise of His Scripture, *"If any man be in Christ, he is a new creature; old things are passed away"*; — the old, repulsive rule of ruin has been broken, *"Behold, all things are become new."*

God's enemies may deny the blessed change which comes through faith in Christ's assurance and the washing of Baptism, but no truth is more positive than this, that by our Savior's grace, sinners, guilty of damnable wrong, can be reborn as God's saints — never perfect and stainless, of course, but always becoming more Christlike. Unbelievers should heed the warning spoken by an old Fiji Island chief who, some years after Missionary Hunt's death, was visited by an infidel English earl. The nobleman could not escape being impressed with the amazing changes wrought on these islands by the Gospel, but he was not willing to concede that Christianity deserved the credit. When he attacked the Bible and belittled the missionaries, the aged native leader, pointing to a near-by stone oven, said: "In that oven we roasted human bodies for our great feasts. If it had not been for the good missionaries, for the old Book, and for Jesus Christ, who changed us from savages into God's children, you would be killed and roasted in yonder oven, and we would feed on your body in no time." In the same line of reasoning we declare: How ugly, sordid, bloodthirsty the world becomes as soon as it rejects Christ! Let those who would overthrow His Gospel tell us what they have done to raise the fallen, cheer the faint-hearted, banish evil, promote good! Has Modernism, denying the Lord Jesus, improved the world, altered men's hearts, curbed evil? Has atheism ever succeeded in beautifying an ugly, misshapen life? But the Savior never fails. He takes men and women who have persuaded themselves that they have no hope, that they have fallen too low ever to be restored — drunkards, prostitutes, murderers, would-be suicides, victims of horrifying vices — and by granting faith in His glorious grace makes them sparkle with radiant purity. The blessed Redeemer, and this is His promise today, has cleansing grace for all who feel that sin has crowded everything good, clean, true, honest, out of your lives, who for years have abused your bodies, poisoned your minds, stifled your consciences, sought to kill your own souls. If you accept His pardon for sin, the Holy Spirit will make you new, glorious creatures in Christ, led by hope in place of despair, truth rather than falsehood, love instead of lust, praying rather than cursing.

You ask for proof, and with overflowing thanks to God I point you to Christ's grace manifestly and marvelously at work in these broadcasts. A Pennsylvania woman, mother of eight children but deserted by all of them, her husband blind, her heart darkened with worry, wrote: "I was about to take my life when I heard your promise of Christ. Now, through Him I have a hold on life again." A prisoner in Michigan testifies: "Through your broadcast Christ has brought peace, hope, and happiness to a tired, weary heart. You have raised a soul from despair, sin, sorrow to salvation." A Minnesota listener declares: "For sixteen years I walked my own sinful way, drinking, gambling, and throwing my life away. Then, two years ago, I heard your broadcasts and saw what a lost and condemned sinner I was. I got in touch with a Lutheran pastor, and we both got on our knees, and he prayed for me. . . . I am a new man." A Connecticut mother joyfully exclaims: "Praise God, your radio messages and the pamphlets have proved a godsend to the young man we took into our home. He was a big sinner and a drunkard. We thank God that he has finally reformed and accepted Christ as his personal Savior." An Iowa pastor relates how he heard the broadcast in the company of an ex-soldier, an alcohol addict, who, after the message, fell on his knees to cry: "God be merciful to me a sinner and save me for Jesus' sake! I mean it! I mean it!" Though penniless, he was, thank God, penitent and hopeful! Christian prayer was offered for him; today he is a new man with a changed heart.

Everyone, without any exception whatever, can be blessed by the same transformation shown in these and hundreds of other radio letters. You young people, tempted to break God's law of purity and decency, urged to throw off all restraints, to revel in immorality, realize what it cost the Lord to free you from past sins, and to strengthen you for firm resistance against future evil! Cling to Christ as His Word appeals, *"Keep thyself pure!"* Trust Jesus! Make Him your daily Companion! Throw away all sex novels and sex stories! Keep a safe distance from suggestive motion pictures! Stay out of taverns, dance halls, every disreputable place where the Savior will not accompany you — and by His grace, He will give you the joy of a beautiful, grace-filled life, and if it be for your spiritual blessing, the happiness of a future home at the side of a clean, consecrated helpmate for life!

You older folks whose home life is marked by hatred instead of love, quarrel rather than quiet joy, give Jesus control over the family, and He will help stifle selfishness, jealousy, faultfinding! His Spirit will show you how husband and wife, parents and children, through faith, can start over again to find harmony and contentment!

You, the victims of drunkenness or destructive personal habits, remember, though everything else collapses, Christ's grace can always help! There is hope for all who trustingly approach the Savior with the plea *"Lord, save us, we perish!"* He can change the blackest heart. Give Him yours! Let Him cleanse it and fill it with pure, holy desires!

You business men who know that the commercial world is filled with fraud, theft, dishonesty; workingmen who during these critical years will be tempted repeatedly to misuse your organized power; servants of the Government who see graft and connivance; the soldiers, sailors, airmen, unselfishly devoting years of your life to the defense of this country, against whom, however, the legions of hell work overtime and with redoubled force; all who are tempted to stoop to the hideous service of sin — to you the call at this crossroads in our national destiny re-echoes, *"Repent ye, and believe the Gospel!"* Accept Jesus, *"fairer than the children of men,"* and from Him learn the beauty of a consecrated life, strengthened to defeat temptation, guided to follow the path of His righteousness!

Oh, how marvelous if the Savior's Gospel could be spread throughout the world and His holiness live in every soul! Perplexed as you are by the spreading war, I tell you that the highest pledge for peace lies in the Lord Jesus. Everyone else has failed. Diplomacy, militarism, appeasement, international treaties, have all collapsed. But Christ can still help. If only trust in His grace would rule in more human hearts, the ravages of warfare would be minimized. Let a man experience the Savior's full mercies and he will stop war-profiteering and cease enriching himself by the suffering of others! He will renounce his lying propaganda, his mania for cruelty, his love of destruction. Put the love of Christ into a statesman's soul, and he will not break his promises or revoke his covenants; he will follow the Scriptural appeal *"Seek peace and pursue it!"*

This is an eleventh-hour plea asking that the beauty of the Lord Jesus Christ and the Gospel of His grace cover our land. How gleefully hell laughs at our world in flames and how restlessly unclean spirits chafe at their leashes, straining to be set loose over the land for the destruction of law, order, civic honesty, morality, religion!

But come what may, we who are the Savior's can still have His grace within us. We look steadfastly to the time when He will appear in His second coming or when we see Him in the resurrection of glory. Then we shall — oh, radiant promise! — *"be like Him,"* our precious Savior, without sin, sorrow, disappointment, death — perfect in the peace of His redemption. Until the dawn of that heavenly radiance and bliss beyond compare, follow Him ever more closely, and as the beauty of His grace reflects itself in our reborn lives, dedicate each day to Him anew through the pledge with which these broadcasts have closed:

> Beautiful Savior, King of creation,
> Son of God and Son of Man,
> Truly I'd love Thee,
> Truly I'd serve Thee,
> Light of my soul, my Joy, my Crown.

O Jesus, grant us Thy beauty, as Thou hast promised! Amen.

WHO IS THIS JESUS?

"Jesus . . . asked His disciples, saying, Whom do men say that I, the Son of Man, am? And they said, Some say that Thou art John the Baptist; some Elias; and others, Jeremias or one of the prophets. He saith unto them, But whom say ye that I am? And Simon Peter answered and said, Thou art the Christ, the Son of the living God." — Saint Matthew 16:13-16

O Jesus, Thou Prince of the Soul's Peace:

Mercifully look down on our torn, bleeding world; behold the victims of war: sailors struggling in the cold seas, aviators with broken bodies, soldiers maimed and crippled, women and children undernourished, starving, families homeless through bombing, hostages innocently killed! Survey the wide suffering, anguish, torture, that men are inflicting on their fellow men — and then, beloved Jesus, give us a true victory over hatred! May the teachings of Thy truth everywhere prevail and the compassions of Thy "new commandment," "that ye love one another," overcome the greed and aggression of power-seeking dictators! Forgive us, we beseech Thee, our many sins, our repeated thanklessness, and for the sake of Thy redeeming death on the cross completely remove all our transgressions! Amid toil and turmoil without, we can have Thy blessed assurance within — peace with our heavenly Father, peace with our conscience, through Thee, our only Savior. We need Thee, merciful Jesus, not only every hour, but during each moment of these trying times. Be with us, therefore, to bless us and in turn to make us a blessing for others! We ask it confidently, because we pray in Thy name and with Thy promise. Amen.

HOW long will the war last? What will be the role of the United States? Where will the young men in our expeditionary forces be sent? — Such are the questions of the hour, discussed throughout the breadth of the land and answered by military experts, newspaper columnists, radio commentators, only too often on the basis of personal bias.

As far-reaching as these critical issues are, many of you

are more directly moved by the perplexities in your own life, the private burdens that weigh heavily on your soul and mind, the restless anxiety about health, home, money, the need of love, companionship, guidance, the mounting fears for the future. Yet, no matter how grave the world problems or how seriously personal difficulties distress you, today this broadcast puts before every one of you a more vital question that centers in eternity itself, an issue of life and death, heaven and hell, everlasting salvation or never-ending damnation, the question concerning Jesus Christ: Who is He? And what is He to you?

This may be the first time many of you have tuned in our broadcast, or it may be the last time for some; but first or last, whoever you are and wherever you may hear these words, the supreme question for every one, irrespective of age, class, creed, or color is not a matter of war or peace, wages or work, health or home, but: Jesus. Who is He whose name is used in prayer and abused in cursing; who is honored by churches built for His worship and dishonored in vulgar cartoons by atheists; the Jesus whom some of His own countrymen have learned to call their Savior, while others still brand Him a satanic deceiver; the Jesus whom Bruce Barton called "The Man Nobody Knows," but of whom Martin Luther said, "So real is Christ to me now as if He had this very hour poured forth His blood"; the Jesus whom certain other broadcasts and churches regard as only another man, but whom this mission of the air exalts as what He really is: God and Savior.

Here, then, as the center of our Bible, our Christian faith, our evangelical churches, is an issue which cannot be successfully side-stepped or completely avoided. Your reply to this question involves your soul, your joy in life, and your assurance in death.

WHO IS THIS JESUS?

For our answer we turn to the source of unfailing truth, God's infallible Word, and there, in the record of Saint Matthew, chapter sixteen, verses thirteen to sixteen, we read: *"Jesus . . . asked His disciples, saying, Whom do men say that I, the Son of Man, am? And they said, Some say that Thou art John the Baptist; some Elias; and others, Jeremias, or one of the prophets. He saith unto them, But whom say ye that I am? And Simon Peter answered and said, Thou art the Christ, the Son of the living God."*

I

HE IS MORE THAN MERE MAN

When Jesus asked, *"Whom do men say that I, the Son of Man, am?"* He was alone with His disciples in the foothills of beautiful Mount Hermon. If Christ withdrew from the crowded, noisy world to teach His followers eternal truths, how much more should we, in this day of increasing tumult and strife, take reverent time to meet Him in His Word, and, cut off from the disastrous allurements of our age, center our thoughts on His promises! The deep-rooted trouble with many churches in our day is this, that their members do not give up all else and at Jesus' feet learn the vital truths of His peace and pardon. They have interest a-plenty for the social activities attached to the congregation's work, ample energy for theatricals, suppers, entertainments, organizational activities, but not even a few spare moments for the study of God's Book, nor a regular Sunday hour to follow the Savior's pointed command *"Learn of Me!"* Instead, church services are shortened, sermons streamlined, the tempo of hymns stepped up, the speed of our whole religious life increased. As a consequence the American pulpit has too often featured snap judgments in place of earnest instruction over which the preacher has studied hard and long. People hear emotional outbursts rather than solid interpretation. They behold Christ in hazy, blurred pictures, not in sharp, clear-cut lines. Millions in this hour — I can sum it up in one short sentence — need to detach themselves from the world and learn the lessons that our Lord, the Master of grace and wisdom, would impart.

Our Lord was resting in Mount Hermon's shadows also because He sought to evade that murderer of John the Baptist, Herod, whose agents now hunted Christ. Even Jesus had to experience the hatred in high places which Saint Paul felt, the opposition of the mighty that sought to destroy Martin Luther, the hostility on the part of world leaders which many Christians feel today. Why is it that when men reach positions of power and fame, they frequently begin to show contempt for religion and are guilty of Herod's readiness to persecute Christ? People who wax wealthy often forget God, boast that they do not need Jesus, even declare themselves open enemies of the Christian faith. The sin against which we must be on guard during these months of easy money, higher salaries, inflation prices, overtime wages, is the conceited pride and its pompous boasting: "We don't need God. We don't want Him."

Perhaps because His disciples were beginning to lose their faith under Herod's steady opposition, Jesus sought to strengthen their trust in Him by asking them, *"Whom do men say that I, the Son of Man, am?"* The answers they gave were not different in principle from the statements we hear today, nineteen momentous centuries later. There was no agreement concerning the Savior then, as there is none today. Some said He was John the Baptist. Among these was Herod, who thought, "The man whom I beheaded has come back to life." His conscience gave him no rest. Day and night he saw that blood-spattered head which in a moment of aroused lust he had presented to a lewd dancer. The memories of that murder were rising up to accuse him, just as the remembrance of wrong relentlessly haunts many of you.

Others said that Jesus was Elijah who, they believed, would precede the Messiah. They concluded that Jesus was too humble and lowly, too poor and persecuted to be the glorious Redeemer of Israel; yet even in His lowliness something strange and compelling about Him made them concede that He might be the Messiah's messenger.

Still others, perhaps recalling the opposition Jesus endured, thought Him to be Jeremiah, the prophet of suffering; while many, having heard with their own ears how Christ preached as no man had ever spoken, were satisfied to call Him *"one of the prophets."*

You find in these contradictory opinions agreement on only one point: public sentiment in those days had a highly respectful impression of our Lord. They ranked Him among the most distinguished figures in Israel's history, just as today every person of sound mind and intelligent judgment has paid Him tribute. People with the average quota of common sense can see that Jesus has showered benefits on the whole race. They recognize that it was He who helped the downtrodden groups of mankind, liberated womanhood from the tyranny of lust, elevated childhood from the depths of despair, turned the toil of slavery into the honor of labor, changed the hideousness of heathendom into decent, progressive society — in short, heaped multiplied blessings on all classes and centuries of men. Nobody except a degenerate atheist, a perverted brute, denies Jesus' greatness. Listen to this testimony: "For the man Christ . . . I have the highest admiration and respect. They crucified a kind and perfectly innocent man. . . . To that great and serene man I gladly pay my homage of admiration and my tears." Do you know who spoke these words? Robert G. Ingersoll, the American infidel who crisscrossed the country and for $250 a night told his audiences that Christianity was a forgery and a sham! Listen to this acknowledgment: "What sweetness, what purity in Christ's ways, what touching grace in His teachings, what loftiness in His maxims, what profound wisdom in His words!" Can you guess who penned those lines? Not a preacher, nor a God-fearing scholar, but Jean Jacques Rousseau, a French scoffer, guilty of serious immorality.

An almost endless list of similar praise even by His enemies shows there should be little difficulty about convincing a normal person that Jesus is at least one of the mightiest figures in history. But this is not enough. Our Lord was not satisfied with such answers, and neither can you be satisfied with only a mortal Jesus. Call Him whatever you want: Teacher, Leader, Master, Guide, Friend, Model; exalt Him to the loftiest heights as the greatest earthly Figure during all the ages, the most magnificent Man, the mightiest Genius ever to be born; glorify His worship with tall cathedrals, erect His statues throughout the world; but when all this honor is given Christ only as a Man, it is futile, false, fatal.

Of what good for your soul's salvation is a merely human Jesus? If the lips that spoke the promise *"Thy sins be forgiven thee!"* are only man's, these words may be wrong and false. If the voice that proclaimed, *"Let not your heart be troubled! . . . My peace I give unto you,"* is but the utterance of another mortal teacher, how can we be sure of its truth? If the arms stretched toward all the weary, burdened souls with the invitation, *"Come unto Me, all ye that labor and are heavy laden, and I will give you rest!"* are only the arms of an earthly Comforter, of what benefit can they be to us in life's repeated trials and increasing sorrows when we need heavenly assurance? If He who was nailed to the cross was only a noble, self-sacrificing sufferer, how can Calvary mean any more to us than Valley Forge, Gettysburg, Flanders Field? If the Jesus who promised, "*I am the Resurrection and the Life; He that believeth in Me, though he were dead, yet shall he live,*" contradicted that pledge with His own death and remained to moulder and decay in His grave, as all men must, then how can we find any positive pledge of the resurrection and the life everlasting?

No man can take your sins away, bear the punishment of your transgressions, become your substitute before the bar of divine justice. None of your fellow men, not even the godliest, can ever remove sin's stain. The purest life, the cleanest mind that human records list, can never make you spotless in God's sight. Plainly and pointedly does Holy Scripture declare, "*None of them can by any means redeem his brother nor give to God a ransom for him.*" A few days ago an airplane hurtled to the ground in Minnesota. It was close to the airport — only two miles away but not close enough, and fourteen passengers met a tragic death. You may be near Christ, but not near enough for spiritual safety if with all your praise you echo the verdict of His countrymen: He is a great prophet but only a prophet.

Our age especially should be ready to welcome One who is more than man, for the deep-rooted trouble with these twisted, tangled years is this, that we have placed our confidence only in earthly guides who, with all their broken promises and pitiful failures, have proved blind leaders of the blind. Every burden in this bleeding age; all the horrors of a Second World War; each conflict between capitalists and laborers; all the battered nations, broken homes, blighted lives in our greedy, gory generation come from rejecting God and relying on ourselves. We have made idols of wisdom, strength, cunning, but we have forgotten God. More than during any other period we, in these frightful forties, ought to confess man's utter sinfulness, the complete depravity of the race, and on bended knees, with folded hands and pleading hearts, beseech the Almighty to forgive us, to grant us divine help, to enlighten us for the one and only true answer to the question "Who is this Jesus on whom our hope of heaven depends?"

Yet how forceful is this Scriptural warning *"Thou hast stricken them, but they have not grieved."* At a time when the very tragedy of a world collapsing about us should drive us to God and to a reverent appreciation of the true Jesus, we must witness a growing determination to keep Christ down on the human level. A recent book, written by a professor of a celebrated Massachusetts college, stated boldly, "The view of Him [Jesus] as the supernatural Being . . . we cannot honestly accept." That college was founded just 150 years ago by Christians who would rather have had the earth open wide to swallow them up than to reduce Jesus to such depths. At this school the first foreign missionary society in the United States was organized; yet now at the same place the brazen denial of the true Lord finds applause. Is it any wonder, with many colleges practical agencies of atheism, that parents have wept bitter tears when their son or daughter, who left home for the university as a child of God, returned, enriched by a degree but robbed of faith? This dethroning of Christ marks our entire modern social system. With a full realization of this indictment, I raise these charges: First, many American churches, especially some of the largest and wealthiest, have brazenly denied that Christ is anything more than man. Second, some Protestant leaders have been guilty of the same damnable sin. Third, church groups, national councils, called "the voice of Protestantism," have chosen officials, printed statements, adopted policies rejecting the truth in a way which leaves no charitable doubt that they have cast the true doctrine concerning the Savior aside. Fourth, some religious broadcasts, which receive chain facilities entirely free (while we pay for every moment on the air), have persistently preached only a human Jesus. Fifth, certain divinity schools, including some of the oldest and wealthiest, systematically teach this pernicious error. Sixth, denominational papers picture Jesus as though He were one of us, and only that. Seventh, the training of our youth in many Sunday schools has the same poisoned basis, with the result that we are educating millions of children who, unless God graciously intercedes, will never know the saving love of Christ who says, *"Suffer the little children to come unto Me, and forbid them not!"*

Facing this widespread denial, what must we who love the Lord Jesus do? To begin with, we should realize the acute danger confronting the churches in the United States and Canada. Sixteen million people over ten years old in the United States cannot read or write, but seventy million are spiritually so illiterate that they have never signed their names beneath an oath of allegiance to Jesus nor read His Gospel. If this rejection of our Lord is not checked, their opportunity for true spiritual instruction will be cut off, as more high places in American church life are usurped by men who bow before a false Christ. Is this country following Europe's destructive example in letting rationalism and religious radicalism assume control? If you who look to Jesus and say, *"I know whom I have believed,"* want to avoid that calamity, pray a hundred times more fervently! Testify! If you do not rise up in protest every time the true Scriptural Jesus is swept aside in your pulpit, you come under this condemnation by our Lord, *"Whosoever shall deny Me before men, him will I also deny before My Father which is in heaven."* Speak up, and if continued protests are unheeded, either you or those who dethrone the Son of God must step out of that church! Benedict Arnold seems a bungling amateur in comparison with some men who receive their salaries from Christian congregations and yet publicly question the Savior's truth and privately ridicule it. A man who insists that Jesus is merely of common human stock cannot be a true disciple of Christ and has no place in His Church. Those who spurn the Scriptural Redeemer have plenty of freedom to form their own religious groups or join with other like-minded apostates, but if they are not honest enough to follow that open course, they ought to be barred from the churches.

II

HE IS THE CHRIST, THE SON OF THE LIVING GOD

How refreshing, by contrast, to hear Peter give the only true, divinely approved answer to the question "Who is this Jesus?"! Without hesitation the eager disciple turns to our Lord and in words imprinted on the souls of millions since that day testifies, *"Thou art the Christ, the Son of the living God."*

The word *Christ* is used so carelessly and so often abused in profanity that most people fail to grasp its full meaning as the *"name which is above every name."* Indeed, there is not a person living, however learned he may be and however imposing the list of degrees behind his name, who can understand or express to others the fullness of grace and glory concealed in this name. Since its full brilliance is too dazzling, we can only single out some of its radiance and say: To be the Christ means far more than to be John the Baptist, Elijah, Jeremiah, or any of the other prophets.   Jesus — this is Christianity's keystone creed, separating it from every other religion — as the Christ is the long-promised, divinely anointed, sin-destroying Deliverer, *"the Lamb of God, which taketh away the sin of the world,"* the Substitute for every sinner, the Ransom for every wrong, the Payment for the entire penalty of our transgressions, the Reconciliation of a race estranged from God, the Restorer of the holiness and happiness lost in rebellion against the Almighty.   Take all your own sins — and before Jesus do not try to parade yourself as innocent of evil, for each one of us, without exception, stands condemned by God's Word for our lustful longings, covetous desires, unclean hearts; take your total guilt, your accumulated soul-terror, the fear that your violation of God's Law and man's will be exposed or their crushing consequences visited on you; bring all this to the Cross, and there through faith in the sin-bearing Deliverer you know that His blood can remove your sins forever. Last week a Pennsylvania invalid wrote: "Can a murderess and an adulteress be forgiven?   This worries me nearly to death.   Oh, pray for my poor soul!   Can you give me any encouragement?"   In the name of the compassionate Christ, I tell that distracted sufferer and every burdened heart throughout the nation, in Canada and Mexico, that every iniquity, however vile and loathsome it may be, can be removed by the grace of Him who says, *"Though your sins be as scarlet, they shall be white as snow; though they be red like crimson, they shall be as wool."*

Christ Jesus is the Savior also of the whole race, with none barred from His mercy.   Heap up the mountains of universal guilt; invite men of every country, color, and condition to bring their transgressions before the Crucified, and His mercy will be so marvelous that again a single drop of the blood He shed in His atoning death can wipe out the world's hideous rebellion against God's truth, love, and purity.

Above all, believe that you yourself may come just as you are, depressed over the repeated victories sin has won in your life, almost desperately eager to find forgiveness, peace for a restless conscience, the assurance of God's love; and at Calvary through faith you learn that while Jesus here *"died for all,"* He died especially for you, to cancel the charges written in the book of justice against your name, to prepare your place in heaven.

This is what the name *Christ* means: complete compassion, limitless love, matchless mercy, glorious grace, free forgiveness. Do you now answer the question "Who is this Jesus?" by exulting, "He is my Savior, my Atonement"? Or — God forbid! — do you behold the writhing agony of the Crucified, suffering for your sins, and then try to laugh this off by rejecting His grace? I read the other day that a group of men sitting on the deck of a steamer on its way up the Delaware River to Philadelphia saw flaming clouds of smoke over the city and paused to discuss that scene of weird beauty. After the ship had docked, one of the men in the party was told, "Your factory has been entirely destroyed by fire!" Unknowingly he had admired a blaze that had wiped out his own business. Yet with even greater tragedy some of you behold the Lord, concede that He may have done good, but detach yourselves completely from His love, little realizing that everything worth while in this life and the next is being destroyed while you are fascinated by the ravages of sin.

Yet, as we ask once more, "Who is this Jesus?" there now comes an answer of glorious climax. — Praised be the love that brought Him from heaven to the shame and agony of the cross! — Christ — Let earth and heaven rejoice, men and angels exult! — is, as Peter triumphantly concluded, *"the Son of the living God,"* of equal majesty with the Father and the Spirit, Lord of lords, King of kings, very God of very God.

Jesus must be God, because only a divine Redeemer can overcome sin; because only One who is Life itself can defeat death; because nothing short of the almighty power of Heaven itself can conquer hell. And Jesus *is* God! Pointing to Christ, the Bible declares, *"This is the true God!"* In the Old Testament Jeremiah called Him *"the Lord"* and in the New Testament Saint John begins his Gospel by stating that He, Jesus, *"the Word, was God."* Our Lord Himself declared, *"I and My Father are One."* He told men that those who beheld Him beheld the Father. In turn, the Father acknowledged Him as His well-beloved Son. Jesus proved He was God by executing the almost endless list of miracles only the Almighty could perform. If the unbreakable Scriptures give Him the names and titles by which men address God; if they ascribe to Him those marvelous powers which can be only God's: eternity, unlimited strength, all-embracing knowledge, and especially the authority to forgive sins; if Christ is honored as God by prophets and apostles, praised as God by saints and martyrs, acknowledged as God both in heaven and hell, the call to everyone of us is to bow before Him and with full reverence of heart, soul, mind, repeat Thomas' conviction *"My Lord, and my God!"*

Some of you demand, "How can you convince me?" In answer, as the Savior told Peter, *"Flesh and blood hath not revealed it unto thee, but My Father which is in heaven,"* so I tell you that the deity of our Lord cannot be proved or disproved by scientific research, technical tests, or elaborate experiments. Only God, through His Spirit, can convince you that what I say is true. Give that Spirit a place in your heart! Ask Him to remove any stubborn resistance, any willful blindness! Yield to Him the direction of your life and let Him persuade you that Christ is your God! — Some years ago Charles Bradlaugh, a blasphemous atheist, challenged a courageous Christian minister to a public debate. Immediately the clergyman accepted, but he specified, "I will bring with me to the debate a hundred men and women who have been saved from lives of sin by the Gospel of Christ. They will give their evidence, and you will be allowed to cross-examine them. I will ask you that you bring with you a hundred men and women who have been similarly helped by the . . . infidelity which you preach." That challenge was never met; and there will be no debate in your mind as to the deity of Jesus Christ when you, saved by the power of His love, know Him as your own.

My fellow redeemed, while the Spirit is close to you and in this moment seeks entrance into your heart, I plead with you who have never known Christ, who have consistently rejected Him, or who, once having pledged Him allegiance, have turned traitorously from His mercy, confess Him your Christ, your Savior, your God! Blessings, endless and immeasurable, for time and eternity, will be yours when your soul rings with Peter's positive acknowledgment of Jesus. What you need, what I need, what this whole bleeding and battered world needs is the answer to our question "Who is this Jesus?" given to the world 400 years ago by the great Reformer and Restorer of Christ's full and free mercies in a ringing statement of faith which I repeat annually as the summary and theme of our broadcasts, this deathless declaration: "I believe that Jesus Christ, true God, begotten of the Father from eternity, and also true man, born of the Virgin Mary, is my Lord, who has redeemed me, a lost and condemned creature, purchased and won me from all sins, from death, and from the power of the devil, not with gold or silver, but with His holy, precious blood and with His innocent suffering and death, that I may be His own and live under Him in His kingdom and serve Him in everlasting righteousness, innocence, and blessedness, even as He is risen from the dead, lives and reigns to all eternity. This is most certainly true."

Who is this Jesus? God grant that you will answer joyfully, "He is my Savior and my God!" Amen.

GOD IS OUR DEFENSE

*"He is my Defense; I shall not be
moved. . . . Trust in Him at all
times, ye people!"* — Psalm 62:6, 8

Holy Spirit, Our Comforter and Sustainer:

*Many powerful enemies have been mobilized against the nation
and the Church. From both without and within our own lives
we feel the attack of dark, hateful forces which oppose the free and
full grace of our Lord Jesus Christ. Forgive us, we beseech Thee,
for the Savior's sake, our many disloyalties, our repeated sins
against Him in whom alone there is heavenly hope! If in our own
strength we seek to resist the foes of the faith, we are lost, for "with
might of ours can naught be done." But be Thou, O blessed Spirit,
together with the Father and the Son, our Shield and Protection
against the onslaughts of hell, the assaults of our own conscience,
and the enticement of a sinful world! Show us that our victory is
granted by our trust in the power of the Cross! Defend our blessed
homeland against all adversaries, the menace of unbelief, rejection of
divine grace, and destructive godlessness! Thou art our Defense.
Hear us and help us, then, for Jesus' sake! Amen.*

TODAY is Defense Sunday, and this is to be a defense
message — but not the kind which certain congregations are featuring and for which many pastors have received especially prepared sermon outlines. True churches of
Christ do not need such reminders of their members' duty
to defend our country and its liberties. It is a vital part
of the Christian creed that we who accept the Lord Jesus
follow His injunction *"Render therefore unto Caesar the
things which are Caesar's!"* obey His word *"Let every soul
be subject unto the higher powers!"* accept its instruction
"Be subject to principalities and powers!" and *"Submit
yourselves to every ordinance of man for the Lord's sake!"*

Those who should receive these defense-talk reminders
are the groups in our country which have repeatedly opposed our system of government. The appeal for whole-

[43]

hearted endorsement of our military, naval, and air preparation should be sent to the Association for the Advancement of Atheism and like-minded infidels who are steadily undermining national foundations. The plea to work harder, longer, more intensively for the protection of the United States should be directed to the Communists, many of whom are pledged to overthrow our American institutions. For unbelievers who reject the Bible and its repeated appeals for loyalty and allegiance to the constituted authorities are those, above all others, who need constant instruction in the duties of citizenship.

My remarks will differ from the opinions some of you heard in your churches this morning, because this broadcast is dedicated to the truth that only in Jesus as the Son of God and Savior of mankind can our age and the millions in our country find sure defense. Men who do not know the Redeemer, who propagate a creed opposed to Christ or who at best omit all mention of the Lord from the sermons they preach on this Sunday, understand neither the greatest weakness of our nation nor the divine help to be found in Jesus and His Word during these darkened days.

Therefore, when military leaders, production experts, and government officials point to the increasing war clouds on the international horizon, the Christian churches should re-emphasize our responsibilities as citizens of this uniquely favored land, unparalleled in its divine blessing; but let Christian pulpits, in addition, call attention especially to the moral and religious dangers confronting us and the necessity of protecting our hearts, our homes, our national institutions against the assaults of unbelief.

So when I speak to you on defense, I want to stress the side that many politicians forget in this crisis, America's need of a spiritual bulwark, the safeguarding of our souls. To that end I give you this divine assurance for the present emergency:

GOD IS OUR DEFENSE —

a pledge from the unbreakable Bible, the words of Psalm Sixty-two, verses six and eight: *"He is my Defense; I shall not be moved. . . . Trust in Him at all times, ye people!"*

I

GOD IS OUR BEST NATIONAL DEFENSE

In a world of international greed, hatred, bloodshed, the United States should have a strong, complete defense. It is the earnest prayer of every American Christian that our country be adequately protected and made too strong for successful attack by any foreign foe. That is in harmony with the Bible — and it is good common sense. The writers of the sacred Scriptures and the founding fathers were not pacifists; and neither should we be. They never entertained the mistaken notion that the world was continually improving and that therefore it was unnecessary for us to have strong military and naval forces; and neither should we, in a world aflame with the fire of war, stop short of protecting our homeland adequately. No sacrifice will be too great to shield our blessings. Those who love God know that He expects them to obey their government in everything — except in any proposal contrary to His revealed will. Christians of America have put their hard-earned savings into Defense Bonds. They have not created bottlenecks in defense work. They love this divinely endowed land, and they will work for it, save for it, fight for it, die for it. True followers of Christ are true patriots. They are like that mighty defender of spiritual liberty Gustavus Adolphus, King of Sweden, who on the battlefield of Luetzen 309 years ago this very day, helped seal modern religious freedom with his blood.

Christian soldiers stood with Washington at Valley Forge. They fought and fell at Gettysburg. They lie buried in the Argonne Forest. Yesterday Saint Louis witnessed an impressive service commemorating the devotion of the first young man from our city to lay down his life during the present hostilities; and Signalman Ralph Kloepper of the ill-fated *Reuben James,* whom we thus mourned, was a member in good standing of our Lutheran Church.

When a nation exalts God and heeds His Word, its people can say in the certainty of our text, *"He is my Defense,"* and be marvelously shielded by the Almighty's guidance. In 713 B. C. the trained armies of Sennacherib, Assyrian king, with regiment upon regiment of fully equipped veterans, came up to besiege Jerusalem. The city seemed doomed, but King Hezekiah, the prophet Isaiah, the priests, and the leaders resorted to the house of God, prayed earnestly for divine help and received His assurance *"I will defend this city to save it."* Despite overwhelming odds, Sennacherib was completely defeated when the angel of the Lord destroyed 185,000 Assyrians. Remember also how in past crisis moments of American history, during Colonial times, the Revolution, the Civil War, our heavenly Father answered the pleas of the masses by delivering our people from overwhelming enemies. God's promise *"Call upon Me in the day of trouble; I will deliver thee"* and these records combine to tell us that where the Lord is honored, the people can say, *"He is my Defense,"* and be comforted by the knowledge that ultimately His good, gracious purpose must prevail.

A country may be attacked not only from without by foreign foes but also from within by even more formidable enemies. Destructive forces, seeking to sap its strength and undermine its resistance, can hew down the pillars which support freedom, blessing, prosperity, rest. Here they are, these powerful but often unrecognized adversaries of a better America: National Enemy Number One: unbelief, rebellion against God. This rejection of the Almighty has no armies to oppose our military forces, no air squadrons for the bombing of our cities, no naval craft to shell our shores; but it has a satanic might more deadly than tanks, airplanes, and cruisers, a force that is not many miles distant, but a spiritual TNT at work now, within our boundaries. The multitudes of Americans who have rejected Christ, His Word, His Church; the pride that boasts, "We don't need God"; the insolence which ridicules the Christian religion; the perjury, blasphemy, and profanity which desecrate God's holy name, the sarcasm heaped on the Almighty in literature, entertainment, often in everyday life; altogether, then, the 50 per cent of America that does not honor God, the ungrateful masses who will not find a moment to remember the Lord even on the two coming days of national Thanksgiving — these constitute the most formidable danger to our country's welfare. The Almighty will not continue indefinitely to bless a people in which unbelief constantly grows bolder. The verdict of His Word and of history is this: *"The nation . . . that will not serve Thee shall perish";* and again, *"If they will not obey, I will utterly pluck up and destroy that nation, saith the Lord."*

National Enemy Number Two: godlessness and crime. Larger than any battalions which can invade us is the army of our past and present criminals, almost five million fellow Americans convicted (and the many others unconvicted) of serious crime: murder, assault, robbery, the heavy sins of violence and greed, the oppression of the poor and underprivileged; the getting rich at the expense of widows and orphans — this can inflict more severe and lasting damage on the United States than any war. For the Holy Word warns: *"The Lord hath a controversy with the nations. . . . He will give them that are wicked to the sword, saith the Lord,"* and again, *"Behold the eyes of the Lord God are upon the sinful kingdom, and I will destroy it from off the face of the earth."* ∠.

National Enemy Number Three: corrupt government. Never before has our country witnessed graft, bribery, official dishonesty on the large scale this generation has produced: judges conniving with criminals, law-enforcement officials working hand in hand with the underworld; legislators selling their votes for patronage and expedience — all this lies over the land as a heavy shadow to forebode evil; for the eternal truth records that while judgment establishes the land, *"he that receiveth gifts overthroweth it."* Again Scripture warns, *"It is an abomination"* for those in authority *"to commit wickedness."*

National Enemy Number Four: unfaithful churches. The studied insolence heaped against the Bible in thousands of American congregations; the rejection of Christ's vicarious atonement at ministerial training schools where not a single faculty member accepts the inspiration of the Bible or the promises of the Cross and the Blood; the worldliness, the lip worship, the *"form of godliness"* even in sound churches — these are disasters far more grievous even than the loss of many a battle. *"Be not deceived,"* the divine Word protests, *"God is not mocked."*

National Enemy Number Five: immorality in the home. We record to our shame that the United States has more broken families than any other civilized nation, excepting Russia; that unfaithfulness between husband and wife is increasing; that young people are constantly lured to break the purity commandment. The loose spirit in our age, the bad example by elders, the ridicule of decency, the spurning of parenthood, the disregard of childhood, all combine to form a menace of tremendous proportions. No country can ever be stronger than its homes. To the extent to which our American households crumble, a vast part of our moral foundation is destroyed.

National Enemy Number Six: anti-Christian education. This tragedy will be more deadly in the years ahead, when today's boys and girls will be tomorrow's fathers and mothers. If our youth is trained to be mentally cunning instead of spiritually good; if its education molds the brain but neglects the soul; if schools refuse to recognize sin and wrong, have no place for God and His grace in Christ, can you not see, should this treachery toward our youth assume control of American education, that the ship of our state may slowly but surely be steered toward destruction on the rocky shoals of unbelief?

National Enemy Number Seven: the disregard of God's law in labor and industry. When, on the one hand, radical elements direct American working men away from the Lord and His will, as the toiling classes are tempted to misuse for selfish interests the power which is theirs in united action; when, on the other hand, the moneyed groups help make the poor poorer and in this day of rising prices, increasing living costs, refuse to share a greater part of their profit with workers, this double disregard of divine instruction may help to produce hard, bleeding days of internal strife and long-drawn class war.

In short, America needs to be defended against itself. Some years ago Sir Edward Arnold told the students at Harvard University: "In 1776 and in 1812 you conquered your fathers. . . . From 1861 to 1865 you conquered your brothers. . . . Your next victory must be over yourselves." He was right, and the conquest over these seven national dangers can be won only by a penitent return to God and His Word, by a widespread spiritual revival which will bring masses to the atoning Christ and His divine protection. We must strengthen the nation from within and build its religious foundation firm and strong.

Because no people can be weak with God on its side, the Christian cry in this crisis hour should be: Defend America by accepting Christ! Every man, woman, and child in the United States who acclaims Jesus Savior and Sovereign can help bring divine protection on this land through personal prayer. If God was ready to spare degenerate Sodom and Gomorrah, provided they contained only ten righteous people, most assuredly He will regard with blessing multitudes which turn penitently to His grace. Besides, every Christian with his regenerated life and his determination to follow the Savior's footsteps, as far as humanly possible, adds to the country's moral strength, increases the righteousness which exalts a nation, and battles against the reproach of sin. No appeal to America in this international emergency is more vital than the plea of our text which, pointing to the gracious God, urges, *"Trust in Him at all times, ye people!"* Look to Christ for the guidance, strength, reliance, that says, " *'He is'* our *'Defense!'* "

Therefore, fortify America by keeping Jesus in the churches built and dedicated to the glory of His name! Every Christian pastor who, seeking to please God rather than men, avoids soft, Christless preaching and instead reveals God's whole truth, the punishment of His Law and the promise of our Savior's pardon, increases spiritual reserve.

Defend America by strengthening Christian homes! Husbands and wives who keep Jesus in their households as the honored Guest, who train the children they bring into the world to be God-fearing, useful, law-abiding, patriotic citizens, do more good than many frequently quoted and frequently married public figures.

Defend America by supporting Christian education! Colleges where the fear of the Lord is still the beginning of all wisdom, where atheists and Christ-deniers are banned from the faculty; lower schools like those conducted by my Church, but open to all, where children are instructed not only in the customary branches, but are daily taught also to love the Lord Jesus, to obey their parents, to thank God for America — these are powerful factors in the promotion of national good and the rejection of evil.

Defend America by putting Christ's teachings into capital and labor! If the American workingman, in conformity with God's Word, gives honest, wholehearted return for his salary, rejects every recourse to violence and oppression, and does unto his employer as he would have the employer do unto him; if capital refuses to exploit the toilers, but accepts the Scriptural program of fair, upright treatment for the working classes, ours will be a stronger and happier country.

Defend America by purifying its political life! Exercise your privilege and responsibilities as citizens! Send men to the legislatures who cannot be bought, who refuse to connive with evil, and will stop the enactment of legislation contrary to divine Law! Give us patriots instead of politicians, Christian statesmen rather than partisan leaders, and America, under God, will be defended.

I do not say that if these principles were followed in our country, we would experience no national difficulty, attacks from without or serious problems from within; for sometimes the Almighty sends reverses to make a people spiritually and morally stronger. But I am equally confident that if multiplied millions of Americans look to the Lord in Christ and say, " 'He is' our 'Defense,' " our heavenly Father will powerfully, if necessary, miraculously, protect and bless us.

II

GOD IS EVERY BELIEVER'S DEFENSE

Many of you, however, desperately need defense for your own personal selves. You are besieged by relentless fears and worries. Your conscience haunts you, as the memories of flaming sins, now after thirty, forty and more years, flare up to mock you with their ghastly horror. You want to get rid of your transgressions, to silence the accusing voice, to enjoy rest for your soul.

No human being will give you that pardon and peace. But Jesus, blessed Jesus, can. When He, God's Son and Mary's, your Savior and Substitute, went to the cross of shame, He took with Him my sins, your sins, the whole world's sins, suffered their appalling punishment, endured their frightful curse, paid their death penalty. By believing this Gospel grace we can find pardon, escape hell's terrors, defeat the grave, triumph over despair. Through this faith we have the immovable, unmistakable confidence that salvation is ours completely, ours eternally; that a special place has been prepared for us in the many mansions; that in the heavens opened by the Redeemer's atonement ours will be the glory — oh, marvelous privilege! — of seeing Him face to face, with endless rapture and adoration.

What matchless love in Jesus! Think of all the vile criminals throughout history who have been sentenced to death, and ask yourself how often you have heard anyone volunteer to take their places at the gallows, the guillotine, the electric chair! But Jesus, merciful Jesus, did even more! He died for the worst of sinners, to save them from the horror of eternal death. Picture the millions in misery all over the earth, either paying the consequences of their own sins or groaning under imposed cruelty. Can you find anyone who has said, "Let me suffer for them, die in their stead, so that they can live in freedom and happiness"? But Jesus, beloved Jesus, did this and more. He went the hard Calvary road to restore to His father's love a world lost in its own wickedness.

Now forget the rest of humanity for a moment and concentrate on yourself! Review your own transgressions, your hate-filled, lust-laden thoughts, your cruel, cutting words, your shameful acts, sometimes hidden from human gaze, but — be sure of this! — known in all their sordid details to the holy God; and as His Word and your conscience remind you that you cannot stand before Him with unforgiven transgressions, I ask you: Do you know any man, saint, or angel who can transfer your guilt to himself? But Jesus, precious Jesus, did: *"His own self bare our sins in His own body on the tree."* His cross is your defense against sin; His blood, your defense against hell; His death, your defense against the decay of the grave. When Christ is enthroned in your heart, you can face an accusing conscience with the triumph: "Jesus *'is my Defense!'*" *"Who is he that condemneth? It is Christ that died, yea rather, that is risen again, who is even at the right hand of God, who also maketh intercession for us."* With the Savior controlling your life, you can reject the coaxing of satanic temptations. When doubts assail you, you can push them aside to declare: "Jesus *'is my Defense!'*" *"I know whom I have believed and am persuaded that He is able to keep that which I have committed unto Him against that day."* If Christ is your Lord, you can face divine justice and though your sins are many, grievous, and disheartening, tell the Judge of eternity: "O Father, Jesus *'is my Defense.'*" *'He was wounded for'* my *'transgressions, He was bruised for'* my *'iniquities.'*"

My fellow redeemed, if you want a sure protection

against evil, acclaim Christ your own Savior! Accept Him now! A day, even an hour's hesitation, may prove too long and too late. If the *Ark Royal* had been an hour or two earlier, it could have been towed safely into the shelter of Gibraltar, only twenty-five miles away. That delay sent the mighty craft to the bottom of the Mediterranean. Some of you have been limping through life, battered and shattered by the enemies of your soul, but now at this moment the refuge in your Redeemer, the Lord Jesus, is close at hand. Will it be life with Christ or death without Him for you? Give the Spirit His way into your heart and declare: From this moment on, despite my past sins, my backsliding, my thanklessness, Jesus is mine, God helping me, forever!

As our Lord is the divine Defense against sin, so He is unfailing Protection against life's sorrows, dangers, and fears. Take courage, you the crushed in spirit who feel yourselves ground under the heel of continued cruelty! His Savior-love is extended especially to the world-weary, the heavily afflicted, the burden-bearers. Look steadfastly unto Jesus, for He not only knows your suffering, since He endured far more than we will ever be asked to bear, but He also promises to help you carry your cross! Through the night of black sorrow, in the depth of depressing gloom, hold your head high because you raise it to Him and repeat the Psalmist's confidence, *"He is my Defense; I shall not be moved"*! Keep your eyes focused on Calvary and remember you are so precious in God's sight that Jesus lived, died, and rose again to free you from the shackles of sorrow! God, the almighty Creator, *can help* you in every need. He *wants to help* you, since He loves you in Christ; He *will help* you even in desperate moments when every human prop gives way!

What, then, are the surrounding afflictions which you

would escape? Are you laid low by sickness? The Savior can be your Rampart against its ravages. He can start where medical science stops. Even more, He can use bodily illness to create a healthy soul. Last week a Christian young woman told me: "I was sick for years, unable to work, confined to my home. But that suffering helped bring me fully to Christ, and if I had to go through all those years of agony again to receive Jesus as I now know Him, I would gladly endure everything once more to have the Savior in my heart." Are you attacked by money troubles, want, poverty? The Lord is your Defense here, too. He who has the riches of all the universe at His disposal can make you prosperous overnight if this is for your good. And if Jesus keeps you poor, He can perform a greater wonder: change this burden to a mighty advantage, transform your earthly poverty to a treasury of spiritual riches. Is your happiness assailed by the tragedy of a loveless family, a broken home, loneliness, desertion? Once again, find sustaining comfort in Jesus! He is able to restore shattered happiness and make it even more radiant. Your own letters testify how divorces were averted and peace restored in your households after Jesus was made the Head of your home. If in His inscrutable wisdom the Lord sees fit to have you suffer under repeated instances of unfaithfulness and continued strife, believe that divine compensation will give you unsurpassable soul peace in the close companionship with your Savior!

Whatever the gloom encircling your life may be, let Christ dispel it! However many enemies may be mobilized against your soul: opposition, persecution, ridicule, cruelty, broken hopes, shattered ambitions, Jesus can repulse every one of them and make life's defeats faith's glorious victories. The Savior will not forsake you as long as you cling to Him — that is your confidence for these clouded years as you go into an unpromising future, overcast with the specters of war and the signs of deeper suffering for all mankind. If in these darkened moments you rely on yourselves, you are lost. But if you trust God in Christ; if you, the unfaithful, who have turned from your heavenly Father, now return to His grace with penitent hearts but with the faith which takes His Son at His Word, then, though the noise of battle roar and hatreds rage, through the wail and woe of suffering, let this be your battle cry, *"He is my Defense,"* and this your triumphant hymn of praise:

> A mighty Fortress is our God,
> A trusty Shield and Weapon.
> He helps us free from every need
> That hath us now o'ertaken.

God grant every one of you that eternal victory through Jesus Christ, the Captain of our salvation! Amen.

GOD, MAKE US PENITENT!

"If ye turn again unto the Lord, your brethren and your children shall find compassion before them that lead them captive, so that they shall come again into this land; for the Lord your God is gracious and merciful and will not turn away His face from you if ye return unto Him." — 2 Chronicles 30:9

God, Eternal and Triune:

We confess to Thee that as a nation, as members of Thy Church, as families, as individuals, we have broken Thy holy Law so repeatedly and grievously that we have no right even to approach Thee. Yet, trusting Thy pledge of mercy, we bow before Thee, contritely and with firm trust. O Father, forgive us all our iniquities for Jesus' sake! O cleansing Spirit, purify our hearts and make us new creatures through faith in His crucifixion and resurrection! O precious Savior, as we raise our eyes to behold Thee on the cross paying the penalty of all sin, drive from our selfish hearts thoughts of pride, demands for recognition, requests for reward! Thou, who art Three in One, teach us rather that without Thee we can do nothing, that Thou art strongest in us when we are weakest! Make us humble, thankful, faithful and keep us for Thee and with Thee through time and into eternity. We ask it in Jesus' name. Amen.

ALMOST 150 years ago, during the administration of John Adams, our second president, the United States found itself confronted by opposition remarkably similar in principle to that which faces us today. Our ships were attacked by French fleets; commerce was virtually cut off; our liberties were threatened by European dictatorship; peace was menaced. In that emergency President Adams did what we have done in this crisis: he enlarged the Army, created a strong Navy, and instituted a firm defense program. But he also went farther than we have gone. He issued a presidential proclamation requesting "a day of solemn humiliation, fasting, and prayer, that the citizens of these states, abstaining from their customary worldly occupations, offer their devout addresses to the Father of mercies." The dominant spirit in the United States at that time was so penitent that it could ask the people to stop their work or play, fast for a whole day, and in solemn church services fall on their knees before God to confess their sins, individual as national. Even more significant is the fact that the people followed President Adam's plea; and most noteworthy of all is the record that war was averted, peace established, and a period of prosperity begun.

During the dark hours of the Civil War, President Abraham Lincoln, who appealed for national prayer more often than any other chief executive, declared that our people should "confess their sins and transgressions . . . pray with all fervency and contrition for the pardon of their past offenses." The great Emancipator expressed the fear — and these are his words — that "the awful calamity of the Civil War that now desolates the land may be but a punishment inflicted upon us for our presumptuous sins." Pointedly he warned the American citizens, "It behooves us, therefore, to humble ourselves before the offended Power, to confess our national sins, and to pray for clemency and forgiveness." By divine grace, when the nation, following Lincoln's guidance, humbled itself before God, the war soon ended, the breach between the North and the South began to heal.

What a contrast all this presents to much of our present-day attitude! We are surrounded by war; labor conflicts increase to menacing proportions; national indebtedness pyramids; industrial and social problems multiply. Our financial outlook, according to some monetary experts, points to inflation, tax confiscation, or even repudiation. Yet at a time when the need for humble, penitent supplication to the Almighty is greater than ever before, we witness an unmistakable religious decline, a more widespread disregard of heaven than in any previous period. Where are the voices like Adams' and Lincoln's pleading for true repentance? Where are national days of humiliation?

Will you not stand shoulder to shoulder with me, then, when I say that the plea in this perilous hour, the necessary appeal of our souls, our families, our churches, our nation, must be

GOD, MAKE US PENITENT!

That is always the earnest petition of every Christian, but it addresses itself to us with particular force on this Lord's Day, set aside from olden times as Humiliation and Prayer Sunday. Today as followers of Jesus bow down before the holy God to confess their transgressions and beseech Christ's mercies, may we similarly humble ourselves to learn the vital lessons of our text, Second Chronicles, chapter thirty, verse nine, *"If ye turn again unto the Lord, your brethren and your children shall find compassion before them that lead them captive, so that they shall come again into this land; for the Lord your God is gracious and merciful; and will not turn away His face from you if ye return unto Him."*

I

WE NEED PENITENCE

This remarkable pledge was written by Hezekiah to the inhabitants of his kingdom. The great, good ruler, who had cleansed Jerusalem of its idolatry and restored the worship of Jehovah, sought to bring all the subjects of his realm back to the one true God. In his zeal for the Lord of hosts, he even planned to reunite all Israel, the ten tribes of the North, and his own southern dominion, not for a political alliance, but for the spiritual unity which would recognize Jehovah and Him alone. Therefore he sent messengers throughout both kingdoms, *"from Beersheba even to Dan,"* calling for a solemn celebration of the Passover Festival such as had not been seen since David's day. This appeal was also accompanied by a plea for repentance. Hezekiah reminded the people of the North and of the South that the Lord was *"the God of Abraham, Isaac, and Jacob."* In truth, what compassionate love the Almighty had showered on the people of Israel! He chose them above all others to be His own, called by His name. He led them out of Egyptian bondage, through the desert's sand and sweat, into Canaan, the happy homeland. He marched before them to protect them against formidable foes, far stronger than they. He gave them His Word in writing, the only people in history thus to be honored. He sent them His prophets; and as the climax of His grace He announced that His own Son, the Savior of the world, would be born of a Judean virgin-mother.

Despite the lavish outpouring of these distinctions, Israel had turned from its God and ungratefully denied Him. Again and again during the seven hundred years from Moses to Hezekiah, the twelve tribes had rebelled against the Lord, their Redeemer. But whenever they repented and cried for mercy, His fatherly compassion forgave and restored them. Now, because of their willful, continued uprising, another punishment, the hardest yet experienced, was to overtake this ungrateful people. They were to be led away into captivity. Yet even then Jehovah's long-suffering and love were not exhausted. He permitted Hezekiah to announce, *"If ye turn again unto the Lord, your brethren and your children shall find compassion before them that lead them captive, so that they shall come again into this land."* Even when it seemed that no hope remained for Israel, they could still regain their lost blessings and the prosperity they had sacrificed through unbelief if through sincere repentance they returned to God. The cry throughout the land, therefore, was, "Back to Jehovah of hosts!"

In all this a powerful lesson presents itself for our country. Gloriously blessed above other nations in our day is America. — This message comes to you from Canada, and for 3,900 miles from Maine to Washington, Nova Scotia to British Columbia, the borderline is undefended. No land mines, pill-box defenses, underground military tunnels, concrete fortresses mark that boundary. By contrast, picture Europe, bristling with fortifications; and remember that while no enemy air-bomb has even fallen on our United States soil, millions in England and on the continent have lost their homes, their entire possessions, in many cases their limbs, sight, hearing, by the air-raids' shattering destruction!

We have food, otherwise unequalled in quality and in quantity, so much in fact that for years the Government, following a philosophy of scarcity, restricted the size of certain crops. But reports from China tell us food is so scarce in Shantung, once the Orient's richest agricultural province, that worms sell for four dollars a quart. Our wealthier classes display silver-fox neckpieces, chinchilla wraps, matched-pearl necklaces, huge, flawless diamonds. But masses of our fellow men in Europe, Asia, Africa, who came into the world just as you and I did, literally wear rags. We have more coined gold than all the rest of the world; and just now the pay envelopes of multitudes are fat and bulging. To appreciate what we have in America, we ought to visualize, for example, the hopeless poverty in crushed France, the regimentation of most workers throughout Europe. We have comfortable homes — at least two thirds of us — the most attractive, convenient houses, on the average, to be found anywhere; but think of the masses huddled in air-raid shelters! And when people open windows to cool a steam-heated apartment, they should picture the long lines in European capitals clutching their ration cards, eager to secure a few sticks of charcoal, so that the whole family can keep warm by crowding into one room.

Or, consider the higher blessings with which the United States has been endowed! We still have a free government, and despite present-day weaknesses of democracy, we are infinitely better off than Nazi Germany and the totalitarian world. We still have freedom of speech; and how much more fortunate are we than some of the belligerents. With our freedom of worship this country is indescribably more blessed, for instance, than Spain, where Protestant churches are banned.

Now, my fellow countrymen, these and many other pre-eminences have been granted us not because our country is racially, morally, or religiously superior to the other nations, but because of God's marvelous mercy in Christ; and the warning of Holy Scripture that bears constant repetition is the reminder *"Unto whomsoever much is given, of him shall be much required."* America has been mightily favored by God, so that it should be a powerful force for God.

How have we responded to this divine generosity? Have we consistently praised Him, from whom all blessings, and particularly national glory, must flow? Has this country of unparalleled favor been unequalled in its devotion to the Almighty? God forgive us! As Israel in haughty pride turned from Jehovah, so we in the United States have encouraged the bloated conceit that we are the creators of our own greatness, the builders of our own grandeur, the authors of our own prosperity. Millions have swept God aside and sought to revoke the Ten Commandments, to nullify the divine will.

What have we done with our money? Luxury taxes are not strong enough to stop the squandering for destructive vices. Even Christians, who repeat, *"God so loved the world that He gave His only-begotten Son, that whosoever believeth in Him should not perish,"* love this perishing world so little that they give only on the average thirty-two cents a year for foreign missions.

What have we done with our home life? In too many instances the Lord Jesus Christ has been completely exiled from American households, the divine laws for domestic happiness completely discarded.

Have we shown our appreciation for free government? Masses of American citizens have not raised their hearts to God in thanks for our liberties or to beseech His divine guidance for the President and the Congress. An increasing number of our countrymen are pledged to radical, revolutionary theories which would overthrow the American form of government. Corruption has sometimes taken the place of political honesty.

Has this nation given evidence of its gratitude to the Lord for freedom of conscience and of worship? Have we come closer to the Lord and devoutly acknowledged His power and grace? You know the answer. Unbelief is on the march. Doubt and denial become bolder even within certain churches, the questioning of the divine Word more frequent in schools, the rejection of Christ's redemption more brazen, the evidence of doctrinal indifference and worldliness more repeated and undisguised. — Let it be said frankly: as a nation we have not grown in faith, progressed in holiness, advanced in spiritual truths!

When multitudes sing lustily, "God Bless America!" it is not easy to proclaim publicly that God will bless only a repentant, contrite America. It is not a light responsibility (when, as last Sunday, a speaker broadcasting after me asserted that we are definitely on the road to universal brotherhood and world-wide peace) to stand before this microphone and tell masses in our country to the contrary, that they are on the road to hell if they do not come to Him who alone is the Way to heaven, Jesus, our Christ. I can imagine a hundred other messages far more popular than Scripture's warning that no nation, no home, no church, no individual, can prosper indefinitely without God. But we dare not seek to please men and court popularity. We who are Christ's are to be watchmen, and if we do not warn sinners of their evil ways, their blood will be on our hands.

Therefore, the message of the Christian Church today must be that of our text, *"Turn again unto the Lord"*! Humble yourselves! Repent, you destroyers of public morals, who with lewd entertainment, filthy books and magazines have increased the love for sin! Repent, you corrupters of the home who have made purity seem old-fashioned and chastity a burden to be scorned! Repent, you rich who have oppressed the poor, and you poor who have hated the rich! Repent, you teachers who lead our youth from Christ! Repent, you adulterous husbands and unfaithful wives, you self-seeking parents and you self-directed children! Repent, you perjurers, blasphemers, abusers of God's holy name! Repent, you public officials who have misused your high office! Repent, you merchants of horrifying death, who delight in war for selfish gain's sake and cloak your lust for profit with the mantle of patriotism! Repent, you scoffers, skeptics, unbelievers, enemies of God, defaming the Lord who made America great! Repent, you preachers of lies who, robed in costly gowns and speaking unctuous words, reject the redemption by God's Son and ridicule His divine Word!

Before all else, however, you and I need repentance for

ourselves. The sins in our own lives that we may seek
to deny, cover up, excuse, laugh away; the transgression
which, unforgiven, will separate us eternally from Christ
and His redeemed — the depravity of our human nature,
our impure desires, hot-tempered words, sinful actions —
Oh, confess them all today! — these should bring us down
on our knees in humility and contrition before the holy
God! A repentant nation is a country in which the individual citizens unmistakably show their sorrow over sin.
Contrition is a personal, not a political matter. Therefore, the admission to be spoken by every American Christian today should embody the full, unreserved acknowledgment of our own guilt and the statement of our faith
in the Savior, taken from the hymnbook of my Church:
"O Almighty God, merciful Father, I, a poor, miserable
sinner, confess unto Thee all my sins and iniquities with
which I have offended Thee and justly deserved Thy temporal and eternal punishment. But I am heartily sorry for
them and sincerely repent of them, and I pray Thee of Thy
boundless mercy and for the sake of the holy, innocent,
and bitter sufferings and death of Thy beloved Son, Jesus
Christ, to be gracious and merciful to me, a poor sinful
being."

II

GOD WILL BLESS THE PENITENT

This confession will help answer the question, What is
real repentance? Do not confuse repentance with fear
for the consequences of your wrong-doing, the dread that
you will be detected, the terror that your secret sins will be
exposed! Some, I know, are burdened by the thought that
you have stolen money over a period of years and that
your theft may soon be revealed. Or you have broken the
commandment of purity and may soon become unwed fathers
or mothers. You have neglected your parents, and people

will soon discover your selfishness. But fear of detection is not repentance. Neither is a sense of disgust over your sins. You are ashamed now when you see the hideousness that sin has produced in your life. You regret the spectacle you presented when in a drunken stupor you made a beast of yourself. You recoil from sordid lusts which in a moment of inflamed passions seemed most enticing. True humiliation, however, means much more. It demands, first, that we acknowledge every sin in our lives, even those which the world applauds. Without reservation or restriction we must confess to God how often, how grievously we have broken each of His commandments, and then declare humbly, *"Father, I have sinned against heaven, and before thee, and am no more worthy to be called thy son!"*

In the second place, true repentance means real, heart-felt sorrow over our misdeeds. Do not get into the habit of blaming the Lord for your errors! People who practice the sins of the flesh often like to say: "I was born with these impulses. They are part of human nature. They cannot be so very wrong. Why did God make me this way?" — when they should fight against this evil that can destroy both body and soul in hell. Yet remorse is not enough. Endless weeping, ceaseless lamenting, moaning through grief-filled days and sorrow-stricken nights will never bring you before the gracious Father. You must know Him who says, *"I am the Way, the Truth, and the Life!"* — Jesus Christ, your Redeemer.

Here, once more, we stand before the most glorious assurance Heaven has ever given mortal men, the pledge which, I pray, will take blessed root in every stubborn, self-righteous soul. Since God is so perfect in His holiness that nothing sinful can ever approach Him, you and I would be cut off forever from the hope of heaven were it not for our blessed Savior. Praise be His endless grace, He not only canceled our transgressions, paid their penalty, assumed their guilt, but He cleansed our sin-marked lives and so completely transferred to Himself our transgressions against God, our fellow men, and ourselves that in our Lord's sight and before the bar of His exacting justice we actually have no sin! Keep this glorious Gospel promise uppermost in your mind: Our righteous God does not simply forget sin, overlook it, smile indulgently at it, discount, or disregard it! He hates it, He damns it. But He loves the sinner with such depth of devotion that in His measureless mercy He has removed our guilt, every part of its eternal punishment, by accepting as our Substitute the Redeemer on whom all our transgressions are laid, Jesus, His beloved Son. When Christ is yours in trusting faith, the way to God is open. His love has broken every barrier down. Despite past transgressions you can bow before Him whom cherubim and seraphim continually exalt, and plead: "My Father, accept me, just as I am, for Jesus' sake! Look upon me, not in my sins, for Thy Son, my Savior, has removed them forever, but behold me with Thy grace!" And as true as God is eternal, all-powerful, and all-merciful in Christ, every penitent, contrite believer whose "hope is built on nothing less than Jesus' blood and righteousness" will hear the God of grace answer, "Thy sins are forgiven fully, freely, forever!" Do not despair of finding a compassionate Lord when you come to bow before Him in that humble, contrite faith! His own Word assures us, *"The mountains shall depart, and the hills be removed; but My kindness shall not depart from thee, neither shall the covenant of My peace,"* the peace purchased by our Lord's anguish and death, *"be removed."*

Genuine repentance, of course, implies sincerity shown by a heartfelt resolve to improve our lives and battle against sin. In the text Hezekiah appeals that all Israel *"turn again unto the Lord."* Their fathers, the verses before our text explain, had despised Jehovah and continued in evil. If now the people's hearts are changed, their hatred of evil should be evident in a God-fearing, reverent walk of life. Hezekiah himself had unmistakably shown His people what it means to *"turn again unto the Lord."* He had hardly assumed the kingship at Jerusalem when, as a young man of twenty-six, he restored the true religion, purified the defiled Temple, banished abominations and immoralities. To him real repentance had to be demonstrated by an improved, cleansed, sanctified life.

Similarly, if you are truly contrite, then on this Day of Humiliation and Prayer, resolve that, God helping you, His Spirit sustaining you, you will break with the evil that seeks to destroy your soul! If you are living in illicit relations, end them today! If you are stealing, stop and begin to make restitution! If you have slandered, curb this ugly sin and, as far as you can, correct every untruth you have uttered! If your heart is filled with hate, ask Christ to cleanse it! Show love to those whom you have wronged! If you have deserted your wife, your husband, or your children, go back to them now! If you are cheating at your work, wasting your employer's time or his materials, quit it and restore what you have destroyed!

If you thus follow divine direction, you will experience a joy of life, a peace of mind which many have never known before. True repentance, then, brings you the assurance of redemption through the Lord Jesus Christ, reconciliation with the Father, restoration to eternal life in heaven. For the sake of your immortal soul, I plead with you, get right with God now!

But more: this humbling yourself before the Lord can be a mighty power for the nation's good. If in place of a regimented America you are eager to preserve a free America; if instead of a war-wracked nation you ask for a country crowned with honorable peace; if rather than class conflict you want class harmony, free government before dictatorship, then bow contritely before the Almighty and urge your countrymen to humble themselves before His invincible power. Let legislatures pass necessary laws, parents make happy homes, teachers maintain good schools, statesmen exert building influences; but more than all else, let us turn to the Almighty in this hour of national need, and we will find divine healing for our land, Heaven's solution to our problems, unfailing answer to our perplexities.

True repentance has the promise of divine acceptance. Pointedly Hezekiah's messages proclaim this truth throughout the land, *"If ye turn again unto the Lord, your brethren and your children shall find compassion . . . for the Lord your God is gracious and merciful, and will not turn away His face from you if ye return unto Him."* It is Christ's repeated pledge that He receives the truly contrite. Isaiah proclaims, *"Let the wicked forsake his way, and the unrighteous man his thoughts; and let him return unto the Lord, and He will have mercy upon him; and to our God, for He will abundantly pardon!"* David assures all believers, *"The Lord is nigh unto them that are of a broken heart; and saveth such as be of a contrite spirit."*

This true humility must be expressed in prayer, the pleading with God, which proves that we completely accept His Word and confide in Him as children trust their father. To go back to the past of American history again, we ought to recall the remarks by Benjamin Franklin at Philadelphia in 1787 before the convention which was to draft our Constitution. For days this group of distinguished Americans had labored almost in vain. The in-

terests of the various States conflicted, and regional prejudices threatened the whole effort with disaster. Then it
was that Franklin, himself no evangelical Christian but
far-sighted enough to recognize undeniable evidence, arose
to declare: "The longer I live, the more convincing proofs
I see of this truth — that God governs the affairs of men;
and if a sparrow cannot fall to the ground without His
notice, is it possible that this empire can rise without His
aid? . . . I therefore beg leave to move that henceforth
prayers imploring the assistance of heaven and its blessings
on our deliberations be held in this assembly every morning."

The deep-seated difficulty, of course, is this, that many
in our country have no desire or time for prayer. They
openly boast that it is childish and unmanly; that it
destroys self-reliance; that God, if there is a God, is too
exalted to be moved by our pleading. If this unbelief
increases, perhaps our country will have to suffer far more
until by the lessons of bitter experience it learns how completely it must rely on the Lord.

Again, others refuse to take time for prayer. They
are not particularly antagonistic to its practice, but because they do not recognize their sins, their needs, and the
assurance of divine power, they never realize the necessity
of pouring their hearts out to the Almighty. Their souls
have shriveled up; their spiritual life is stunted, and when
they stand before heavy afflictions, they are bewildered and
helpless.

Prayer is often misdirected. To begin with, many do
not know to whom their pleas are spoken. They picture
God as a vague, impersonal, abstract force, unknown and
unknowable, when in truth Jesus has clearly revealed the
true God who is no hazy, undefinable force, but the Father,
together with Christ and the Spirit, the holy Trinity in
blessed Unity. Only He is worthy to receive men's praise,

and only He can answer their petitions. The one who can help America and in whom alone there is deliverance and salvation is the God of the Bible, the God of Christian truth, the God of the Apostles' Creed, Father, Son, and Spirit.

Others similarly misunderstand prayer because they have not learned that we must beseech the Almighty in Christ's name, that is, with trusting faith and unquestioning acceptance of His blood-bought atonement, life-giving death, and heaven-assuring resurrection. When we come to the mercy seat with that triumphant faith, we have the Savior's own assurance *"Whatsoever ye shall ask the Father in My name, He will give it you."* Therefore it is doubly to be regretted that men in public life, often in prominent circles, omit the ever-blessed name of Jesus Christ in their public prayers because they hesitate to mention Him before His enemies. How pointed the warning raised by our Lord Himself, *"Whosoever shall deny Me before men, him will I also deny before My Father which is in heaven"*!

Prayers are also unanswered because they are spoken from hate-filled hearts, while our Savior warns us that we cannot expect to find forgiveness if we willfully withhold pardon from those who have transgressed against us. Our prayers are often not heard because we ask something destructive, injurious to soul or body, and of course our gracious Father will not give us the means of harming ourselves eternally. Frequently, too, we pray merely by rote and rule. We insult God when we address Him, because our thoughts wander far away, as our petitions become mere recitations.

True Christian prayer always brings God's blessed answer. I am firmly convinced that if all over the blood-soaked earth human hearts were regularly, earnestly raised to the Almighty in Jesus' name, beseeching His help, without any thought of personal or national gain, but with intercession even for our enemies, as Jesus commanded, we would have a mighty power for ending this war and establishing peace.

Humiliation and Prayer Sunday, then, reminds us "what a privilege it is to carry everything to God" in fervent pleading. If for your own heart and life you want the joy of Christ's salvation, then approach your Savior now in prayer! No matter how unwelcome you may be to others, He is ever ready to receive you provided you come repentant and rely on His full mercy. You need bring no credentials, no one to intercede for you, no record of past performances; for if, kneeling in contrite faith, you pray the publican's prayer, *"God, be merciful to me, a sinner!"* you can rise with the assurance that your transgressions have been washed away, the horrors of hell removed and heaven assured you. If you want Christ's peace and blessing in your home, make your dwelling a house of prayer! Have parents and children assemble each day for family worship, and Christ, who in the days of His humility entered Palestinian homes to bring salvation, health after sickness, life after death, will now in the glory of His exaltation, enrich your household far beyond your understanding. For a better America, pray as you have never prayed before that God in His mercy for Jesus' sake would save us from enemies without as from treachery within and continue the outpouring of His miraculous, undeserved, and often thanklessly received mercy! If you want peace — and I mean helpful, co-operative harmony, with tyranny, selfish class-interests, national hatred subdued, the mutual rights and needs of nations respected, a peace with a far better basis for understanding between peoples than we have yet seen — then beseech God for Jesus' sake to grant us that grace! For He who *"maketh wars to cease unto the end of the earth"*; He who *"breaketh the bow and cutteth the spear in sunder"*; He who *"burneth the chariot in the fire"* can, if it be His will, grant the world years of necessary reconstruction.

What, then, can we do in this crisis day — both those who have long loved the Lord and those who, by the Spirit's power, now resolve to accept Him as their Ransom and Redeemer? What, if not humble ourselves in penitence and prayer? What, if not proclaim this divine assurance by God Himself for blessing in our souls, our homes, our country, our churches, *"If ye turn again unto the Lord, your brethren and your children shall find compassion, . . . for the Lord your God is gracious and merciful and will not turn away His face from you if ye return unto Him"*? God grant you this true penitence and the promise of salvation by faith through Jesus Christ, our Lord! Amen.

TRIUMPH OVER TEMPTATION!

"How . . . can I do this great wickedness and sin against God?" — Genesis 39:9

God of All Grace and Truth, Father of Our Lord Jesus:

We come before Thee to thank Thee for the manifold outpourings of Thy bounty upon our country, especially for the saving knowledge of Thy Son, Jesus Christ, our Redeemer from sin and death. Send us Thy Holy Spirit now so that throughout this broad nation many hearts may be turned from sin to grace by receiving Jesus, the Advent King of glory! We entreat Thee to guide our youth and lead them to follow Him who lived and died for all mankind. As we are met in one of the nation's military camps, we implore Thee with redoubled petition, heavenly Father, to watch over the young men and women in our military and naval service. Show them that if they keep Christ in their contrite and trusting hearts, they have forgiveness, power, and the pledge of their redemption! Guard them against sin; preserve them against temptation! May they always be true to their parents, their Church, their country, and their Savior! Help us all "fight the good fight of faith"; assure us of the eternal victory in heaven won by Christ for those who are His! We plead for this in Jesus' blessed name. Amen.

TODAY for the first time in radio history a religious coast-to-coast broadcast originates in a United States Army post, at the headquarters' chapel, Fort Leonard Wood, in the heart of Missouri's Ozark Mountains. We dedicate this message to our American youth, especially the several million young men in our Army, Navy, Marine, and Air service, the volunteers and selectees who have left farms, factories, schools, business offices, in many instances sacrificing high positions and professional careers, to give themselves for our country's protection. We want all our young people to know that the Church is deeply, prayerfully concerned about their souls' welfare, and we are eager to offer them the divine strength and guidance of the Lord Jesus Christ. To the slogans now displayed throughout the land: "Keep Them Flying!" "Keep Them Rolling!"

we add: "Keep Them Clean!" "Keep Them Safe!" "Keep Them True to Christ!" Side by side with allegiance to the United States and the flag, we want our young men and women to show loyalty to Christ and His Cross. Besides training for national defense, we want to extend help for spiritual struggles far harder than the conflict on any battlefield.

Only the great God and our young people themselves, particularly these military men, know how much they need counsel and courage to repel the forces of impurity and lust which assail them from within and without. If you think it strange that I speak so plainly and pointedly on this question of youth's chastity, let me tell you that an authority no less than the Surgeon General of the United States, Thomas Parran, has helped write a startling book which reveals a shocking increase in diseases caused by impurity. If even medical experts issue such undisguised warnings, can the Savior's Church remain silent and indifferent, when not only the bodies but also the souls of the nation's youth are in danger? Must we not plead, with all the power Heaven gives us, for purity, and at the same time outline constructive help from God's own Word? Today, then, as I appeal:

TRIUMPH OVER TEMPTATION!

remember, young men and women of America, I voice this plea not only in behalf of your parents who are constantly praying that you be kept clean in Christ, not only for the young person with whom you will share your life and who likewise wants you to guard your chastity; I address all of you, young and old, also in the name of our sinless Lord Himself, and on the basis of the words in Genesis, chapter thirty-nine, verse nine, *"How . . . can I do this great wickedness and sin against God?"*

I

YOUTH MUST EXPECT SEVERE TEMPTATIONS

Many of you know the remarkable story from which this exclamation has been chosen. A Hebrew slave, Joseph, is tempted by the wife of his master, Potiphar, to commit adultery with her, but he repels her advances and, triumphing over temptation, speaks these words of protest, *"How . . . can I do this great wickedness and sin against God?"*

Here, then, is an ancient record, more than thirty-three hundred years old, yet with a modern, up-to-the-minute plot. Manners, customs, styles may change, but not human nature. The scene is far-off Egypt, but lust knows no geographical limits. Immorality is America's besetting sin; and because this allurement is in principle similar to the enticement confronting everyone of you, stop to picture the tremendous moral difficulty Joseph had to face! Here was an unmarried young servant, perhaps twenty-six or twenty-seven years old, not a cold, unfeeling automaton, but a normal man, held and swayed by those powerful emotions which the almighty Creator Himself implanted to prevent the race from dying out, the mysterious energies which through sin, can become treacherous, destructive passions, especially during the throbbing, pulsating years of youth. Some of you young people who spurn the very suggestion of stealing, who recoil from the mere thought of injuring your fellow man, to whom slander and profanity are repulsive, who zealously maintain a loyal interest in your home and church will agree that among all temptations those which lead to the violation of purity have the most penetrating persistence and assail your highest resolve with battering, shattering attacks.

The force of Joseph's temptation was increased by the fact that he was far from his home, alone in a strange land, separated from his mother, who could have supported him in this crisis, cut off from his father, who himself had once seen Jehovah face to face. Similarly millions in training camps and government service, in defense work, college, or business, are away from home — and away from its protection. The danger for many is that, "out of sight, out of mind," you forget parental love and teachings. You start going with a fast crowd. You tell yourself, "When in Rome, do as Romans do!" But how thoughtless and cruel that is! The best friends you have are your parents. No one has ever gone wrong by following the counsel of a Christian father or mother. And while some of you hardly take time to write your family, back home your mother is on her knees praying for your soul, your father beseeching the Savior to strengthen you against evil.

Joseph's battle was the harder because Egypt was a country of loose morals. Its ancient records and its painted walls show the debauchery and perversions of the age. For about ten years Joseph, living in these surroundings, had seen enough to know that if he consented to his master's wife's proposition, he would be acting in accord with the popular spirit of that day and land. You, too, live in the midst of an adulterous and perverse generation which often smiles at unchastity and applauds impurity. The printed pages rolling off huge presses, the books and magazines eagerly read by millions in our country are often sex-drugged. The moronic motion picture, with its risqué plot and attacks on marriage, is a major moral hazard, a source of incalculable evil, to be shunned by every self-respecting young person. Colleges and universities have sometimes given room to instructors who encourage premarital unchastity and free love. Married life in America has suffered under the growing attacks of easy, dishonest, anti-Scriptural divorce and the blight of sinful birth control. The number of unwed mothers, illegitimate children, and abortions is startling; and with all this, many young people are beginning to think that they can do anything provided they do not get caught and know how to avoid consequences. What is more, certain misguided city governments are making immorality easy and accessible. In this national crisis especially we should have emergency legislation abolishing all commercialized vice, as far as possible removing that damnable temptation. During these difficult times we ought to close every saloon and dance hall where the morals of youth are attacked. We should ban every lascivious magazine from the mails and public distribution. The Government should clamp down on the licentious entertainments. With every power at our disposal as citizens and Christians we should help clean up these appalling conditions and reinforce our national reserve of righteousness.

The brunt of Joseph's temptation was made the more severe by the fact that it came from the wife of his master. Had Joseph been guided by a worldly-wise policy of "get what you can," he might have considered the invitation a steppingstone in his career, an opportunity to gain the favor of one who could further his ambitions. A similar situation is created today in the allurements which come from high places. Here is a young man, reared in a Christian home, confronted in his classroom by that complete denial of personal purity which some widely applauded sociologists advance. If an uncouth, long-haired radical would expound these doctrines from a soapbox on the street corner, the danger would be reduced, but because these attacks on Christian ethics come from those in positions of recognized authority, they are doubly dangerous. Or there is a young woman, approached by her employer with dishonorable intentions; a conflict arises between following Christ and perhaps losing her position or, on the other hand, rejecting Jesus and securing personal advancement.

Added to the lure of Joseph's enticement was the fact that it came repeatedly. *"She spoke unto Joseph day by day,"* we read; and nothing is more deadly in its devastating force than such continued, relentless hammering against good intentions and high resolves, especially if it comes from a woman. It is bad enough when a man becomes a slave to his passions, but somehow it seems immeasurably worse if a woman, with the gentler nature and the finer feelings of her sex, wantonly serves as an agent of hell in leading others into vice. Women of America, you have within your grasp the power, under God, to elevate our country's moral standards or tear them down, to help promote purity or assist in the breakdown of decency. Do not abuse this power through immodest dress, wanton talk, suggestive actions! Pray God in Christ's name to make and keep you clean and honest!

II

YOUTH CAN DEFEAT ITS TEMPTATIONS —
THROUGH CHRIST

As we find a deep warning in Joseph's temptation, so we should learn important lessons from his reply. First of all, he does not stop to consider and debate this unholy proposition as though there might be something good in it; and neither should you or I dally, once we know that according to God's holy will these sins of the flesh are condemned. *"Flee . . . youthful lusts,"* His Word demands. Get away immediately from every contact with uncleanness! Break off every unholy connection now!

Joseph rebukes the temptress with this pointed charge: *"My master . . . hath committed all that he hath to my hand; there is none greater in this house than I; neither hath he kept back anything from me but thee, because thou art his wife.*" By yielding to her he would violate his trust and injure his master. If only each of us were moved by this firm sense of loyalty to others! If only every young man would see that the sins of the flesh can bring unspeakable misery on innocent victims! Those who break the commandment of purity, besides running the risk of ruining their own bodies with the most loathsome diseases, poisoning their minds and destroying their souls, may also bring suffering to others, physical torture to their husbands or wives, unspeakable handicaps to their children who may be born blind, diseased, maimed — soul agony and shame to their nearest and dearest.

Yet, the real reason Joseph spurned this temptation lies deeper and is expressed in his words *"How . . . can I do this great wickedness?"* He calls adultery by its right name. It is a monstrous evil, a *"great wickedness,"* so vile that it provokes some of the most abhorrent punishments: disease-ridden bodies, peace-robbed minds, accusing consciences, sin-crushed souls. Today, in shocking contrast, certain teachers glorify the very sin Joseph spurned and declare, "Abstinence is nervously and mentally undesirable." I want you young folks to know that the best modern medical opinion contradicts this claim and asserts: "A clean moral life . . . is not prejudicial to the health but on the contrary is to be recommended from a purely hygienic standpoint. . . . This is the consensus of most of the great medical thinkers." The more clean and chaste our young people are, the healthier and stronger — as a whole — they will be.

In spurning this temptation, however, Joseph was moved by motives even deeper than the thought that impurity does not pay. Most intelligent persons, even many enemies of the Christian faith, will agree that lust often exacts terrifying ravages. But when Joseph protested, *"How . . . can I do this great wickedness* AND SIN AGAINST GOD?" he showed the most vicious and damning side of unchastity. It is a rebellion against the Almighty, a brazen uprising against His holy will. Joseph knew how much he owed the Lord. God had given him life; God sustained him while his own brothers sought to destroy him; God marvelously strengthened him in the dungeon and brought him forth safely; and the same God, holy, sinless, perfect, demanded a clean, chaste life and would punish in hell every unforgiven sin of impurity. *" 'How then,' "* Joseph concludes, *" 'can I do this great wickedness and sin against God,'* the God who made me, who loved me, and who can destroy me?"

With even greater clearness we should understand how the Almighty hates these sins, for we have a guide which Joseph never knew — the whole Bible. Listen to these clear-cut statements in the Word which has never made a mistake and never will: *"Flee fornication!"* *"Be not deceived; neither fornicators nor idolaters . . . shall inherit the kingdom of God!"* *"This is the will of God, even your sanctification, that ye should abstain from fornication."* *"Fornication and all uncleanness or covetousness, let it not be once named among you!"* *"Adulterers God will judge."* When our heavenly Father speaks in this unmistakable condemnation and with such dread-filled threats, it should be understood that illicit relations before or after marriage cannot be lightly dismissed; for these sins, if not removed, are damning, soul-destroying transgressions leading to eternal punishment, from which no brains, money, influence, no prayer can offer escape.

Besides, we can now see clearly in fulfillment what Joseph could perceive only dimly in prophecy — Christ suffering for my sins, yours, and the transgressions of the whole world. Anyone who has beheld that Savior during the dark, desperate hours of anguish in Gethsemane, witnessed the unplumbed depths of His suffering on Calvary, heard His dying cry of agony break out over that rumbling darkness on Golgotha — should recognize personally how God hates sin and how terrifying are its consequences, since we can be saved from their penalty — not by a lifetime of repayment and regret, not through the merits and intercessions of a whole army of saints, but only by the precious blood of the Lord Jesus Christ, God's Son, our Savior. He had to become our Substitute on the cross to pay the full, final penalty for all human iniquities, the Innocent suffering for the guilty, the Sinless for the sin-cursed. Therefore, my fellow redeemed, young or old, can you, knowing how God abhors sin, how He punishes it, what an overwhelming price He paid to free us from it, behold the bleeding head, the blanched face, the nail-pierced hands and feet of that pain-racked Sufferer on Calvary, tortured in our stead — and still think lightly of your misdeeds, still continue in sordid sin? Can you behold your wounded, dying Savior and, turning away from Him, sneer, "What is that to me?" Can you knowingly crucify Him anew by a lust-filled life? God forbid!

On the contrary, let us follow Joseph by viewing our transgressions in their relation to the Almighty! For then — blessed assurance! — we also find that our heavenly Father, for Jesus' sake, is ready to forgive freely and to remove completely every transgression of His holy law, no matter how degrading and unforgivable these sins may seem. The loving Redeemer who refused to cast a stone on a woman taken in adultery but graciously pardoned her, though others sought to destroy her, is still the same ever merciful Christ who would fill your hearts with the feeling of repentance and a deep-rooted trust in His power to save to the uttermost. Come to Him, although you scarcely dare to lift your head, even if your whole life up till this moment has been lived against Jesus and your transgressions seem too vile, too repulsive, to be forgiven!

Only your own refusal to accept Christ can keep you from His pardoning grace. For here is His promise, *"Though your sins be as scarlet, they shall be as white as snow; though they be red like crimson, they shall be as wool."* Whether you need forgiveness for a single rash act or for a lifetime of shame; whether you are troubled by lustful thoughts, evil desires — and who would dare say that he has not thus been besieged? — or whether you now shrink from a long list of shocking wickedness, Jesus is ready to forgive you freely, if only with faith in Him as God's Son and your Redeemer you penitently beseech His mercy. Anyone can come to Christ, no matter how high or how low he may be in the scale of human favor; everyone, but particularly you; any time, but especially now, when the Spirit knocks at your heart, can be the right time to approach Him for His pardon and His blessed peace; in any place you can come close to Jesus — in camp, on shipboard, at home, in a hotel; anywhere, but notably the spot at which you now find yourself, before your radio, with the promise of divine mercy directed especially for your needs! Kneel before the Christ of all compassion with trusting faith, and you will rise restored to God, your sins completely removed!

But more: our blessed Savior, whose mercy is so magnificent that we can never even begin to exhaust its promises, not only remits your transgressions, redeems your soul and reunites you with His Father; almighty God that He is, He gives His own new strength to resist temptation and to follow Him along the pathways of purity. If these sins of the flesh seem to have secured a strangle hold on your life; if with all your good resolutions you fall back into the very evils you seek and pray to avoid; if you have read many books on personal chastity and find these human remedies helpless in emergencies, then come to the Lord Jesus with this ancient prayer for purity, *"Create in me a clean heart, O God, and renew a right spirit within me!"* and the God who promises, *"A new heart will I give you!"* by the Holy Spirit and the miracle of the second birth will make you a new creature in Christ, with heavenly power to resist evil and triumph over your temptations! No matter how many times you have already tried and failed; regardless of the clutching grip bad habits may have on your life; in spite of the fact that Satan may even now be whispering into your ear: "This is too late for you! You have gone too far! You have dropped too low! There is no help for you!" Jesus, blessed Savior, can still make you clean.

Can you not see, therefore, that the great purpose in your life must be to cling close to the Lord Jesus and employ His divine aids to a clean, happy life? And here they are, His powerful helps to purity: First: The Bible, which, as no other book, has within its covers a heavenly strength. Read Scripture every morning and every evening! Read it even though scoffers may make fun of you! Read it reverently and build up your spiritual reserve! Second: Baptism and the Lord's Supper — these holy ordinances, which, through faith, can help strengthen and preserve you against temptation. If you have never been baptized, write now and let us help you! Third: The divine power of Christ-centered prayer. Jesus promised, *"Ask, and ye shall receive!"* and does not He who understands the problems of youth better than youth itself mean especially that if we ask for power to resist temptation, He will grant it? So pray fervently and in Jesus' name!

Invoke Christ's presence in every household, whether torn by dissension or blessed by peace! Fourth: Attend a true Christian church regularly! If you really love the Lord Jesus, you will not be satisfied until you join others in Christ-dedicated worship and hear God's Word expounded! We will be glad to assist you in finding a real spiritual home. Fifth: Busy yourself with Christian work which will bring the Savior's promise of grace to others or help the destitute and distressed in the spirit of the Savior's charity! Once you start testifying of Christ, unsealing lips which have never yet spoken in His behalf, you will find, as a blessing from above, that your faith is fortified, your resolution steeled to meet temptations. In this connection I plead with the Christians of America to open their homes to the young men and women in the nation's service and provide wholesome influences for those who are making heavy sacrifices in our behalf.

The struggle against sin is never easy, and in the eyes of the world it seldom brings reward. Joseph was thrown into prison because he spurned the call of lust; and sneering skeptics who saw him languishing in the Egyptian jail might have asked cynically: "Well, what did the saint get for his purity? Had he been wiser, he might have had everything his own way." In our lives, too, it may seem at times that we lose by rejecting temptation; yet purity always pays rich, repeated compensation. If Joseph had not been imprisoned, he could not have been exalted to the second highest rank in all Egypt and to the position of food director in the seven years of agricultural depression in the Nile Valley. True, we can promise youth today little of material blessings if they remain loyal to Christ. Before us stretches a future which can bring more hardships, fewer opportunities, heavier burdens for the rising generation than any previous period of American history. But come what may, young people who have the Lord Jesus Christ enshrined in their hearts will be able to find strength to triumph over whatever difficulties may seek to overwhelm them.

Men of Fort Leonard Wood, soldiers, sailors, air men, marines throughout the country; youth of America, youth of Christ: for pardon and strength in your own lives, for the sake of your devoted Christian parents, in behalf of your future husbands and wives, in the name of your unborn children, for our country's defense, since righteousness is our greatest asset, for the upbuilding of Christ's Church, I ask you, standing in spirit with me beneath the flag of our glorious nation and beneath the cross of our Savior, to repeat this declaration of loyalty: " 'I pledge allegiance to the flag of the United States of America and to the Republic for which it stands, one nation indivisible, with liberty and justice for all'; I also pledge allegiance to the Cross and to the faith for which it stands, one Savior — King eternal — Jesus Christ, with grace and mercy for all. So help me God!" Amen.

BRING BACK THE BIBLE!

"Hilkiah the high priest said unto Shaphan the scribe,
I have found the book of the law in the house of the
Lord. . . . And the king went up into the house of
the Lord, and all the men of Judah and all the in-
habitants of Jerusalem with him and the priests and
the prophets and all the people, both small and great;
and he read in their ears all the words of the book
of the covenant which was found in the house of the
Lord." — 2 Kings 22:8 and 23:2

Blessed Lord Jesus, Our Advent Glory:

Long years ago Thou didst come into this world of woe to save
us from our sins; and Thou wilt soon return in the majesty of
Thy Second Coming to judge unbelievers, but to take Thy children
home to Thee in heaven. Until that final triumph, daily enter our
hearts by Thy holy Word! O Jesus, we thank Thee for Thy
Gospel with its promise of full, free, final forgiveness of our sins;
and we praise Thee for all the Bible translations, the printing and
distribution of the Scriptures, notably the freedom that is ours in
reading Thy Word. Repeatedly have hatred and unbelief sought
to destroy Holy Scripture; but wicked plans have not succeeded
in removing the precious Book from the face of the earth. Thine
almighty power has prevailed. More than ever before, men are
able to read in their own language Thy heavenly assurance of
eternal pardon, unfailing guidance through all the suffering and
problems of life's pilgrimage to the prepared places in Thy Father's
many mansions. Forgive us our neglect of Thy truth and bring
the Bible to millions in this nation, to churches, homes, souls, that
have turned from its comfort! Revive us, O Christ, and we shall
indeed be redeemed from death! Amen.

AMERICA'S most destructive danger is the growing
indifference to God's Word, the sullen sneering at
the Bible. In a critical moment like the present, when our
country gropes on the jagged edge of long, protracted warfare, we ought to realize that neglect of divine instruction
and opposition to sacred Scripture can pull down in one
swift generation all the noble achievements which the

founding fathers and their successors laboriously produced through a dozen generations.

It was, therefore, with deep regret and alarm that I read the brazen assault on the Bible recenly published in the CIO *News,* the Congress of Industrial Organization's official weekly organ. Prominently displayed on its first page was a large-type item headlined "The New Twenty-third Psalm," a current version of that old shepherd-poem which many call their favorite Scripture passage. As a parody on the beloved lines of *"The Lord is My Shepherd,"* this publication suggested that we now read: "The CIO is my shepherd. . . . They prepare a raise of my salary in the presence of my foreman. They anoint my check with raises; my expense goeth down. Surely the union and my wages shall follow me the rest of my days, and I shall dwell in a house of my own forever." Now, I am not indicting the whole CIO for such blasphemy nor singling it out for particular attack. I also know that the same ridicule of the Bible is widespread in other organizations. I do feel, however, that when an official paper prominently endorses the sarcastic, Communistic delusion that a labor group takes God's place as the *"Good Shepherd";* when the union and the salary check push divine *"goodness and mercy"* completely aside, Christians affiliated with such movements should protest, call a halt to abominations like these and remove from positions of leadership all atheists and Communists — and there are 2,000 of the latter class alone, according to a recent Washington report.

In contrast to this rejection of God's Word let us on this Sunday, which ushers in National Bible Week, study an outstanding instance when workers, carpenters, masons, with fervent faith and untiring zeal helped restore the Scriptures! I point to a startling Old Testament incident recorded in Second Kings, the twenty-second chapter, verse eight and the twenty-third chapter, verse two, from which these words have been chosen as our text: *"Hilkiah the high priest said unto Shaphan the scribe, I have found the book of the law in the house of the Lord. . . . And the king went up into the house of the Lord, and all the men of Judah and all the inhabitants of Jerusalem with him and the priests and the prophets and all the people, both small and great; and he read in their ears all the words of the book of the covenant which was found in the house of the Lord."* As we learn modern lessons from this ancient rediscovery of the Scriptures, let this be our cry:

BRING BACK THE BIBLE!

— back to American churches, back to American homes, back to more of our American schools, back to our whole American life!

I

WE HAVE NEGLECTED THE BIBLE

When Josiah, of whom our text speaks, was crowned King of Judah as an eight-year-old child, the religion and morals of his people were at their lowest ebb. The Temple at Jerusalem had been hideously desecrated; ugly altars to heathen idols were erected in the place where only God was to be worshiped. The sanctuary had become a center of money-making. Throughout the land pagan altars were built on high places. Astrologers, fortune tellers, spiritist mediums flourished. Yet Jehovah, the Lord of hosts, who had mercifully chosen Israel for His own people and Zion, the mount for His Temple, that great and glorious Creator and Sustainer, was forgotten by the leaders and the masses.

Unbelief always goes hand in hand with impurity, and the more brazenly Judah rebelled against the Lord, the more bestial the people's conduct became. Unmentionable sex sins were practiced within the very Temple bounds; commercialized vice for priestly profit was the least of these immoralities. With religious leaders catering to lust, what could be expected of the people? Outside the city walls, in the notorious Valley of Hinnom, they offered their own flesh and blood, helpless children, as burning, shrieking sacrifices to the hideous idol Moloch.

Added to degeneracy and desertion of God were the national burdens under which the country and its capital, Jerusalem, staggered. These were hard, crushing times, bordering on destitution for many, since the Assyrians with whom, overriding divine protest, Israelite kings signed an unholy alliance, had made Judah a vassal state, robbed it of its liberties, and forced it to pay enormous tribute. A royal, cuneiform inscription, uncovered near Nineveh, still bears emphatic testimony to the folly of leaning on man rather than trusting God. This monument states plainly but ominously, "I, Esarhaddon . . . overthrew Manasseh, King of Judah."

How, we pause to ask, can we account for these desperate days of national suffering, moral decline, and religious collapse, when Judah could have been the happiest, most prosperous and blessed place on earth? There is one answer for the whole debacle: Israel forgot Jehovah, pushed His revealed will aside. Even the priests, pledged to execute their sacred duties according to Old Testament specification; the prophets, who were to preach, teach, explain, and apply God's Word; the scribes, whose privilege it was to copy and publish Holy Writ — these high servants of the Almighty traitorously discarded His Scripture. No longer did the Temple resound with the singing of David's psalms; no longer did Aaron's blessing re-echo through the sacred place; no longer did the high priest, with promises concerning the coming Christ in his heart and on his lips, enter the Holy of Holies to make atonement for the people's sins. If even the sanctuary had removed the divine oracles, certainly the common people, who only too readily follow the bad examples of their leaders, had long accustomed themselves to neglect divine instruction completely.

Do not accuse me of pessimism or exaggeration when I now tell you that the same destructive, anti-Biblical tendency confronts the United States today. We are in the midst of an unmistakable religious decline. A deplorable number of churches as well as entire denominations within our borders are constantly losing members. Those who had hoped that this era of two world wars would purify the nation's spiritual life ought now in all honesty confess their mistake and admit that this country witnesses more unbelief, brazen challenging of the Almighty, organized assaults on Christianity, worldliness in religious circles now than before World War I. Many church buildings have become centers of illegal money making. If their members raffle automobiles, conduct lotteries, feature games of chance, against God's Law and man's, are they any better than the grasping, greedy Temple officials at Jerusalem? Above all, when they reject Christ as the only and complete Savior; when they teach a fatherhood of God and a brotherhood of man which, despite these highsounding words, simply means that all religions must finally be regarded as the same, that Jews, Mohammedans, Confucianists, Christians, Animists, Buddhists, Taoists are traveling toward the same goal, only along different roads, although Jesus sharply protests, *"I am the Way, the Truth, and the Life; no man cometh unto the Father but by Me,"* and His Word uncompromisingly teaches, *"Neither is there salvation in any other; for there is none other name under heaven given among men whereby we must be saved"* — when masses today put the God of the Bible on the same low level with the gods of the heathen, are they any better than the ancient Israelites who bowed before the Baals and the Astartes, idols of their heathen neighbors?

Whenever worship of God declines, morality sinks with it. True, American infants are not offered to Moloch, but pagan practices prevent multitudes of children from being born or, after they have come into the world, help poison their souls with unbelief. Sins of the flesh increase in number and boldness as young people give way to passion, their elders deliberately plan secret affairs, and the Christian ideal of keeping clean and chaste before marriage, true and faithful after, is laughed away.

Besides, we find ourselves in the midst of accumulating problems and growing burdens. How sadly the best efforts for improvement have failed! Through tireless medical research and the self-sacrifice of the nation's physicians, the death rate of infants has been cut drastically; yet the suicide figure for adults — more than 20,000 each year — has steadily increased. We have a better knowledge of the brain than any previous generation; yet we have greater worries, more nervous breakdowns, larger insane asylums. We build the best schools, yet produce formidable armies of juvenile criminals. We have the most attractive and commodious homes men have ever known; but America has more broken families and disrupted marriages than any other comparable nation. We institute far-reaching welfare efforts, like the Red Cross, designed to save men's lives; but at the same time we record higher murder ratios than any other country, 12,000 plus every year. We have more churches than any other nation, but, excepting Russia, more unchurched. We boast of impressive financial reserves; yet we list the heaviest national debt. We exalt our democracy; however, unquestionably we have sustained a serious loss in representative government.

Why these glaring contradictions? Write this down as

America's number one transgression: We, too, are despising God's Word. In this divinely enriched nation, where President John Quincy Adams declared, "I say to you, *'Search the Scriptures'!";* where Andrew Jackson proclaimed, "The Bible is the rock on which our Republic rests"; where President Ulysses S. Grant appealed, "Hold fast to the Bible as the sheet anchor of your liberties!" God's Word is as completely rejected by millions as in the days of Israel's deep decline. Skeptical ministers in modern congregations belittle, attack, and even ridicule God's Word. It used to be the work of loud-mouthed infidels — this discrediting of the Scriptures; but today many a theological professor opposes the Bible as persistently as did Bob Ingersoll — at the same time accepting his salary from Christian contributors or a Christian endowment. Your letters likewise reveal that in some churches Scripture is practically a closed and sealed book. Sermon texts, if any, are chosen from recent best sellers, four-starred motion pictures, or current events. Baffled men and bewildered women who attend services to hear a promise starting with this assurance *"Thus saith the Lord,"* must listen instead to discourses which feature statements by men, at a time when merely human utterances must be regarded with suspicion and distrust.

If the Bible is banned from the pulpit, we must not be surprised that it has given way to nature stories and "pep" talks in the Sunday school; that private Bible reading in the home has suffered serious setbacks. How many families are there in this vast mission of the air, from the Atlantic seaboard to the Pacific Coast, in which the family finds time to *"search the Scriptures"?* I have before me a Bible printed in 1541, just 400 years old. Prepared only fifty years after Columbus' first voyage, it contains a map of the world, grotesque in many respects and significant because it omits North and South America entirely. Despite the changes that have intervened in these four centuries, neither the basic needs of humanity nor the power of the Scriptures to meet these needs has fundamentally changed. Originally, this ancient Bible, large and cumbersome, cost at least twenty dollars; today a Testament — with accurate maps — can be bought for a fraction of a dollar. Nevertheless, stolid indifference to the divine Word reigns in many hearts and homes. Movements are organized to destroy the Bible. Our youth is being coaxed from its truth, many churches directed away from its power. At a time when America sorely needs divine, unfailing direction, we are forced to admit that millions are perpetuating the same traitorous and fatal mistake which helped to cast Israel prostrate in its darkest day.

II

WE MUST RESTORE THE BIBLE!

In this crisis we must follow Josiah, a God-fearing young man. As he increased in years, his devotion to Jehovah was likewise strengthened. When he was twenty-six years old, in the prime of his young manhood, he started to repair and rebuild the Temple. There were no strikes or labor troubles in that reconstruction, because the builders, doubtless chosen from the faithful, were earnest and sincere workers, adequately paid and so thoroughly trusted by the king that he demanded no accounting of them. There would be no strikes today and no labor legislation required by Congress if this same mutual esteem existed between employer and employee and both regarded their duties as a divine trust.

In the course of Josiah's operations a startling discovery was made. Accidentally, it seems, the workmen uncovered an ancient manuscript, a scroll that had perhaps been deposited in a wall when the Temple was built 350 years before or that had been contemptuously cast aside when Jehovah was no longer worshiped as the true God. At any rate, Hilkiah, the high priest, immediately recognized the remarkable document. He cried to Shaphan the scribe, *"I have found the book of the law in the house of the Lord!"* The scroll was read to the king. When Josiah heard what the holy God demands of His people and then contrasted their repeated, protracted sins, he tore his garments in distress and ordered that the rediscovered Word of God be read to all the people. In one of the most remarkable public demonstrations in history, so we are told, *"the king went up into the house of the Lord and all the men of Judah and all the inhabitants of Jerusalem with him and all the priests and the prophets and all the people, both small and great: and he read in their ears all the words of the book of the covenant which was found in the house of the Lord."* That reading of the Scriptures had a startling effect. The people made a solemn pledge to God, promising faithfully to obey His Word. A passover festival was held — greater than any since the early days of Israel — and a cleansing instituted in which the Temple was purged of false worship, the idolatrous priests removed, all immorality banned from the sanctuary grounds, every false priest throughout the land thrown out of office, and the cruel sacrifices of children in the Valley of Hinnom stopped. In short, one of history's great reformations began, and it started when the Bible was brought back to the rulers, the priests, and the people.

Today, if America is to have a thorough, effective reformation — and God knows we need it! — we must start where Moses started, where Josiah, Saint Paul, Luther began — at the Word of God and in the churches. Say what you will about our country's various needs, the supreme necessity for this perilous hour pleads, America, bring back the Bible! Banish the enemies of God's Word from Christian pulpits! Exclude the opponents of the Scriptures from Christian theological seminaries and colleges! Stop the printing and dissemination, under Christian auspices, of books and periodicals that put question marks behind the clear, sure statements concerning our Savior's death and atonement! Do what Josiah did, and that means, have the great masses of the 70,000,000 Americans who bear Christ's name turn completely from the denial of Scripture and rededicate themselves to the task and privilege of restoring the Bible to their hearts, their homes, their churches — and we will witness a sweeping reformation!

However, Scripture must be brought back, not merely as "The Good Book," a collection of pious, helpful thoughts, a volume that *contains* God's Word, but as the Book that *is* God's Word, in at Genesis and out at Revelation, the divinely inspired and errorless Record which has never made a mistake and which will never be rightfully charged with error, the only decisive Source of Christian doctrine, the one infallible Guide for Christian life. Because most Americans are not willing to declare the Bible, as originally given by God, without error; because even some Lutheran groups (not united with us) will not accept its full, literal inspiration, let me repeat the reasons which should lead us to rely unquestioningly on Scripture as divine Truth. First of all, the Bible, unlike all other writings, repeatedly claims to come from the Almighty. More than 3,100 times writers in the Old and New Testaments assert that their utterances are God's utterances. Have you ever heard of another volume which makes like claims?

The Bible proves itself God's own Word particularly by the power of prophecy. Read the predictions concerning

Babylon, Nineveh, Syria, Egypt, Palestine; study the verdict of history which shows how clearly these have been fulfilled; and then ask yourself again whether this unique volume must not come from the Almighty and All-knowing, since only He can foretell the future with such startling faithfulness!

The Bible must come from Heaven because only a divine volume could victoriously conquer the unparalleled, vicious opposition it has suffered. Copies of it have been burned, thrown into the ocean, ground to pieces; yet the Bible is sold in greater numbers today than any other book; translated into a thousand different languages and widely distributed over the face of the earth. Bob Ingersoll once stated in Denver that within fifty years the Bible would not have fifty believers left in that city. A half century has elapsed. Last week I wired the secretary of the American Bible Society in Denver to see whether Ingersoll was right and Scripture was an unknown book in that metropolis of the Rockies. He replied that in the last year almost 38,000 Bibles and Testament parts had been distributed in this city, one for every ten Denver citizens. Recent newspaper reports tell us that in Fascist Spain a shipment of 110,000 Bibles has been confiscated by General Franco's totalitarian government and that they have been ground to pulp. But God's Word cannot be destroyed in this way nor by the persecution and imprisonment of its readers. One nation rejects it, only to have another accept it. From war-torn China come unprecedented demands for Holy Writ.

We believe that the Bible is God's Word because of its divine power exerted on every page of history. A hundred years ago, after the first missionaries had brought the Word to Africa, a Hottentot delegate to a London missionary society reported: "When the Bible came to us, we were naked, we lived in caves and on the tops of mountains, we painted our bodies with red paint. The Bible charmed us out of our caves and from the tops of the mountains. Now we know there is a God." The Maharajah of Travancore, India, paid Scripture this pointed tribute: "Take it and read it, examine it and see whether it is good! Of one thing I am convinced, do what we will, oppose it as we may, it is the Christian Bible which will sooner or later work out the regeneration of our land." Survey the blessed influence of Scripture on womanhood, childhood, labor, education, government, charity, the arts, on nations as a whole, and you ought to be fair enough to realize that these startling improvements have come, not from politics, Christless religions, atheism, Communism, legislation, conquest, evolution, but from the Book of all books. If only the Bible completely controlled the hearts and minds of the world's leaders and all its peoples, we could have Bibles instead of bullets; Scriptures, not sub-machine guns; the Gospel, not gunfire; Testaments, rather than tanks!

Particularly, however, do we believe that Scripture is God's Word because of its miraculous influence on human souls. It has done what no college degree, no code of law can accomplish. It has changed, ennobled, and uplifted the human heart. When Stanley lay on his sickbed in Africa during his first attack of jungle fever, he wrote: "Then verses of Scripture rang iteratingly through my mind as applicable to my own being, sometimes full of flowing promise, often of solemn warning. Alone in my tent, unseen of men, . . . I flung myself on my knees and poured out my soul utterly in secret prayer to Him who had led me here mysteriously into Africa, there to reveal Himself and His will." The Bible changed Stanley into a believer. Rabbi Slostowski, a professor of the

Talmud in the rabbinical seminary at Tel Aviv, Palestine, as an orthodox Jew hated the Lord Jesus Christ. Riding in a railway train from Haifa to Jerusalem, he noticed a young man on the seat opposite him who was reading a New Testament in Hebrew. So great was the learned Israelite's resentment against Christ that he took it upon himself sharply to criticize the young Jewish convert. The young man replied by giving Slostowski his copy of the New Testament. That very night the rabbi, alone in his room, read on in the Gospels until three o'clock in the morning, with every passing page, he reports, increasing the deep conviction that Jesus Christ was the promised Messiah. For the first time in his life he fell on his knees and prayed in the name of Christ. And today he writes: "I have already found more than 200 passages of the New Testament which prove beyond a doubt that truly Jesus is the Messiah."

The Scriptures have this remarkable power since they testify of Him to whom each of our broadcasts is dedicated, the Lord and Savior. Because the Bible in the marvelous provisions of the Old Testament and through its system of sacrifice pointed to *"the Lamb of God, which taketh away the sin of the world";* because the New Testament portrays Jesus as true God and true man, the Son of the Almighty and the Son of the Virgin Mary, the crucified Savior and the resurrected Redeemer, the Servant of servants, yet the Sovereign of sovereigns, the Christ who on the cross pleaded for all men and who still makes intercession with the Father for us, the glorious Lord of grace and mercy once born in the lowliness of Bethlehem but who will soon return in His glorious Second Coming — and a score of evident signs foretell this — as King of kings and Judge of the quick and the dead; because this Savior calls the Scripture God's Truth, we should accept the Bible, trust it, cherish it, defend it, and ceaselessly spread its message of grace and truth.

When we cry out, "Bring back the Bible!" we also add, "Bring back the Bible's Savior!" As Christmas approaches and the Advent cry resounds, *"Behold, thy King cometh!"* may we be given the grace to prepare our hearts worthily to receive the coming King of grace! However disheartening the burden of your sin, bring it all to Christ! He has never spurned anyone who has come with a broken, contrite heart. When you are the weakest and smallest, His mercy is the strongest and greatest. However pressing your personal problems may be — and I know they weigh you down with unusual heaviness during these otherwise happy weeks of Christmas preparation — may the promise of His grace make you realize "what a Friend" you "have in Jesus, all" your "sins and griefs to bear"! His glorious Gospel, penned for all men, yet written by divine inspiration especially for you, contains this climax of divine truth: God not only loved the whole world with such heavenly devotion *"that He gave His only-begotten Son"* as the Ransom for every sinner, but this mercy is offered you freely, without any condition or credentials, without any payment or prerequisite, without any thought of reward or recompense — for what have we, with all our transgressions, for which we could expect recognition in the sight of a holy God? — solely by the Savior's limitless love. By His pledge *"Behold, all things are become new"* I promise you that if you come face to face with Jesus on the pages of Scripture, you can have incomparable joy. Listeners from New York State write us that after hearing our broadcast they bought two Bibles — one in English for the daughter and one in French for the parents, who preferred that language. They explain, "We never read the Bible before we heard your message; but now we read it regularly and attend a true Christian church. Today we feel like a new family." Every home in this radio assembly can likewise experience in Christ renewing power. Take time to bring Jesus into your household through daily Scripture reading! Fathers and mothers of America, during these pre-Christmas weeks find at least five or ten minutes in each twenty-four hour day to explain to your children the real significance of Christ's compassion! As you make ready to adorn your dwellings for these holidays, first of all prepare your hearts with the cleansing of His purifying Word!

Jesus is calling you, asking for faith in Him and His Word, for loyalty to His promises and His Scriptures, for faithfulness to the cross and the Bible. Because there can be no more important appeal, either for the nation as a whole, for the churches, for our homes, or for our own souls, in His blessed name and for the spread of His truth, I beseech you: Bring back the Bible! Restore it in Christless churches; in unhappy, strife-torn homes; in benighted, sin-clouded hearts; in our own souls, so that in these desperate days God's truth may continue to march from victory to victory, the only hope for inner peace in a war-wracked world, our one assurance of pardon and blessing for earth and heaven! The mightiest movement for the spread of the Scriptures was started 137 years ago in London, at a time when England appeared to totter on the brink of ruin as Napoleon's army, across the channel, threatened invasion. Amid wars and the proud boastings of atheists, the British and Foreign Bible Society began its work. If only during these years of mass slaughter and devastating destruction that can engulf our country there were a nation-wide determination to teach, publish, spread, read, cherish, and obey the Scripture truth as never before! O God, we ask in Jesus' name, bring back the Bible to us, and bring us back to the Bible! Amen.

AMERICA, EMBATTLED, TURN TO CHRIST!

"When ye shall hear of wars and rumors of wars, be ye not troubled; for such things must needs be." — Saint Mark 13:7

Heavenly Father, Lord of the Nations:

A crucial moment has come for our country, with the reports of enemy bombardment; and we flee to Thee for refuge, strength, and the hope of victory. Humbly we bow before Thee, in Jesus' name, to beseech Thy guidance during the heavy days before us. Direct the President, the Congress, and all responsible for the nation's future course along paths pleasing to Thee! Teach us individually to understand that we may be called to sacrifice life's most precious possessions for the defense of America and for the defeat of those who threaten to bring destruction within our borders! O God, who canst still break the bow and cut the enemies' spear asunder, we commit our cause to Thee, as we humble ourselves to confess our sins and for Jesus' sake beseech the pardon sealed in His blood. Help us in this crisis hour to love Thy truth! We know from Thy blessed Word which never makes a mistake that Thou canst deliver us and, clinging more resolutely to our Savior, we declare, "If God be for us, who can be against us?" Therefore, O Lord of hosts, be with us now as Thou wast with our fathers! We ask it contritely because we pray in Jesus' blessed name. Amen.

"IF *God be for us, who can be against us?*" May this divine truth strengthen the souls of millions throughout America as our beloved nation finds itself treacherously attacked in the first week of a destructive war. We dare not make the fatal mistake of assuming that we can succeed without God or be victorious against Him! Our enemies are numerous, powerful, prepared; they will wage a long-drawn, hard-fought contest. Those who only a few days ago predicted that the Japanese Empire would be smashed within six weeks will be forced to revise their opinion. This struggle may last six years or more. Before

us, my countrymen, is a heavily weighted future, the end
of which can be foreseen by no scientist, however learned,
no statesman, however experienced, no economic expert,
however renowned. Earnest appeals are made to patriotism; and may the love for America now ring clear and
true in every heart! But patriotism will not be enough.
We will be called upon to practice self-denial, and because
of the rich blessings the United States has granted each
one of us, we should be eager to forego luxuries and non-
essentials; but self-denial will not be enough. As the
struggle continues, we will be asked to sacrifice time,
energies, money, perhaps even our lives; and who, reflecting
on the privileges, the opportunities, the freedoms which
are ours, will shrink from doing whatever is humanly possible to transmit the heritage of liberty, received from our
fathers, to our children? But even sacrifice will not be
enough. We need the Almighty. Spiritual defense is as
vital as military defense. We must turn to the Lord and
exult, "A mighty Fortress is our God, a trusty Shield
and Weapon!" Millions from coast to coast will require
redoubled soul comfort and guidance during the heavy
sieges of this conflict. As the Old Testament prophets
during periods of national visitation were commanded,
"Comfort ye, comfort ye My people," so the consolation
and strengthening which comes from faith in the redemption purchased by Jesus Christ, not the message of any
counterfeit gospel, must be the keynote of wartime
preaching.

Today, then, on National Bible Sunday and the first
Lord's day in radio history on which a vast coast-to-coast
broadcasting system can be employed in bringing the
Savior's promise to the people of the United States at war,
may God's Spirit mightily bless this appeal:

AMERICA, EMBATTLED, TURN TO CHRIST!

Accept His divine instruction and comfort given in our Scripture for today (Saint Mark, chapter thirteen, verse seven), which with heavenly understanding of our problems, individual and national, says, *"When ye shall hear of wars and rumors of wars, be ye not troubled; for such things must needs be."*

I

JESUS INSTRUCTS US IN THE REASON FOR WAR

Reviewing the events of the past several days we are startled by the suddenness with which war began. A weekly confidential bulletin issued by financial advisers in Washington, dated December 6, expressed the opinion that conflict with Japan might be avoided; at worst, it was some distance away. Yet, on December 7 Japanese planes attacked our island outposts. A magazine dated December 12 and purporting to give the last word in national affairs likewise predicted that hostilities, if they were declared, would be postponed for some time. Before that magazine reached its readers enemy bombs had taken their toll of American lives. On the very morning, just a week ago, when the struggle broke, a feature writer for New York's largest newspaper voiced this opinion, "Japan does not want war." But, even as people were reading these wishful thoughts, American youth was being killed on our Pacific islands. While human predictions — and there were many other similar mistakes — have collapsed notoriously, God's prophecies have never failed. Every one among the hundreds of Scriptural predictions referring to history, past or present, has been literally, exactly fulfilled. With all the mockery evil-minded men heap on Holy Writ, they have failed to produce a single volume from the millions written since the earliest days which has foretold future events with only a fraction of the accuracy and detail found in Bible prophecies. It has always seemed to me that if men would use good, common, unbiased sense, they would come to the conclusion, on this basis of prophecy and fulfillment, that the Old and New Testaments must be, as no other book ever written or read, divine revelation. The basic trouble, however, is this: Usually the enemies of the Bible do not take time to read the writings they condemn. If they did and thus gave the Spirit a chance to work in their hearts, they could come to the conclusion reached by the famous British poet Cowper when he wrote, "If the prophecies have been fulfilled (of which there is abundant demonstration), the Scriptures must be the Word of God; and if the Scripture is the Word of God, Christianity must be true."

Thus when Jesus tells us in our text, *"Ye shall hear of wars and rumors of wars,"* that prediction, now 1900 years old, has never been realized as forcefully as now in the most widespread of all wars. For years unbelieving men, with their little prides and puny prejudices, sought to discount this forecast of *"wars and rumors of wars."* In opposition they taught that the race was constantly on the upgrade, steadily elevating itself by its own bootstraps. As the "human animals" — for so are men called by this delusion — steadfastly lifted themselves from the lower beast level, crime would be checked, lusts restricted, greed controlled, hatreds removed, and, this is the repeated promise, bloodshed completely banished. I submit to you that no other generation in American history should be more ready than ours to cast aside completely these rosy promises, dangerous and destructive, every one of them, because they contradict divine truth. At a time when culture, education, science, and invention have reached their height, international morals are at their lowest, international strife at its widest. Twenty-three years ago the first world conflict was concluded, the war that was to end all wars; but while that struggle involved sixteen nations, the present list of belligerents already numbers thirty-six, and many more may still be added before the victory is ours. Thus, while men, wise in their own conceit, have prophesied, *"Peace, peace!"* Christ has predicted, *"Wars and rumors of wars."* His Word alone is the immovable, unalterable, unbreakable Truth of all truths. Therefore, believe with all your hearts that the thunderous denunciations of God's Law: *"The soul that sinneth, it shall die." "The wages of sin is death." "Ye shall die in your sins,"* are not theory, guesswork, speculation. *"Heaven and earth shall pass away"* before *"one jot or one tittle"* of these utterances is proved false. By the same heavenly power every promise of grace, every pledge of mercy that Jesus, God's Son and the world's Savior, offers you — assurances like these beloved passages: *"God so loved the world that He gave His only begotten Son, that whosoever believeth in Him should not perish but have everlasting life." "Come unto Me, all ye that labor and are heavy laden, and I will give you rest." "If a man keep My saying, he shall never see death." "I am the Resurrection and the Life"* — these pledges are the sure, eternal, triumphant truth of *"Jesus Christ, the same yesterday and today and forever."* My countrymen, turn to Him for His changeless grace, for everlasting verity!

The Savior also declares in our text that wars *"must needs be."* In explanation, the Bible, honored throughout America today, asks pointedly, *"From whence come wars and fightings among you?"* and answers, *"Come they not hence, even of your lusts?"* In other words, Scripture teaches that bloodshed is provoked by sin. Examine every conflict since the cradle days of humanity, and behind each struggle you will find overreaching greed, the desire for more territory, more trade, more natural resources, more

profit, more power, and with it, envy, jealousy, race prejudice, hatred, oppression, conquest.

Besides, God often uses war as a chastening and a visitation of His outraged justice. If people live in the unbroken peace and the carnal security that forgets the
Almighty; if atheism flourishes in universities, unbelief in
high schools, disregard of the Creator even in grammar
schools; if pulpits are polluted with the denial of God
and His Christ; if the Scriptures fall into neglect within
buildings once dedicated to their teaching; if even homes
are marked by irreligion, families forsake the faith, live in
legalized lust with utter disregard of the divine standards for
domestic honesty — then He whose justice and righteousness prevent the sins of an individual, as of a nation, from
remaining unrebuked often intervenes and the horror of
war begins its devastation.

"Such things must needs be," the Scriptures echo, also
in the United States. This is not the hour, with American
shore-cities darkened by blackout, American defense seriously threatened and American lives at stake, to speak in
boastful, boisterous tones as though this nation did not
need the Almighty. But it is the time, high time, for
masses in America to approach God, to fall on their knees
before Him in full confession of their sins, to find pardon
and power through Christ. Over the clamor of this disturbed hour, at the beginning of a war that will cost us
more in men and money, toil and tears, than we now can
measure, the momentous call, from heaven itself, resounds
across the land, "America, get right with God!" We must
understand that this conflict did not break on us simply
through our enemies' planning and treachery. All the
sweat and sorrow, the blighted hopes and bitter bereavements this struggle can produce, are to remind us as
individuals, families, church groups, as a nation, how re-

peatedly we have disregarded God's Word, rebelled against His instruction, rejected the precious Gospel, ridiculed the message of Christ's cross and His blood. Instead of shouting, whistling, screaming as many did last Monday when war was declared, Christians in this country know that for them the cry of this crisis is: "On your knees, America!" "Pray, America, pray!" With their reconciliation assured through faith in Christ's atoning love they can rise, ready to battle courageously for the defeat of our enemies. For God Himself promises, *"If My people, which are called by My name, shall humble themselves and pray and seek My face and turn from their wicked ways; then will I hear from heaven, and will forgive their sin and will heal their land."*

In another sense this conflict *"must needs be,"* for in the chapter from which our text has been chosen Jesus reveals that *"wars and rumors of wars"* are to foreshadow the beginning of the end for mankind. It is Bible truth that this old, sin-encrusted world will not, yes, cannot endure forever. Since the days of Cain, the earth on which men walk is too soaked with the blood of the legions murdered by their brothers, of the myriads killed on battlefields or cut down in brutal massacres; the clean air God gave us has been breathed by too many who are moved by hatred, lust, covetousness, degenerate passions; the skies above have looked down on the vileness and depravity of the whole race too long to permit a world like ours to last eternally. It must end. Indeed, the Scriptures foretell in scores of clear passages that this entire globe, with everything on and in it, will be destroyed when Christ at His second coming appears to judge the quick and the dead.

In order that believers, instead of being caught unawares when Jesus comes, may be fully prepared to meet

Him, the Scriptures present a long list of signs, describing in detail church and world conditions which are to precede Christ's return in glory. Particularly prominent is Jesus' warning of *"wars and rumors of wars"* with His explanation that *"nation shall rise against nation and kingdom against kingdom"* — a prophecy now more clearly fulfilled than ever in past ages. We witness other evidences of this approaching end. Famines are predicted, and impoverished people by the millions in the small occupied countries of Europe, not to mention multitudes more in China, will not have enough to eat during the coming winter. Pestilences are foretold; physicians are forecasting epidemics which will sweep across nations after this conflict just as the dread influenza scourge accompanied World War I. Earthquakes are to come; and it is on record that recent years have witnessed the most disastrous of such upheavals. In these last times, we are warned, *"false prophets shall rise."* Have they ever been as numerous before? *"Iniquity shall abound."* — Our crime records are at their highest figure. *"The love of many shall wax cold"* — How true, when we see the worldliness in many churches or survey the number of those who have turned from Christ! Listen to Saint Paul's description of conditions before judgment breaks upon us: *"This know also that in the last days perilous times shall come. For men shall be lovers of their own selves, covetous, boasters, proud, blasphemers, disobedient to parents, unthankful, unholy, without natural affection, truce-breakers, false accusers, incontinent, fierce, despisers of those that are good, traitors, heady, high-minded, lovers of pleasure more than lovers of God, having a form of godliness, but denying the power thereof, . . . ever learning and never able to come to the knowledge of the truth."* A score of sermons can be based on these twenty charges. How readily we should conclude that if the primitive Christian Church proclaimed, *"The Lord is at hand,"* then assuredly today, after 1900 years, His Second Advent is upon us. He will come at any time.

May He not find us unprepared! The lessons of last week's attack at Pearl Harbor showed us how destructive it is to imagine danger far off. Therefore, as God's Word calls out: "America, turn to Jesus! He is coming soon!" let us keep ourselves in constant readiness for that hour which will bring terrifying rejection to those who have spurned Jesus, but a home-coming in joy and unspeakable glory, a day of release from worry and war, an eternity of bliss beyond compare for all who humbly, sincerely, trustingly acclaim Christ their Savior! If we could only realize what indescribably radiant blessings Christ's return will bring those who are His, every heart throughout this broad land would constantly repeat the prayer of the early Church, *"Even so, come, Lord Jesus!"*

II

JESUS GIVES US COMFORT IN TIME OF WAR

Until this glorious Advent we must work and hope, watch and pray amid life's sorrows and its joys. If this conflict continues to rage, year after year, we must be ready — and the Government has issued this warning — to give up many comforts and luxuries, to adopt a lower standard of living. Who knows whether that will be the end? Grave questions of inflation, serious problems of postwar reconstruction, the whole readjustment of our American life — all this puts everyone before the most deep-rooted difficulties we, as a nation, have ever faced. More penetrating will be the personal grief, when war demands the limb or the life of a son, a father, a brother. The first days of fighting have made many gold-star mothers and brought bereavement into hundreds of American homes. While we pay tribute to the devotion and heroism of those who have died fighting our battles and resolve that, God helping us, their sacrifice will not have been made in vain, we must expect that as the war progresses casualty lists will be far longer and more of the sons to whom you parents waved a brave farewell will never return.

Now, where can we find unfailing solace, unchanging consolation, unfaltering assurance? Where, if not in Him who is the Hope of the ages, the Help in every need, the Comforter for every distressed soul — Jesus, our Christ, who today tells us, *"When ye shall hear of wars and rumors of wars, be ye not troubled"*?

Had anyone else written this, *"Be ye not troubled!"*; were this the claim of a mortal leader, the wishful thinking of a social expert, we would shake our heads and turn away, unconvinced. Too often have men been tortured by the glib promises and false predictions which abound in our age. But take heart! Remember who spoke these words! No dreamer, no enthusiast, no mistaken optimist, no irresponsible fanatic! This is the pledge of Jesus Christ, who is more than all men, saints, or angels; He is the very God together with the Father and the Spirit, the ever-blessed Trinity in ever-holy Unity. The modern denial which makes our Lord only an exalted teacher can help us nothing. The suffering world cries out for *divine* comfort and direction. And here it is in the words of One who never spoke an empty promise nor raised an unfulfilled hope, Jesus, who declares, *"When ye shall hear of wars and rumors of wars, be ye not troubled!"* America, turn to that Christ, the King of kings, Sovereign of sovereigns, Lord of lords, the very God of very God!

The truth of this *"Be ye not troubled,"* is also assured us because Jesus, as approaching Christmas reminds us, is our Savior. He grants real assurance, unfailing strength, true courage, even for the worst that may confront us, because He, blessed Redeemer of our souls, has removed completely the evil responsible for fear, doubt, and dismay. It is the unspeakable glory of His love for us that while we were yet in our sins, shaking our puny fists against the Almighty, speaking words of blasphemy against His holy name, thinking thoughts of lustful desire and covetous greed against His divine law; while we were sending our souls to hell, swinging the doors of heaven closed by our repeated transgression, condemning ourselves utterly, hopelessly, and eternally, Jesus took from us all our sins, including especially those which seemed too vile to be forgiven, made each of those transgressions His own, and suffered their guilt, their curse, their punishment, their death, when He *"died for all"* on Golgotha's gory cross, *"the Lamb of God, which taketh away the sin of the world."* No matter what others tell you, no matter how vehemently the church you attend may deny this claim, no matter whether high authorities protest against your repeating this Bible truth, believe Jesus when He assures you that the pardon purchased by His blood, the life restored by His death and resurrection are yours, not as a reward for your good works or anyone else's; not as a compensation for your self-denial or sacrifice; not in answer to your parents' pleadings or your pastor's prayers, but simply as God's marvelous gift, granted by Christ's unearnable, unpurchasable grace and His pure, unconditioned mercy. America, turn to that Christ of all compassion!

Particularly let every soldier or sailor who may be summoned to fight the life-and-death struggles of this war accept Jesus now, before facing the brunt of battle, so that in the midst of tumult and strife faith in His constant companionship will bestow this assurance, *"Being justified by faith, we have peace with God"* — the inner peace *"which passeth all understanding"*!

"When ye shall hear of wars and rumors of wars, be ye not troubled!" because a Christian never need be troubled. If everything else crashes about him, with increasing power he feels the Savior's closeness. We who acclaim Jesus our only Redeemer know that the Lord, without whose will not a sparrow falls to the ground, has numbered the very hairs on our head. From the moment our lives are *"hid with Christ,"* heaven's angels in their legions are ready to protect us. Therefore I said at the beginning, *"If God be for us, who can be against us?"* When Jesus rules your heart in a personal, pulsating faith, you can stand confidently in stormed trenches as the din of hell itself appears to loose its fury around you. You can crouch securely in blacked-out cities, while bombs seem to blast away the earth beneath you. You can face hidden perils above and below the murky ocean with a bravery that is highest when true Christian faith is strongest. This is not fatalism nor irresponsible recklessness. It is rather the blessing which comes from the assurance that the Redeemer who died for us, now lives for us and with us, constantly ready to protect us.

Sometimes, of course, it may be God's inscrutable will that we fall in life's battle. Rather than accuse our Father of cruelty, question His ways, drop into unbelief or snarling blasphemy, we need the faith which guarantees us that *"whether we live . . . or die, we are the Lord's"* and which assures us that *"all things,"* even the most terrifying disasters the war may produce, *"work together for good to them that love God."* In our shortsighted vision we may not be able to grasp why God took this promising young man or that exemplary young woman from our midst.

Deep-rooted reliance is required to believe that the losses this war may bring will become spiritual gain for those who are Christ's. But the Almighty has compassion on us in this respect, too. He assures us, *"What I do thou knowest not now; but thou shalt know hereafter."* In heaven's hallowed bliss when we come to claim our prepared place in the many mansions — and all that we need for a title to our portion in the Father's house is this personal trust in the Lord Jesus — we will be able to survey God's marvelous dealings with us. The mists will clear, and as we see the harmony in the design of life He has helped us weave, there will be no more tears nor sorrows. We will exult, *"He hath done all things well!"*

It is to this faith in the crucified, redeeming, comforting, sustaining Christ that we pledge these broadcasts anew in an hour of crisis for the American nation. With God's help we will continue to preach nothing but His Word and to apply it to our multiplied needs. We are planning to bring these Gospel messages to the military youth in ever-widening range, since in times of stress like ours young people bear the brunt of the struggle and often find themselves confronted with redoubled temptation. Our transcriptions are being heard on certain battleships and at land stations.

I plead with *all* you who love the Lord — who know that this broadcast, though it is called and in truth is "The Lutheran Hour — Bringing Christ to the Nations," is fighting the battle for conservative, Scriptural, fundamental Christianity throughout the land. — Stand by us during the coming months with frequent, fervent prayers, with generous financial assistance! It costs us $8,000 each week to glorify Christ over this vast radio system. If we are to answer fully the challenge of this hour, we need a larger network, more outlets. Before *"the night cometh when no man can work,*" we must send out the message of salvation, life, hope, and a blessed eternity in the Lord Jesus Christ with greater force and penetration. Stand beside us, then, as we begin our wartime broadcasting with the plea "America, turn to Christ!" and the prayer "Christ, turn Thy mercies to America!" For in Jesus, our God and Redeemer, there is pardon, peace, and power — for the nation, for the Church, for every believing heart. — God grant you this saving faith, for the Savior's sake. Amen!

GOD, GRANT US TRUE CHRISTMAS PEACE!

"On earth peace!" — Saint Luke 2:14

Blessed Babe of Bethlehem:

Raise our hearts above all the sorrows, hatreds, lusts of this grief-filled hour and grant us that true, inner joy of salvation which is ours when we kneel in faith before Thy manger to worship Thee as our God and Savior! By Thy Spirit help every sin-laden soul to approach Thee for cleansing, every burdened heart to find comfort in the glorious Christmas Gospel! Be with our beloved nation during this time of testing! Protect the military and naval forces that would protect us! Bless those called to guide the United States with wisdom and the determination to do Thy will! At Thy birth the angels caroled, "On earth peace!" and we beseech Thee to enrich us with the rejoicing and calm of soul which that celestial hymn promised. Yet, O Lord of all power and mercy, if it be Thy will, give us also a just and honorable peace between nations! Defeat all proud men who rise against Thee! Help us worthily to receive Thee and make this a blessed Christmas for many, especially the poor, the forsaken, the distressed! We ask this by the promise of Thy manifold mercies. Amen.

TWO weeks ago, when sudden death treacherously rained down on American troops near Honolulu, many of us began to wonder whether for the coming birthday of Christ anyone could honestly speak the customary greeting "Merry Christmas!" Today, when we are told that not 300, as first reported, but close to 3,000 of our military youth, physically the best specimens of American manhood, were killed and wounded in that outrageous attack; when all but the stupid must foresee that we are in the first battles of a conflict which, week after week, month after month, and it may well be year after year, will destroy more youthful lives; it will be hard, often unspeakably hard, to greet friends with the usual "Merry Christmas!"

There will be plenty of hilarity during these next days, to be sure, overplenty of drunkenness and debauch. National magazine advertisements feature a glass of whisky enshrined in a halo, the circle of light which reverent artists place about Christ's head. And how true to modern life that blasphemy is! Millions, instead of kneeling before Bethlehem's Babe, are serving sin, crying out in dull fatalism, "Let us *'eat, drink and be merry,'* for who knows what tomorrow's war will bring? But that kind of merriment is never acceptable Americanism, especially not this year, and it always contradicts Christian faith.

Can I be merry when I think of the shallow graves at Pearl Harbor? Be merry when a recent graduate of Concordia Seminary, whom I helped prepare for the ministry, a young pastor appointed naval chaplain, lies wounded in an Hawaiian hospital? Let children enjoy the season to the fullest! Let their laughter ring unrestrained, for who knows what the future will bring them? But the rest of us ought to be mature and intelligent enough to realize that not since 1777 and the piercing, desperate winter at Valley Forge has there been a more perilous Christmas in the United States than the festival which comes this week or those in succeeding years until God makes us a repentant nation and grants victory with righteous, equitable peace.

What shall we do, then, with Christmas? Was Clarence Darrow right when, shortly before his death, he called it "a humbug, a public nuisance," declaring, "People would be better off if they paid no attention to it." Was George Bernard Shaw right when he labeled the festival of the Nativity an "unbearable nuisance that ought to be abolished"? God forbid! This year many of us feel the need of the Christ Child, perhaps more than ever before. Through Him ours can still be a blessed, though saddened Christmas. Despite the inferno which may surround us with blood and disaster, famine and disease, murder and torture, bomb and blasting, the first carol, particularly the promise, *"On earth peace!"* (Saint Luke, chapter two, verse fourteen) can re-echo in our hearts, whether the future may bring prosperity or adversity, joy or sorrow, health or sickness, life or death.

Come, then, throw off dark, morbid thoughts! Cast fear away! And as you prepare to adore the newborn Savior, let the angelic announcement *"On earth peace!"* bring this prayer from your heart:

GOD, GRANT US TRUE CHRISTMAS PEACE

— peace in our souls, peace throughout the world!

I

HOW GLORIOUS THE GRACE OF THIS CHRISTMAS PEACE!

For a message as glorious, radiant, heavenly as this, *"On earth peace!"* God chose glorious, radiant, heavenly messengers. No high priest from the near-by Temple; no prophet — and were he gifted as Isaiah, compassionate as Jeremiah, loyal as Amos — was worthy of bringing that marvelous promise. Celestial voices were required, *"the multitude of the heavenly host,"* and in a vast, unnumbered chorus of angels and archangels such as the world had never heard before and will never hear again their sanctified voices proclaim, *"On earth peace!"*

For this Christmas no immortal messenger will appear to you with the glad tidings of peace in Christ, but the Nativity news is imprinted in your Bible with the same divine force and unbreakable truth as though cherubim and seraphim had sung their carols directly to you. If your Christmas is to be a day of peace, then first of all resolve to take God at His word, and with a faith that hurdles every doubt declare, "Because my heavenly Father sent His holy servants to announce the birth at Bethlehem; because my Bible, God's inspired, infallible Word, records the Christmas glory, with my whole heart and soul I accept this double assurance that the Babe in the Judean manger is my Prince of Peace." Do not let anyone discourage you by asserting that this faith is puerile, unacceptable to thinking people! A few days ago death came to the great Russian author Dmitri Merejowski in Vichy. Exiled from the Soviet country because of his religion and political persuasion, that scholar, a man according even to newspaper reports, "whose equal in knowledge and diligence has rarely appeared," found unusual strength in the Bible. Referring to his own New Testament which had been in his possession for thirty years, he wrote in one of his books: "I read it daily and shall continue to read it as long as my eyes can see and by every kind of light, by rays coming from the sun or from the earth, on brightest days and in blackest nights, happy or unhappy, sick or well, full of faith or of doubt, full of feeling or devoid of feeling. And it seems to me there is always something new in what I read, something unfathomed, and that I shall never plumb its depths or reach its end. The gilt edges of the leaves are tarnished, the paper is yellow, the leather binding is coming to pieces and the back has come unstuck. Some of the pages are loose; it ought to be rebound; but I cannot find it in my heart to send it away. Indeed, the thought of being separated from it even for a few days frightens me. What shall be buried with me in my coffin? The Book. With what shall I rise from the grave? With the Book. What did I do on earth? I read the Book." — Marvelous words! If the mighty intellect of Dmitri Merejowski paid the Scriptures such unstinted tribute, has anyone in this audience the right to put a question mark behind the peace promise chanted by the angels? What grace to have this immovable assurance for our faith!

Noteworthy, too, is the place where the announcement of this peace was made! The angels spurned the seven hills of proud Rome, the market places of learned Athens, the pyramids and the sphinxes of Egypt; they passed by the imposing Temple at Jerusalem and came not even to the heart and center of Bethlehem, insignificant as it was, but to an empty pasture outside the village, to show all later ages that God, almighty and all-gracious as He has shown Himself in Christ, will come to any place, no matter how remote and unimportant it may be. Ten thousand communities in the United States are too small or too distant to have a church of their own. Many of you now tuned to our broadcast feel yourselves out of touch with the world and sometimes begin to think you are beyond God's reach; but recall how that bare shepherds' field was exalted by celestial messengers, and believe that the Father, through Jesus, is indeed a *"God at hand and not a God afar off"!* What grace that Christ's peace will come to every place!

Again, it is not accidental that the first to hear these heaven-sent tidings were shepherds. Christmas art has glorified these men, depicting them as clothed with colorful, costly raiment; yet in truth their calling was ill-paid and hard. They represented the working classes. Nevertheless, God chose these sons of toil as the first to hear of peace in the newborn Christ Child. Learn the lesson the Father would teach you through this! In His endless compassion His merciful heart loves all men, particularly the poor. He has grace and mercy for the whole race, especially for those who must gather the crumbs, while others feast in luxury. However severe life has been for you, however downtrodden you may feel, when, like the shepherds, you are given only the lowly tasks of life, listen closely as the divine anthem sung by angels over Bethlehem's star-lit fields rings through the centuries to tell all — you in hospitals, public and private institutions, in prison; you far from home in a cold, cynical world — that the Savior, whose birth was first announced to these herdsmen, today seeks entrance into your heart with the promise of peace that only He can give! What grace that Jesus came for all, even the humblest!

Now just what is the Christmas assurance? Not a genial, jovial holiday spirit; not the satisfied feeling that the year's Yuletide business has been the best ever, with profits proportionately greater; not the indifference to a world of suffering or the unconcern about personal needs which comes with drunkenness and carousal; not a treaty made at diplomatic tables, dictated by the victor, a truce during which the nations can gird themselves for heavier conflict! When Jesus promises, *"My peace I give unto you; not as the world giveth, give I unto you,"* He reminds us that only He can enrich us with this blessing, which is serenity of soul, peace of heart, mind, and conscience — all because He, God's Son, was born at Bethlehem of the Virgin Mary to save us from our sins, banish fear from our lives, reconcile us with His Father, and end the conflict between the holy God and His unholy children.

"Being justified by faith," the apostle exults, *"we have peace with God."* Because Christ came from heaven, assumed our flesh, lived among us, and, though rejected by those whom He would help, died for every one of us, the transgressions which destroy our calm have been removed forever. God becomes our loving Father, not our stern Judge. Heaven becomes our promise instead of hell our

penalty. If your conscience seeks to accuse you, you can point to the Child cradled at Bethlehem and declare triumphantly: "He came for me, to take my place in suffering the punishment for all my wrongdoing — and His Word has promised me, *'There is therefore now no condemnation to them which are in Christ Jesus.'* " If dark doubt whispers that you have transgressed God's holy Law so carelessly, with such destruction to yourself or suffering to others that there can be no pardon, then as you kneel before the Christ Child, this questioning of God's grace will stop. You will know that because Jesus was born at Bethlehem, crucified on Calvary, and resurrected from the garden grave, He has plenteous grace for every transgression, mercy in overabundance for all sin. Perhaps modern unbelief has made you uncertain whether the whole Christmas story is true or false. You may be one of those people who insist that every article of faith has to be proved before you accept it, who protest that you cannot understand how Christ as God could be born of a virgin mother or how His suffering and death can give assurance of heaven. If so, give the Holy Spirit free reign in your soul! Let these days bring you to Jesus in trusting humility, and by faith you will understand why the Scripture records, *"His name shall be called Wonderful"*! God's Spirit will testify that Jesus in all truth is the Miracle of the ages. Doubts will vanish, questions will be answered, and with the fullness of victorious faith you will say, *"I know whom I have believed!"*

Of course, you will never be able to understand Jesus completely, nor measure His magnificent mercy. Men have penetrated fourteen miles up into the stratosphere, but what about the myriads of miles above that? We bore small holes into the ground, but we know nothing of the mysteries buried far below in the core of this sphere. Amundsen discovered the South Pole, and air flights have taken explorers over great sections of the Antarctic wastes; yet who can say what actually lies concealed in the frozen grasp of that silent vastness? How much less, as the approach of Christmas reminds us, can we measure the height, the depth, the contents of this marvelous mercy by which Christ loved us *"while we were yet sinners"?* All we can do — and this we must do if the Nativity blessings are to be ours — is bow down in spirit before Bethlehem's Babe and with repentant, yet grateful hearts exclaim, *"Thanks be unto God for His unspeakable Gift!"*

Because Christ was born as our Peace-bringer, the appeal of the Christmas season asks you to accept Him. Since He purchased you with His blood, you belong to Him and ought to serve Him. In the heart of darkest Africa, Amelia Buchanan translated the New Testament into a native dialect, but she had difficulty in finding words meaning "Savior" or "to save." One day, however, when a woman slipped from a tree-trunk bridge into a swollen stream, a bystander jumped in and rescued her. Intense excitement gripped the natives, and they cried in frenzied chant: "She belongs to him! She must be his slave forever, for he saved her!" "And then," writes Amelia Buchanan, "I found the word that unlocked the New Testament translation. . . . We belong to the Savior, for He has saved us." You, too, can make the angels in heaven rejoice once more this Christmastide if you, especially the unbelieving, the preoccupied, the unfaithful, will realize that you belong to the Prince of Peace, since He saved you. Make this a blessed festival by accepting Him fully and unconditionally as your personal Redeemer, believing that He came into this world, lived, died, shed His blood for you!

The time is short, and amid all the uncertainty of life as we now live it delay is dangerous. On Christmas Day about five hundred of our countrymen will be killed in household, highway, or other accidents. About fifteen will be suicides, about thirty cut down in cold-blooded murder. Yet these losses, as shocking as they are, can hardly be compared with the spiritual destruction resulting from the neglect and misunderstanding of the real Christmas message. Now, while God gives you life and breath; while the Spirit urges you, crown Him the Prince of your peace! Without Him you are without hope. There is no other pathway to the soul's peace besides Jesus since He says, *"I am the Way, the Truth, and the Life. No man cometh unto the Father but by Me."* You have no other Redeemer by whom you can be saved, for His Word states clearly, *"There is none other name under heaven given among men whereby we must be saved,"* no other basis on which your hope and assurance may be built, for Saint Paul writes emphatically, *"Other foundation can no man lay than that is laid, which is Jesus Christ"!* No other message of salvation because the apostle warned, *"Though we, or an angel from heaven, preach any other Gospel unto you, . . . let him be accursed!"* No other peace for you except in Jesus since the Scriptures recognize Him alone as the Mediator who *"made peace through the blood of His cross"!*

Come to Him, then, for harmony with your heavenly Father instead of discord! Come contritely but joyfully, for the greatest Gift that God Himself could offer, a blessing so precious that in contrast all the Christmas presents exchanged in this year of unparalleled war prosperity are only glittering baubles and tarnished tinsel! Come to the Savior for assurance, since the testimony of His truth declares, *"He is our Peace!"*

II

HOW GLORIOUS THE BLESSINGS OF CHRISTMAS PEACE!

This inner peace seeks outward expression, and it is the glory of our Christmas Gospel that with the Christ Child to guide, strengthen, and uphold us, we can find contentment in a discontented world, comfort in a cruel day, companionship in loneliness, sustaining power in weakness, soul happiness amid bodily pain, a serene faith though surrounded by chaos: peace, blessed peace, amid the agony of a world aflame with war.

Is not this the spiritual security, the soul quiet everyone of us needs for the testing time ahead when everything for which we strive and save, all that we hold high and precious: our homes, American liberties, Christian faith, the happiness of our youth, will be assailed with a force of destruction hitherto unknown in our country? But come what will, may God imprint on your heart with letters of living faith the heavenly assurance that if you have Christ, you can face even the hardest, cruelest, most powerful of enemies, death — the end of human hope, the *finis* to our lives and ambitions, the cutting off forever of earthly happiness — and still have the divine peace which the angels caroled over Bethlehem's shepherd fields!

Courageous Christians have proved this. Dr. Georges Regard of Geneva, Switzerland, who died five years ago, was a surgeon of outstanding skill and ability, and for his valiant service to the wounded during World War I the French government made him a member of the Legion of Honor. When that conflict ended, he began to publish scientific books, one of which brought him the coveted prize from the Academy of Surgery in Paris. Honors were showered on him, yet he remained a staunch Christian and wrote two books on the defense of our faith. He died at the early age of forty-six, and his last words were: "Jesus

Christ is coming. There is nothing except Jesus Christ. There is only Christ." This remarkable statement he asked to be read at his own funeral: "Being a physician, I knew from the beginning of my sickness what it was. Now in the face of the grave, open at my feet, and before the sight of death which is tracking me — a sight given to physicians alone, I must state that I have not even seen the king of terrors. I have seen only the Savior." In the Christ Child's name I promise that if you likewise will see only Jesus, you will also have the peace which can change human defeats into divine victory, the agony of death into the joy of eternal life.

Another blessing of this Christmas calm with our God is the happy harmony it produces with our fellow men. Because you who are Christ's know what it cost Jesus to leave the heaven of matchless magnificence to descend into this sin-cursed world of vice, greed, hatred, poisoned passions, and on the cross to shed His holy life-blood for your redemption, you want every one, including the worst enemies, to be saved. Because Jesus forgave us the ten thousand talents, the immeasurable debt our sins incurred, should we not readily cancel the few pennies others may owe us? Should we not strive to maintain peace, first of all, in our own family circle? If we cannot find a refuge and haven of rest in our homes, where can we find quiet? However, it is a strange proof of human perversity that just as soon as American families enjoy larger incomes, as now, domestic trouble increases. Are you living in a house where discord reigns instead of love? Believe me when I tell you that Christmas comes with the offer of special blessing for you! If you truly accept Christ and invite Him into your dwelling, His presence will bring love. Christmas, more than any other Church festival, emphasizes the home. It glorifies motherhood, exalts childhood, depicts the Holy Family;

it should bring love and understanding to the whole household. Therefore, take time in these overbusy hours, despite the competition of giving and receiving, the planning and fulfilling, the strain of sleeplessness and the stress of haste, to make your home a sanctuary for the newborn Savior! When the "holy night" comes, may none in your family be too tired or irritated to thank God for the Christ Child! If even the world takes time to feature sacred seasonal music, how much more should each Christian household carol its praises to the Babe of Bethlehem!

The Nativity peace and good will should extend far beyond our homes, even — and I say this deliberately, in the Savior's name — even to our enemies. Dr. Schneller, pastor of the Lutheran Church at Bethlehem, told of a remarkable Christmas Eve there. After his simple Arabic services were concluded, an English missionary who had attended stood with him on the balcony overlooking the little town, which during these days becomes the center of Christian thought. The missionary, Bishop Hannington, on his way to Uganda in the heart of Africa, was a man of wealth and learning, who had given up a brilliant career to dedicate his life to Christ. The hour of worship in Bethlehem mightily strengthened him. But that Christmas was his last on earth. Before another year passed, this brave witness, only thirty-six years old, was captured, tortured, and sentenced to death. With a prayer for the spiritual deliverance of Uganda he knelt down and bared his breast to the spears of the savages.

Oh, that in this world of hatred there were more of that Christlike love and self-sacrifice! Let me remind you that this is the Savior's plain, repeated instruction: *"Love your enemies!" "Pray for them which despitefully use you and persecute you!"* You cannot argue this out of the Bible. The trouble with too many of us is that we wilfully disobey Jesus and substitute hatred for compassion. While we despise tyranny, dictatorships, oppression, militarism, aggression, totalitarianism in every form; while we must be ready to defend our nation with all our possessions and, if need be, with life itself, we cannot, would we be true to Christ, hate our fellow men, even though we must battle against them. May the American Christian pulpit never forget this truth! Headline preachers who during these days have been discoursing on subjects like "To Hell with America's Enemies!" are rendering no service either to the country or the Church. The Christian cry must be, "To Christ with Our Enemies!" in the hope that He, acclaimed their Savior, will change their hearts.

Ten years ago the Christmas issue of the London *Star* printed a feature article entitled, "The Man Who Nearly Stopped the War." The story described the Christmas Eve of 1914 in the Ypres salient where the British and Germans lay in trenches separated by only a narrow strip of contested territory. Toward midnight, strains of Christmas carols rose from the German trenches, to be answered immediately by English Christmas hymns. That sacred music softened the soldiers' hatred, and when Christmas morning broke, greetings were shouted from one trench to the other. Soon a venturesome German lad raised his head over the parapet, declaring that he was going to visit the British trench, and to show his sincerity, he threw down his rifle. Soon others followed; and in a few minutes, as the newspaper had it, "the two opposing armies rushed forward to meet with handshakes and Christmas greetings, in No Man's Land." Gifts were exchanged. Photographs of wives, sweethearts, children were shown and politely admired. For days everything remained peaceful, until an inspecting officer came along, saw two soldiers outside their trenches, and, learning that they were enemies, commanded sharply, "Corporal, shoot those two men!" The corporal had to obey; war began again.

People throughout the world want peace; yet sometimes war is a protective necessity. When, with the Scriptures, we ask God to rebuke those who delight in war, we plead that the power of faith in the Christ Child may mightily spread among men and nations, so that after the present conflict — and, O Father, may it end soon and with the complete overthrow of those who seek our harm! — men in the opposing trenches of class warfare, race conflict, religious hatred, and international struggle, may be drawn more closely to Thy Son, the only and last Hope of the human race. Then, indeed, can the Christmas carol, *"On earth peace!"* exert new blessing throughout the world. Therefore, with hearts again directed to Bethlehem, with a faith that finds in the Prince of Peace, despite the lowliness of the manger, our Lord, our Savior, our King, let our prayer, long after the Christmas greens have faded and the lights darkened, constantly ask, "O God, grant us perpetual Christmas peace by the promise of the Christ Child, our only Redeemer!" Amen.

———————

THE CHRIST CHILD — MIGHTIEST
OF MARVELS!

"His name shall be called Wonderful." — Isaiah 9:6

Blessed Christ Child:

On this day which recalls Thy birth at Bethlehem, we give Thee glory across this continent for the marvel of Thy mercy. Humbly we bow at Thy manger to pray for peace on earth, but first for Thy peace in our hearts, and to ask Thee that by Thy power men of good will, all over the world, may help bring a constructive end to this destructive conflict. We open our hearts to Thee, Lord Jesus. Enter with the assurance that by the compassion of the first Christmas, by Thy living and dying for our salvation, our sins have been removed, the strangle hold of hell broken, and death's dominion shattered for those who accept Thee as their God, their Redeemer, the Sovereign of their souls! Give us true Christmas faith, so that in a penitent nation we can be confident of Thy guidance, in afflicted homes know the real Christmas comfort, in sin-marked or burden-weighted souls, have the joy in spirit only Thou canst give! Hear us, O holy Babe of Bethlehem, and despite the outward sorrows of this day, make it a radiant Christmas, particularly for every darkened life in this audience! We ask it by the eternal promise of Thine Incarnation. Amen.

A BLESSED, Christ-centered Christmas to all of you across the continent! A *blessed* Christmas, I say, for no matter how heavy our individual and national prospects may seem; regardless of the increasing burdens to be heaped on us; despite the black clouds forming on the uncharted horizons of the future, the anniversary of the Savior's birth can always bring comfort, strength, and a joyful heart.

We may well recall that this day, to us the most radiant of the entire year, was often a time of testing and anguish in the early Christian Church. Ancient records testify that Telesphorus, valiant witness to the Lord Jesus in Rome, was put to a martyr's death, among other reasons, for insisting on the observance of Christ's birthday. Though his loyalty cost him his life, the assurance that Jesus had been born for him was so convincing that in his dying hours he could sing hymns of exalted praise. Similarly, when Diocletian, Roman emperor, blood-mad archfiend, found a vast congregation of believers celebrating Christmas, he had the doors and windows in their assembly place barred to prevent their escape and then ordered torches applied to the overcrowded building. Even the roar of angry flames was not loud enough to silence the hymns which those martyrs sang to the Christ Child. — Ask God for such triumphant trust, you whose faith is ridiculed, or who are persecuted because of your devotion to the Lord Jesus! As Telesphorus and that loyal congregation found unspeakable joy in the newborn Savior and through Him the power to conquer agony and torture, so real reliance on the Christ Child can help you repel every opposition.

On another Christmas, in 496, twenty years after the Roman Empire had collapsed, Clovis, King of the Franks, together with 3,000 warriors, confessed Christ and was baptized. A hundred and one years later, likewise on Christmas, Ethelbert, King of Kent, together with 10,000 subjects, pledged allegiance to the Savior and likewise received baptism. For these soldiers the day of the Savior's birth became the day of their own rebirth, just as I pray God that this message may touch the hearts of many, particularly of you, the nation's military men, and bring you contritely but confidently to the manger.

Again, we think of that Christmas Day in the life of the Reformer, Martin Luther, when he brought into the parsonage a fir tree which, so the records indicate, was destined to become the first Christmas tree. Perhaps it was at this time also, while rocking one of his babies to sleep, that Luther composed the melody and the words of the carol which has since sung its way into the hearts of millions in many Christian creeds and lands, "From Heaven Above to Earth I Come." Those were trying times for that man of God. He was overworked, underpaid, misunderstood, and opposed, but at Christmas he found rest from his ceaseless toil; he wanted joy to reign in his whole household. Similarly, if some of you have been hard pressed and overtaxed; if, instead of appreciation, your efforts have met only rebuff and sarcastic challenge, let each decorated tree recall the radiance of Him who is the Light of the World, and its evergreen branches symbolize your evergrowing hope in Jesus! Let the carols help banish worries and strengthen you to face courageously each day's new tasks!

Thus the record of one Christmas after the other can prove that no problem is too hard for solution, no suffering too intense for relief, no pain (including overwhelming grief sustained by parents who lost their sons in enemy attacks) too crushing for healing — provided you know the true meaning of this blessed day. To that end kneel reverently at the manger and ask the Spirit's help in acclaiming

THE CHRIST CHILD — MIGHTIEST OF MARVELS!

We take our Christmas text from the prophecy which Isaiah recorded seven centuries before Bethlehem, when, beholding the Christ Child even at that distance, he exulted (chapter nine, verse six), *"His name shall be called Wonderful."*

I

HIS MARVELOUS PERSON

The English word *wonderful* hardly does justice to the prophet's original term. We find the deep, divine meaning of Isaiah's Christmas forecast when we translate

"*His name shall be called* Miracle!" And assuredly Bethlehem's Babe is in every sense of the word the Miracle of the ages, the most amazing Wonder men and angels have ever beheld.

Think of His miraculous birth! You and I are born of earthly parents. Yet while Mary of Nazareth is His mother, the Lord of hosts is His Father, and His coming into the world we call *the* Virgin Birth because of all who have ever lived on earth only the Christ Child came into existence without a human father. Now, since the Virgin Birth has been fiercely attacked outside the Church and because from within religious leaders have sweepingly denied it, we emphasize that our "Bringing-Christ-to-the-Nations" mission unhesitatingly accepts and proclaims the Virgin Birth of Jesus Christ. Why? First, the Old Testament foresees this truth. Isaiah, chapter seven, verse fourteen, definitely declares, "*Behold, a virgin shall conceive and bear a Son and shall call His name Immanuel.*" Second, the New Testament teaches this truth. Read the opening chapters of Saint Matthew and Saint Luke! Third, the whole Christian Church from the first Christmas until today — Protestants and Catholics, Lutherans and Reformed — has clung to the fact which the Apostolic Creed frames in the words "born of the Virgin Mary." Not one Christian denomination in the United States officially refuses to accept this clear-cut Biblical truth, although too many tolerate and even applaud leaders who point-blank reject this revealed miracle. Fourth, we believe in the Virgin Birth because Jesus had to be born in a superhuman manner if He was to be without inherited sin and guilt. The unbroken rule for the whole race is, "*That which is born of the flesh is flesh.*" If Jesus had been conceived and born as men are, He would have been conceived and born in sin. Then, burdened with the same corrupted nature you and I have, He could not be the sinless, spotless, stainless Savior of mankind. Then there could be no essential difference between Jesus and any human being!

But, praise God today! Jesus, the Miracle of the ages, is Virgin-born; and He is more than man, more than superior men, more than the supreme men of our day. He is (and now we are to see even more clearly why *"His name shall be called Wonderful"*) God in the real, full sense of that word, our all-glorious, almighty, all-merciful God. Isaiah, to take only one Old Testament prophet, called Him divine, for he says not only that *"His name shall be called Wonderful,"* but the words following our text also acclaim Him as firmly and sharply as language permits *"the mighty God."* When the fulfillment of this prophecy came to Bethlehem, the herald angels announced that He would be *"the Lord,"* the Sovereign of the universe. Saint Paul, reviewing Christ's nativity, exclaims, *"God was manifest in the flesh,"* and again, beholding the Mightiest of miracles, he acclaims Jesus *"over all, God-blessed forever."* Our Lord, as the Babe in the manger, the Lad in the Temple, as the unparalleled Preacher on the highways and byways of Palestine, Jesus as the Sufferer in the Garden, the Sin-bearer on the cross, death's Victor before the tomb, our Intercessor at the Father's throne, is, in the Nicene Creed's summary of Bible verity, "God of God, Light of Light, Very God of Very God."

Can you not see at this wartime Christmas that we need a divine Christ? When war broke out I stated that the motto of American Christians should be, *"If God be for us, who can be against us?"* Are we ready to substitute anyone else or anything else for God in that assurance? Are we willing to say: "If our military strength, air power, naval might be for us, who can be against us?

If our scientists, financiers, laboring forces be for us, who can be against us"? No, we want God for us, and it is the Christmas miracle, the amazing wonder of heaven and earth, that Christ is our God, an almighty Helper for all who truly love Him.

Do not repeat the old, threadbare objection that you cannot understand Christmas or account scientifically for the Savior's being both God and man! Of course you cannot! *"His name"* would not be called *"Wonderful"* if He were not so far beyond our human comprehension that we shall never even begin to understand what the sacred Scripture calls a complete *"mystery."* Take Bethlehem's miracle on faith! You constantly accept a score of unexplainable facts in the physical realm of everyday life. Why balk at the heavenly wonder of Jesus' life? While men with third- and fourth-rate minds scoff at the Christmas story and object that it contradicts science, first-rate minds do not usually share this protest. Dr. Arthur Compton, Nobel Prize winner and discoverer of the cosmic ray, a scholar in the forefront of American research, pays his tribute to the Savior's birth in this remarkable statement: "Christmas is totally in keeping with science. . . . One of the very first laws of science is that of cause and effect. When we see the finest cultures and civilization ever known to the world . . . dating back to Christmas Day, when we see art and music reaching their most exultant heights under the resistless drive of Christmas faith, we can but say, 'The deeper spirit of Christmas and the real spirit of science are one.'" Some distance down a Grand Canyon trail a reverent tourist inscribed on a perpendicular rock wall these challenging words in large letters: "In this place doubt is impossible. Else why all these wonders, this surpassing beauty, this silence of deep peace, this confident repose? Here is the Spirit of

God. Here one must believe." Similarly at Christmas, when the Holy Spirit takes full possession of our hearts on faith's pilgrimage to Bethlehem's manger, we, too, can say: "In this place doubt is impossible! Here one must believe!" Whatever may have been given you, the richly remembered, on this blessed day, or whatever may have been withheld from you, the poor and the suffering, oh, pray with me that the Giver of *"every good"* and *"perfect gift"* may grant you a firm faith in the divine Christ Child, the Son of God as the Son of Man! Before this day passes into history and brings you a step closer to eternity, yield yourself to Him! Kneel in spirit before Him to banish all indifference and doubt with this unreserved acclaim, *"My Lord and my God!"*

II

HIS MARVELOUS GRACE

Even the glory of the Holy Infant's deity does not exhaust the Advent miracle; it is only the start of the ageless mystery. Isaiah foretold, *"His name shall be called Wonderful,"* also because of His miraculous grace. Many things are uncertain about that first Christmas. If we ask, "When exactly was Jesus born?" historians will start a lengthy debate and answer with various conflicting dates. Should we inquire, "Where precisely in Bethlehem was Jesus born?" we likewise receive contradictory replies. Yet, if we raise the most important question, "Why was Jesus born?" we have positive, heavenly certainty. An angelic messenger told Joseph, *"He shall save His people from their sins."* Another celestial herald assured the shepherds, *"Unto you is born this day in the city of David* A SAVIOR, *which is Christ the Lord."* The very name given the Child, *"Jesus,"* implies "salvation," and from these infant days through His entire career, from the earliest passages in the Gospels to the latest in the epistles, in Old Testament prophecy and New Testament fulfillment, the one purpose of His coming stands out clearly: He was born — let the Christmas bells ring out these *"tidings of great joy,"* the Christmas lights reflect this radiance, and the gifts recall this matchless grace! — to save sinners! The heart and climax of the Christmas message promises: "Jesus came to save you and me!"

No wonder He is called the Miracle, when He offers such marvelous mercy! He loved us, when we hated Him. He, Lord of lords, forsook His glorious heaven to come into the world of woe that rejected Him. Yet, even more marvelous, He *"who knew no sin"* became *"sin for us . . . that we might be made the righteousness of God in Him,"* when He suffered for the very men who persecuted Him and who still rebel against Him. And it is the absolute height of miraculous compassion that Jesus died for all sinners, including His enemies who nailed His hands and feet to the cross, so that through faith in Him as *"the Lamb of God which taketh away the sin of the world"* we could be freed forever from the terror of eternal death.

Never has the world witnessed any grace as sweeping as our Lord's on Christmas. On that day, in 1868, President Andrew Johnson issued a remarkable amnesty proclamation in which full and unconditional pardon was extended as the document reveals, to "all who directly or indirectly participated in the late rebellion," not excluding even Jefferson Davis, the president of the Confederacy. That pardon was certainly pledged in the spirit of the Christ Child's mercy; but how much greater is the peace Jesus offers! President Johnson's amnesty embraced one group of people involved in a single rebellion, while the Savior's grace is offered to all groups of people in every uprising against God and His holy will. *"He shall save*

His people *from their sins,"* and *"His people"* are those who trust in Him as their Savior, especially the poor in spirit, the downtrodden, those who think that they are beyond help and hope.

It was during the darkness of night, when such heaven-sent news would least be expected, that the angel chorus intoned its promise, *"Unto you is born . . . a Savior";* and it is midnight for many of you, when the light of hope flickers and fails. You do not know whether you want to see the beginning of another day. You are like a distressed listener who, his self-respect gone and courage completely vanished, writes: "I shouldn't waste your time. . . . I'm not worth it. . . . I have lost faith in everyone. . . . I cannot get hold of myself. . . . I wish I would die and get out of this awful world. I'm only twenty-six years old but feel like a hundred. . . . Life holds nothing for me. . . . I wish I could meet my death very soon. . . . I won't blame you if you don't write me, because I am not good for anything. I never was and never will be." Oh, take heart! It is not too late to find peace in Christ! Clinging with personal, trusting faith to Him, you can know that no matter how hard and hopeless your life's course may seem, at Bethlehem you learn that this Child is Heaven's Light for dispelling darkness, brightening your pathway, and finally leading you to celestial glory, where gloom shall be no more. What marvelous grace to know that Jesus will grant us His pardon and peace always, especially when we need it most!

III

HIS MARVELOUS POWER

Combined with the Savior's miraculous mercy is His marvelous power. If we read the section of Isaiah from which our text has been taken, we see that He *"shall be* called *Wonderful"* also because *"the government shall be upon His shoulder."* Contradicting human reason, but concordant with Heaven's truth, is the assurance that He who was born in Bethlehem as a helpless Babe is in truth the Ruler of the universe to whom has been given *"all power . . . in heaven and in earth."*

What comfort this promise offers! We need divine help for the increasing burdens of our perplexed day. Anyone who thinks that the postwar world will be one of tranquillity and plenty is simply practicing wishful dreaming. But you, the skeptics, who deny that, however great the difficulties may be, the Lord God is greater, are guilty of a far more serious error. Can you not see, therefore, why the whole world needs the Christmas power; why in our beloved country the seventy million who have never acknowledged Jesus as their Savior should bow before Him? Christ, who, as the apostle reminds us, *"though He was rich, yet for your sakes He became poor, that ye through His poverty might be rich,"* has the resources of heaven at His command required to supply all your personal needs, whether they be of soul, mind, or body. Whatever your individual difficulty may be today, questions of food, shelter, warmth, clothing, money, business, health, Christmas emphasizes this divine pledge, sealed in the Savior's birth at Bethlehem: through trusting faith *"God shall supply all your need according to His riches in glory by Christ Jesus."*

His bounty offers far more, however, than the necessities for our daily existence. His divine guidance includes the entire direction of life for those who acclaim Him their only Redeemer. Many of you write for the assurance that your sons in the armed forces will be spared injuries and death; that even now, though you have received no word, they may be safe on our Pacific islands. While no one can promise that your boys will escape injury or even death, the Christ of Christmas who says of His faithful, *"neither shall any man pluck them out of My hand,"* can shield your Christian son in the midst of raking gunfire or on the deck of a sinking ship. If, however He calls home a beloved one who persevered in the faith, then remember also how marvelous is His mercy when He transports a soul immediately, without delay or further trial, from this sin-crushed earth of suffering to the radiant realms of heaven!

The blessed Lord Jesus not only provides and protects, He also improves, rebuilds, restores. How mightily He has changed human affairs since that first Christmas! Everything noble, elevating, constructive the pages of history record since His appearance must be traced ultimately to His manger in Bethlehem. If only in the conflict of this disquieted day men would fully turn to Christ who can restrict the battle's terrors and rebuke those who delight in war or profit from its prosecution! Missionary Nott, who worked in the South Seas, once came to the Island of Tubooi to find the whole population in a state of siege. With a remarkable bravery he and his fellow workers offered themselves as mediators, brought the leaders of the contending armies together, and under the prayerful invocation of Christ removed their difficulties. Peace was declared. The armies threw down their weapons. Soldiers cordially embraced each other, and together, friend and foe alike, attended divine services to hear the Savior's Gospel of brotherly love. Missionary records are full of similar instances in which Christ the *"Wonderful,"* Heaven's Prince of Peace, has helped to avoid bloodshed. Pray for His presence in the hearts and lives of those responsible for this war! Pray for His presence in the repentant souls of our people, so that this conflict may soon end and peace, blessed, righteous, constructive, co-operative peace, may reign!

The marvelous Savior who can change the course of nations can also alter the lives of men. It is the promise of His sacred Word that *"if any man be in Christ, he is a new creature,"* and if you are dissatisfied with your life; if you see too much of sin and selfishness, failure and fraud, dishonesty and distrust, approach Jesus in His Gospel and experience His purifying, ennobling grace! The *Bible Society Record* tells of a criminal called "Santa Claus" because he had stolen a Christmas tree and had also taken a handbag containing a New Testament. Back in his room, when he examined the loot, he started to read God's Word, and by divine direction he was led to ponder particularly the study of the Prodigal. He began to realize that he was the ungrateful son who had wasted his life in sin. Led by the Holy Spirit, he fell on his knees, confessed his guilt, sought forgiveness from Jesus and promised to make restitution. None of us needs steal a Bible to learn of the Spirit's wondrous power in remaking our lives. On this day of the Savior's birth — and what occasion could be more appropriate as the birthday of your new life in Christ? — let us approach Him with His blessed assurance to strengthen us, *"Him that cometh to Me I will in no wise cast out"*!

Whatever Christmas brings, may it mightily help us to adore the Holy Child whose name was called *"Wonderful,"* the mightiest Miracle of the ages; and having bowed contritely and with the inner conviction of His divine mercy, may we — everyone of us — follow the shepherds, who returned *"glorifying and praising God for all the things that they had heard and seen"*! God grant everyone of us the Miracle of this Christmas mercy! Amen.

JESUS — THE NAME ABOVE ALL OTHER NAMES!

"Thou shalt call His name Jesus: for He shall save His people from their sins. . . . And he called His name Jesus." — Saint Matthew 1:21, 25

O Jesus, Our Christ, the Same Yesterday and Today and Forever:

As the close of another year approaches, we humble ourselves before Thee to confess all our transgressions against Thy holy will and to admit, reviewing the past twelve months, that often, by word and action, we have denied Thee who didst come into this world for us and whose very name means "Salvation." Forgive us, we beseech Thee, by the repeated pledges of Thy full, free grace! O Jesus, through Thine enlightening Spirit touch many hearts in this mission of the air! Show all the distressed and disillusioned that knowing Thee as their God and Redeemer, they are prepared to start the new year with hope because they begin in Thy name! Bless our nation during this crisis with deep repentance and sincere dedication to Thee! Protect the young men who are defending our cause! Guide all Government officials according to Thy truth, and, O Savior, grant us soon a true peace! We ask this according to Thy will, by Thy promise and for Thy name's sake. Amen.

THERE is a name — and only one name — that can bring peace to bewildered minds in the madness we call modern civilization. It does not designate a military leader, because even titled strategists can fail in an emergency and be deposed under the pressure of heavy charges, as the past days have shown. This marvelous name does not denote a diplomatic genius; for the plans of statecraft can bog down completely, as the present conflict reveals. Again, this most notable of names does not mark a scientific inventor or a famous scholar, since almost every discovery has been misused in the destructive service of sin; with the cultured nations at each other's throats, we must realize that far more is needed than brain power, high intelligence quotients.

At first glance the Name which alone holds hope — and I believe the last hope — seems completely out of joint with our modern ideals and ambitions. It represents earthly poverty, while we crave riches; emphasizes purity and chastity, though the world pursues lust and licentiousness; urges humility, and our age applauds pride; pleads for blessed peace, but this generation wallows in war. Yet it is eternal, unchanging in a day when mighty world figures have altered their names. In more than a thousand languages it is adored by men who differ in race and color. It is the holy, peerless name given the Babe of Bethlehem soon after His birth. It is — thank God that we with our sinful lips can speak it! — the name of names: *Jesus!*

Historians tell us that often when ancient Greek orators found their audiences inattentive or sleeping, they used one word by which interest could be reawakened and enthusiasm sustained. In the midst of important orations they would stop suddenly to cry out, "Marathon!" and the people, recalling their glorious national victory at Marathon, would listen with renewed attention. How much more do we need the name *Jesus* for our sleepy, self-indulgent world! Cry out *Jesus!* in the midst of heathen darkness, and idols, with their vile worship and hideous superstitions, crumble. Proclaim *Jesus!* throughout America, let that Savior be accepted by the masses, and this nation will become morally mighty, spiritually unconquerable! Preach *Jesus!* in decadent churches, and they revive with fresh zeal and power. Exalt *Jesus!* throughout the world in the perils of the postwar period, when atheistic Communism, I firmly believe, will be more securely entrenched than ever before, and the Christian masses can be strengthened for loyalty and ceaseless testimony. Put *Jesus!* into the hearts of sin-stricken humanity, the homes of the suffering and sorrowful, the lives of those embattled against God, their fellow-men, their own better selves, and amazing peace will reign supreme!

Because Christmas is too radiant to be dismissed with a single day, we linger one Sunday longer at Bethlehem to hear more of this name at which, according to Holy Scripture, *"every knee should bow, of things in heaven and things in earth and things under the earth"* — the password through the sentries of death to the gates of heaven,

JESUS — THE NAME ABOVE ALL OTHER NAMES!

which our text (Saint Matthew, chapter one, verses twenty-one and twenty-five) explains in the words: *"Thou shalt call His name JESUS; for He shall save His people from their sins. . . . And he called His name Jesus."*

I

HOW THIS NAME WAS GIVEN

There is a glorious history behind this glorious name. It was sent from heaven. A holy angel came to declare, *"Thou shalt call His name Jesus!"* Because of its celestial origin, no human title ascribed to Christ can ever be as blessed and powerful. Designations used by the world today — the Carpenter's Son, the Great Galilean, the Judean Teacher, are earthly; the real and most appropriate name, *Jesus,* was given by God Himself and transmitted by a heavenly messenger.

Significantly the angel brought this announcement to Joseph. We know little about the Savior's foster father, but the few facts the Bible supplies lead us to understand that Joseph was indeed well chosen for this distinction. He was a devout, God-fearing man. Almost every time he is mentioned in connection with our Lord's infancy, angels address him as the responsible head of the Holy Family, one deeply concerned about the divine Child whom Christmas day had put under his charge. — American fathers should similarly realize that the Lord has ordained them as the heads of their households, not merely the breadwinners, but as spiritual leaders who are to bring up their children *"in the nurture and admonition of the Lord."* If outside activities take them away too much from their home and the guidance of their sons and daughters, fathers should drop these external interests to provide sound training and assure Christian example for their boys and girls.

Note well Joseph's implicit obedience to the angel's *"Thou shalt call His name Jesus"*! In fulfillment, as in obedient echo, we read, *"He called His name Jesus."* The New Testament records that whenever the Savior's foster father received divine direction, he followed unquestioningly. An angel explains the mystery of the Virgin Birth, and Joseph accepts it. An angel warns him to flee from Herod's murderous vengeance, and unhesitatingly he arises at night, starts the perilous journey into Egypt. God give us fathers today who will courageously follow His guidance! By contrast, our age sees many men who think themselves too virile and masculine to attend church, but regard drinking, cursing, carousing, as evidence of manhood. What destructive examples they give their own children! Young minds are molded much more by parental influence and home habits than by schools and even some churches. "My father does this!" "My father says that!" "My father told me!" — These eager, frequent exclamations by growing children show what a force for good or evil the father can be. — Men of America, at a time when our country's tomorrow is overclouded as never before in the 165 years of our national existence, the Lord expects you to show the spirit of Joseph in your home. It is terrifying enough when you yourself without Christ are lost, but how appalling to drag your own flesh and blood down to spiritual destruction! Ask God for the strength required to put Jesus in your heart and keep Him in your home!

According to Saint Luke the Virgin Mary had also been told that the Christ Child's name was to be *Jesus*. Perhaps this is to show us, even if incidentally, that husband and wife are to share the family plans. In any event, Mary likewise accepted this name from heaven and here, too, gave a high example of Christian womanhood. Today our country needs mothers who will follow the divine will for American home life. Figures compiled in New Jersey already point to the increase in divorces which the State authorities specifically ascribe to higher pay and the more luxurious life resultant from the increase of war prosperity and creature comforts. As money continues to grow more plentiful under wartime emergency the family ties will correspondingly become weaker.

How directly children are influenced by their parents' spiritual strength or weakness! Some time ago an automobile mechanic came into my office accompanied by his little girl. She was dressed as neatly as though she had stepped out of a bandbox, while the father still wore his garage overalls, black with grease and grime. But his eyes sparkled with love as he spoke of his child. Before they left, I gave the lassie one of our golden crosses, the emblem of this broadcast, and I asked her, "Do you know what this is?" Immediately she replied, "That's where my Jesus died!" The father was a hardworking man with only a grammar-school education, but he knew a father's responsibility to his household. By contrast I thought of another home, comfortably situated and fashionably furnished, in which a son asked his father, "Daddy, is it better to kill a man with a gun, a dagger, a blackjack, or a big dose of poison?" He had been reading so-called comic strips and cheap magazines, while his father had lost the necessary contact with him.

Now, "the child is father of the man," and if parents fail to heed God's Word in their home life, whom but themselves have they to blame if their children become scoffers, sneering sophisticates, or lawbreakers? A few years ago an unbeliever in Finland left a will bequeathing his farm to the devil. After his death the court decided to carry out his wishes by permitting the land to remain completely untouched by human labor, so that it would be overrun with weeds and wilderness growth. Any prison warden will tell you that when youthful souls are left alone without parental direction, they likewise revert to an untamed, wild, passion-filled existence. Yet the most some young people can say of their mother is something like this: "She taught me how to use make-up, how to hold a cigarette, how to attract attention." The most some young men can say of their father is: "He showed me how to play cards, how to make a shrewd bargain, how to smoke."

We are witnessing the tragic consequences of such parental neglect. During the last year almost 1,500,000 serious crimes — murder, manslaughter, rape, robbery, burglary, criminal assault — were committed in our country, not to count the 13,000,000 smaller cases of fraud, forgery, embezzlement, vice. This distressing picture recalls the world before Noah's flood, Nineveh before its bloody destruction, Rome on the eve of its fall, France on the brink of the ruthless revolution. — But do you know that one fifth of these major crimes was perpetrated by youths under twenty-one? As J. Edgar Hoover, director of the FBI, warns, because fathers and mothers often evade their responsibilities, the life-pathway of too many boys runs from the high chair to the electric chair. We cannot correct these startling conditions only by bemoaning them, passing laws against them, or instituting educational campaigns to offset them. We need Christ in the family with His purifying, strengthening power. The 30,000,000 homes in the United States require the constant contact with God which the Holy Family enjoyed, the obedience to the divine will which Joseph and Mary showed in following the divine direction, *"Thou shalt call His name Jesus."*

II

WHY THIS NAME WAS GIVEN

I need hardly explain, even if you are not a Christian, that this name is of the utmost importance. All intelligent persons, whether they accept or reject Christ, should understand that He is the most important Figure in history. *Jesus* occurs more than six hundred times in the New Testament; and while some two hundred titles are otherwise given Christ, *Jesus* is the real name of our Lord, His name when earthly existence began for Him at Bethlehem and when it ended on Calvary where Pilate wrote as the superscription on the cross, *"Jesus of Nazareth!"* It is His first and last designation in the New Testament, and, whether spoken in English or in any other language of our Babellike world, it should be the first and last on every believer's lips.

He is not, however, the only person to be called by this name. The Hebrew form for Jesus was also given to Moses' successor, Joshua, and to many others in Jewish history. There is a lesson in this, too. So completely did Jesus become man that He took a name common among men. He was as one of us in everything except sin; and in His complete humanity He knew our weaknesses and sorrows. He understands our temptations, for He was tried as we are. He sympathizes with us in every need, for we are never forced to tread any pathway, however hard and apparently cruel, where Jesus has not gone before us.

Yet it is remarkable that after our Lord became known as *Jesus*, the name fell into disuse among His countrymen, as though it were a title to be reserved for Him. In truth, He alone could fully live up to its meaning. Our English word *Jesus* is taken from a Hebrew term which really means "the Lord is Salvation." And assuredly He, as no one else can ever be, is both our God and the Redeemer of our race. Every time you hear His name, you should also perceive the promise of divine redemption in this glorious word. David Strauss, German rationalist, paid imposing tribute to Jesus when he described Him as the "highest model of religion"; but that is not enough. Benjamin Disraeli, Jewish prime minister of England, acclaimed Christ when he wrote that "He has made Jewish history the most important history in the world." Neither is that enough. Thomas Carlyle, British man of letters, once exclaimed, "Jesus of Nazareth, our divinest symbol!" But Jesus must be more than a symbol. Benjamin Franklin conceded, "His system of morals and His religion . . . are the best the world ever saw." But the devils in hell will sign their name to that. Robert Ingersoll, Number 1 American atheist, was forced to admit that Jesus was "a great and serene man, kind and perfectly innocent"; yet nineteen centuries before Ingersoll, Pontius Pilate said practically the same thing. All such praise is empty because, like most of the modern biographies of Christ, it deliberately omits the true meaning of *Jesus* and refuses to confess that He is, as His name implies, "the Lord is Salvation." So, call Christ, occasionally if you must, Master, Teacher, Leader. But let His real name, the one you repeat and love, ever be and remain for you *Jesus*. There are other masters, teachers, leaders; but there can be only one Jesus, one Lord and Redeemer.

When the angel announced the name to Joseph, he explained its meaning in this promise, *"He shall save His people from their sins."* In other words, Jesus is called Salvation because He *is* our salvation. There is no misrepresentation or exaggeration here. When the grandson of Italy's king was born a few years ago, he was called Victor and given eleven other names. There is grave doubt, however, that he will be a victor. But Christ is called Salvation because He is in absolute truth heaven's only Redemption.

Now, *Jesus* is a name above all others because the deliverance which it signifies is the highest, deepest, widest love the great God Himself could show. May you never lose sight of this all-vital truth: Our heavenly Father was not — and in His holiness could not be — satisfied with smiling at our violations of His Law, as an indulgent parent amuses himself at a baby's mistakes! He could not overlook our transgressions, as a kindly teacher closes his eyes to a pupil's hasty error. He could not forget our iniquities, as a Christian wife might overlook a husband's unfaithfulness. God is so holy, just, and perfect that every transgression must be punished; yet while He hates sin and demands the full penalty for His broken Law, He loves His fallen children with such devotion that He sent His Son to become the sinner's Substitute, the universal Ransom.

Have you ever taken time to measure, as far as the mortal mind can, the matchless mercy God showed in sending Christ? Last week a distracted mother wrote me that her son who had just been discharged from the Army would doubtless be recalled almost any day. Shuddering over that prospect — as many mothers do who are without Christ — she confessed: "How can I let him go? I don't want him to kill, and I don't want him to be killed." But how indescribably much more it cost God to send His Son into certain death, not in behalf of friends or of country, but for the benefit of His enemies! What love beyond measure we can find in that name *Jesus* when we see the Savior, unresisting and uncomplaining, go unswervingly to Calvary for us!

Jesus also means *completed* salvation. When our Lord, nailed to the cross, bowed His head in death with the cry *"It is finished!"* He left nothing undone for our redemption. We *"are complete in Him."* Our deliverance has been definitely accomplished, now and forever. You cannot add anything to what Christ has already achieved. Those, I care not who they may be, who teach that His divine love must be supplemented by human endeavor, either do not know the true Jesus or deliberately reject Him.

Therefore, *Jesus* means *free* salvation. If you had all the money stored in the world's great treasuries, the hundreds of millions daily spent for war's destruction, you would not have enough to purchase forgiveness for a single sin. But what all financial resources can never buy, the cleansing of your soul, is offered freely through Christ's heavenly mercy. *"By grace are ye saved,"* the New Testament summarizes, *"and that not of yourselves; it is the gift of God, not of works, lest any man should boast."* I have constantly tried to emphasize the sacred truth that you, my fellow-redeemed, can come to Christ just as you are, trusting only in His compassion, which is strongest when you are weakest. You may be deprived of much in life, even of some necessities, because you have no money to pay for them. You may be prevented from cashing a check because you have no credentials or endorsement to present at the bank. You may stand far away from the world's high and mighty since you have no one to introduce you.

But may God's Spirit help you realize today that, simply by faith, you can have pardon without money, blessing without payment, access to the throne of Christ's mercy, without any human intermediary!

Jesus means *universal* salvation, redemption offered everyone. When a child is born in a royal family, especially when a successor to the throne has been long and eagerly awaited, a selected list of prisoners receives a reprieve or pardon; but when Jesus was born *"in the fullness of time,"* after long centuries of expectation, liberty was promised not to a chosen few, but to the whole race. *"God so loved the* WORLD, *that He gave His only-begotten Son, that* WHOSOEVER *believeth in Him should not perish, but have everlasting life."* You have not fallen too low, sinned too frequently, transgressed God's holy Law too brazenly to be received, forgiven, and restored by Christ's universal, all-embracing, non-excluding grace.

Jesus means our *only* salvation. Call that narrow and bigoted if you will, but God's Word declares with Heaven's authority, *"There is none other Name under heaven given among men, whereby we must be saved."* Jesus is the one Way from earth to a blessed eternity, and every other road is the devil's detour leading to hell. Our Lord is the one Truth, and everyone who contradicts Him teaches damnable falsehoods. He is the one Life, and everything that rejects Him paves the way to death.

Jesus means *comforting* salvation. John Newton (on whose grave this inscription has been carved: "John Newton, clerk, once an infidel and a libertine, a servant of slavers in Africa, was, by the rich mercy of our Lord and Savior, Jesus Christ, preserved, restored, pardoned, and appointed to preach the faith he had long labored to destroy"), who saw life at its lowest and ugliest as he lived in unspeakable misery and vile sins, looked to Jesus and found the comfort that made him write among a score of his hymns:

> How sweet the name of Jesus sounds
> In a believer's ear!
> It soothes his sorrows, heals his wounds
> And drives away his fear!

May God grant that some of you who have been fighting Christ will now, by the same grace, hear the sweet name of Jesus appealing to you, *"Come unto Me, . . . I will give you rest,"* and accept that invitation!

Jesus means *unchanging* salvation. The names of men, even the greatest, are often forgotten. When Longfellow died, Ralph Waldo Emerson was among the notable mourners at his bier. Weakened by advancing age, his memory had left him. After looking down into the dead face of the man who had been his friend, he turned away, puzzled. Those near the casket heard him say, "The gentleman we are burying was a sweet and beautiful soul, but I forgot his name." As long as you look to the Savior, you will never forget His name or His mercies. They will be renewed to you every morning in such an impressive way that you will daily grow in grace.

Jesus means *sure* salvation. There is no guesswork about His Gospel. His mercies have been proved in too many millions of hearts; His power, as century is heaped on century, too constantly changes the lives of men, too repeatedly gives them calm in the chaos of world strife, to be denied or even questioned. The longer and more intently you behold the Son of God, work with Him and for Him, the more deeply you immerse yourself in His Word, the more clear your conviction grows that He is what His name, *Jesus,* implies: Salvation, Deliverance, Atonement, Redemption, Pardon for all the world, especially for you.

III
WHAT MUST WE DO WITH THIS NAME?

What, then, does the Name of names mean to us? Appropriately this message comes on the last Sunday of a year that will be remembered for its sorrow, a year that points, unless God is overgracious, to a future with even graver difficulties. Unless He intervenes *"who breaketh the bow and cutteth the spear in sunder,"* this will be a long, disastrous war before victory is ours. While many issues of this struggle are problematical, we fear that because of atheism's growth and its blatant revolt against the Almighty, Christian churches over large areas of the world's surface may be attacked and closed. But whatever happens, *Jesus* should always loom before us with Heaven's own pledge for our eternal salvation.

In taking a spiritual inventory, we remember our grievous weaknesses, our smallness of trust, our misuse of the Savior's name, our refusal to spread abroad the marvels of His mercy; in short, our many, frequent, daily, repeated sins. In deep humility we approach the Lord to plead for mercy instead of justice and, blessed Savior that He is, He assures us that no matter how marred and spotted each of the 365 daily entries are, the handwriting against us is blotted out. His precious name proves the truth that *"He shall save His people"* — and through faith you, too, are His inseparably, His eternally — *"from their sins."*

With your pardon sealed by the Redeemer's blood, I ask you to show your heartfelt regard for His redemptive love by keeping the name *"at which every knee should bow"* in holy reverence. It should not require a public admonition of this kind to urge a God-blessed America to avoid blaspheming the Savior; but as a consequence of the moral letdown caused by the war, we are beginning to witness an increasing abuse of the divine names. The stage has become notorious in this respect, and the plays that run the longest usually are the worst. Seldom do God's forbearance and patience seem greater than when a filthy-minded, foul-mouthed scoffer lets loose a string of curses or unmentionable profanity; and we, expecting a flash of lightning to strike him dead on the spot, find instead that our merciful Father has granted time for repentance. But every unforgiven misuse of this Name will ultimately bring eternal punishment.

We should accept the name *Jesus* as the pledge of our own salvation, defend it whenever attacked, and make it the center of our prayers, believing His promise *"Whatsoever ye shall ask the Father in My name, that will I do."* New Year's Day, in response to presidential proclamation, is to be marked with special prayer for our nation — and I hope you will not be kept away by New Year's Eve's revelry, particularly inappropriate now when American young men are dying in the Philippines. As you bow before God and plead with Him to bless our country, speak your petitions in Jesus' name! Pray contritely! Acknowledge your own sins and our country's shortcomings! Before God confess that these United States, with more light, blessings, privileges, opportunities than almost the rest of the world together, have transgressed grievously, repeatedly, ungratefully; that despite our many, deep-rooted iniquities, we look to Jesus and His atoning love for the assurance of pardon, for the courage to meet the hardships before us and overcome our enemies. If in America there are thus truly repentant millions who love the Savior, who live for Him, who testify to Him, we will have divine, invincible power. But if we neglect and reject the Son of God and lean on the arm of flesh instead of trusting Him who can do all things, no one can tell to what depths of suffering we may be brought.

Therefore let His name ring throughout the land! Let church leaders go all the way in acclaiming Christ both God and Savior! Let the churches return to a full acceptance of Jesus as the Redeemer who *"shall save His people from their sins"!* Since the present emergency calls particularly for the comfort and strength that our Lord alone can offer, our pulpits should echo and re-echo with Jesus' name, which to the believer is balm and healing for his soul.

On the last Sunday of a dying year we think also of our last moments and find courage in Christ's promise that we shall *"live through His name."* During these Christmas days the music probably most featured on the radio, in churches, by oratorio societies, has been the marvelous creation of Haendel, *The Messiah,* in which that eminent composer pays his spiritual and artistic tribute to Jesus. Haendel, however, should be known not only for this musical masterpiece but also for his trusting faith. When he felt his last hour approaching, he summoned his servant and asked to hear the Ninety-first Psalm. "That was beautiful," Haendel whispered when the reading was finished. Then he continued, "Oh, that is food that nourishes! That is refreshment! . . . What a splendid thing it is to be sure of one's faith! How glorious to be a member of the Church which preaches the free grace of God through Christ as the only hope of the sinner! If we were to depend on our good works . . . what would become of us? Truly, Dr. Martin Luther discovered the sound Gospel — that only faith in Christ receives salvation! Grace is a gift." His dying words were: "Lord Jesus, receive my spirit! Oh, let me die with Thee and rise with Thee!" And as Jesus answered Haendel's prayer, so, whether this be the last year of temporal life or the first year of spiritual life in Christ, you, too, have the assurance that through our Savior, in God's good time, you shall go from this earth of sin and suffering to the heaven of hallowed bliss and glory, there to sing your praise in strains far grander than even Haendel's "Hallelujah Chorus." Until then, with *Jesus* in our hearts and on our lips, let us sing:

> Dear name! the Rock on which I build,
>   My Shield and Hiding-place;
> My never-failing Treasury, filled
>   With boundless stores of grace!
>
> Weak is the effort of my heart
>   And cold my warmest thought;
> But when I see Thee as Thou art,
>   I'll praise Thee as I ought.
>
> Till then I would Thy love proclaim
>   With every fleeting breath;
> And may the music of Thy name
>   Refresh my soul in death!

Amen

STRENGTH IN SORROW

"When" Joseph *"arose, he took the young Child and His mother by night, and departed into Egypt: and was there until the death of Herod: that it might be fulfilled which was spoken of the Lord by the prophet, saying, Out of Egypt have I called My Son."* — Saint Matthew 2:14, 15

Beloved Lord Jesus:

Fortify us with the courage to face bravely all the sorrows Thy wisdom may permit to burden us, and so deepen our reliance on Thee that in every trial we, as Thy redeemed, discern only Thy compassion for us! Keep us from doubt and despair whenever grief assails us! Constantly remind us that Thou didst suffer the punishment of our sins! In Thy mercy restore us to Thy Father and thus remove forever the penalty incurred by our many transgressions of the divine Law! Bless the millions of our nation with faith and trust in their hearts, love and truth in their lives! If it be Thy will, grant us a speedy victory with honor and justice! Comfort all who mourn in consequence of war's horror; feed the hungry; provide for the shelterless; mercifully relieve the wounded; cheer the suffering; sustain the poor; lighten every burden of those who seek refuge in Thee! Grant patience to the convalescent, healing to the wounded, Thy presence to the dying! We ask this confidently because Thou hast invited us, "Come unto Me!" and now, Lord Jesus, in these days of world-wide sorrow we come! Receive us, by Thine eternal mercy! Amen.

A blessed New Year to everyone of you! Come what will, may these twelve months bring you closer to the Lord Jesus Christ — eternal praise be to Him, our only Savior!

This is also an appropriate time for me to thank you from the bottom of my heart for the support you have given this mission of the air. We are now in our ninth season; but in all these years your help has never been as generous nor the visible blessings of God as astonishing as in these past weeks. Some of you must have been praying

[158]

very hard, for the mail following the last broadcast brought 13,000 letters in four days. Continue, I ask you, in Christ's name, with your intercessions, gifts, and testimony in behalf of the only and glorious Savior whom alone these messages exalt!

Difficulties have presented themselves, of course. Our Far East broadcasting has suffered severely. Advices from Manila tell us that the powerful station there, which carried our message throughout the Philippine Islands, East Indies, south into Australia and New Zealand, and north into China, was dismantled shortly before our enemies took the city. The work in Shanghai, China, has been interrupted. Similarly, the stress of official transmissions has stopped our Asiatic short-wave transmissions from San Francisco. Pray God that in our Father's best time and by His perfect will the evangel of the crucified Christ may not only be returned to these stations, but may find scores of new outlets in the Far East, in the Near East — over this entire sin-cursed world!

There have been compensations for these war losses. Since I last spoke to you, a station in Nova Scotia has asked for our message. More stations have been added in our own country. You will be thrilled to hear that finally, after much difficulty, our Portuguese broadcasts will soon begin over the powerful Quito, Ecuador, station, and the 45,000,000 people of Brazil, a country as large as ours, will have the opportunity of receiving by radio the promises of Christ, Son of God, Son of man, Comforter of all the disconsolate, Savior of the world.

You can see, then, why we need your continued, increasing help. This broadcast in twenty-five countries outside the United States has become, under God — and only to Him be glory! — a mighty missionary factor, which, with your aid, may be destined to serve as the greatest single agency — I say it with reverence and awe — for the spread of our Redeemer's eternal Gospel and the comfort of His love.

It is this sustaining power, which Jesus alone can give, that offers you for this darkened day

STRENGTH IN SORROW

We find our text in the words of Saint Matthew, chapter two, verses fourteen and fifteen: *"When"* Joseph *"arose, he took the young Child and His mother by night, and departed into Egypt: and was there until the death of Herod: that it might be fulfilled which was spoken of the Lord by the prophet, saying, Out of Egypt have I called My Son."*

I

WE MUST BE PREPARED FOR SUFFERING

Herod, cruel and crafty, had commanded the Wise Men to bring him exact information as to who the newborn King, the Infant Jesus, was and where He could be found. But whoever the Magi were and whatever their previous religious training may have been, they showed the sincerity of their faith by returning from Bethlehem without satisfying Herod's murderous curiosity. By the same loyalty to the Lord we, too, must reject always and unconditionally any command that would injure His cause. The divine decree that today, after nineteen centuries, stands above civil law and governmental authority, wherever and whenever these rise up against the Almighty, is the apostle's resolution, *"We ought to obey God rather than men."*

Herod's rage at the secret departure of the Magi was terrifying; and with the mania for massacre often found in the lives of fiends, he proposed to destroy the Child whom his warped mind feared as a rival, but who in truth had come to be his Savior. So Herod planned a bloody persecution — the first instance of governmental interference with the Christian cause. From that time on until now the same spirit of official control over conscience, State tyranny in matters of faith, has wrought unspeakable horror, more misery than can be told. During the sixteenth century alone the number of martyrs whose lives were demanded by such interference in religion was, it has been estimated, no fewer than 900,000. Today the spirit of governmental intrusion into the realms of religion is growing. In Spain a woman was recently thrown into prison because she expressed the belief that the Virgin Mary had other children besides our Lord. In Quebec those who distribute Protestant tracts are arrested. In Italy non-Catholic churches and preachers suffer severe discrimination. In Germany, as a Lutheran leader recently protested, the Gestapo terrorizes many church members, and the Nazi philosophy works particularly disastrously among the young people. In Russia atheistic tyranny has forever stained its hands with the blood of Christian martyrs. God keep all this far from America! One hundred and fifty years ago the far-visioned founders of our nation were so concerned about the separation of Church and State that the first provision in the American Bill of Rights and the First Amendment to the Constitution required that "Congress shall make no law respecting an establishment of religion or prohibiting the free exercise thereof." These provisions, made at a time when our country was recovering from the Revolution, must be kept, now that we are engaged in our latest struggle, when fundamental principles may easily be forgotten while hysteria takes the place of sound judgment. To counteract this may we do our full duty as Americans by working, giving, and praying as

God requires and the interests of our nation demand! And in return may we continue to employ and protect with ceaseless diligence our heritage of religious freedom! It is said that when American troops first entered Manila during the Spanish War, they found many imprisoned for what was called "political offense." This, somehow, included reading Holy Scripture. Hardly had the American flag been raised over the Philippines when the cell doors were unlocked. Then it was that a native approached an American missionary with this whispered question "Is it true? Can I now read the Bible without fear of imprisonment?" Pointing to the Stars and Stripes, the clergyman assured him, "As long as you see that flag floating over your country, you can sit on the ridgepole of your house, if you want to, and read your Bible; no one can molest you." We thank God for that freedom! Pray for those who have been robbed of that liberty! Beseech the Lord of the nations to preserve inviolate this blessed possession for us and our posterity!

To escape Herod's hatred, the Christ Child had to flee. God could have struck the royal wretch with quick death and removed the necessity of that flight, just as He could, if it were His will, take every difficulty from our pathways. Yet if peril confronts us, we, too, must use the means God gives us to escape. In the early Christian centuries some believers held the mistaken idea that instead of fleeing from the Roman authorities they should surrender to them, earn a martyr's death, or have God miraculously intervene. Today, too, many regard medical care as unnecessary even for serious sickness or accident, and still others maintain that they could fondle cobras, rattlesnakes, copperheads, cottonmouths, and suffer no harm. All this, however, is against good common sense, against the requirements of

Scripture, and, so our text clearly instructs us, against the example of Christ Himself.

It was no easy journey from Bethlehem into Egypt. True, ancient tradition, which often speaks when the Bible is silent, says roses sprang into blossom wherever the Holy Family went, lions and leopards rushed out of the wilderness to bow in adoration before the Christ Child, and date palms bent low to provide the necessary food. Now, you mothers know how difficult travel with a small child may be, even with the conveniences of modern transportation. How much more arduous that slow, dangerous flight, and what mercy we must find in each moment of its pain and peril! It was not enough, according to the divine plan of our redemption, for Christ to leave His radiant heaven and live with us in this world; from His early years He was also to endure suffering. The loneliness, the weariness, the repeated perils of this exile, were to be only the introduction to a life of love, a career of heavenly compassion, in which He would live and die for the redemption of mankind.

No wonder reverent artists have repeatedly portrayed the sojourn in Egypt, often in connection with the mighty monuments of that country! What contrasts those canvases represent! Here the mysterious Sphinx, the riddle of the ages; and there the Christ of God, with Heaven's own answer for every question concerning soul and body, time and eternity! Here the massive pyramids, supposedly to protect the bodies of the pharaohs, and there the Christ Child, through whom even the lowliest outcast can be assured of an eternity these Nile rulers never knew. Here pyramids built by the brawn and blood, the life and death of 200,000 slaves over a period of thirty years, and there, resting in their shadow, the Christ Child, who was come to redeem the downtrodden masses and save their souls for eternity! The very land where His own countrymen had groaned under centuries of bondage now sheltering Him who was to be the Liberator of all human souls!

This flight into a strange land was a severe test to His mother's faith. The angel had promised Mary marvelous blesssings; yet now she experienced exile and persecution at the hands of a cruel king. And how much this banishment cost the Savior's foster father! A celestial messenger had promised Joseph that the Babe should be called Jesus because *"He shall save His people from their sins,"* and now Joseph had to flee to save the Child's life, leave his home in the dark of night, part from his acquaintances without a word of farewell, give up his trade, sacrifice his income — in short, lose almost everything for the Infant Jesus.

Yet in God's plan that loss was necessary. The Christ Child had to be removed from the reach of murderous men; and often those who love the Lord Jesus must similarly seclude themselves from the world. The warning of His Word, *"Come out from among them and be ye separate!"* is often pushed aside when the line separating the Church and the unbelieving world is steadily being erased. The trouble with too many who call themselves "Christians" is that they do not want to be separated people, except on Sunday morning. Otherwise they crowd the same night clubs, lounge around in the same taverns, regularly visit the same public dance halls, read the same *risqué* magazines, tell the same suggestive jokes, sing the same sophisticated songs, follow the same practices of sin which mark unbelievers — just as though they had never been *"bought with a price,"* the Savior's holy, precious blood. The trouble with too many churches which have lost their power comes from conformity to the world. Instead of acclaiming Christ the one and only Hope of humanity for earth and heaven, they disclaim Him. In place of exalting His name in Law-and-Gospel sermons, they exclude His name in man-pleasing talks. Rather than emphasize Bible texts, they use devious pretexts to foretell the course of war and the principles of peace from their pulpits. They go the way of the unbelieving world by conducting raffles, bingo games, questionable theatricals, minstrel shows. The call in this crisis is for reborn, separated Christians; reborn, separated churches; reborn, separated preachers. The clergy should remember that they are exempted from the draft and military danger, not because they are heads of organizations which give sauerkraut suppers, socials, and Saturday night dances — you do not need a theological education for that! — but because prudent American policy holds that during war this nation must have men at home as with our armed forces who will build up a spiritual defense. For that reason I ask you who are ministers of our Lord to preach the glorious Gospel of the crucified Christ with greater power and persistence than ever before!

It will be hard to break away from the world. Sometimes this separation means suffering and loss, as in the case of Joseph and Mary. Indeed, often the closer people are to Christ, the more they must suffer. If some of you have not known reverses and afflictions; if your life's course has been smooth and unruffled progress from prosperity to prosperity; if the world does not assail you, then God is either exceptionally merciful in having spared you the pain many others have endured for years, or your Christianity is so weak and unrecognizable that even the devil does not bother to oppose you. Especially in years when cults spring up overnight to lure dissatisfied, disillusioned men and women with the hope of an easier, softer existence, we ought to be clear on this: Christ tells us that if we are to receive the crown of glory, we must bear the cross of affliction. How else can we understand His clear-cut requirement of everyone who would be a true member of His Church, *"Let him take up his cross and follow Me!"?* Scientific theories may be revolutionized; political philosophies discarded; national boundaries altered and realtered; but in all the upheaval from the first century to the twentieth, the divine ultimatum remains unmoved, *"We must through much tribulation enter into the kingdom of God."*

We are in war, and it should not be difficult to convince this audience that hardships hitherto unknown will soon confront us. We hear grumblings now because automobile tires are almost unobtainable. But such inconvenience; the taxes we must pay as the nation girds itself to spend half of its income for victory; the ration cards; the unemployment many of you must endure; the restrictions which necessarily fall on small business — put them all together, multiply them as you will — are not to be compared with the sorrow, suffering, and death awaiting multitudes who will be called upon to face danger on distant lands, on the deep seas, in the uncharted air. Unless God in His mercy intervenes — and let us constantly pray He will! — the casualty lists will be longer, the number of bereavements greater.

Inevitably, it seems, we must face new afflictions. The history of past struggles has shown us that the forces of hell will work in day and night shifts to lower morale and morals. More homes will be broken than in peacetime. The lure of lust will be stronger and more relentless. Especially must we be prepared for the fact that when this war is over, the influence of atheism will sweep over large sections of the globe, notably the defeated areas of Europe, as well as over groups in our country who with a hatred like Herod's will try to destroy Christianity.

II

WE CAN FIND STRENGTH IN THE SCRIPTURES

How did Joseph and Mary find courage to bear up under the exile in Egypt, its loneliness, hardship, and dangers? How can you and I receive strength for the sorrows that may surround us? Studying our text, we understand that these parents did not simply rely on their own ability to endure difficulty. They did not face their trials with the bravado noticeable today when people who boast that they can "take" anything life may bring often collapse under the first impact of affliction. Nor were Joseph and Mary fatalists who resigned themselves to whatever might come with the declaration of defeat: "Everything in life is prearranged and predetermined. All we can do is accept our fate with a protest." Some might have charged God with unfairness and cruelty. Had He not promised Mary that she should be *"blessed among women"*? And now she was a refugee! Some would have sought solace in fortune tellers or tried to find courage in the counsel of superstition. Not Joseph and Mary! As they were strengthened for their ordeal, so you and I can discover sustaining grace for our trials — in one unfailing, unchanging source, God's own Word. Not only did the Almighty send His instruction through an angel; as our text explains, this exile also *"fulfilled"* that *"which was spoken of the Lord by the prophet, Out of Egypt have I called My Son."* In this passage from the prophet Hosea the flight into Egypt was foretold more than seven centuries before it occurred, in accordance with God's plan. Similarly, divine revelation can show you, once you are Christ's, how sorrow is a helpful, remedial part of His program for your life.

The Old Testament passage in Hosea concerning Christ, at first glance, seems to be anything but a prophecy.

Yet the Holy Spirit assures us and the early testimony even of Jewish authorities agrees that these words *"Out of Egypt have I called My Son"* foretell the coming Deliverer's sojourn in Egypt. What marvelous assurance in this truth! The Bible is a source of inestimable hidden wealth. The words which read like an ordinary verse are actually a marvelous, golden prediction. No one can plumb the depths or measure the heights of Scripture.

Many plans and programs are devised today for the purpose of helping people solve their complex difficulties. If they leave Scripture out, disregard its principles, reject its help, all their proposals are doomed. In this crisis, patriotism is not enough. Courage is not enough. Military, naval, and air forces are not enough. Without God, the strongest defense can crumble, and our present emergencies demand that we resolutely heed this warning *"Cursed be the man that trusteth in man and maketh flesh his arm and whose heart departeth from the Lord!"* Even prayer is not enough, for there are a dozen different kinds of false pleading, and the Scripture declares, *"He that turneth away his ear from hearing the Law, even his prayer shall be abomination."* The Book we need today above all other books, the Word more vital than the pronouncements of statesmen and diplomats, the Truth with priority over every other claim, the Direction which alone can show faltering, groping men the way to light and hope — that Book, Word, Truth, Guidance, is found solely, but — Thank God! — assuredly in the Holy Scriptures. Only the Bible explains the cause of sorrow and suffering, national or individual; offers the way out of our difficulties, collective or personal; builds up the inner spiritual power required to face bravely and confidently deep-rooted perplexities surrounding us.

Never before — and I measure well this sweeping statement — has the urgency been as great to plead with the masses in our country: Read the Bible! Investigate its assertions! Examine its truth! Memorize its promises! Apply its remedies! *"Search the Scriptures"* in personal study, in Bible classes, especially at the family altar! Within the covers of Holy Writ are God's own solutions to the troubles now upon us. We are engaged in a bloody, destructive conflict, and we ask, "Why must we endure the hardship and heartache this struggle will impose?" If you think that World War II was forced on us only through the attack of crafty enemies, you understand merely part of the answer. Read the twenty-sixth chapter of Leviticus, the twenty-eighth of Deuteronomy, the first of Isaiah, the fifth of Jeremiah, and a score of other passages which, as clearly as language can express it, reveal that the horrors of war, even if it is necessary, justified or in self-defense, may come to a people because it forgets God and spurns His love!

This, therefore, is no hour for boasting or the preening of our American virtues. We ought rather to admit in this God-blessed nation that we have too frequently built schools without spiritual training, homes without Christ, churches without the Scriptures. We have often striven for wealth without work, sought to build industry without equity, encouraged politics without principle, condoned marriages without life-long faithfulness, science without service to humanity, carnal pleasures without the restraint of conscience. We have seen capital and labor organized without the support of mutual sacrifice, promises made without fulfillment, culture developed without character. For many folks Sunday is a time for recreation without spiritual rededication, religion a creed without the Bible. They have a Christianity without the real Christ, a Christ without the true cross, a cross without the saving blood, the blood without the atonement. For this reason God now speaks to America in actions that the Bible clearly outlines, just as it pointedly describes the one and only means of help and hope. God can permit this nation to crash and smash its way to victory through a long struggle by the sheer weight of its industrial strength, manpower, natural resources, and unparalleled wealth. But that way will demand an appalling cost in the lives of our youth and the loss of other blessings. The Almighty can help us to a quicker, surer, more lasting peace. We read in the Book of Judges that when Israel returned to God, *"the land had rest."* We, too, can have rest, by His will, if the watchword of millions from coast to coast becomes "Repentance!" "Return to God in Christ!" "Reconciliation with our heavenly Father through the Lord Jesus!"

There, in Christ and His Word, we can find individual answers to the disconsolate "Why?" of our personal sufferings. We should read the Bible, as the flight into Egypt reveals, to find Christ in the Old Testament and the New, in the Psalms and the Prophets, in the Gospels and in the Epistles, from Genesis to Revelation. When we thus know the real Jesus, who pervades the entire Scriptures, we understand the secret of our own suffering; the mystery of our many afflictions is solved; we know that through the divine, redeeming Christ the adversities Heaven permits us to encounter are but the evidences of the Father's love.

No other religion teaches this sublime truth that the sorrows we endure can be manifestations of mercy instead of the punishments of wrath; but no other religion has the assured hope of a Savior like the Lord Jesus. Until you know what Christ has done for you and then accept Him as your Savior, you are under divine wrath and must pay the penalty for your transgressions. I owe it to you who are living without Jesus to warn you that because of your rejecting the Redeemer, all the bitter griefs you endure come from God's retributive justice as an unmistakable punishment pointing to the eternal penalty which inescapably awaits you if you continually deny your Savior. — Thank God, the Bible also explains that when a man, encumbered with the heavy weight of his sins, burdened with crushing sorrows, comes to Christ, he finds undeserved grace, unmerited compassion, unearned pardon, such as he can never measure nor describe! May the Spirit help you believe this eternal, supreme, and saving truth that here in Christ there is love, divine, all-embracing love, unconditioned, assured love for every trial of this life! See how Jesus suffered, beginning with the flight to Egypt; follow Him through the persecution, slander, ridicule He endured at the hands of those whom He had come to save; through the unspeakable agony of body but the far greater torture of His soul in Gethsemane, in the repeated trials of corrupted justice! Behold Him on the cross atoning for your sins! And then believe that the Savior who is proved to be the Son of God by His own words and miracles, by the infallible truth of His almighty Father, by the divine names and honors accorded Him in the unbreakable Scriptures, by the homage of men and angels; who promises you through mercy, not through merit, *"Thy sins be forgiven thee!"* also pledges you, *"If ye continue in My Word, then are ye My disciples indeed, and ye shall know the truth, and the truth shall make you free"* — free from sin, free from its punishment, its curse, its hell and death, free forever for heaven and its blessings! Know that you, too, were released from the punishment of God's anger, since your heavenly Father, who loved your soul enough to send Christ to the cross, will extend His mercies also into your everyday affairs and by the marvels of His grace turn each affliction into a blessed advantage!

Cherish this blessed truth for the dark days ahead: In Christ *"God is Love,"* and everything which happens to you comes from His compassion and His tender kindness toward you. Only at the cross, where you know you have been washed by the cleansing blood; only when you look to Jesus and say, " *'Behold the Lamb of God, which taketh away the sin of the world,'* and particularly my sins," can you grasp this truth and the comfort of such remarkable passages as *"Whom the Lord loveth, He chasteneth."* It will take a deep and heroic faith like that of Mary and Joseph for you to accept tribulations as tokens of God's deeper love. Our constant prayer, therefore, should repeat this ancient petition, *"Lord, increase our faith!"* so that we may submit to His perfect will, not grudgingly, but gratefully, and with Job trust Him though He slay us. We must cheerfully accept God's direction even if we cannot understand His plans. — During the gold rush to California, ships leaving New England for the Pacific Coast would often carry in their holds the framework and structure of entire houses made in Massachusetts and knocked down to be shipped in sections. If a casual visitor had examined the cargoes on those Yankee Clippers at Boston, he would have seen only huge piles of variously shaped lumber and panels. But at the end of the voyage, in some West Coast town, he could have observed that these curiously shaped piles had become re-assembled dwelling places. — At the end of life's journey the Spirit will help us assemble the loose and disconnected parts of the structure we call life into a *"building fitly framed together."* Then we will understand that sometimes God permits visitations to come upon us to weaken our reliance on ourselves and deepen our trust in Him; to subdue our desire for the tinsel and tarnish of human pleasure and increase our longing for heavenly joy. We will realize that we had to be humbled so that we could be exalted; that we had to know what it means to suffer so that we could sympathize with others; that we had to lose our earthly home in order to gain the heavenly mansions; that we had to see one near and dear to us in this life taken by death, so that we could meet him in the next. For the Christian even the graves at Pearl Harbor which cover the remains of soldiers who fought *"the good fight of faith"* under Jesus, the Captain of their salvation, finally become evidence of the Savior's love.

So dry your tears, you, crushed to earth by the impact of suffering; you, the bereaved, to whom dark and destructive forces whisper, "There can never be any more hope or happiness for you!" No matter how far you have been exiled from happiness, in God's perfect schedule and by His heavenly guidance you can return to everything good and profitable for your soul. The cross of Christ is a pledge that God will take care of you. His mercies, as His miracles, will be renewed every morning in carrying out His gracious purposes. Have you ever wondered how Joseph and Mary supported themselves in a foreign country? The Bible does not tell us, but it seems to me God timed the arrival of the Magi so that, laying their gold, frankincense and myrrh at the Savior's feet, they could give Him the means of providing the necessities for the stay in Egypt. God will likewise help you in Christ. Our text concludes with the statement that the Holy Family remained in Egypt until Herod's death and then returned; and you, too, can be assured that every enemy of your soul will be defeated while you cling to Christ. When God's clock strikes the last hour for you, He will lead you out of a world of tumult and strife which to the Christian seems strange and foreign — as Egypt must have appeared to Joseph and Mary — and bring you to the glorious homeland of the redeemed, where, because you are Christ's, you shall endure no more suffering and pain.

My fellow redeemed, receive this blessed Christ now as your Savior and Strength in suffering! If one of the mighty world figures called out in speaking of the defense of an empire, "There is not a week, not a day, not an hour to be lost," I beg you in Christ's name, for the sake of your soul, worth all the empires in the world, "Is there a moment to be lost in the assurance of your salvation?" Write me now that you, your family, your community — if it is without a church — want this Christ! Because He is the Son of God and the Savior of the world, His benediction *"My peace I give unto you!"* the promise of His Word *"All things work together for good to them that love God,"* the exultation of His mighty apostle *"I glory in mine infirmities,"* will give you *"the peace which passeth all understanding,"* courage in a world of international conflict, heavenly wisdom in a bewildered, disconcerted age, a hymn of praise in your heart and on your lips even during the deepest adversity. As He now calls, tenderly, pleadingly, *"Come unto Me!"* promising, *"I will give you rest!"* approach Him, penitently, trustingly, completely, and His strength, His joy, His heaven are yours! God grant you this, for the Savior's sake! Amen!

ARE YOU "BORN AGAIN"?

"Whosoever believeth that Jesus is the Christ is born of God." — 1 John 5:1

Purifying, Strengthening Spirit of God:

Make us new creatures in Christ through the mercy and marvel of the second birth! Show us again today that as soon as we find in the Lord Jesus the atonement for our sins, the cleansing for the stains of our guilt, the ransom from all punishment, we who were children of wrath have — by the miracle of the new birth — become children of a loving heavenly Father! Help those who know their Redeemer to face every adversity bravely and walk resolutely in the Savior's footsteps! Especially do we beseech Thee mightily to spread the glorious promise of Gospel grace. Convict many of their sins and bring them contritely to their Savior! Guide our country and those responsible for its policies; enrich us with true repentance, and according to Thy good will grant us genuine peace! Destroy the evil plans of selfish, unbelieving men who promote aggression and hatred! Be with us, strengthening Spirit, as Thou wast with our fathers, for Jesus' sake! Amen.

IN 1858 thirty-four-year-old John Paton left Scotland for the New Hebrides Islands in the South Pacific Ocean. Words cannot begin to describe the lust for blood, the shocking vice, the satanic practices, he found on his arrival among the naked, treacherous cannibals. Blood flowed so freely that sometimes even the springs were discolored by its crimson, and Paton had to use rainwater for drinking. The devilish desire for human flesh drove the natives to dig up decaying bodies and to consume the rotting remains. When one of the savages died, his wife was choked to death. If a chief took sick, three women were sacrificed to secure his recovery. The entire island was ruled by bestial superstition, sorcery, and the cringing fear of demons. Yet, before thirty years elapsed, when this brave man left the New Hebrides, the fiendish fury of the inhabitants had been completely and miraculously transformed. The chiefs had pledged themselves to avoid war, women and children were no longer murdered, sorcerers and witch doctors were banished, nakedness outlawed, fear supplanted by happiness, and in a hundred other astonishing ways these people had been freed from the hideous slavery of vice and literally changed into new persons.

What was the secret of this startling success? Was Paton a military genius, acquainted with the strategy of slaughter? Did he follow dictators' methods by killing masses and forcing survivors into subjection? As far as his life story shows, Paton never raised a rifle to his shoulder. Did he produce this phenomenal change by making people physically better, removing tonsils, adenoids, head bumps, instituting new diets, explaining vitamins and calories, teaching eugenics, demanding health examinations? He never dreamed of all this. Did he write a new code of laws, establish a police force on the islands or seek to elevate the minds by holding lectures on culture and civilization for the cannibals and thus argue them out of their vicious habits? Did he try to socialize them into progress and prosperity? If you have ideas like these, you do not know John Paton. You cannot understand this South Pacific miracle or the same wonder perpetuated in 10,000 other places unless you realize that instead of force he used love. Instead of trying to alter the body or influence the mind, he sought to change the heart, to purify the soul. For Paton was a missionary of the Lord Jesus Christ, and by his preaching the glorious Gospel of free, full, final forgiveness through faith in that Savior, the Holy Spirit cleansed the blackened hearts of those natives and made of them new creatures in Christ.

The same wondrous grace of rebirth in Jesus has been repeated millions of times throughout history whenever a sinner has come to Jesus in trusting reliance on His mercies. But far more important than other instances of conversion and regeneration through the Savior is the matter of *your* rebirth. Pay close attention, then, as in our Lord's name I put this pointed question before every member of our coast-to-coast radio mission:

ARE YOU "BORN AGAIN"?

May the Holy Spirit so enlighten the hearts of multitudes from the Atlantic to the Pacific that today — and O God, let it be a time of glorious grace for thousands! — many may believe this promise of our text (First Letter of Saint John, chapter five, verse one): *"Whosoever believeth that Jesus is the Christ is born of God,"* with repentant faith give themselves to Christ and through His Spirit become totally *"new creatures"!*

I
YOU "MUST BE BORN AGAIN"

When Saint John here speaks of being *"born of God,"* he tells us that there is a second birth, marvelous and beyond human understanding. As all who come into this world of physical life must be born of human parents, so all who would enter the next world for spiritual and eternal life must be *"born of God."* Don't think that this rebirth is merely a pretty thought, a pleasant phrase, a pious wish, yet empty of practical value! When you see drunken blasphemers permanently sobered into courageous witnesses for Christ, wife-beaters become loving husbands, murderers remade into true Christians, South Sea Island cannibals into self-sacrificing believers, African child-killers into devoted parents, sworn enemies of Jesus into His avowed friends, snarling atheists reborn as contrite confessors, devil worshipers as children of God, you are confronted by reality, positive and assured.

Even unbelievers have often admitted the truth and power of regeneration in Christ. Charles Darwin certainly was no Christian; and his claim that man is descended from apelike creatures, together with his further rejection of the Bible, has helped to send many souls to hell; yet he conceded openly in his writings that no other power could alter human hearts and lives so completely as conversion to Christ. Darwin traveled to Tahiti, saw the startling missionary transformation on that island and wrote in his *Journal of Research:* "Human sacrifices, unparalleled profligacy, infanticide, and bloody wars had been abolished, dishonesty, intemperance, and licentiousness greatly reduced by the introduction of Christianity." He went to New Zealand and, beholding the conversion of the natives, wrote: "The lesson of the missionary is the enchanter's wand. . . . The march of improvement consequent on the introduction of Christianity throughout the South Seas probably stands by itself in the records of history." He sailed to the southern tip of South America and, dumbfounded by the moral, social, spiritual improvement in Christianized Patagonia, recognized the renewing power of the Gospel by sending an annual check to the Patagonian mission. Now, if this man, whom militant atheists have exalted as one of the Bible's most destructive enemies, thus freely conceded the electrifying changes Christianity brings, should not those who bear Jesus' name unhesitatingly express their faith in its regenerating strength?

We know, of course, that this truth has been violently attacked even by churches. When asked to explain his refusal to preach on the new birth, a Christ-denying pastor sneered, "I will have no obstetrics in my pulpit." We had learned to expect such ridicule and blasphemy from Modernists; but it is even more discouraging to see how many Gospel churches neglect this teaching. In protest, note the repeated emphasis God's errorless Scriptures place on this truth. No fewer than seventy Old and New Testament passages explain, exalt, exemplify the new birth. If the Bible speaks only once, that should be sufficient authority for all men; but how unusual the stress when the Scriptures speak seventy times in the words of prophets, psalmists, evangelists, apostles, and particularly in the sacred utterances of the Lord Jesus Christ Himself!

Do you know that according to the Gospel records rebirth in God was the first great doctrine Jesus explained at length? When our broadcast is over, take your New Testament — and if you are too poor to own one, let me send you a copy! — turn to the third chapter of Saint John's Gospel and read of the remarkable visit paid to our Lord during the darkness of night by Nicodemus, teacher and leader of Israel. How solemnly, how unmistakably Christ taught the reality and necessity of the rebirth! Read these verses carefully, and you will see that four times the Savior says, *"Verily,"* as though He were taking a repeated oath to stress the truth. Once again, if the Son of God speaks, that should settle the issue, but when He uses four *"verily's"* (I know of no similar number of verses in the whole Scripture with this quadruple emphasis), He speaks with compelling power. Pay close attention, therefore, when the Redeemer tells Nicodemus and you, *"Except a man be born again, he cannot see the kingdom of God"*; when the Savior repeats, *"Except a man be born of water and of the Spirit, he cannot enter into the kingdom of God"*; and when, for the third time in five verses, Jesus decisively insists, *"Ye must be born again."* May that *"Ye must — ye must — ye must — be born again"* be dinned into your very souls! Wealth can never buy the key to God's kingdom. High position and authority will not unlock the door to heaven. Old age and white hair cannot bring you a step closer to God. Church membership is no assurance of your salvation. You need far more than leading offices in the congregation. Even preaching from pulpits gives you no title to a prepared place in the many mansions. You may come from a Christian family with a long list of churchgoing ancestors; you may have a devout wife, a consecrated husband, but all these, unmistakable blessings that they are, will never bring you before the Throne of Mercy. You may show the close acquaintance with the Bible which enables you to cite book, chapter, verse; you may display medals for Sunday-school attendance or certificates for teaching; you may wear a robe and sing in the choir; you may be generous with your gifts, sympathetic with your fellow-men, abounding in so-called good works — but this is not enough. Men have enjoyed such preeminences and still gone straight to hell! Jesus tells us, *"Ye must be born again."*

Because this rebirth is so vital, forget the war for a few moments and think of the struggle in your soul, as well as your own personal need of being born again! Realize immediately this basic, inescapable truth from which our haughty, self-righteous world constantly recoils—the shocking reality that men without Christ live in repeated, grievous sin, held and swayed by envious, covetous, lustful, hate-filled thoughts and cruel, dishonest, destructive actions! Take Christian influences from our modern culture, and unbelievers in principle would not be different from those hideous savages who opposed John Paton in the New Hebrides Islands! Take God out of men's hearts, and they will be devoted to evil instead of good, to hatred much more than love, to war in place of peace, to lust rather than purity, to falsehood before truth, to kicking their helpless fellow-men instead of helping them! At the beginning of this twentieth century, scoffers, without the churches as within, insisted loudly that mankind was really good, that the whole race was improving, that human affairs were on the upgrade toward beauty, truth, happiness. The Bible passages which declare, *"All have sinned, and come short of the glory of God,"* or, *"There is not a just man upon earth, that doeth good and sinneth not,"* were laughed away as outworn, pessimistic errors. At the heyday of that delusion came World War I, and after just enough time for another generation to arise, World War II with greater hatred, brutality, mass destruction, murder of innocent hostages, suffering on the part of non-combatants, than any war between cannibals has ever witnessed. And unless God is undeservedly merciful, in the year 1965, or thereabouts, if this earth can stand that long, World War III will be in the making, with even more shocking destruction.

Survey our reaction to the heaped blessings God has showered upon us! Ungratefully men have rebelled against the Almighty and employed His benedictions in sin's service. They have used their brains and intelligence, the faculties of schools and colleges, to attack His Word and banish God from modern life. They have poisoned home happiness with adultery, lust, unfaithfulness, strife, unbelief. Many churches have become campaign headquarters for assaults on the Scriptures. Newspaper columns, as here in St. Louis, advertise material which champions atheism and free love. Across both oceans, in Europe and Asia, dictators restrict the course of the Gospel. Crime soars to the zenith in American history, and those who are aware of these trends ought to be convinced that the whole human race without God is an ugly, sordid, selfish, sensual aggregate; that men who reject Christ are truly murderers of their own souls.

It is not easy for me to use this microphone and vast network to tell you, the self-respecting, substantial, esteemed, and applauded, that you must be born again if you would behold God, that lacking the new birth, you are still children of wrath; but in the eternity awaiting every one of us I do not want you to point a finger of scorn at me and say, "You had that coast-to-coast radio hook-up, and you never told me that I was lost in my sins, that I had to be born into a new existence before I could see God." Every one of you ought to realize in an intimate, direct way that daily you commit transgressions which invoke divine wrath.

While most people are ready to admit that not all is right in their lives, yet nothing is harder to wring from the heart of an unconverted man or woman than the confession "I have sinned before my God." One of the supreme needs of this spiritually decadent day is to call sin by its right name, to recognize every violation of God's Law as an iniquity capable of sending the soul and body to hell. Many deluded individuals, particularly church-members, can become so blinded to God's truth that they seek even to glorify sin. Some of you labor under this curse when the divine Word plainly brands your actions as sin and you try to justify yourself by disguising iniquity as virtue. But you will never succeed. If you are not born again, you are spiritually dead. You face complete and everlasting rejection by the Almighty, eternal death and banishment from heaven, the pain and penalty of hell itself. To escape that terror, to enter God's kingdom, to be assured of heaven, you must — O Father, engrave it on our souls! — *"be born again,"* or in the words of our text, be *"born of God."*

II

YOU CAN BE "BORN AGAIN"

As I now repeat this direct question, "Are you *'born again'*"? I thank the Lord that the blessing of this re-birth can be yours through the Savior's grace and might.

If it were not for this power, of course, you would be help-less, hopeless, lost forever, unable to lift a finger, move an eyelid, whisper a plea that would help change your hearts or purify your lives.   True, modern science and industry can produce amazing transformation. Visit a paper factory and you will see how dirty rags, thrown into a large hopper, cut into pieces, treated with acids, finally emerge as white, spotless sheets. But no industrial process can take human beings despite claims of many righteousnesses — the Bible calls these *"filthy rags"* — and make them clean, stainless. By the marvels of modern chemistry coal tar, black, sticky, smelly, altogether unpromising, can be converted into a rainbow of wonderful colors, an array of perfumes, a num-ber of useful plastics, an assortment of explosives, and many other materials.   But the soul will not yield to such treat-ment, and neither education, medical care, social improve-ment, can transform black, sordid, corrupt characters and endow them with beauty, strength, and power.   At best, evil may be concealed or disguised; but as little as you can restore a rotting, worm-eaten apple by polishing its skin, purify water by painting the pump; bring life into a corpse by putting rouge on its cheeks, so and even more impossible is it to change the soul by culture, medical or social science. You need God for that!

Thanks to His endless compassion, you can have God in the Lord Jesus Christ.   When we are crushed by the weight of our sins; when we grovel in damning, degrading vices; when in human blindness we grope for safety and salvation, only constantly to find ourselves farther from the goal, then what glory beyond compare to know, as I now assure you, that our heavenly Father in the magnificence of His divine mercy has sent every one of us a Savior!   This Re-deemer — oh, for a thousand tongues, ten thousand radio stations, a universal hook-up throughout every nation, to sing His blessed praise! — is God's own Son, Jesus, the Christ, who alone could fulfil the Law we had broken, suffer the penalty we had deserved, die the death that should have been ours. This Savior gave Himself, His holy, divine Self. He was nailed to the cross, the accursed tree, to which the lowest criminals were sentenced. There He shed His blood, suffered the agonies of excruciating pain, the torment of ridicule, and, above all, the anguish of soul torture — for this sacred, heavenly, compassionate purpose, — to remove once and forever the entire burden of men's sins, with their ugly guilt and the dread damnation to which, if unforgiven, every transgression must lead. Whether you have heard this before or not; whether you now believe it or not, *"Christ Jesus came into the world to save sinners,"* to save *you.*

Such glorious grace, however, does not exhaust the Savior's mercy. Besides redeeming us for eternity, His love also remakes us entirely, for as soon as we penitently confess Him our Ransom and Redemption, sincerely crown Him the Sovereign of our souls, contritely cling to Him as the immovable Rock of Ages, the Holy Spirit has begun His marvelous work in our souls by which we, children of wrath, become children of grace; sinners in the eyes of men, but now saints in the sight of our heavenly Father — all in fulfilment of the sacred promise *"If any man be in Christ Jesus, he is a new creature."* We look the same after this rebirth as before, but we cannot act the same. A real change has come from within. We who hated God begin to love Him. Those who ridiculed and rejected Christ now show Him reverence. Those who served sin now serve Jesus. Habitual drunkards write us to testify that after hearing the broadcast Word the power of alcohol has been broken. Self-confessed atheists testify that they have become humble believers; would-be suicides that they have found life eminently worth while when lived for Jesus. Scoffers have converted their blasphemy to testimony, their foul-mouthed profanity to praise for Christ. Parents who wickedly plotted to destroy their unborn children have learned to stop this murder, welcome and cherish the baby that came to them as God's gift. In hundreds of ways by the Spirit's power working through these broadcasts, lives have been remade, the desires of the heart directed from sin to the Savior, the understanding of the Scriptures opened and simplified, as men who before their conversion had sought contradictions in the Bible now bow before its harmony.

With this new birth comes a new power to walk in the footsteps of Jesus, to lead clean and pure lives, never perfect, it is true (since we are still in the flesh while here on earth), yet always, despite serious lapses, progressing toward holiness. With this new birth comes new courage, fortitude required to face the difficulties that will confront many of us during the post-war crisis, the bravery with which Chrysostom, fifth-century pulpit orator and witness to the Lord Jesus, could face threatened exile and exult: "Should the Empress banish me, let her; the earth is the Lord's and the fulness thereof. If she cast me into the sea, let her; I remember Jonah. — If she cast me into the fire, the three Hebrews were there. If she throw me to the wild beasts, Daniel was among the lions. If she stone me, I shall stand with Stephen. If she behead me, I am the Baptist. If she takes all — naked came I into the world, and naked leave it."

I ask you once more, "Are *you 'born again?'*" Remember that the blessings of the new birth are assured you in heaven's highest mercy. Our text promises, "*Whosoever believeth that Jesus is the Christ is born of God.*" That blessed "*whosoever*" includes you, for whom life may have little attraction, who may be suffering under racial prejudice, social injustice, religious discrimination. Here before the Lord Jesus Christ — all on the same level — are men of various colors, conditions, and countries, men of all creeds which proclaim Jesus as the only Savior. Before Christ there are no Protestants, Catholics, Lutherans, or Reformed, no denominations or divisions within denominations; but *"whosoever,"* wherever and whatever he may be, *"believeth that Jesus is the Christ is born of God."*

And what marvel of mercy radiates from that word *"believeth"!* It implies the supreme glory of our Christian faith which enabled Saint Paul to exult, *"By grace are ye saved, through faith,"* and which gives us the assured conviction that while this whole world of striving men could never heap up enough wealth, perform sufficient penances, earn the merits required to pay for a single sin, Jesus by the shedding of His blood, His atoning death, has earned and paid all a holy God requires for the remission of our sin. We need only believe, only approach Christ, our compassionate Redeemer, with contrite, trusting hearts to have pardon, peace, and power.

Think of the blessings which could come to our world in these days of deep-rooted sorrow if millions who now reject Christ could be *"born again"* in Him and if those who confess His name would show their new birth! We could then be assured, for example, that the terror of war would be reduced. Men reborn in Jesus are reborn to peace with their God and, as far as in them lies, with their fellow-men. Wherever true missionaries of our Lord have planted His cross, they have checked bloodshed. If only the churches of Jesus Christ could proclaim His good news to men throughout the world, so that Christian faith would produce an increasing number who live, work, and pray for peace, blessed peace! Perhaps this war is to remind us as

American Christians, with our advantages in men and money, that we have been remiss in our missionary duties. Who knows, had we really made sacrifices in the past and brought the Gospel with greater intensity to Japan, whether much of international misunderstanding could not have been removed, some of the cause and spirit of aggression retarded?

I come back, then, to this vital question, "Are you *born again*'?" If you are and can testify that everything I have said is God's holy truth, then show the world that you are "*born of God*"! With all your heart get behind the spread of the saving truth by which others may be reborn! Work for missions! But if you do not acclaim Christ your own Savior and must confess, "The black powers of darkness still control my life," then let me ask you in the most vital question ever directed to you, "What keeps you from Jesus?" In stubborn pride do you insist you have no need of a Redeemer? The last person who told me that was a derelict in the shelter for homeless men here in Saint Louis, and he was in a drunken, slobbering stupor, as he struggled to his feet to say he had never done anything wrong.

Swinging to the other extreme, do you think you have been guilty of sins too terrifying to be forgiven; that you are so steeped in iniquity that you can never be cleansed? Hear David, after his adultery, pleading, "*Create in me a clean heart, O God, and renew a right spirit within me!*" only to receive the promise of pardon and purity! Recall skeptical, sword-bearing Saul, transformed into penitent, believing Paul; Augustine, the sensualist, remade into a saint!

Have you refused to accept Christ and His new birth because you cannot understand the unsearchable love and power of this grace? But you do accept the mystery of this physical life though neither you nor anyone else can explain it. Why, then, reject the divine processes which no physical instruments can measure and no laboratory analyze?

Have you postponed your desire to accept Christ, hoping, in common with many deluded people, for a more convenient time, a day which may never come? For the sake of your soul, now, today, while the Spirit urges you, give Christ His blessed way in your heart! Welcome Him as your own Savior! Receive Heaven's own Redeemer, sent to the world for all men but particularly for you! Resolve today that with divine assistance you will take time for instruction in the Christian faith, to read the Scriptures, to be baptized for the washing away of your sins! Let me send you a true man of God, a pastor and spiritual guide who preaches the same messages I have broadcast to you for nine years! Give us your children for our Sunday-schools and Christian day-schools! Welcome Christ into your family circle! And as you accept Him, by the Holy Spirit's indwelling, you will be *"born again," "born of God,"* born into everlasting life. O Father, may this day be the spiritual birthday, the beginning of a new, reborn existence for multitudes in this mission of the air! We ask it in Jesus' name and by the restoring, re-energizing, renewing power of the Holy Spirit. Amen!

KEEP AMERICA CHRISTIAN!

*"Turn Thou us unto Thee, O Lord, and
we shall be turned; renew our days as of
old!"* — Lamentations 5:21

Our God and, through Jesus Christ, Our Father:

*In this hour of our country's need we come before Thee to im-
plore Thy guidance and Thine almighty power for the welfare of
our nation, for victory with a just, righteous peace. We know,
however, that Thou art pleased only with those who love Thee,
follow Thy Word, and seek to do Thy will. Therefore, as we
behold sin and wrong in our lives and unbelief rampant in America,
we approach Thee for mercy, beseeching Thee, by the power of
Christ's cleansing blood and His life-giving death, to forgive us,
restore us, strengthen us. We have not deserved Thy compassion;
but Thou hast promised to be gracious to us for Jesus' sake, and
we rely wholly on Thy Word. Lay on us whatever Thy wisdom
decrees may be necessary and helpful for us; but, O God of endless
love, bring many to Christ, keep those who know Thy Son as their
only Redeemer faithful to the end! Make us a thoroughly Christian people! Bless the preaching of Thy pure Gospel throughout
the world! We ask these favors and Thy benediction upon this
broadcast for Jesus', our glorious Savior's, sake. Amen.*

FOUR thousand billion dollars! Who among us can
really understand that staggering sum? Yet a Harvard professor of economics recently told those worried
about our growing national deficit that within fifty years,
provided the Federal income continues to increase as it has,
the United States will be able to sustain an indebtedness of
that inconceivable amount. Four thousand billion dollars!
Who knows whether this figure, cruelly fantastic to many
of you who would thank God if you had four dollars,
represents the breaking point in American financial power?
An army of experts, I suppose, will contradict this claim;
moreover, we should realize that a nation's existence is
not guaranteed by the amount of its money nor its destruc-

[189]

tion sealed by financial loss. A country can rebuild, some-times better and stronger, after complete bankruptcy. The wildest inflation, when people pay hundreds of thousands in paper money for a loaf of bread or a quart of milk, need not mark the utter end of any nation.

Similarly, if we ask ourselves, What is the worst disaster that can overtake our beloved land? we ought to agree that the most devastating danger comes not from without, but from within. Just as a man can recover from ghastly surface wounds, broken or even amputated limbs, while below-the-surface diseases, like cancer or internal injury to the vital organs, prove fatal, so a nation, with its cities, towns, and villages, can regain its peace after the chaos and upheaval of war; it can be restored to health after wide epidemics of influenza or typhus; it can rise victoriously from the ashes of fire, the debris of flood, earthquake, tornado, the ruin of bombs and cannon. Yet history testifies that there is one inner loss which is final, that can remove national glory forever and permanently reduce any country, however rich and powerful. That deadliest danger is unbelief, ingratitude toward God Almighty, the blasphemous ridicule of His Word, the rejection of the Lord Jesus Christ, the denial of the cleansing blood, the contempt for the Gospel, and with this, the carnival of crime, the sweeping rule of sin, the glorification of evil. God's truth, majestic in its plain, unalterable force, warns, *"The nation and kingdom that will not serve Thee shall perish,"* and every time an empire has collapsed — review this parade of fallen kingdoms: Egypt, Babylonia, Syria, Media, Persia, Greece, Rome, and, above all, Judah — the truth of that warning is fulfilled.

The most vital necessity for America today is, there-fore, trust in the Lord Jesus Christ's power to forgive sins and restore us to God. That truth was recognized when the United States was founded; but because the opposition to our Lord and His Church is steadily increasing, while sinister anti-Christian forces attempt to destroy the faith which has been the heritage of millions, I appeal to you in Christ's name:

KEEP AMERICA CHRISTIAN!

For our text we turn to the closing words in the Book of Lamentations (chapter five, verse twenty-one), where Jeremiah, surveying his people's unbelief and their sorrow, cries out, *"Turn Thou us unto Thee, O Lord, and we shall be turned; renew our days as of old!"*

I

WE ARE LOSING OUR CHRISTIAN HERITAGE

In this plaintive plea, *"Renew our days as of old,"* the prophet recorded his sorrow over the tragic fact that Israel, blessed by Jehovah above all other nations; Israel, protected by divine might and heavenly love since its earliest days; Israel to whom alone God sent His prophets, His Word, and the promise of a coming Messiah, had forgotten its Creator and Redeemer. The ancient days during which the people stood close to their God had given way to a new, sin-marked era in which the Lord was ungratefully cast aside. Recalling David's golden age when Israel loyally acclaimed Jehovah; Solomon's temple, where swelling psalms joyfully sang the Almighty's praise; the reign of God-fearing kings, when Old Testament Scriptures were held in high esteem, sacrifices performed with humble repentance — and contrasting with those distant, happy days the worldliness, unbelief, rebellion against God which aroused divine wrath and summoned Nebuchadnezzar's Babylonian hordes to lay Jerusalem waste, Jeremiah breaks out into this plea: *" 'Renew our days as of old'!* Bring back those glorious years when Israel gladly served God!"

Need I remind you that a similar, lamentable contrast exists between the America of today and of our founding fathers; that we, too, must pray with deep-souled appeal, "O God, *renew our days as of old*!" The Book of Judges points to grave national calamities which began when *"another generation"* arose *"which knew not the Lord, nor yet the works which He had done for Israel."* Similarly a new generation has now arisen within our boundaries which does not know the God who made America great nor recognize His overbounteous mercy toward our country. Despite everything radicals may try to tell you, keep this basic truth firmly implanted in your mind: Our colonies, later the States, were settled by men and women who were Christians, who came to our shores, among other reasons, because they could here spread the Gospel, erect Christian churches, and worship the Savior according to His Word! Those early pioneers had their faults, of course, and I am not endeavoring to glorify something so far distant from us that its frailties cannot be seen; but for the most part, the people who built America were outstanding in their devotion to Christ. The Charter of Virginia assures its colonists the right to live together in "Christian peace" and instructs them to help "in propagating . . . the Christian religion to such people as yet live in ignorance of the true knowledge and worship of God." The Plymouth Charter specifies that the colony is established "to advance the enlargement of the Christian religion, to the glory of God Almighty." The Delaware Charter defines one purpose of that settlement as "the further propagation of the Holy Gospel." Maryland's Charter explains that its first settlers were moved by a "pious zeal for extending the Christian religion." The Massachusetts Bay Charter emphasizes that Boston was founded by men who wanted to bring the new world "to the knowledge and obedience of the only true

God and the Savior of mankind." The early settlers of Pennsylvania came to America, according to their own declaration, for the spread of the "Christian religion." The Rhode Island Charter commits its people to the "true Christian faith and worship of God," and in the Rhode Island Compact the signers declare, "We submit our persons, lives, and estates unto our Lord Jesus Christ, the King of kings, and Lord of lords." The Connecticut Constitution in its preamble pledges the settlers to help "preserve the liberty and purity of the Gospel of the Lord Jesus Christ." The first article in the New Hampshire Charter begins: "We . . . in the name of Christ and in the sight of God." The oath that this instrument requires was to be administered in the name of "the Lord Jesus Christ, the King and Savior of His people."

Similarly, in the early days of our War for Independence, although freethinkers sometimes occupied high places, an unmistakably Christian note rang through the official proceedings. The closing words in the Declaration of Independence confessed the nation's dependence on God. The first American day of humiliation, fasting, and prayer, in 1776, was appointed by Congress so that the colonies might "through the merits and mediation of Jesus Christ, obtain His pardon and forgiveness." The first Thanksgiving Day, ordered by Congress in 1777, asked the people's prayers for God's solemn blessing and "the penitent confession of their manifold sins . . . and their humble and earnest supplication that it may please God, through the merits of Jesus Christ, mercifully to blot our sins out of remembrance." President John Adams proclaimed a country-wide fast, asking the citizens to admit their sins before the "Most High God" and with the sincerest penitence implore His pardoning mercy through the "Great Mediator and Redeemer for our past transgressions." In the midst of the Civil War, 1863, the United States Senate passed a resolution suggesting that our people seek God's help "through Jesus Christ." In a hundred different ways, it could be shown, the America of yesterday exalted Almighty God as the Supreme Ruler of our commonwealth, taught that in the Scriptures His will is revealed for the infallible guidance of men, and that Jesus Christ is the divinely appointed Mediator between God and the men who make up nations.

I am not now discussing the relation of Church and State nor pleading for intolerance or religious discrimination, both of which are condemned by true Americanism and true Christianity. I am trying to show you that the founding fathers in America were not atheists, skeptics, unbelievers, pantheists, freethinkers, Mohammedans, Buddhists, but (despite their denominational differences, which I would in no way minimize) Christians who built their hope on the Lord Jesus Christ. Here and there, in the course of years and with the freedom America offered all men, a settlement of unbelievers and atheists did spring up. For example, when the city of New Ulm, Minnesota, was planned, its founders boasted that in this community the folly of religion would be revealed by the success of irreligion. Yet New Ulm and a few other similar experiments failed dismally to function as centers of antireligious agitation. Today a Lutheran college and church steeples show Christ's victory over unbelief. On the whole, the pioneers along our Eastern seaboard, the men and women who built cities and towns in the Colonies, the first to cut down forests in the Northwest Territory, to cross the Alleghenies, to sail down the Ohio and up the Mississippi, the early farmers on our Midwestern plains, the hardy adventurers who drove covered wagons to the Rockies and then fought their way over desert or mountain passes through blister of heat or blizzard to the slopes that drop into the blue Pacific, were close to the Almighty in those days when most of our congregations were established, most of our mission groups, Bible societies, Christian charitable and educational institutions founded.

Now, however, the scene is changed. We have more churches, but not stronger churches. The clear-cut acknowledgment of the Lord Jesus Christ which marked the original American way of life is subdued. Public orators speak of God, it is true; but have you noticed how woefully infrequent is the reference to *"the Name which is above every name"?* In some instances men of prominence deliberately refuse to mention Christ. Certain fraternal organizations, called "Christian," systematically bar His name, perhaps because they are afraid of incurring the disfavor or losing the support of anti-Biblical elements. Even some religious groups which during the hard, formative periods of this country were outspoken in their loyalty to Jesus have gone over to the left wing of Modernism. They have imposing buildings, well-paid choirs, celebrated pulpit orators, élite membership, social halls, gymnasiums; but they are without Christ, the Son of God, the one Savior. They have lost the faith of their fathers, they have compromised when God's Word demanded opposition to error and warned, *"Whosoever shall deny Me before men, him will I also deny before My Father which is in heaven."*

At the same time, other countermovements have been set in motion against our Lord. Atheism has been systematically organized. Communism — and I mean the Bible-ridiculing, Christ-blaspheming sort — has made startling headway in the United States during the last two decades, and we may well expect that it will go forward in greater strides after the war. American Christians should realize that every atheistic Communist has sworn hostility to the Gospel of Jesus and that the higher his rank, the greater his influence, the more dangerous his hatred of the Savior.

When we thus behold the denial of the Lord Jesus in this blessed nation, generations ago dedicated to faith in His redemption; when we see the America in which, while strange, foreign sects and cults become firmly rooted, half of the entire population belongs to no church whatever and, therefore, comes under Christ's verdict *"He that is not with Me is against Me,"* do you not agree that the prayer to be spoken from our innermost hearts must repeat Jeremiah's plea "O God, *'renew our days as of old'* "? Bring back the America that was not ashamed to confess the Lord Jesus; the America that had days of fasting, humiliation, and penance; the America in which Sunday was a time for church attendance by the whole family; the America that wanted sermons instead of sermonettes, that listened to preachers who called sin *sin;* the America in which frontier settlers shared their homes with circuit riders or traveled for days to hear a preacher expound the Gospel; the America that had no streamlined trains, no airplanes, no radios, no electric power, no steam heat, no modern plumbing, no production lines, yet that had the Savior, and, having Him, was victorious over its enemies!

"Renew our days as of old!" we repeat as we recall the startling change which has overtaken American education. The first schools founded on this continent taught the Christian religion and were based on the Scriptural maxim *"The fear of the Lord is the beginning of wisdom."* Today much of public education is pointedly antireligious, with a deep-rooted determination on the part of many teachers (whose salaries are paid from public funds) to poison young minds against the Bible. Most of you have no idea of the startling extent to which textbooks used in many public schools feature an away-from-God tendency. While

recent years have witnessed a remarkable increase in school building and enrollment, on a steadily mounting scale we have been forced to erect more prisons in the battle against juvenile crime. In many cities we are training children to be mentally shrewd rather than morally good, cute and cunning instead of honest and straightforward. Because the collapse of morality and reverence constitutes a serious menace to the future of the nation, we ought constantly to ask the Almighty for a return to the early American educational ideals. They had no modern theories of training in those pioneer decades, no "progressive" systems, no theories of self-expression; but they kept first things first. For them no training was complete without the study of the Bible, the memorizing of its passages, the exalting of its truth.

True, we can never fully recapture that early American ideal since our public schools, attended by children of various, conflicting creeds, cannot give spiritual instruction or require Biblical training; but the Christians of our country can return to the colonial practice — and the conditions after the war may make this necessary — by which the churches built their own elementary schools to insure religious instruction. My own Church annually spends millions of dollars to maintain and expand a system of child training which helps the pupils keep the Lord Jesus uppermost in his mind. We gladly pay our taxes to support the public educational system; but we also believe that the nation and the churches require hearts and minds illuminated by the Holy Spirit, souls daily instructed in Biblical truth. Therefore we maintain hundreds of Christian day schools throughout the land, offering more than secular culture can legally give — a sound, Scriptural training. These schools are open to your boys and girls. Give us your children so that we can help give them to

Christ! Juvenile court statistics show conclusively that youngsters thus trained have a moral and spiritual force in their lives which goes far in keeping them away from crime and closer to Christ.

Similarly, we need a return to the spirit of Christian higher education which marked our country's yesteryear, when colleges and universities were founded for the defense and spread of the true faith. Read the records of the seventeenth, eighteenth, and nineteenth centuries to remind yourself that the oldest, largest, and best universities were dedicated to the Savior in their charters, on their seals, and in their Scripture-centered instruction! Deeply we regret that many of the colleges thus called into existence by humble, Christian faith, built by Christian funds, endowed by legacies from Christian friends, have forsaken this foundation. In too many cases such schools have become hotbeds of infidelity and hatred of the Redeemer. As some of you parents know from bitter experience, young people who enter colleges as happy, trusting believers, leave as dissatisfied, sophisticated skeptics. Particularly in times like these, when the nation needs spiritual strength for its first line of defense, we must keep Christ in culture. Therefore, if you fathers and mothers want your children to attend a college in which Biblical religion, far from being assailed, will be exalted, write me for a list of spiritually accredited colleges connected with my Church!

Similarly, the plea *"Renew our days as of old!"* arises from a dozen different sectors of our life. Give us the early American household, with large families, mothers devoted to their home, fathers conscious of the fact that they must be God's priests among their own, children who are obedient and respectful; homes, in short, with Jesus the constant Guest and His Spirit the consecrating Power! Think of it, Christian marriage was so sacred in the

Plymouth Colony that during its first seventy-one years only six divorces were granted, and these on Scripturally justified grounds! Contrast with this the reports of fifth, sixth, and seventh marriages in the United States and a divorce rate which now seems primed for a startling increase!

This *"renew our days as of old!"* should be spoken with redoubled sincerity now, when the burdens of war begin to press heavily. Listening to some speakers, one would imagine God plays no part in the triumph of our forces or in the just and righteous peace for which we pray. "We must win this war," it is said, "because we have the will to win." But we need more than the armies, navies, air armadas; more than hundred-billion-dollar expenditures; more than organization and strategy, bravery and sacrifice! My fellow countrymen, we need God; and since He is with those only who accept Him in humble, trusting faith, let us seek Him penitently in Christ and recognize how earnestly He speaks to us in war's visitation. Church papers do well in featuring these paragraphs spoken by a preacher in Bournemouth, England, to his congregation: "We have ignored the ringing of the church bells calling us to worship. *Now* the bells cannot ring except to warn of invasion. We have left the churches half empty when they should have been filled with worshipers. *Now* they are in ruins. The money we would not give to the Lord's work, *now* is taken from us in taxes and higher prices. The food for which we forgot to say thanks, *now* is unobtainable. The service we refused to give to God, *now* is conscripted for the country. Nights we would not spend 'watching unto prayer,' *now* are spent in anxious air-raid precautions." Similarly, of our own country it could be said: We have used our automobile tires to take us away from church on Sunday, and *now* many have no tires for the whole week. We did not send enough missionaries to convert the Japanese, *now* we must send soldiers to destroy them. We have not trained our youth for the Savior; *now* we must train them for slaughter.

II

WE NEED GOD TO PRESERVE OUR CHRISTIAN HERITAGE

We should, however, do more than cry out, "Keep America Christian!" We must act! Everyone who knows the Lord Jesus and the magnificence of His grace in reconciling a lost world to His heavenly Father must be ready to assume individual responsibility. Jeremiah does not primarily seek to start a mass movement nor ask others to act for him. He recognizes his own share, his personal duty. May the Holy Spirit awaken men with the courage of that mighty prophet who, as few others, protested ceaselessly against evil, defended the faith at all costs, resolutely championed his Lord and continually sounded the necessary note of repentance and contrition! Let American clergymen make this fearless man of God their model by clinging to the whole Word of Truth! Such loyalty may produce opposition, just as Jeremiah had to fight the chief priests and the officials in the ecclesiastical system of his day. Dare to be a Jeremiah, and you will have a Jeremiah's blessing — deliverance in danger and persecution! If necessary, the Almighty can invoke His heavenly power to sustain you in any struggle.

Laity of America, read these Old Testament prophecies to find strength and courage during disturbed days! You are not too small, insignificant, isolated, to be heard or have your objection to apostasy sustained. The man with the Almighty on his side is still a majority. Therefore, if you hear any attack on Christ, cry out in rebuke! If in church circles you meet denial of the faith, any contradiction of God's truth, raise your voice in disavowal! If in the realm of politics attempts are made to discredit the divine Word; for example, if efforts are made to introduce anti-Biblical, anti-American, evolutionary, Communist books, reading guides or courses into the public-school system of your community, start a petition to prohibit them! Take the lead in eliminating violations of Scriptural teachings and our constitutional rights! Some of you business men, blessed with a clear-cut understanding of the Savior's teaching, should enter the nation's political life and contribute the uplifting power that Christian leadership can offer. Today there is a marked need in the weighty public offices — especially those dealing with the lives of our military youth — for many more far-sighted men who know Jesus and His exalting righteousness.

Jeremiah, realizing that without God all his protests would be of no avail, turned to the Almighty in the prayer of our text. Oh, that millions from coast to coast would likewise find refuge and strength in true petition and bring down God's benediction through fervent intercession! America on bended knees, with folded hands, bowed heads, and humble hearts could win victories over foes a thousand times stronger than our enemies across both oceans. So, pray, America! Pray penitently! Beseech God in your own room, your household, your church, wherever you may be! Pray persistently, with trust which can never be defeated because you know *"with God nothing shall be impossible"*! By the omnipotence of heaven, if it be His will and for our individual and collective best, He can change our sorrows, stop this war, and give the world a true and righteous peace, with all oppression defeated.

Especially, however, pray as Jeremiah did when he pleaded contritely, confessing the sins of his people as well as his own transgressions!   Multitudes across this nation should repeat his prayer *"Turn Thou us unto Thee, O Lord, and we shall be turned!"*   Come before God, you among the unconverted who have never accepted the Redeemer!   Ask the Almighty, "Turn me from sin, from hell, from eternal death!   Turn me from my own sinful flesh, from my own lustful thoughts, my own selfish, hateful, revengeful self!   Turn me from the lure and lust of temptation!   Turn me from the despair over my transgressions, from the accusation of my conscience, from the fear of death!   Turn me from Thy wrath, and for Jesus' sake bring me into Thy love!"   When you plead with this complete trust which takes Christ fully at His Word; when you know in the positive assurance of the Holy Spirit that the suffering which Jesus endured, the blood He shed on Calvary, the cry of anguish which there escaped His parched lips, the death He died on the cross, was all for you, so that by the humble acceptance of Him as your Savior you could be turned from sin to salvation — you are saved for earth and heaven.   Then, while you cling to Christ, no power of men or devils combined can tear you from His hands.   You have been born again into a new existence that has turned you to God!

Many of you (I know from your letters) could now testify that God has marvelously turned you; that the Spirit has changed men who have beaten or deserted their wives and made them repentant, loving husbands. Some of you had to be imprisoned to meet Christ and find the new life in Him; now — praise God! — drunkenness, envy, malice, unmentionable sins, have all been forgiven and conquered in your life through the Spirit who has turned you to the Father by the power of His regeneration.

Do not let anyone or anything keep you from Christ's love!   Ask God to turn your mind so that instead of doubting, you gladly accept the glorious truth which even mighty intellects have acclaimed!   Beseech the Spirit to direct your heart from the treacherous clinging to worldly treasures!   Last week a sailor on the doomed tanker *Allen Jackson,* instead of fleeing to a lifeboat when the torpedo struck the ship's side, remembered eighty dollars left in the locker and ran to salvage his wallet.   But he sold his life for money he could never enjoy.   While his shipmates escaped, he was drowned.   To avoid spiritual death, beseech your heavenly Father for the strength required to cut loose from all destructive entanglements!   Ask God to turn your life from the slavery of sin to the service of your neighbors and your country in this hour of its need, so that perishing souls may be restored by a word of Christ's grace and truth you may be privileged to speak!

Plead with God in the faith of Jeremiah to turn you wholly to the Savior in body, soul, heart, mind, and spirit! My fellow redeemed, may the joy of a saved, sanctified life be yours!   By the power of rebirth and reconciliation to the heavenly Father, you, as believers in Christ, can be a mighty force in restoring the *"days as of old,"* in keeping America Christian.   God bless you in your love for the Savior, and God bless a Christian America, for Jesus' sake!   Amen.

ALMOST PERSUADED

"Agrippa said unto Paul, Almost thou persuadest me to be a Christian." — Acts 26:28

Lord Jesus, Our Only Redeemer:

Show us today that we must go all the way with Thee; that almost believing Thy grace is not enough; that we cannot be saved unless we accept Thee unconditionally as our divine Savior from sin, our never-failing Friend in every need! We confess that too often we have doubted when we should have believed, questioned the Cross when we should have affirmed its truth. For Thy mercy's sake, forgive us our sins of pride and vainglory. Dwell in our hearts constantly! May our faith increase, looking to Thy guidance in this life and the assurance of everlasting blessedness in heaven with Thee! Sustain our broadcast throughout the country, and in many homes make this a day of decision for Thee! Defend our mission of the air against the special dangers threatening it, and let America's Christian forces help build the righteousness which by divine grace can exalt the nation with true and victorious peace! Hear us, O Christ of endless compassion, and bring us, especially also the burdened, the bereaved, the grief-gripped, altogether, all the way, to Thee! Amen.

IN the early part of the sixteenth century two men, in different countries of Europe, each named Martin, came to the same glorious knowledge that they were saved, not by their good works, but by grace through faith in the Lord Jesus Christ. With the same marvelous opportunity of making that message of mercy known to their fellow men, what did they do? — The one Martin, fearing public disfavor, wrote these words on parchment: "Oh, most merciful Christ, I know that I am saved only by the merit of Thy blood. Holy Jesus, I love Thee, I love Thee!" Then he secretly hid the parchment behind a stone in the wall of his chamber. Hardly one of ten thousand has ever heard of him and one in a million may know the details of his life. He was Martin of Basel, and it was only accidentally that, several hundred years after his death, his hidden testimony to Christ was discovered. Meanwhile the victorious promise of full justification by faith, which he in fear had concealed, was heard through the civilized world. Why? The other Martin, as soon as the light of saving grace illumined the night of his despair over sin, threw caution to the winds. He cried, "My Lord has confessed me before men; I will not shrink from confessing my Lord before princes and kings." Impelled by the love of his Savior, he used every means within his grasp — the pulpit, lecture hall, printing press, schools, universities, churches, music — to spread the Gospel of salvation. With a courage unintimidated by threats of persecution and a loyalty unchanged by the promise of high honors, he preached, wrote, published, proclaimed Jesus Christ, eternal Son of God and incarnate Son of Mary, as the divine, complete, never-failing Redeemer of the whole race. That second Martin, I hardly need tell you, was Luther, the mighty Reformer, from whose world-moving testimony to Christ we date our modern era. — Martin of Basel was *almost* a mighty man of God. Few men in all history have ever been offered the opportunity within his grasp. Yet he failed, as some of you have failed, because of fear and weak faith.

Yet a tragedy still more grievous than such refusal to exalt Jesus is the unwillingness even to accept Him, though the Spirit of God testifies that He is the Atonement and Redemption of our souls. Modern Chinese history knows two men who illustrate this truth. Both were officers serving their country. Both were well educated. Both had become interested in Christianity. When one was invited to make a decision for Christ, he told the missionary: "I'll see you tomorrow morning at eleven o'clock." Before that same day closed, he was assassinated. This man, apparently only a few hours distant from Christ, yet in reality an eternity from him, was Admiral Chen. The other national leader was urged by his mother-in-law to read the Bible and pray God for enlightenment. He followed her advice, and his private, early morning devotions brought the Holy Spirit into his heart, made him study the entire Bible, convinced him of the baptismal blessing, and finally led him all the way to the Lord. That man of the hour, a humble Christian who can pray, as visitors testify, even for enemy airmen circling over his city with the avowed purpose of destroying him, that convert to Christ for whom *"almost"* was not enough, is Generalissimo Chiang Kai-Shek, leader of 400,000,000 Chinese.

Because indecision, the refusal to accept salvation now, this coming close to the Kingdom but stopping short of the final step, is a soul peril which hangs heavy over many, I want to show you the folly and tragedy of being

Almost Persuaded —

"almost" but not completely convinced — that Christ is your atoning Lord. To learn this vital lesson read — and may your doubts there be changed to faith! — in the Book of Acts (chapter twenty-six, verse twenty-eight), *"Agrippa said unto Paul, Almost thou persuadest me to be a Christian"*!

I

THE FOLLY OF "ALMOST" AND ITS CAUSE

Few scenes even in the swift-moving New Testament history are more powerful and electrifying than the account from which this text has been chosen. Saint Paul, mightiest of Christ's missionaries, had been imprisoned at Caesarea for two long years, guilty — O blessed guilt! — of preaching the reconciling Gospel and of showing his countrymen how the Old Testament prophecies were fulfilled in Christ.

The governor at Caesarea must have believed his prisoner innocent of the fraudulent charges; but shrewd, graft-loving, money-grasping politician that he was, he thought he could demand a price for a release. After two years he was succeeded by the new governor, Festus. Paul's case was brought before him, and, convinced of the apostle's innocence, Festus arranged for King Herod Agrippa, who ruled a section of Palestine through the favor of the Roman conquerors and who was visiting Caesarea, to hear Paul.

What a striking spectacle ensued! With royal pomp and elaborate ceremonies King Agrippa, his sister Bernice, Festus the governor, Caesarea's military and civic leaders, royalty and officialdom, were assembled amid the display of the palace luxury to hear the Savior's Gospel and the defense of His persecuted disciple. Not often have enthroned kings thus faced Christ's ambassadors. Throughout the centuries men who have wielded immense might, including power over the life and death of their subjects, have satanically misused this control simply because they have spurned the Christian faith and utterly rejected our Lord. Oh, that in today's world, leaders of human affairs would take time to consider and apply the Savior's teaching! Among the notable blessings of our American government, for which we cannot sufficiently thank God, is this that we have had in the presidency many men who have been humble followers of Jesus. And while Christians have always prayed for the chief executive and the nation's leaders, the heaped perils in the present crisis make that intercession doubly, trebly necessary. No one realizes how, particularly in wartimes, national leaders are beset by multiplied problems and overtaxing burdens. The least we can do, and what we as Christians must do, is to intercede fervently and constantly for the government of the United States, asking that all, especially the President, his cabinet, the

Congress, be guided continually by divine wisdom, truth, and righteousness.

God give you who know the merciful Savior's love the same desire to testify to His grace which moved Saint Paul before that impressive assembly! You may never have the apostle's opportunity of speaking to kings, but you can bear witness to others. If you are a maid in a non-Christian home, you may be able to speak of Christ to your employers, courteously but courageously, as Paul did. An unnamed Hebrew servant girl, as the fifth chapter of Second Kings tells her story, directed mighty Naaman, the commander in chief of the Syrian armies, to God's prophet for healing and salvation. If you work in an office, factory, store, you can tactfully but determinedly acknowledge your faith in Christ before those in higher positions. If you are a Sunday-school teacher in search of more children for Christ, do not skip the fashionable sections of your community because you may be afraid to talk to important people! Often they need the Gospel more than others. I personally know a remarkable instance in which a family, frequently featured by the nation's newspapers, was led to affiliate itself with a Christian church largely because of the aggressive, bring-the-Gospel-to-everyone spirit shown by a Lutheran pastor and his Sunday-school canvassers.

Even more impressive than the fact that Saint Paul addressed this royal assembly is the way in which he brought his message. We can almost see him there, erect, majestic, as he looks into Herod Agrippa's face or turns his penetrating gaze to the others seated before him. His eyes flash. His hands move in emphatic gestures. Words roll from his lips. Conviction speaks in his sentences. God's Spirit fires him with startling eloquence. Festus, the governor, unable to explain the power blazing from the apostle's

words, interrupts him to cry out loudly, *"Paul, thou art
beside thyself; much learning doth make thee mad."* But
no one has ever been saner than Paul in that moment. He
knew whereof he spoke. No "perhaps" or "maybe," no
theories, guesses, or wishful thinking mark his defense.
His words were uttered with personal conviction. Forty-
two times in the twenty-six recorded verses he refers to
himself as he describes the way in which the Almighty
brought him to Christ. May divine goodness likewise give
us many men as spiritual shepherds who have not merely
a head knowledge, a book understanding, but heart assurance that they themselves, born in sin, doomed to death,
have been completely saved by faith in Christ's cleansing
blood; preachers and teachers who understand how mercifully God has dealt with them, so that they may help
persuade others to receive Christ's redeeming grace!

Paul went back to Moses and the prophets. He delivered a Scripture-grounded, Scripture-supported, Scrip-
ture-exalting sermon. In this respect, as has well been said,
Paul, the preacher for kings, remains the king of preachers.
God give us men in American pulpits who draw their
sermons from the Bible, the whole Bible, and nothing but
the Bible; who speak with authority because they declare,
"Thus saith the Lord!" During this emergency help us
keep our churches *churches,* that is, houses of the Lord,
where God's Word is explained and applied! We have
public forums at which political views may be aired; legis-
lative chambers for the discussion of new laws and social
codes; libraries where the latest books are reviewed; places
of amusement for dispensing humor; college classrooms
for expounding new theories; but for soul guidance and
the spiritual defense of millions in this nation today we
should guard our churches as God's sanctuaries where His

Word, not man's, rules; where Christ's eternal verities, not human guesswork, reign supreme.

Note especially, however, that throughout the whole discourse Paul's purpose was to win Agrippa and the others in that palace for Christ! The Savior's suffering, redemptive death, resurrection, reconciling the whole world to God, formed the climax and center of his entire plea, the startling truth that made Festus, the governor, charge him with madness. Today, too, every loyal evangelist must expect to be denounced if he preaches the final, full, free message of the Savior's redemption. Let him be denounced! On the great day of His appearing Christ will bring those who have been faithful unto the end to His Father with the declaration, *"Well done, thou good and faithful servant!"* It is not enough that sermons have Scripture texts. It is possible to take passages, for example, from Proverbs and Ecclesiastes and for years offer moralizing messages without mentioning the Savior. Verses featuring the Lord Jesus may be selected and then misinterpreted so that nothing is left of our blessed hope in our blood-bought salvation. But Saint Paul could not deliver a sermon without asking a decision for Christ, and neither should you and I in any way neglect or ignore Him, the blessed Foundation of our faith. A hundred other activities can crowd into our religious work, but the one purpose of every truly Christian church is to tell all men that while without Christ they are hopelessly lost in their sins, with faith in the same Jesus they are eternally redeemed from their transgressions.

Nor should we overlook the personal, direct force of the apostle's plea to the whole assembly. Six times he speaks straight to King Agrippa, and though it is not given to me now to look into the face of everyone in this audience who has not received Christ, I want you to accept these words as directed to you individually. Your heavenly

Father wants *you* to be saved. As Saint Paul put this pointed question before his royal judge, *"King Agrippa, believest thou the prophets?"* and hoped the ruler would answer, "Yes, I believe the prophets and the Messiah of whom they have prophesied," so I ask you: "Do you believe the Bible and the Savior of whom the entire Scripture testifies? Do you acclaim this Christ as your own Redeemer?"

God grant that you give a better answer than Agrippa's reply *"Almost thou persuadest me to be a Christian"*! Although this remark has been variously interpreted, his words certainly imply that a man has to be persuaded to become a believer, and yet, as a matter of fact, discipleship with the Lord Jesus Christ is the most marvelous blessing we can ever experience. You do not have to convince a drowning sailor to grasp a life line. You do not need a long, elaborate discussion to show a man that he ought to step from the path of an onrushing automobile, argue a starving man into accepting food, a lost traveler into following a forest ranger to safety. Why, then, must people be persuaded to accept that which is incomparably greater than the mightiest benefits man can ever give his fellow man?

If people today would only take time to study our Christian faith and recognize the help it imparts, our churches would be overcrowded, the Bible universally read, the name of Jesus not abused in profanity but spoken with reverence. For, think of the glory that comes to those who pledge Christ their allegiance! His compassion answers all questions disturbing to the mind, removes each difficulty that distresses our thoughts, lifts every burden weighing heavy on our souls. Christian trust acknowledges that we are not accidental atoms of humanity, changed by chance from a lower brute stage, but creatures of God, the masterpiece of His almighty wisdom. Christian truth reveals whither we are bound. It assures us that we have been freed from the consequences of our sins by the self-giving, the suffering, the bleeding, the dying of the Lord Jesus as our Substitute. Our souls are so precious in His sight that He constantly guards and guides us along the paths of heavenly rightness, and always for the blessed purpose of directing us to our eternal salvation. Particularly in trying days like these it should not be difficult to bring men and women to the cross, there to acclaim the crucified Savior their own, since only in Him is there a complete refuge from fear and weakness, a satisfying source of strength to withstand the stress and strain of sorrow, the one true solution to suffering. Restored to grace, reconciled to God, we have this pledge in Jesus: Our heavenly Father loves us with such deathless devotion that the very hairs of our heads are numbered. As long as we are Christ's, no evil will draw nigh us, and everything we may be called upon to endure becomes the evidence of His love by which He would fortify our faith, reinforce our reliance on His mercy, purify our desires, and daily draw us closer to Him. When we are Christ's and He is ours, we can rejoice in affliction. If all else seems dark and hopeless, we have light and assurance in the victorious truth that *"with God nothing shall be impossible."* His limitless love overnight can change tears into gladness. You ought to accept Jesus without any lengthy appeal and repeated plea, for He alone solves the mystery of the grave and answers your question "What becomes of me after death?" While other creeds refuse to reply or offer vague, deceptive theories, Jesus declares with His divine authority: *"I am the Resurrection and the Life: he that believeth in Me, though he were dead, yet shall he live. And whosoever liveth and believeth in Me shall never die."* He promises world-weary believers, *"I go to prepare a place for you,"* and His holy Word reveals, as far as the mortal mind can grasp, the glory in a heaven of unspeakable bliss, a celestial radiance beyond compare; eternal companionship with the redeemed before the throne of the living God; heaven without tears and toil, without agony and grief, without pain and loss, sickness and infirmity; heaven with Jesus. You should be willing to give up everything you possess, sell everything you own, pay everything you earn to make these blessings of Christian faith yours. But when I tell you once more in the Savior's name that His love is granted you freely by the magnificence of His mercy; that this redemption is yours, wholly, unconditionally, assuredly, by faith, why does everyone of you not agree that instead of arguing whether or not you will accept Christ, you should fall on your knees and cry out, "O Jesus, I am not worthy that Thou in Thy holiness shouldst even look at me in my sins; but by the promise of Thy love, as by Thy bitter suffering and death on the cross, receive me, wash me, cleanse me, make me Thine forever!"?

Why was it, then, that Agrippa came close to confessing Christ, yet failed to take the last, decisive step? Why is it that some of you hear this appeal pointed directly at your souls, yet turn away from the outstretched arms of Christ? The Book of Acts gives no explanation for Agrippa's action, but his motives were doubtless the same as those now influencing many people. Perhaps he feared the consequences of confessing Christ. It meant that he would be scorned, hated by his royal friends. He would have to substitute faith for reason, and this he was unwilling to do. Becoming a Christian meant changing his life; and because he was living in sin; because he condoned immorality, he would not pay the price. Accepting Christianity might involve the loss of his royal office, being stripped of gold, silver, precious stones; and he was too selfish to take up that cross, as Jesus commanded.

Are not these the very stumbling blocks which keep people from turning to Christ today? They feel inwardly that the Bible is the truth. They cannot deny or disprove its statements. They are unable to raise a justified charge against it. They have a good word and a kind thought for Jesus. No one else who ever trod the face of the earth was His equal, they admit. They see that Christianity works. Yet in the decisive moment, when they are to declare Jesus their Savior and say without reservation, "I am a believer," it is either the dread of ridicule, the fear of loss, the love of sin, the refusal to live as Christians or the reluctance to take reason captive — which helps make them deny Christ, forfeit their hope of salvation, close the gates of heaven against themselves.

II

THE SORROW OF "ALMOST" AND HOW TO AVOID IT

For, to be only *"almost"* persuaded really means to be lost. *"Almost"* is never enough. The airplane that *"almost"* clears the mountain top is destroyed. The city that has *"almost"* enough defenses will be captured. The reprieve from the death sentence which comes *"almost"* in time, only a minute late, will not save the prisoner. "Dereliction of duty," neglect of watchfulness, such as reported at Pearl Harbor, has a spiritual counterpart when modern men and women are only *"almost"* prepared to resist the onslaughts of treacherous enemies.

It is not enough to call the Lord Jesus the most outstanding Person of the ages, the most unselfish Hero men have ever known, the greatest Benefactor our race has ever had. You must go all the way and, pointing to the Crucified, say, "He is my God and my Savior!" It is not enough to hear the story of His atoning love and then wonder whether or not there is grace for you, forgiveness for your transgressions. You must take the final step and believe that you, too, are saved, since no sins are too scarlet, no iniquities too abhorrent to be removed by the compassionate Redeemer. It is not enough to think you can be saved provided you earn your entrance into heaven by a long list of penances, good works, and self-denials; you must trust altogether in Christ and know you are *"justified by faith, without the deeds of the Law."* Jesus paid your entire ransom from sin, hell, and death's despair.

Herod Agrippa missed the opportunity of becoming a Christian, and never, as far as we know, did he embrace the faith. And finally he faded from the historical records of his day — an insignificant failure. Had he been fully persuaded to acclaim Jesus his Savior; had he been ready to take up Christ's reproach, his name would have been honored by hundreds of millions throughout the succeeding centuries. What is of far greater importance, Jesus would have acknowledged him before His throne. Unknowingly he missed the greatest moment in his life, just as others have lost mighty blessings. Some years ago a young man of prominent social standing in Philadelphia killed a friend. He was arrested, tried, convicted, and sentenced to death. Powerful influences soon sought to have Governor Pollock commute the sentence, but he refused. Finally the mother of the condemned murderer journeyed to Harrisburg to plead with a mother's devotion for her wayward child. When Governor Pollock told her that he could not change the sentence, she fainted and fell limp to the floor. The governor then turned to his secretary and said, "One thing I can do; I will see the boy and prepare him for death." So he went to the cell and without revealing his identity spoke to the young man of God's promises in Christ to every penitent sinner, prayed with him, heard the condemned youth say that he was not afraid to die, and then left. A few moments later the prisoner called the warden to ask, "Who was that man who just now left my cell?" In surprise the warden exclaimed, "Why, he was Governor Pollock." "O warden," the prisoner cried, "the governor in my cell — and I did not know it! If only you had told me he was the governor, I would have thrown my arms about him and never let him leave the cell until he had given me my pardon!" One incomparably greater than any governor now stands before you, with free and full pardon for all your transgressions, offering you the commutation of that terrifying sentence which Scripture places on every unforgiven wrong when it warns, "*The soul that sinneth, it shall die.*" God grant that you will not permit Jesus to pass out of your lives without receiving the joy of your salvation! Say to Him now, as Jacob said to Jehovah of old, "*I will not leave Thee, except Thou bless me!*" This may be the last broadcast you will hear, the final appeal for Christ ever directed to you. Do not make the fatal error of continually postponing your welcome of His mercy, of remaining an "*almost*" persuaded man or woman, until death makes it impossible for you to be altogether persuaded! You need Christ for this life, particularly in view of the uncertainties of the conflict years now upon us. Most urgently, however, you need Christ for the next world, since His own words insist: "*I am the Way, the Truth, and the Life. No man cometh unto the Father but by Me!*" Therefore to be only "*almost*" persuaded means to miss the right way, lose the truth, forfeit the blessing of the heavenly radiance. To avoid such tragedy, that most terrifying loss, learn to know Christ! Come to Him in His Word, you who have neglected or despised the Gospel! Take the sacred Book, read it without prejudice, and let God's Spirit work in your hearts! His divine Volume has turned many a skeptic into a saint, removed the "*almost*" and made it an "altogether"! M. L. Bautain, a French professor of philosophy, was an unbeliever until he studied the Scriptures. And then he wrote this remarkable confession: "A single Book has saved me, but that Book is not of human origin. Long had I despised it, long had I deemed it a classbook for the credulous and ignorant, until, having investigated the Gospel of Christ, with an ardent desire to ascertain its truth or falsity, I found that its pages proffered to my inquiries the sublimest knowledge . . . and at the same time the most exalted system of moral ethics. Faith, hope, and charity were enkindled in my bosom; and every advancing step strengthened me in the conviction that the morals of this book are superior to human morals as its oracles are superior to human opinions." In the same way the study of your Bible, the preaching of God's Word in true churches, the help of a real Christian pastor, your prayers in Jesus' name can take you, the "*almost*" persuaded, and by the outpouring of Heaven's highest grace, help you join the mighty apostle in declaring, "*I am persuaded that neither death nor life nor angels nor principalities nor powers nor things present nor things to come nor height nor depth nor any other creature shall be able to separate us from the love of God, which is in Christ Jesus our Lord.*" God grant that today many of you will thus come all the way to Christ! Amen.

THE WHOLE FAMILY FOR CHRIST

"They" [Paul and Silas] *"spoke unto him"* [the jailer]
*"the Word of the Lord and to all that were in his
house. And he took them the same hour of the night
and washed their stripes and was baptized, he and all
his, straightway. And when he had brought them into
his house, he set meat before them and rejoiced, believing
in God with all his house."* — Acts 16:32-34

Gracious God:

*I*nto Thy watchful, loving care we commend the homes of our
people. Protect them against invasion with its bombings and
blastings, fire and destruction! O Thou who dost neither slumber
nor sleep, guard our families by day and night! We beseech Thy
goodness in Christ to speed the course of the Savior's Gospel, so
that entire households may be sustained by His blood-bought pardon
and find joy of soul despite future sorrows! Rebuke the forces of
lust and impurity which seek to destroy Christian marriage and
home life! Bless husbands and wives with self-sacrificing devotion
to their privileges and duties! Implant in children a spirit of obedience to their parents! In this time of trials, when our nation needs the
inner support of homes hallowed by Thy presence, we implore Thy
fatherly goodness to send Thy Spirit across our broad land, so that
in many more households Scripture reading and prayer will find an
honored place. Strengthen many with the assurance that through
Jesus they will finally be part of the whole family in heaven! We
ask this by His unfailing promise. Amen.

DURING the battle of Yorktown, the last and decisive
struggle in the American Revolution, it became
necessary to dislodge the enemy from a prominent house
occupied as headquarters. By coincidence this was the
residence of General Nelson, Governor of Virginia, a leader
of our Colonial troops. With the full knowledge that he
was ordering the destruction of his own dwelling place,
General Nelson turned to his artillery squadron and gave
this quick order, "Sergeant, train your cannon on my
home!" The battery roared in obedience, the cannon balls

struck their mark, the enemy was driven out, and the victory that was to help seal our independence brought closer — all by the patriotism of a man who sacrificed his cherished possession, his home, for American freedom.

Others have been ready to give up their dwellings in the nation's interest. When President Garfield was shot by an assassin, his physicians sought a cool, quiet spot, where he could find the required rest for healing. Finally they selected Elberon, New Jersey; and since the town had no railroad connection, engineers planned to build a rail spur from the main line. The right of way, as they plotted it, was to run over the front lawn of a certain farm house. At first the owner refused to permit the railroad passage over his property; but when told that this was part of an effort to save Garfield's life, he answered: "Oh, that is different! Why, if the railroad is for the President, you can run it straight through my house!"

Now, if these men were willing to have their homes destroyed for the country's welfare, should we not be ready to build our households for the nation's strengthening by consecrating our families to One incomparably greater than any President of the United States — Jesus Christ, Savior of our souls? Domestic life with Him the constant Guest, families with time for reverent prayer and Scripture reading, these are bulwarks of national defense, a firm foundation for the Church's growth, an uplifting power for all that is good. During war, with its stress and strain, home ties are often loosened. In England, as our newspaper correspondents cable, people are learning that the most menacing danger to the British family has come not through air-raid damage but by a growing spirit of irreligion, indifference to parental authority, and the unmistakable lowering of morals. Similarly on this side of the Atlantic the cry resounds: "Guard your homes! Protect your families! Reinforce the ties binding together parents and children!"

How, you ask, can we defeat the mobilized enemies of the American home during the dark hours of this struggle and amid the difficulties of postwar reconstruction? How can we secure positive solutions for domestic problems, unfailing help in family sorrows, blessed assurance when sickness, accident, or even death itself crosses our thresholds? I thank God that I have the privilege of answering across the continent by pointing to the Lord Jesus Christ and pleading not only that you dedicate your home to Him in a general way, that parents *or* children welcome Him, that *some* members of your household accept His mercies — far more than that; the Savior wants — and in His blessed name I ask it —

THE WHOLE FAMILY FOR CHRIST

This appeal is strengthened by the Scripture passage chosen as our text, these words of Acts, chapter sixteen, verses thirty-two to thirty-four: *"They"* [Paul and Silas] *"spake unto him"* [the jailer] *"the Word of the Lord and to all that were in his house. And he took them the same hour of the night and washed their stripes and was baptized, he and all his, straightway. And when he had brought them into his house, he set meat before them and rejoiced, believing in God with all his house."*

I

OUR MODERN FAMILIES NEED CHRIST

This account concludes one of the happiest New Testament stories. It all started in a dungeon at the Greek city of Philippi, the last place in the world where we would expect Christ's mercy and power to be revealed. Paul and Silas had been beaten and thrown into prison. Why?

Only because the apostle had cleansed a slave girl by banishing a destructive spirit of divination.

The disgrace and pain of this imprisonment would have made many other men give up their discipleship and object, "If that is the price I have to pay for Christianity, I am through with Jesus!" Some of you have left the Church because of slight reverses and disappointments in small matters. The solo part in the choir that you wanted for yourself was given to another singer; someone else was made chairman of the committee which you planned to head. You have been mistreated by one churchmember and bitterly you conclude that all are hypocrites. You expect people in your congregation to make their purchases at your store, and if one of them deals with your competitor, you are through with religion. Now, while you have a small grievance — it may be well founded — and you risk your soul's salvation by cutting yourself off from the Church, the apostles, their backs crisscrossed with deep wounds and their pain-racked bodies locked in instruments of torture, never once bemoaned their suffering nor charged God with injustice. Instead they lifted their voices — oh, think of this! — *"and sang praises unto God,"* hymns of thanksgiving that could be heard throughout the whole prison. When the black midnight of sorrows overtakes you, sing out courageously, and you, too, will have the blessed assurance that the hardest afflictions can become the strongest advantages. Paul and Silas were to make this remarkable discovery, for while their praise songs reechoed through dungeons and damp cells, suddenly another sound grew louder and louder until, rumbling like thunder, it silenced their hymns. It was the shaking, quaking, of the earth itself. The very foundations of the building swayed. The doors opened. The bonds sprang from the prisoners' hands and feet.

That earthquake, which brought the thrill of freedom to the prisoners, produced the threat of disgrace to the jailer. Philippi was a Roman colony, and under the Roman law, in the event criminals escaped, the responsible official suffered the penalties to which his captives had been sentenced. Fearing that the worst had happened and that all had run away, the distracted warden saw only one way to avoid dishonor. It was a popular method in the ancient pagan world, well-known in Philippi and widespread even in our modern enlightenment: he planned to take his own life. Yet as he drew his sword and prepared to send his soul to hell, a voice stopped him. It was the warning by Saint Paul *"Do thyself no harm!"* and the assurance *"We are all here."* A light was quickly brought. The apostle's words were true. None of the prisoners had taken flight. Instead of being merely gratified by the startling turn of events, the warden was seized by dread concerning his soul. He knew that these two prisoners, for whom Heaven's omnipotence shook the earth as the human hand plays with a ball, were not ordinary men. They conquered pain and chanted their praises to God while others would have cursed and screamed in agony. They had been called *"the servants of the most high God"* by the demoniac slave. The jailer realized that despite darkness Paul had been able to see his evil intentions and had saved his life. He felt himself confronted by a higher power and in the presence of God's ambassadors. So the Roman officer who had previously been unconcerned about his soul's salvation now falls down before Paul and Silas — the warden before the prisoners. Pleadingly, penitently, he cries out in that question of all questions, the personal, pivotal request, which I pray God many of you will repeat today, *"What must I do to be saved?"* Almost in an instant, it seems, he was led to understand that he was on the swift, sure way to his soul's destruction. His whole life, it suddenly dawned on him, had been lived in the wrong way. The restless, relentless inner voice reminded him that he must get right with the God whom these men represented; and from a heart conscious only of its guilt, its helpless, hopeless, lost, and damned condition, he begs Paul and Silas to reveal the road to his redemption.

The apostles' answer is the very cornerstone of our faith and the keystone of its arching promises. Listen attentively to their reply as I now repeat it under the guidance of the same Spirit who blessed the Philippian jailer, the pledge of salvation in one short sentence of eleven words, *"Believe on the Lord Jesus Christ, and thou shalt be saved!"*

Measure each of these blessed words! Start with *"Believe!"* and let me assure you that you need have only faith — the knowledge, acceptance, trust which comes with unquestioning reliance on your heavenly Father's mercy in Christ. God asks not for good works, for payment, contribution, cooperation, not for meeting Him halfway, one quarter of the way, one short step of the way, not for good intentions or resolutions. No other human being can intercede for you. In the widest, highest, deepest grace of Heaven itself, pardon and peace are yours completely when with all your heart and soul you believe in the Lord Jesus Christ, confessing that He, the Son of God, is your Savior and Substitute who went the way of suffering to Calvary's cross and there, on that gory altar, sacrificed Himself as the Atonement for all humanity's sins. Acknowledging the wrong which springs from your heart, speaks from your lips, and shows itself in your actions, build your hope, the assurance of pardon for every sin, solely but entirely on Jesus' self-surrender to death. By that faith, through God's infinite grace, you, too, will be *"saved"* from the consequences of your sins, *"saved"* from the punishment of divine wrath in this life, "*saved*" from death's eternal doom. What must you "*do to be saved*"? So that you will make no mistake in this most vital issue, so that you never can protest, "No one ever told me the way of salvation!" hear this answer once more, "*Believe on the Lord Jesus Christ, and thou shalt be saved!*"

To this promise the apostles purposely added the words "*and thy house.*" They were concerned about the jailer's family. At the rumble of the earthquake the warden's household was filled with terror. Now, after hearing of the way to heaven, they "*rejoiced.*" A few hours earlier the Philippian prison keeper had been utterly unconcerned about his prisoners' suffering; now, through the rebirth by faith, he was a new man, bent on helping his fellow men in Christ's spirit. He started with the beaten, bleeding apostles and "*washed their stripes.*" Before midnight the members of that household were pagan. After midnight, when they had accepted the Savior's redemption, they were baptized and, through that washing of regeneration, became members of Christ's glorious Church. What a difference the Spirit of Jesus made in that home!

What a difference the Savior can make in our families! The basic needs in our households are still the same as during that first-century day. Our American homes should have — beyond education, culture, domestic-arts programs, the conveniences of modern architecture, the axioms of twentieth-century psychology — the presence of the Lord Jesus. When He enters any family circle, His peace replaces trouble, care, and burdened anxiety. Happiness reigns instead of bickering and strife. Contentment takes the place of worry. Calm overrules the passionate outbursts of selfish assertions. Inner spiritual joy overtowers earthly sorrows. We cannot assert, of course, that Christ's presence is a divine guarantee against every grief. On the contrary, in His inscrutable wisdom God often sees fit to lay increased burdens on Christian homes. But whether these visitations be harder or lighter, the Savior can relieve sorrow, as He did after that memorable midnight at Philippi. Is your household burdened by constant quarreling and jealousy? Let Jesus in to check the ravages of self-centeredness, to give husband and wife, parents and children, the power for restraining all unworthy desires, and His promise *"My peace I give unto you"* will be fulfilled. Without Him little faults and failings are magnified, just as a new microscope recently perfected makes a single hair look like a tree branch. But with Christ frailties and failures are overlooked, and as a modern searchlight can be focused on an object of joy and beauty, so faith magnifies good qualities and virtues.

Has the devil of drunkenness taken cruel possession of a father or a son? Do warnings seem useless, cures hopeless? When Jesus is granted control of any drink-addicted life, He breaks its treacherous tyranny. Has disease imposed its pressing burden? Let Jesus step across the threshold of any sickroom, and He can give the sufferer sweet patience, with the privilege to be an example for others. If it be His will, He can remove the illness, or, for higher purpose, call the sufferer home to unspeakable glory. In the loneliness following the bereavement some of you now endure, the Savior's presence can be of real, lasting comfort, besides turning death's sorrows to faith-strengthening ends. A brilliant attorney used to keep a pair of baby shoes on his desk and tell inquirers: "Until the little feet that fit those shoes were taken to walk in Paradise, I never believed. Now heaven is near, and Jesus is my all in all."

Particularly when disaster suddenly looms close, can Jesus offer the cheer that His benediction brought to the jailer's home. At a terrifying mine accident a few years ago in Belgium the wives and children of the entombed men stood near the top of the shaft and wept loudly. One woman, however, a widow whose only son was trapped below, stood apart, serene and undisturbed. She explained: "My comfort is this, that my son was a reverent Christian. If he has been killed, he is with God in heaven, where I shall soon meet him again. If he is alive, God is with him and will see that he comes back to me safely." Is not this the confidence many of you parents need during the days when your sons are called to our country's defense? If they have Jesus, whether they are now in distant lands, in the air, on the ocean, under the sea, God Himself is at their side. He can protect them, if it be for their soul's welfare, against bombing and blasting, injury and death. If He wants to show them special grace, He can give them heaven's glory and the unspeakable radiance of the blessed homeland where there shall be no more separation or suffering, no more havoc of war's destruction. No problem ever is too great for Him. By faith you will understand that *"the things which are impossible with men are possible with God,"* that our Father never makes a mistake; His ways with His children, though we may not understand them, are always the paths of truth, blessedness, peace.

But you say, "There are no apostles today as in that period when Paul on his missionary journeys could visit the homes of the believers." Are you sure? Thousands of pastors working together with me are eager to knock at your door and to be welcomed into your family circle, for the one purpose that they, too, may speak *"the Word of the Lord"* and bring the Savior into your household as surely as He accompanied the imprisoned apostles into that Philippian dwelling. No family in the United States or Canada need be without Jesus or lack the guidance of a true minister of His Church. We are deeply interested in bringing you His sustaining promise.

You can also welcome the Savior by honoring His Word in your household. The family altar, that is, joint Scripture reading and prayer by parents and children, has been a notable force in the nation's past crises, and today it should be the rock on which people found their home life to withstand all future trials — and who can look into the days before us without realizing that America needs this? Think of the appalling difference that Christ's presence or absence makes in any family! An Arkansas pastor testifies: "When I was the chaplain of a penitentiary in Arkansas, out of 1,700 convicts I found only one that had been brought up in a home where they had a family altar. I heard since that he was pardoned, as he was found innocent of the crime with which he had been charged."

Jesus was brought into that jailer's home, and He can be brought into your house through the blessing of Baptism which, by faith, cleanses you of your sin. Modern theology belittles this Sacrament; even in many churches its washing of regeneration is neglected. Perhaps this disregard helps account for the loss of power in many Christian groups. The Savior's command is clear, *"Go ye, therefore, and teach all nations, baptizing them in the name of the Father and of the Son and of the Holy Ghost!"* The Bible itself assures us in words which all should accept that this ordinance is a means of divine grace, since the apostle declares, *"Baptism doth also now save us."* Therefore the appeal of this hour is identical with the plea which rang out in the early Church, *"Repent, and be baptized every one of you in the name of Jesus Christ for the remission of sins!"* Since our Lord Himself instituted Baptism, since He requires it of all who know His grace, I ask you, young and old, who have never received the strengthening Sacrament to write immediately: "I want to be baptized! Tell me more about it! Send someone who will explain its blessing to me!"

You young folks especially should understand how all-important it is to give Christ the decisive place in your future home. We witness a wave of hasty marriages. Such weddings, especially when prompted by the desire to avoid military service, are often without spiritual foundation and therefore frequently preludes to marital disaster. Despite everything you may hear to the contrary in a day when evolutionists, Communists, Modernists, radical theorists, religious extremists, attack the Christian code of marriage, build your home with Christ! Follow the rule: *"Whatsoever ye do"* [in courtship and marriage] *"in word or deed, do all in the name of the Lord Jesus."* Make Him the Counselor in your wedding plans! Focus your marriage ideals on this central, pivotal point: My home must be a church of God, a temple of His truth! From your first wedded days until the last, in sunshine and shadow, in health and sickness, in prosperity and poverty, let Christ be the Head of your home, the unseen Guest at every meal, the silent Listener to every conversation! Keep Him as the uplifting, refining, selfishness-destroying power, so that, instead of insisting on rights, you live in and by the Spirit of the humble, self-giving Savior! Continually seek His guidance in all problems and perplexities! Follow His instructions concerning parenthood and childhood; then, come what may, your home will withstand the formidable difficulties which may yet be mobilized against it.

II

THE WHOLE FAMILY NEEDS CHRIST

Now, it was the apostles' hope and plea that the whole family at Philippi should be brought to Christ. This is emphasized three times in our text. First, Paul spoke the

Word of the Lord *"to all that were in his* [the jailer's] *"house."* Secondly, we read how *"he and all his"* were baptized; and, thirdly, how *"all his house"* believed in God. Nor was this the only instance in which the entire family was sought and won for Jesus. Repeatedly in the brief New Testament accounts we find missionaries teaching, instructing, baptizing, the whole household, parents, children, relatives, servants, and friends.

Every time I read these records in the Book of Acts testifying that everyone in a certain home was baptized, I ask myself: If the apostles baptized complete families — and it cannot be that all these homes were without boys and girls — why should some churches today demand that children be excluded from baptismal blessing? If the Old Testament had a special rite for infants, why not the New? If Jesus insists, *"Suffer the little children to come unto Me,"* why bar them from Baptism, when the Church in the second and third centuries regularly baptized the sons and daughters, even the youngest, in the families of the believers?

The apostle's chief purpose in winning the whole family for the Savior was basically the driving desire *"that the world through Him might be saved."* And our concern in helping to bring the members of our households to Him must of course be a personal interest in their souls' salvation. Life knows few sorrows deeper than that of a consecrated wife, for example, who sees her husband remain in cold, sneering unbelief, or of parents whose children steadily turn from the Lord. How reassuring, by contrast, to know that those whom we love most dearly are all in the Savior's grace!

We follow the apostles in asking the whole family to accept Him also for the tranquillity and happiness He bestows. When both parents, with their children, are

Christ's in true, trusting faith, the home has a radiance which no money can purchase, no culture bestow, no modern experiment impart. The family circle united in the worship of Jesus may be poor, humble, unnoticed; yet in His sight these lowly believers are so high and blessed that He grants them an overflowing measure of His mercy in contentment and rest.

When sorrows enter the home with the impact of unexpected blows, the family completely consecrated to Christ is strengthened by the mutual trust that the God of grace *"hath done all things well."* Death snatches a child in the joy of its young life, but the bereaved father can take his wife in his arms, and because they are the Lord's, he can say: "My beloved, we will face this together with trust in our Savior. Because we both belong to Him, because our child believed in Jesus and was baptized, we know that *'all things,'* even this sudden, crushing death, *'work together for good,'* to our dear child and to us." — Contrast with this the hopelessness of an atheist father who stands beside the casket of his little one and can only stammer meaningless generalities or groan in unrelieved despair!

The family should be united in its allegiance to the Lord because Christless parents or children often exert a destructive influence on the faithful members. Many a young woman, resolute, determined, outspoken in her spiritual loyalty, has seen her assurance slowly but surely grow weaker through daily life with a husband in whose heart Jesus had no part whatever. At first she attended church every Sunday, but gradually either outspoken dissatisfaction, carefully planned coaxing, or day-by-day assault on her faith weakened her resistance, made her drop church work, skip attendance at services, and finally produced total indifference. Because Christ loves us too much to see those for whom He shed His blood led into unbelief, His Word pleads that those who live together worship together.

The family, above other forces of human society, should be united in acclaiming the Savior, so that the spiritual life of the children entrusted to its care may be safeguarded. Repeatedly the Old and New Testaments direct parents, in effect, to bring up their children *"in the nurture and admonition of the Lord."* When Jesus is the Head of the home, that command is followed; parents teach their children to pray, tell them what Jesus has done for them, bring them to Baptism, see that they attend Sunday school and, whenever possible, offer daily religious instruction. Especially do Christian fathers and mothers give their sons and daughters a good example in regular, reverent church attendance. But picture the houses divided against themselves in religious matters. When Sunday comes, the boys see their father shun the church; or the girls soon notice that their mother has only a smile of contempt for the faith. From the first moment the children sense this opposition to Christ's Gospel, the seeds of doubt are sown in their hearts. Soon they form the conclusion, very logical to them: "If father or mother does not attend church, why should I?" — the practical reasoning that keeps millions of our children away from every contact with their Savior.

For a dozen different reasons we repeat the plea: Bring the whole family to Christ! You young folks who know the Lord, earnestly resolve that you will never marry an unbeliever, no matter how insistent and repeated his pleas of love may be! To those living without Jesus or against Him I say: "Don't ever ask a Christian girl to be your wife! Don't think of a Christian boy as your husband! You will probably cause them more misery than you can imagine. If you persist in rejecting your Redeemer, then

marry someone who shares this unbelief! But don't spoil
a Christian life or endanger the devotion of those whom you
profess to love!"   Still more, however, I say to them:
"Have you ever taken time to meet Jesus on the pages of
the Bible, to study the blessing and promise of His Gospel,
the sacrifice of His own holy body for your sins? Be fair
enough at least to examine His truth and give the Spirit
a chance in your heart! He is *your* Savior! He wants
you at this moment. He pleads with you through this
message, Be reconciled to God through faith! In His
name I promise that when you kneel before Him, convinced that He is your Redeemer and your God, then peace
that you have never before dreamed possible will be yours.
Then, too, you will be ready to take a Christian as your
life's companion and establish a home where the Savior
will reign supreme.

To believing young men and women I add: "Never
marry anyone who does not completely share with you
this unity of Christ-centered truth!" It is not enough
to say: "Even though my sweetheart is Catholic and I
Lutheran, we both believe in Christ." These religiously
mixed marriages are often the source of deep sorrow.
I am not speaking in theory, but on the basis of facts which
have come to me from many hundreds of cases. I doubt
whether anyone in the United States has reviewed as many
instances of mixed marriages as are locked in my files;
and on the basis of these documents I tell you that such
marriages often lead to misunderstanding, quarrel, separation, divorce, and, what is even worse, to the neglect and
denial of the Lord Jesus Christ. Make this your prayer
and resolution: "God helping me, I will marry only a true
Christian!" Everything you do in maintaining your faith
will bring His rich, repeated blessings.

To you parents God says: "Take time for your children! Give them the guidance, companionship, discipline, they require! Watch over them by day and night, particularly during these years of unrest, when sinister forces try to coax them from Christ! Show them how Christians should live! Sit with them in the family pew! Let your prayers continually ascend in their behalf to the throne of divine mercy!" If you are Christ's, you must plead powerfully and persistently before the Lord for your child's soul, for its usefulness in this life, its blessing in the next!

Let us make American homes — dear Father, place this resolve into many hearts throughout the land! — havens of the Savior's peace and blessing, so that, come what may, we are always ready to receive Him! When the Prince of Wales visited a town in the Midlands, he selected a typical laborer's home at random and entered unannounced. The next day the workman told his friends: "I did not expect him, nor did my wife. The house was untidy, and I hadn't washed. We shall never forgive ourselves. If we had known he was coming, we should have been ready for him." After what I have told you today, you should be ready to receive more than any earthly ruler the Prince of inner peace, Jesus, the Friend of sinners. From this moment keep your home in readiness to welcome Him who promises, *"Behold, I stand at the door and knock: if any man hear My voice and open the door, I will come in to him and will sup with him and he with Me."* Ask yourself, you who know the Lord Jesus, these questions suggested by the Bible itself: *"Is it well with thy husband? Is it well with the child?"* Is it well with thy wife? God give you the strength and courage resolutely to work and pray for the conversion of all your relatives! Then, when it may be said, adapting the language of our text, that those who are in your house hear *"the Word of the Lord"*; when all have been baptized; when your whole household believes God in Christ, you will have this radiant assurance: In heaven, when Jesus' promise *"I am the Resurrection and the Life"* is magnificently fulfilled, you, as part of *"the whole family in heaven,"* will be reunited with those who are yours and Christ's on earth. The span of this life passes far too swiftly to be marred by unbelief. Relatively few couples enjoy more than thirty or forty years of married life. Golden weddings are exceptional, diamond anniversaries great rarities. Oh, let these fleeting years be a period of preparation for the never-ending joys of the heavenly homeland, where we shall be with the Savior and together with the loved ones who have died in the faith! God give us all that supreme glory by keeping Christ first, last, and uppermost for the whole family! We ask it in His name. Amen.

HEAVEN'S HELP FOR TROUBLED HEARTS

> *"Let not your heart be troubled; ye believe in God, believe also in Me. In My Father's house are many mansions; if it were not so, I would have told you. I go to prepare a place for you."* — Saint John 14:1, 2

God, Our Gracious Father:

In our deepening sorrow help us believe confidently that there is "a better country," a heavenly homeland, for all who accept the Lord Jesus as their Savior from sin, the Victor over the grave and its terror! Let Thy Spirit teach us that day after day we approach more closely the inescapable moment when life ends and we must face Thy judgment! Without Christ, who died and rose again for everyone of us, we are doomed to eternal death; but, O Father, we thank Thee that by trusting the Redeemer with our whole hearts we have a prepared place in the many mansions of heaven. Bring multitudes to the faith through this broadcast! Call sinners to repentance! Lighten the load of the heavily burdened! Relieve the suffering! Abide with us as our country's God! Forgive our sins for Jesus' sake, and grant us more of that righteousness which alone exalts a nation! Hear us, O merciful Father, and in Thy time bring us all together before the throne of Thy celestial majesty, through Jesus Christ, Thy Son, our heavenly Redeemer! Amen.

AN early missionary to Tierra del Fuego, the tip end of South America, tells us how every morning the natives of that barren country greeted the sunrise with piercing howls and shrieking lament. As he later learned in seeking an explanation for this weird rite, so much misery crowded into the lives of the Fuegians that they viewed each new day with horror, every sunrise as the beginning of added evil.

We are separated from Tierra del Fuego and those missionary days by 8,000 miles and many long years; yet too many people in our country and this modern era, gripped by the same fear which tortured those savages, likewise greet each dawn with grim forebodings. They have endured such unspeakable agony of body, mind, and soul; they have beheld so much misery on all sides, that each morning, instead of breaking with joyous hope, seems only to add grief to grief.

The number of these, the heavyhearted, will increase during the burdened months before us. The fall of Singapore, it is predicted, will add another year to the world conflict — twelve months more of killing and being killed. The American people, we are warned, do not yet realize that we are in the midst of a devastating war. As the millions of men who today and tomorrow register for the draft are called into military service; as the casualty lists gradually increase in size and frequency, masses in this country will need help to keep them from doubt, distrust, and despair.

Men are asking themselves: "Where can we find unfailing comfort during this crisis? In pleasure?" As late as Wednesday of this week tea dances catered to large crowds in the Raffles Hotel at Singapore; people stood in long queues waiting to buy tickets for their favorite entertainment. Last night Singapore fell. Can forgetfulness of sorrow be found in drunkenness? Positively not! The growth in liquor sales throughout the United States is so staggering that it ought to recall the prophet Nahum's warning concerning Nineveh, which was to be destroyed after drunken carousal. More than ever we need clear-thinking men and women whose perceptive powers have not been befuddled by overindulgence in alcohol. Can money purchase release from fears and worries? Jay Gould, American multimillionaire, lamented on his death-bed, "I am the most miserable man on earth." Will unbelief, the denial of Christ, the overbrave reliance on self, conquer human miseries? Skeptical, sneering Voltaire cried out, "I wish I had never been born." Can courage be found in an alert, trained mind, the calmness of a pleasing personality? These advantages melt away quickly under the heat of affliction. In these days of trying men's souls, as promises prove unreliable, hopes misplaced, our own strength insufficient, we must turn penitently, pleadingly to God in Christ.

Whatever our individual troubles may be, let us find sustaining strength in faith! Through Christ we are in God's hand. For every perplexity believe that in Jesus there is

HEAVEN'S HELP FOR TROUBLED HEARTS —

the comfort pledged by our Lord Himself in the words that have brought light and life to millions of sin-darkened souls, the radiant promise of Saint John, chapter fourteen, verses one and two: *"Let not your heart be troubled; ye believe in God, believe also in Me. In My Father's house are many mansions; if it were not so, I would have told you. I go to prepare a place for you."*

I

IN CHRIST WE HAVE THE ASSURANCE OF GOD'S HELP
FOR THIS LIFE

Remove all doubt from your minds that there can be any exaggeration in these words! People are suspicious today. Again and again within this generation they have been led to expect happier times with the blessings of peace, but throughout the world they face sorrows deeper than they have ever known. Diplomats break their word; politicians prove unreliable; scientists make bad guesses; prophets of new cults raise the hopes of their fellow men to the highest pitch, only to fail cruelly in producing real help. Yet this utterance of the Lord Jesus, as all His pledges, are divine truth, immovable, unchangeable, eternal.

By His own declaration *"heaven and earth shall pass away, but My Word shall not pass away."* Christ's promise can never fail. Let that be our sustaining assurance! The Bible, as God's revelation, must prevail.

Our age particularly ought to be impressed with this sacredness of Holy Writ. Just a hundred years ago, in 1842, the first systematic excavations were undertaken in Bible lands, and the intervening period has indeed been a century of progress in defending Scripture. Archaeologists working in the ruins of ancient cities, especially in Assyria, Babylonia, Egypt, Palestine, have uncovered historical records, now three and four thousand years old, which remarkably support the Bible and corroborate its claims. Not, of course, that we need such human endorsement! Through the Holy Spirit the Christian knows God's Word is true; but how timely and helpful that just in these days of brash unbelief the promise has been fulfilled, *"The stones shall cry out"!* Therefore when you face the cutting criticism of the Bible, remember how often those who had been the most bitter in assailing Christ's pledges, once they have really become acquainted with their truth, have defended the Scriptures. George Romanes, the British biologist, wrote a book to support atheism. He explained, "I took it for granted that the Christian faith was played out." When, however, he saw that Christianity worked; that many eminent men, some the most illustrious in the fields of science, had ranged themselves on the side of the Gospel, he resolved to let the Bible speak for itself. As a result of his studies he wrote a book called *Thoughts on Religion,* showing why, from the merely human viewpoint everyone should be a Christian. He concluded — and now he speaks to you who have placed a question mark behind the statements of Holy Writ, "Unbelief is usually due to indolence, often to prejudice, and never a thing to be proud of."

"Let not your heart be troubled!" — This word offers added comfort since it is among our Lord's final utterances, spoken on the last night of His earthly life, shortly before He began the ordeal which was to end with His death on the cross. Jesus left His followers nothing of wealth or earthly value; but in this sacred pledge He bequeathed them and us the heritage of untroubled hearts; and within less than one day after speaking this promise Jesus sealed it with His blood, died to prove its truth.

"Let not your heart be troubled!" Jesus says, for He recognizes the severe trials which burden our souls. Those who give counsel for the distressed often do not understand the problems they promise to solve, Christ knows our every sorrow. He was born in a stable and understands the needs of the poor and the outcasts. To save His life He had to flee into a foreign country! He can measure the suffering of refugees, religious and political exiles. He spent the greater part of His earthly existence in lowly work and more than any expert in labor or industry He realizes what the laboring man requires. He suffered from hunger, thirst, weariness. Has anyone a better insight into the privations to be endured by millions of the famished and undernourished? He was persecuted by those whom He had helped; and because He felt the pains of spurned devotion, He can sympathize with you who have been deserted by someone whom you loved and for whom you labored hard and long. He was slandered and defamed, although He was absolutely innocent of wrongdoing: and whenever false accusations blacken your character or baseless rumors disturb your peace, confide in Christ and know that He felt, though in a far deeper degree, the cruelty inflicted on you. What comfort, too, when faced with coaxing, tugging enticements for evil, to know that *"He was in all points tempted like as we are"!* He was made

to bear the unspeakable anguish of bodily suffering as the lash cut its furrows on His back, the blunt nails were hammered through His quivering flesh, and the tortures of crucifixion crushed out His life. When you toss on your sickbeds, broken by accident, consumed by wasting diseases, turn to Him for sympathetic love! He was burdened above all by inner agony in that unfathomable rack and torture of His soul when He cried, *"My God, My God, why hast Thou forsaken Me?"* If it ever seems that God has left you; if you begin to doubt whether there is any salvation for your soul with its sins; if you verge closely to despair, then, what an understanding, compassionate Friend Jesus proves Himself!

Much more than sympathy, however, is found in Christ. He can say, *"Let not your heart be troubled!"* because He has removed forever the cause of fear and worry. Everything which disturbs your peace of mind, each affliction that has brought trouble into your home, every burden you must bear, is to be traced, finally but definitely, to sin, the transgression of which you or someone else is guilty. This war comes from sin. The tragedy in your home starts with selfishness. Your money losses originate in dishonesty and fraud. The sorrows you young people meet in courtship often begin with unfaithfulness and untruth. Even the sickness which lays us low, the injuries that seem to come merely by accident, are ultimately traceable to evil.

All glory to the Lord Jesus that He, Christ, forever broke the power of sin and completely removed its curse! Clinging to Him, we can exult, *"Sin shall not have dominion over you: for ye are not under the Law, but under grace."* No dictator with the combined powers of Hitler, Mussolini, Stalin, Franco, has ever exerted the complete sway over mankind and the full control over souls which mark the tyranny of sin. It locks us in its iron grip. You and

I were born under its rule, and without Christ we die in its slavery. It burdens your conscience, robs you of your peace, and makes life a continued series of griefs, death a terrifying horror. Yet with Jesus — eternal praise to the compassionate Christ! — sin's curse has been removed from your life if only you will believe this divine assurance *"He hath made Him to be sin for us who knew no sin, that we might be made the righteousness of God in Him."* How did Jesus remove your sins? Not by overlooking, forgetting, simply canceling them, but by suffering for them, paying the price of every transgression, satisfying the demands of a just and holy God, giving Himself as the redemption for all iniquity, the sacrifice for the appalling total of human transgressions; by shedding His holy blood, the divine cleansing for each wrong; by laying down His life as the ransom price demanded for our liberation! You will not be able to understand how Christ could take away your sins. It is too miraculous, too marvelous, too merciful. Believe God and this promise of His Word, *"There is therefore now no condemnation to them which are in Christ Jesus"!* When you give your heart to the Savior, your sins are removed *"as far as the East is from the West."* You are restored to grace, reconciled with God, reborn into a new, blessed existence.

"Let not your heart be troubled!" Jesus assures you, because the same love that removes your sins can make the hardest blows the tenderest caresses, use the galling bitterness of affliction for purposes of sweet, bounteous mercy. That is why a soldier leaving for distant fronts could write me, "It took this war to bring me to Christ." By the same love for your soul Jesus promises, not that you will escape trouble, that life will be a round of unbroken pleasure (on the contrary, He still warns you, *"We must through much tribulation enter into the kingdom of God"*), but that

through faith, *"sorrow is turned into joy"* as *"all things work together for good to them that love God."*

"Let not your heart be troubled!" — This comfort is doubly sure because it comes not only from Jesus, who is our Christ, *"the Lamb of God, which taketh away the sin of the world,"* but also from Jesus, who is our God. Plainly He declares, *"Ye believe in God; believe also in Me!"* He asks men to trust Him as they trust the Almighty. What a powerful prooftext with which to confound those— and their number is increasing! — who are willing to pay our Lord almost every tribute except to admit that He is God, together with the Father and the Spirit, the ever-blessed Trinity! *"Ye believe in God,"* He says; *"believe also in Me!"* for, as He states elsewhere, *"I and the Father are one."* Jesus, according to His own words, according to Old Testament prophecies and New Testament epistles, the proclamation of His Father, the adoration of the angels, the verdict of His miracles, is God almighty, with the resources of heaven itself at His command; God omniscient, who foresees the path we must take as the road to glory; God the ever present, whose pledge *"Lo, I am with you alway, even unto the end of the world"* must be of out-standing consolation for millions subjected to the perils of war and its destruction; God all-merciful, to forgive us our selfishness and hatred, our impurities of thought and action, our rebellion against His grace, our refusal to help our fellow men. Jesus is all this, nothing less, yet much more. He is — hear it, believe it, trust it! — your God and your Savior. The Lord who can help us and whom this groping, bleeding age needs with double necessity is the divine Christ. Tens of thousands of men have been nailed to crosses, though their suffering affects us little now. The day before yesterday 130 students at our seminary gave of their blood, the largest single group of blood donors

on record in this part of the country. While many lives may be saved by the transfusion of these gallons of vital life-fluid into broken, anemic bodies, all the human blood throughout the world can never cleanse a single sin-stained soul. Increasing numbers of American youth are laying down their lives in the nation's defense. God grant that their sacrifice will be rewarded by a true, righteous victory! But no man can give his life to pay for iniquity. Only God could do that; only God did do that when Jesus, our divine Savior, atoned for all sin.

Therefore His appeal *"Ye believe in God; believe also in Me,"* is directed both to the young in the prime of hopeful lives, as they gird themselves for the service of war and to the aged, who are passing the last milestones on life's long journey. *"Believe . . . in Me!"* He says to those who have placed their reliance on everything else except His grace — only to see their hopes completely shattered, *"Believe . . . in Me!"* He repeats to you who have found life easy and prosperous, but for whom the next years may bring sudden, complete reverses, *"Believe . . . in Me!"* He entreats those who have steadfastly spurned His outstretched arms, rejected every overture of His mercy, *" 'Believe . . . in Me!'* Accept Me as your Savior! Trust Me sincerely, perpetually, and your hearts will not be troubled!"

With faith in Christ, what can destroy your peace of mind, rob you of inner joy? Questions of money or of health, good name, quarrels in your home, losses in your business, matters of physical or mental health, the fear that your sons may never return from the battle lines? Listen to this promise: *"If God be for us, who can be against us? He that spared not His own Son but de- livered Him up for us all, how shall He not with Him also freely give us all things?"* Whenever the burden seems too heavy, the way too steep, the night too dark, the pain too torturing, turn to Jesus! If He loved our souls so much that He gave His own body to rescue them for eternity, certainly He will take care of the comparatively small details of our earthly needs and use them for uplifting purposes.

Why are we so fainthearted, so reluctant to go all the way with the Savior? People in Saint Louis tell of a traveler who in the early days came to the banks of the Mississippi during a hard winter, when the river was completely frozen over. Not trusting the strength of the ice, he began to crawl on hands and knees from the Illinois shore toward Missouri. Every advance was made slowly and cautiously. After covering a few hundred feet you can imagine his surprise when, hearing a loud noise behind him, he turned to see a wagon, loaded with heavy logs and drawn by two horses, move quickly over the frozen stream. In much the same way many of you are crawling on your knees, beset by worry and care, when, if you would only take God at His Word in Christ, you could walk safely across icebound rivers of doubt or affliction with the assurance of a blessed eternity constantly to strengthen you.

II

IN CHRIST WE HAVE THE PLEDGE OF GOD'S MANSIONS
FOR THE NEXT LIFE

It is in this promise for the hereafter that the Savior's grace reaches its glorious climax as it triumphs over the most fearful of terrors, death's paralysis. Men love life so dearly that they cringe in horror before the judgment beyond the grave and go to almost any extreme in avoiding the grim, clutching power of death. They will cling to rafts during thirst-crazed days and delirious nights; they will hastily throw away the earning of a lifetime if this weights them down in their race for safety; they will end raving, chattering, cursing in despair, as they see life slip from their grasp and know that before long they must face God. Add all other sorrows men endure, and their appalling total is not to be compared with the dread of the end! No scientific theories can offer any comfort here. No speculations, however learned, will dry tears at the side of a casket. No spiritist séances can ever remove the numb, aching pain of bereavement. Despite the systematic study of the circumstances surrounding thousands of deaths, science knows no more of the next life than did the ancient Egyptian pyramid architects or the Babylonian tower builders. The Bible is the only source of positive assurance regarding the hereafter, since it is the one Volume that offers God's revelation and Christ's assurance. If it were not for our Jesus and His divine comfort *"Let not your heart be troubled!"* men would be cringing creatures, far worse, with this fear, than the dumb animals.

Through our Savior, however, we can exult: *"O death, where is thy sting? O grave, where is thy victory? . . . Thanks be to God, which giveth us the victory through our Lord Jesus Christ!"* See how clearly our blessed Redeemer relieves death's pain! He tells His disciples in the Upper Room a few hours before He sets His face toward Gethsemane: *"In My Father's house are many mansions. . . . I go to prepare a place for you."* He was going, first of all, to the cross, but beyond Calvary's shame and agony He was directed to heaven. How overfilled are these words with personal comfort! He speaks intimately of His *"Father's house,"* and He assures those who believe that there is a blessed existence for them after the grave. Cling closely to each word in this promise, especially during these doubt-filled days when the statements concluding the Apostles' Creed, "I believe . . . in the resurrection of the body and the life everlasting," are assailed with new, destructive hatred or laughed at in ridicule. We need a ban on every allegedly humorous reference to heaven. Public or private slurs on Bible teachings concerning the life to come are always objectionable, but doubly so in an emergency like the present when masses of American youth defending our country may be close to death on land, in the air, at sea. Men by the millions are killed in world conflict, laid into hastily dug graves, their bodies drowned in the deep sea or exposed to the devastating elements; and that, unbelief sneeringly claims, is the end. How bitter and cruel life would be if it were! Instead, we ought to find constant comfort in the fact that through Christ death is only the beginning of glory incomparable, immeasurable, unutterable.

One of our Lutheran families in Omaha had the harrowing experience of being informed soon after Pearl Harbor that two sons, both volunteers, had been killed aboard a battleship in Hawaiian waters. What anguish must have shaken the souls of that father and mother, even though their sons had died defending the nation! Now, as you try to feel the heartbreaking sorrow of those bereaved parents, you can begin to understand the rejoicing which must have been theirs when recently they received the electrifying report that the death notices were mistakes, since the two boys had been found safe and secure! Few people, I suppose, have ever thrilled with such deep-souled rejoicing; yet everyone of you, my fellow redeemed, accepting Christ's resurrection, His death-destroying love for the world, can have the far greater joy of knowing that whenever unbelief says your dear ones, asleep in Jesus, will never live again, this is a lie. In God's good time you, too, will learn the full truth of the Savior's pledge *"If a man keep My saying, he shall never see death,"* the eternal death. Here, then, is the first promise Christ gives you today: The grave does not end all. There is a future life, an eternity, which the Lord of life Himself has won for us by removing our sins and destroying forever the power of eternal death.

We have only begun to survey the glories of His promise. Jesus also tells His disciples, and He includes all who receive Him as their Redeemer, that they shall be in His *"Father's house,"* in heaven. What unspeakable bliss! To be face to face with God the Father who gave us our existence; to sing our praises to God the Savior who redeemed us by His own life-giving atonement; to exalt God the Holy Spirit who gave us the new birth in holiness and righteousness — can any earthly privilege even approach this unspeakable joy?

Perfection, sinlessness, absolute holiness always dwell with God. Therefore the Scriptures want us to believe that in the celestial city we will experience no sorrow or grief, no pain or broken hopes, no partings or tears. There, in a radiance we cannot describe or understand, all our frantic, unrewarded toils, the aching anguish of broken hearts, the sorrow of sin, will utterly vanish under the realization that *"the sufferings of this present time are not worthy to be compared with the glory which shall be revealed in us."* Though we cannot even faintly picture its dazzling splendor, let us rest with the assurance that if this world, despite sin, contains marvels of breath-taking beauty — the towering mountains etched against the flaming sky, the amethyst-green surf, the ocean's fringe dashing restlessly on our shores, the rainbow arching its spectrum of color across the land — the celestial realm must be magnificent.

In His *"Father's house,"* Jesus says, *"are many mansions,"* a vast number of heavenly dwelling places. These everlasting homes will not remain empty; they have been reserved for the mighty host, the ten thousand times ten thousand, the myriad times myriads, who have been faithful unto death and have received the crown of life. You may be crowded out of many places on earth, but there is room for you in heaven. Jesus promises, *"Where I am, there shall also My servant be."* Before the throne we shall meet those who have likewise died in the faith, the prophets and the apostles, the disciples and the evangelists, as well as those who *"as a firebrand"* have been *"plucked out of the burning,"* rescued in the last moment, as the thief on the cross. Especially, however, will we be reunited with those Christians whom we knew in this life. Earthly relations like marriage will stop and give way to a higher, more blessed existence. For the comfort of those still wounded by recent bereavements, let me say that the Scriptures contain no word which keeps us from believing that in heaven we shall be reassembled with those who have gone before us in the faith. What an incentive to remain true to Jesus! What a compelling reason for each member of the family to accept Him as the Savior!

Note the personal, pointed *"I go to prepare a place for* you." Jesus died for all the world, but I tell you individually that He gave Himself for *you.* He shed His blood for *you.* He was crucified for *you.* He died for *you.* He rose again for *you.* Christ deals with the world through individuals; therefore *your* faith counts, not your church's, your parents', your wife's. *Your* name must be written in the Book of Life. How comforting in days like these when all else gives way to think of heaven not merely in a vague, indefinite sense, but as your *"Father's house"* with a special place prepared by Christ Himself for you!

"I" [Jesus] *"go to prepare a place for you"* helps an-

swer the question "How can I be sure of my prepared place in the many mansions?" Some people try to earn their title to this heavenly dwelling, pay their way or have someone else pay it; pray themselves or be prayed into heaven. They want the blessings of the *"Father's house"* to be theirs in reward or recognition. But this is not Christ's teaching. He told His disciples on that Thursday night that *He,* as our Forerunner, our God and Savior, would make our place ready. How He fulfilled that promise and marked a celestial place with our names, what fearful price *He* paid to serve as our Way to heaven, is told in the story of Lent, which the Christian churches begin to commemorate this week. May it be a blessed season for all of you! May you learn to believe that by the shedding of His blood, His dying on the cross, His resurrection from the sealed grave, Jesus gives you, even now through faith, the indescribable blessings of eternity!

Why, then, with heaven as our real home, should our hearts be troubled? Why weep at funerals as those who have no hope? In the second century a Greek named Aristides wrote to a friend concerning the early followers of our Lord: "If any among these Christians passes from this world, they rejoice and give thanks to God. And they escort his body with songs and thanksgiving, as if he were setting out from one place to another near by." God grant you the same resolute faith, so that when death takes a beloved one or finally comes to summon you, you may rejoice in spirit even though in tears of human sorrow! Clinging to the resurrected Christ, may you look forward joyfully to the *"Father's house,"* with its *"many mansions,"* the reunion with all God's children, and particularly to our own personal prepared place, where we shall behold our Savior. *"For we shall see Him as He is."* O God, bring us all to that glory for Jesus' sake! Amen.

"NOT MY WILL, BUT THINE
BE DONE"

*"Father, if Thou be willing, remove this
cup from Me: nevertheless not My will,
but Thine be done!"* — Saint Luke 22:42

Christ, Our Lord:

*Thou Lamb of God that takest away the sin of the world, have
mercy upon us and grant us Thy peace! As we prepare to follow
Thy footsteps from the gloom of the Garden to the death cry on
the cross, help us stifle every suggestion of self-righteousness as we
find in Thy suffering the appalling price Thou didst pay to free
us from our sins! Come especially to the discontented, the disillusioned young and the world-worn old, to the restless and tor-
mented, burdened of soul and conscience, to those who have religion in their heads but no true faith in their hearts! Enable us
all to submit ourselves to Thy perfect guidance and repeat the words
Thou Thyself didst pray, "Not My will, but Thine be done!"
Grant that during these months of war the work of Thy Church
throughout the world may not be hindered! Send Thy Spirit to
accompany all Gospel preaching, so that sinners are brought to repentance, doubting hearts strengthened, distressed souls fortified! We
ask this, together with a prayer for the nation's victory, according
to Thy will, assured by the promise of Thine atonement and the
power of Thy cleansing blood! Amen.*

LAST week in hundreds of American communities religious and lay leaders of Protestant, Catholic, and
Jewish groups issued a signed statement featuring seven
articles of faith, called "The Foundation of Our National
Life." It contains approximately 450 words, but not once,
directly or indirectly, is the Lord Jesus Christ mentioned
by name or reference — as though He had never been
born at Bethlehem or nailed to the cross at Calvary, there
to shed His blood for the cleansing of all sin.

In the light of Bible teaching, such declarations which
refuse to recognize Christ and deliberately omit the *"Name
which is above every name"* are not acceptable to the

Savior who says, "*Without Me ye can do nothing*," and who instructs us to confess Him openly, boldly, persistently. Today, while America is engaged in the most dangerous struggle of its entire existence, we who have pledged ourselves to the Lord Jesus should know that it is not enough to cry out, "Back to God — any God!" We must say, "Back to the God revealed in Jesus Christ!" It will not help us to resolve, "Back to religion — any religion!" Some creeds can destroy rather than build, as we were reminded only a few days ago when the two founders of a California cult were convicted of fraudulent use of the United States mails. Nor can any help and hope be found in crying, "Back to the church — any church," for the certainty of prevailing victory is granted, by divine promise and history's verdict, only to those who love Jesus Christ and cling steadfastly to His Word.

This may appear narrow and bigoted to some of you; yet it is in harmony with good Christianity and certainly not in conflict with good Americanism. The Savior Himself warned, "*No man cometh unto the Father but by Me.*" Again, "*If ye believe not that I am He, ye shall die in your sins.*" Again, "*Whosoever shall deny Me before men, him will I also deny before my Father which is in heaven.*" And the first President, whose birthday the nation oberserves today, supports these statements. If millions of American defense workers tomorrow show their appreciation of George Washington by working instead of taking a holiday, then let millions of American citizens devote at least a few moments to honor George Washington by reaffirming their allegiance to the Savior. The Father of our Country was not ashamed of Jesus. As a youth of twenty he acclaimed Christ when he wrote into a booklet called *Daily Sacrifices* prayers like these: "Be our God, and guide us this day and forever for His sake who lay down in the grave and arose again for us, Jesus Christ, our Lord!   Remit my transgressions, negligences, and ignorances, and cover them all with the absolute obedience of Thy dear Son! . . .   Be merciful to me, O God, and pardon me for Jesus Christ's sake; and so into Thy hands I commend myself, both soul and body, in the name of Thy Son Jesus Christ!"   Throughout his life he definitely acknowledged the Savior.   In a later prayer Washington plainly stated that unless we follow Jesus' example "we can never hope to be a happy nation."   Religious leaders, searching for a better day in our country, may sign their names to a document which ignores the Lord, but Washington reminds us that we can never be a "happy nation" without the Redeemer.

Similarly I tell you that unless *you* learn to follow the Savior's footsteps you will miss the true joy of life. For the future, heavy with grievous burdens, you should subject yourselves to God and walk in Christ's footsteps, as Washington pleaded in his prayer.   And how, amid ascending dangers, can you more assuredly show your love for your Lord than by making the very words He spoke your own, turning to the Father in His name and praying:

"Not My Will, but Thine be Done!"

Let this be the subject of our first Lenten devotion, as, reviewing the opening scenes in our Savior's suffering, we read, Saint Luke, chapter twenty-two, verse forty-two, and repeat, *"Father, if Thou be willing, remove this cup from Me: nevertheless not My will, but Thine be done!"*

I

WHY WE SHOULD SUBMIT TO THE DIVINE WILL

The Garden of Gethsemane, where Jesus prayed these words, is the only place in the entire record of our Savior's passion which can be identified today almost with certainty; also the one spot mentioned in the Lenten record that probably has escaped the ravages of destruction. The Cedron Valley, winding at the foot of Olivet, has been covered with ruin and wreckage, while God's wrath has repeatedly loosed its fury against thankless, stubborn, self-willed Jerusalem. But the Garden where Jesus *"ofttimes resorted . . . with His disciples"* and where He spent part of the night before His death has remained unharmed for nineteen centuries with their bloody battles. It is as though our heavenly Father had purposely preserved that sacred site to retain within the limits of battle-scarred Judea one area to which men could point with considerable certainty and say: "Here God's Son and the world's Savior knelt in prayer. Here began the agony that was to end in our redemption."

To speak merely of "agony," however, does not begin to describe the overwhelming anguish which in Gethsemane almost crushed the Christ of God into death. Before blasphemous hands bound and struck Him; before the lash cut into the flesh of His back; before the thorny crown was pressed onto His head, He had to endure torture no other sufferer has known. It was not merely the fear of the cross nor the terror of death which gripped our Lord in the Garden; for if men can face death bravely, certainly He could. If Christians in the early Church so readily surrendered themselves to their executioners that at one time a law had to be passed preventing believers from deliberately seeking a martyr's death, assuredly the Lord of life and death could be expected to show unflinching fortitude in His last hours.

Nor is the unspeakable, unparalleled agony in Gethsemane to be explained by the fact that Jesus, alone in His death vigil, was assailed by unrelieved loneliness. The companionship of the disciples whom He had selected to watch with Him would indeed have offered strength and comfort; yet even His closest friends were so utterly insensible to the weight of His woe that they slept in heavy, almost stupefied slumber. This, of course, pressed heavily on our Lord; but the wound which tore at His heart and made Him gasp, *"My soul is exceeding sorrowful, even unto death,"* was the curse of sin that He there started to bear, the penalty of all the world's transgressions for which He prepared to atone with His life.

Picture to yourself the shocking consequences which may follow a single violation of God's Law: the banishment of peace, the insistent charges by an outraged conscience, the threatening of hell itself — the restless anguish that can drive sinners to despair; add the grief which your transgressions have heaped up during your own life, the sleepless nights, the distress of mind, the fear of God's justice and its punishment; try to visualize the appalling total of sins in your home, community, state, the whole nation; go to the earth's limits and the bounds of the past and the future to heap up the iniquity that has cursed the race, and then believe that for all these sins Jesus — may you ever praise His mercy! — made such complete atonement, that through faith you have no sins in God's sight! Now, if our Savior thus carries the weight of human guilt — and the Scriptures clearly teach that He is *"the Lamb of God, which taketh away the sin of the* WORLD," that *"He was wounded for our transgressions, He was bruised for our iniquities"* — can you not understand why with the punishment mankind should have endured sweeping down on Him, with hell's furies loosed on his soul, suffering as His has never been seen elsewhere? Great drops of sweat, as blood, begin to run down His pallid face. In His agony He falls headlong to the ground. Three times He raises His voice in piteous entreaty to pierce the silence of the darkened Garden with the plea "Oh, My Father, if it be possible, let this cup pass from Me!" The heartbreaking, soul-racking torture was so overwhelming that Jesus could not be fully human without begging God to stop the racking, tearing, crushing of His soul that almost killed Him. Yet Jesus could not be true God if at the height of His anguish He had not added to His "Father, . . . remove this cup from Me!" this victorious cry of submission, "Nevertheless, not My will, but Thine be done!" What holy self-surrender! What complete obedience to God!

At no time will you and I face any sorrow which even resembles Gethsemane's ghastly horror. The worst that life and death itself will ever inflict on us should not be mentioned in the same breath with Christ's anguish. The time will come, however, for everyone of us, when our burdens prove too hard, our grief too heavy, our pain too agonizing to endure, when we cry, "O God, remove this cup of suffering!" In those agonized moments think of our Savior, grief-gripped in Gethsemane, and remember that Jesus, so perfect that men have never been able to raise a true charge against Him, submitted to heavenly direction, praying, "Thy will be done!" How much more should we, with all our frailties and weaknesses, follow His sacred example by discarding our wishes in favor of divine wisdom!

"Not My will, but Thine be done!" we, too, should pray, realizing that our will is often marred with mistakes. A renowned surgeon at one of the nation's leading medical schools was asked to remove a diseased, lightless eye from a patient. However, he made the tragic error of destroying the sound, healthy eye and left the patient blind. Even with our best intentions we often do the wrong thing. The guns at Singapore were directed seaward to prevent a naval attack, but the assault came from land, and those eighteen-inch guns were useless. So it often happens in life that despite the utmost sincerity our purpose is diametrically opposed to our own good.

Again, we should ask for God's leading since man's will is thoroughly selfish. Even in these war days when almost every freedom we love is at stake, when millions of American young men are being summoned by law to risk their very lives in our country's defense, we witness the driving urge of personal gain which produces war profiteers, men obsessed with the mania that they must get richer while the war makes most of us poorer.

"Not my will, but Thine be done!" we should repeat because our will, enslaved by evil, is directed toward destructive ends. Many in the godless masses deliberately devote themselves to the enjoyment of lust. Consequently bodies are wrecked, mental powers impaired, souls sent to hell. We have it on the authority of leaders in military circles that the heaviest losses suffered by the United States Army result from impure living. In fact, the whole World War has been provoked by the fatal tragedy that multitudes have changed the words of our text to read, "Not Thy will, but mine be done!" Aggression, militarism, dictatorship, disregard of the divine law, ingratitude for Heaven's blessings have placed man's desires over God's, and for generations we must continue to pay the penalty of this folly.

"Not my will, but Thine be done!" we should pray, because we are too shortsighted to see the far-reaching sequel of our own folly or to measure the wide extent of divine mercy. We clutch at momentary enjoyment instead of seeking everlasting benedictions. Like children who cry for those things that can bring harm and injury, we want the sweet, easy pleasures of life when we need bitterness, hardness, the friction and pain of reverses to strengthen us,

the fire of trial to purify us. God's marvelous mercy in Christ grants what we need instead of what we blindly want. Only by His grace are we saved from ourselves. Think what would happen if our misdirected desires, selfish ambitions, sinful cravings were granted free reign! The horrors we witness in this world of war would be increased a hundred times. All peace, calm, and rest would be banished under the clash of our restless cravings.

How imperative, therefore, that we learn of Jesus how to pray, *"Not my will, but Thine be done!"* and know that God's intentions for His children are always right! To shortsighted human vision it may appear cruel for the Lord to have permitted that excruciating agony in the Garden, but how glorious was the final outcome of the Savior's self-sacrifice! It offered complete pardon to every penitent sinner, liberation from the dread tyranny of sin, victory over hell, restoration to the Father, benediction of an abundant life amid rankling disappointment, triumph over death, promise of an eternity with God. If the Lord had not permitted Christ to suffer, these unsearchable riches of His mercy could not be ours. Jesus had to be crucified if this world was to be saved. By the same principle of divine love God's will toward you in Christ is directed toward your salvation. Until you acclaim Jesus the Savior and Sovereign of your soul, you are sentenced to rebuke and rejection by the Almighty. The sorrow you suffer is one of the penalties (however small in comparison with those which are to come) you pay for your unbelief, stubborn rebellion against God's grace. But from the very moment the Savior enters your heart, your life is divinely controlled, your destiny directed toward heaven, and everything you experience, the good as well as the sad, is part of an infallible plan by which your heavenly Father constantly draws you closer to Him.

Be sure of this, the divine will toward the redeemed is always perfect, errorless. Sometimes the all-knowing God has to use harsh, strong means to carry out His blessed program. A few days ago, the newspapers told of a sailor from a torpedoed ship who found that some of the crew in his lifeboat were being overcome by the numb drowsiness which precedes death by freezing. He deliberately struck these men, aroused their anger, made them fight back for the purpose of keeping their blood in vital circulation and preventing icy death. So God often lets conflict come to arouse you from the stupor of sin, save you from self-indulgence. He permits your faith to be attacked so that you will be driven to defend it and in so doing search the Scriptures to find spiritual reserve.

It has been hard for some of you mothers to give your sons for the nation's defense. Everything for which you hoped and prayed, worked and saved, as you planned what you thought best for your boys seems to have collapsed. Yet, every soldier who has Christ in his heart, who can truly point to Jesus and say, " '*If God be for us*' — and I know that He is because He sent His Son to redeem me — '*who can be against us?*' " will experience that these years of military training, with all the perils of land, ocean, and air, can become a design in God's perfect pattern for life. Our chaplains write us that men in the armed forces are being converted to Christ. Despite the hazards of army camp life, Christian selectees are being deepened in their faith. After this war, when we can view God's ways with us from that higher level, multitudes will thank the Almighty for taking the course He did to prove in an unmistakable manner that "*all things work together for good to them that love God.*" Almost with every mail I receive letters from young folks who face the alternative of marrying now or of waiting until peace has been declared, and many of these couples feel themselves the victims of cruel circumstances. What if you cannot marry now? Do you not believe that the God who gave you the Savior is powerful enough to make up for months and years of married happiness you may lose? Perhaps postponement of your wedding, as unbelievable as this now seems, may give you greater happiness. Trust God's will in Christ to use even delays and hindrances for glorious purposes! When Bishop Gobat was working among wild tribes of the Druses, he was invited to visit the chief whose support he had long hoped to win. Before he could accept, he took sick. He was likewise obliged to decline a second invitation. When the third came, he set out with a native guide so that he would not miss the chief's home. But the leader lost his way and refused to advance. Completely disappointed, Missionary Gobat had to forego his visit. Later, however, he learned that the chief had set a trap for him and that three times a group of murderers waited to destroy him. The influence which the missionary hoped to exert by personal contact was secured even without seeing the chief, for the tribal head acknowledged, "That man must be the servant of God, for though I sent messenger after messenger to bring him, he was always hindered."

Through Christ, life's heaviest adversities can become part of God's wonderful guidance. When Dr. Moon, a twenty-three-year-old physician in England, lost the sight of both eyes, his friends must have concluded that only death itself could be harder than total sightlessness. But Dr. Moon was a Christian. Although prayers seemed unanswered and medical help failed, he cried out: "O God, I thank Thee for the talent of blindness. May I so use it that at the coming of our Lord Jesus Christ He may receive His own with usury!" Dedicating himself to the

Savior, he produced the Moon system of script for the blind, which has been used in 492 languages and dialects to help bring thousands of sightless to the Lord Jesus. Even in the deepest of all sorrows, when death enters a home, through Christ we can rest with the assurance that God's will, as contrary to reason as this sounds, is but the proof of His love. Your letters testify to the fact that it took a sudden death, perhaps of a devoted husband or wife, to shake some of you out of indifference into the realization of your lost and hopeless condition. It may be that God called a beloved one because in His overmercy He wished to spare His child much earthly anguish, save it from over-whelming temptation, and early grant it the happiness of the heavenly homeland.

In short, God's will, however it may manifest itself to the believers, is always for our salvation. As the magnet attracts steel particles, drawing them straight toward it, so His love, as it molds our lives through pain and pleasure, seeks to draw us to Christ and His inexhaustible mercy. Our age has witnessed many philanthropies, gifts of billions of dollars for the advancement of the race, to cure its ills and solve its social problems. But everything men have to offer, in comparison with the Savior's marvelous grace and the wondrous ways of His will, is but as a small, evaporating drop of water in relation to the ocean's fathomless depths. Grace, pardon, peace, assurance, divine help, heavenly, unfailing wisdom — all these are ours when, loving Jesus with contrite, cross-centered faith, we submit to God and say, " '*Thy will*,' not mine, '*be done!*' "

Before us in the United States lie days, months, it may be long years, of deep-rooted difficulties. Some believe that the America we have known in the past is gone forever. They question the continuance of our free institutions and visualize the darkest days this country has ever known, as they forecast the triumph of Communist principles and their destructive practices. Self-appointed prophets have predicted a war of five, ten, twenty, even thirty years. As we pray God that He who overnight can change the tide of battle grant us a righteous peace and true tranquillity, let us remember that there is only one way in which Christians should face both national difficulties and personal reverses! That is not the path of fatalism which stolidly sneers: "Life is against us! The cards are stacked for evil! Our whole existence is a gamble!" Such folly offers no consolation during the crisis hours of life and death; rather it proves its own futility. Nor can there be any real help in the false bravado which boasts that it fears neither God nor man, that it can defy life's hurricanes, bending but not breaking under their force. How often have agnostics who spoke the language of that taunting self-sufficiency ended as shivering, shaking cowards! One and only one route leads to inner peace amid war's ravages, to soul-calm in the chaos and confusion of this wicked world, and that is the road of resignation to God, by which we say, " *'Thy will,'* " not mine, *'be done!'* " For then we have the assurance that as our Savior, submitting to divine direction, was gloriously rewarded with the ingathering of unnumbered souls, cleansed in His blood, forgiven by His grace, restored by His atonement, so the cheerful *"Thy will be done"* can bring us the highest joys the heavenly Father has prepared for His children.

II

HOW WE CAN SUBMIT TO THE DIVINE WILL

To be blessed by this Christian resignation you must first of all learn to know as much of the divine will as God's wisdom has revealed. You must study your Bible, the sustaining Guide for America through the dark hours of this emergency. I am not asking you to place confidence in earthly help or cure; for the blind reliance on widely heralded agencies has repeatedly betrayed our trust and steadfastly failed to meet the real needs of the masses. Scientists, even experts of great renown, have made bad guesses and aroused false hopes which have often turned to rankling disappointment. Prophets of new cults raise enthusiasm to high pitch only to fail cruelly in producing practical help. The only promises on which we can rely completely are Christ's assurances. His are the words of Heaven's truth, immovable, unchangeable, eternal. All the critical examination of the Scriptures has never produced a single false or misleading statement. If you are to find the assurance for your own life that will enable you to bear one blow after the other and still pray, *"Thy will be done,"* you must go back to God's Word, which, according to the apostle, *"is able to build you up"*!

While our age has much praise for the Bible, while American statesmen have paid lavish tribute to Holy Writ, how deplorable is the spiritual ignorance and Scriptural illiteracy shown by millions of otherwise intelligent Americans! The most powerful indictment of militarism, the most scathing denunciation of the "might-makes-right" policy, which today rules our world, is found in the Book of Nahum, only forty-seven verses, which can be read thoughtfully in six or seven minutes. I recently told a newspaper reporter that not one in a thousand St. Louisians knows this book of sacred Scriptures. And after more deliberate thought I am ready to say: Not one in ten thousand throughout the United States is personally acquainted with the teachings of that prophet. It is high time to take our Bible seriously, to study it personally, at home, in Bible classes, throughout the land. May one of the happier results of the present conflict be this that it will bring millions from coast to coast back to the divine authority of the Scriptures, so that we learn with increasing clarity what the divine will is and how earnestly our heavenly Father asks for real repentance, contrite hearts, surrendered souls, submissive lives!

After you know what God requires of us, you must turn to the Lord Jesus Christ for the salvation His mercy grants us. You can never truthfully say, "'Thy will,' not mine, 'be done!'" unless in heart-deep faith you have knelt in spirit at the cross to cry out: "He is my Savior. His blood was shed for me. His hands and feet were pierced so that I could escape the punishment of my sins. He was crowned with thorns that I, faithful unto death, might receive the crown of life. He endured agony beyond description or measure to free me for glory beyond earthly beauty and power of expression." Therefore, my fellow ransomed, for whom the Lord of life died the anguish of all death, let these Lenten weeks draw you closer to Him! Pray with us that, following the Savior from scene to scene in His suffering, many of you will accept His pleading invitation "Come unto Me!" and approach Him for pardon and the resigned peace that asks, "O Father, 'not my will, but Thine be done!'" Jesus has everything you need for the greatest joy possible in this life or the next. He offers His Gospel grace to the whole world, but in this moment especially to you. He bestows His rich blessings freely, without charge, by the sheerest mercy that even Heaven knows. God grant, as Jesus' arms are extended to you, burdened with your sins, worries, hardships, you will now resolve that, the Father helping you, the Son accompanying you, His Spirit sustaining you, you will break the tyranny of sin over your soul, dispel its gloom of fear from your life, remove the weight of worries from your heart, and say with hope-filled faith: "O Jesus, Thou art my Re-

deemer!   Nothing can happen to me as long as I am
Thine, except it come from Thy love to chasten, purify,
strengthen.   I give myself to Thee and pray, Abide with
me, bless me, make me in turn a blessing for many!"
And that Savior, whose Word is truth itself, will enrich
you with the joy of salvation, guidance for each perplexed
pathway, Christian courage in every danger, and the submissive love which constantly prays, "Not my will, but
Thine be done."

It takes a strong faith thus to resign oneself to God.
But everyone of you can find Heaven's help, as Jesus did,
in communion with the Father.   How lamentable that while
prayer should be highly prized, it is often ridiculed!   Be
sure of this, however: The time is coming, and it may not
be far distant, when millions in America will learn to pray,
when they will not have to be urged to fall on their knees
before the Almighty.   Again and again in accounts of
ships lost at sea, survivors tell us of petitions to God that
could be heard above the turmoil of disaster.   Do not wait
until danger brings you on your knees!   Beholding the
Savior in the Garden as He prayed with agonized earnestness yet with submissive trust, you are reminded that He
still wants His followers to watch and pray with Him!
Before the sleep of indifference overtakes you, kneel in
spirit beside Him and there in dark Gethsemane "learn of
Jesus Christ to pray!"

Our Lord's pleading was answered when the Father sent
a strengthening angel to attend His Son.   Our entreaties
for a deeper, fuller trust will likewise be fulfilled whenever
they are spoken in Christ's name, that is, in full reliance
on His cleansing blood and whenever we ask, "Thy will
be done!"   As Jesus could rise, fortified in spirit for the
ordeal awaiting Him, never again during His trials or the
convulsing pain of the crucifixion to plead, "Remove this

cup from Me," so you and I can emerge from the fires of affliction purified, steeled against every adversity. We can face the worst that earth or hell can direct against us with the same deep-rooted faith through which God's children have triumphantly braved all danger. Such implicit trust is still found today and in unexpected places. A Chinese missionary tells of his humble native servant, a Christian, who during an errand to the market was caught in the terrors of an air raid. The roar of the Japanese planes became louder and louder, but the servant only smiled at the terrified group locked in a store with him. When one of his heathen friends demanded: "Are you not afraid? Do you not know that all of us may be killed in two minutes?" he replied: "Why should I be afraid? I am a Christian, and God will take care of me." "But they may drop bombs upon us, and you may be killed," the others objected. Calmly he answered, "In that case I will go to heaven, and that will be even better than being here."

Therefore when the storms of disaster swirl down on your happiness, bringing sorrows you never dreamed possible, do not clench your fist against the Almighty! If the tremors of disaster shake your home and seem to destroy the foundation of your family life, do not surrender to despair or moan, "What's the use anyway, what good is my faith now?" Your health may break or accidents on the highway inflict life-long injuries; yet, though the doctor shakes his head, admitting that he knows no human cure, you must not sink into dark, sullen rebellion against the Almighty! Should death, unannounced, snatch your loved one from your side, don't charge God with cruelty! Instead, go into the Garden with Christ, and as faith triumphs over doubt, repeat the prayer that has brought happiness and help to myriads, " *'Oh, my Father,'* if it be

Thy will, Thy gracious will for my good and the blessing of others, 'remove this cup' of suffering 'from me: nevertheless,' O Father of all mercies, 'not my will,' my blind, sinful, selfish, shortsighted will, 'but Thine,' Thy holy, perfect, loving, salvation-bringing will 'be done,' both now and forever!"   And the same God who brought Jesus through Gethsemane and Calvary to the triumph of His resurrection will lead us through the small, short afflictions of life to the incomparable "glory which shall be revealed in us" because we are Christ's.

O God of all grace, hear us as we pledge ourselves anew to Thee and ask, for Jesus' sake, with His faith, and in His own words, "O Father, 'not my will, but Thine be done!'" Amen.

THE SAVIOR'S MATCHLESS MERCY

"If, therefore, ye seek Me, let these go their way!" — Saint John 18:8

Beloved Lord Jesus:

Receive our thanks for the immeasurable mercy by which Thou didst willingly, yea, eagerly, tread the path of suffering! Let Thy readiness to endure shame and anguish be a strengthening example for us when our burdens become heavy! Open our eyes first to our lost, helpless condition without Thee, but then to our assured salvation with Thee. More than ever before in these beclouded days we need the trusting faith in Thy compassion even unto the cross and the courage to take refuge in Thy never-failing love! Show us that Thou didst permit Thyself to be captured and bound so that we might be freed from the rule of sin, the tyranny of worry, the dominion of death! Save us from stubborn doubts or willful contradictions of Thy Word, and by Thy Spirit nurture within us a childlike trust in Thy mercies! Keep firm on our souls the imprint of Thy love! Fill us — and many others in our country — with true penitence and a Heaven-sent determination to walk in Thy footsteps! Grant us all a joy-instilling, life-giving faith, precious Savior, for Thou alone canst help us! Amen.

WHEN Japanese bombers last week struck heavily in northern Burma, our newspapers cited two women for "coolness and heroism." Fifty civilians had been killed and many more wounded at a railroad station; but these two women, spurning danger, helped carry the maimed to safety "from a platform slippery with blood." Tirelessly they bandaged the injured, held flashlights while surgeons operated and amputated, took charge of a school with sixty-nine children whose teacher had been blown to bits. Now, who were these heroines, and why, instead of fleeing to shelter, did they sacrifice every personal interest, risk their own lives to help the natives? Not travelers in search of adventure, not local air-raid wardens, not the mothers of the wounded, not professional nurses working in line of duty! These two fearless messengers of mercy were American missionaries of the Lord Jesus Christ, who, forsaking ease and comfort, went to the Burmese hinterland and there dedicated themselves solely to serve their fellow men in the Savior's spirit.

The annals of Christian missions are filled with countless instances of the same devotion. We shun homes placarded with "Scarlet Fever" or "Diphtheria" signs, but servants of Jesus, forgetting their own health, enter leper colonies and daily come into contact with that loathsome disease because the love of Christ constrains them. David Livingstone, invading the dangerous cannibal regions in darkest Africa; Allen Gardiner, laying down his life on the bleak shores of Patagonia; Hans Egede, fighting his way through ice floes to Greenland — these and ten thousand other missionaries following Christ's example have undergone indescribable hardships and thus given the world the high example of lives, energies, talents, wholly directed to help perishing humanity.

Our cold, cruel age cries out for such love and compassion. One of the basic conflicts today is the struggle between Christian self-sacrifice and the growing philosophy of selfish materialism. As we witness international warfare, systematic destruction, class hatred, the stubborn insistence, "Might makes right," and, "Only the fittest should survive," we ought to realize that we are far from a world in which men serve, rather than kill, each other, or nations co-operate honestly instead of competing treacherously. We want a world with the harsh caste and class systems broken down by mutual assistance among men, with the rich sustaining the poor, the learned devoting themselves to the unlettered, the powerful supporting the weak. We need homes in which the husband, in place of playing cards with his cronies night after night and spending a large part of his income purely for his personal pleasure, loves his wife and children, gladly shares everything he has with them, and ceaselessly labors for their happiness; families in which the wife understands how, in trying times like these, God expects her to make the home a haven of peace and rest for husband and children. For our own individual lives we need, not the "get-yours-while-you-can," "I'll-stick-to-my-rights" attitude, which, like murderous Cain, sneers at the thought of being our brother's keeper. We want — and our whole age pleads for this — men and women, young and old, who learn from Christ that earth's highest joy comes from serving and helping save others.

The uplifting power by which we can dedicate ourselves to our fellow men, go as missionaries into unknown and incalculable dangers, sacrifice our money, time, strength, if necessary even our lives, for the benefit of the race, comes directly or indirectly from Jesus. Therefore, to receive more of His heavenly grace, to see how He willingly offered Himself in our behalf, let us, in our second Lenten message, study

THE SAVIOR'S MATCHLESS MERCY

as this is recorded (Saint John's Gospel, chapter eighteen, verse eight) in Jesus' own words, *"If, therefore, ye seek Me, let these go their way!"*

I

HE SUFFERED WILLINGLY

Hardly had our Lord finished His pleading prayer in Gethsemane, asking that the cup of suffering be removed, yet adding, *"Not My will, but Thine, be done!"* when, strengthened by the ministering angel, He arose, divinely fortified for the ordeal awaiting Him. He clearly foresaw each separate sorrow ahead of Him: the cruelty of His arrest, the binding of His hands, the repeated trials before His own countrymen and the Roman authorities, the abuse at the hands of coarse soldiers, the mockery with purple robe, reed scepter and crown of cutting thorns, the frightful scourging, the crucifixion itself with its crushing agony, and, far more terrifying, the torture of soul and mind that He would have to endure before completely atoning for the sins of the whole world. He knew all this in advance, and it would have been easy for Him to escape under the cover of night. Within a few hours He could have hidden away in one of the secret caves high in the stony Judean highlands. But these thoughts never entered Jesus' mind. He loved us with such self-giving devotion that, banishing every suggestion of flight and personal safety, He advanced resolutely to meet the Roman soldiers and the Temple guards, come to capture Him. With a majesty men have otherwise not beheld, He stepped forward to greet the heavily armed group with the quiet question *"Whom seek ye?"*

We wonder why the soldiers failed to recognize Christ immediately. It has been suggested that perhaps the darkness in the Garden prevented their identifying Him; yet we read that they carried lamps and torches, and even in that flickering light the Savior could easily have been discerned. Most likely these men did not know Jesus. Doubtless most of the Roman soldiers had never seen Him and even the Temple guards had paid Him scant attention. Therefore they had to have Him pointed out by a faithless wretch who would betray his Master with a kiss.

Does this ignorance concerning our Lord not picture much of modern unbelief? Men arise to attack Jesus, but actually they do not know who He is. Some of the most vicious enemies of His truth are spiritually ignorant and must confess that they have never personally studied His Word. Some of you set yourselves against Christ without ever having approached Him earnestly, honestly, in an unbiased, open mind. If we were to stand at Times Square in New York City, on Michigan Boulevard in Chicago, on Market Street in San Francisco, and ask those passing on these busy thoroughfares who Christ is, we would soon discover that although more books have been written about the Savior than anyone else, although more schools have been built for His cause and more houses of worship erected to His name than have been dedicated to any other person, there is still a widespread ignorance concerning our Lord which keeps multitudes from Jesus and His salvation. If only you, the skeptical and the sworn enemies of our faith, would take time to meet Him in His Word, to learn of the rich blessings He has brought everyone, your questions of doubt would be answered and your sullen hatreds removed.

Acquaint yourself with Christ before you condemn Him! Meet Him face to face in His Word before you reject Him! Behold the Savior in the Garden, as His enemies, armed with swords and staves, encircle Him and their flaming torches light up His countenance! Though you may not have seen Jesus in this light before, look at Him there! Though you may never have known it and you now seek to contradict it, this Sufferer in Gethsemane, serene even in the face of persecutions soon to break upon Him, is far more than a victim of priestly jealousy, a target of popular hatred, a misunderstood genius, a self-sacrificing idealist. He is rather — and I call as witness the sacred Scriptures with their repeated endorsement of this truth — the Savior of the world, but especially your own Redeemer. Give Him your heart! Let Him control your life!

When the soldiers, answering the Savior's question *"Whom seek ye?"* replied, *"Jesus of Nazareth,"* and our Lord quickly answered, *"I am He!"* these few words suddenly hurled the guards to the ground. You see, then,

Christ did not need to escape. If one short sentence could cast His enemies prostrate, another sentence could have destroyed them. In Jesus there is an unseen power of God, a source of immeasurable divine strength that helps you defeat the foes of your faith. When boasting, taunting men arise to challenge the Lord, some weak Christians often wonder whether God has been defeated, whether reason has triumphed over divine revelation. Yet the same Savior who threw His adversaries on their faces can and actually does intervene today in frustrating the designs of evil men. Before God's inescapable judgment every unrepentant person who has clenched his fist against Christ and spoken words of defiant unbelief will be cast down in eternal defeat before our royal Redeemer.

Jesus not only permitted the Temple guard and the Roman soldiers to scramble to their feet; He also refused to summon for His own aid the twelve legions of angels at His beck and call, the 72,000 heavenly messengers, each capable of destroying all the armies in the world. Our Lord deliberately rejected every possibility of avoiding the cross, saving Himself from its rack and torture. For — here is matchless mercy, love such as only a divine Savior could show, grace so deep that we could not believe it, were it not the truth of Heaven itself — Jesus *wanted* to suffer. He willingly laid down His life. The salvation of a perishing world was of such supreme concern to Him that nothing could keep Him from that pathway of anguish. He saw the cross ahead, and no one will know as Jesus knew what excruciating agony Calvary meant; yet beyond the cross the blessed Savior saw you, and He loved you with such intense, heavenly self-giving that He could even glorify His Father in His suffering for the redemption of mankind.

Never has there been a compassion as magnificent as

this. We give our deep-rooted thanks to the guardians of safety, the policemen and firemen, public servants who protect us and our homes. Yet when they risk their lives, they do it in line of duty. They are paid for their services. Jesus did not have to suffer and die. We had no claim on Christ that would bring Him from the radiance of heaven to a sin-cursed earth. He had nothing to gain, humanly speaking, for Himself by being born in a stable and dying as a criminal on the cross. The only earthly payment He received was jeering ridicule, stinging sarcasm, the "*Crucify Him! Crucify Him!*" of those whom He had come to save. Yet His love for us was so endless and depthless that no mortal power could have kept Him from the cross.

We have high regard for the millions of men who have been selected for the nation's defense. They go for us, and our prayers should continually ascend to the Throne of Mercy in their behalf. Yet, while they are summoned by law, Jesus was called by love. They are drafted and go because they must; but no compulsion drove Jesus to the pathway of pain indescribable, nothing except the divine, never-to-be-fathomed compassion for our souls.

Nor was there anything haphazard about our Savior's suffering and dying. People sometimes give their lives unintentionally for others. A few years ago in Florida when an assassin's bullet, aimed at President Roosevelt, killed Mayor Cermak of Chicago, the dying man expressed his thanks that he had been struck, and not the President. No element of chance, however, nothing haphazard or accidental lingers in our Savior's anguish. Ages before you were born, He knew you and loved you with such tender, limitless affection that He would not stop short of the cross; instead, He was determined to give Himself in the mightiest sacrifice even He could make for your salvation.

Words are woefully weak in describing our Savior's incomparable mercy. He bore His never-to-be-fathomed grief willingly, moved not by duty, necessity, chance, but by the marvel and miracle of His heavenly compassion, His sacred longing to have you with Him in eternity. As we can never express the height and depth of this voluntary, self-giving love, so we can never understand why Jesus unhesitatingly yielded Himself to the shame and agony of the crucifixion for our sakes. But why try to comprehend and analyze this unconditional readiness to complete our redemption? Believe it! Trust His grace! Take Christ at His Word, and you will experience that His willingness imparts itself to your life, enriching you with a sacred readiness to suffer and serve! That is one of the supreme needs for our disquieted day, this eagerness to promote the welfare of our fellow men. If the present is disturbed and distracted, what of the future? If, as we are told, the hearts of men are being tried now, then in the question-marked tomorrow, when we begin to pay for today, the souls of men will be doubly tried in affliction's fires. This country, which, generally speaking, has enjoyed more of life's bounty while enduring far less pain than any other people on earth, may yet be brought to grips with the cold, cruel, ruthless battle for existence. In England the pinch of hunger is driving people to eat sparrows, starlings, crows. In some of the Axis-controlled territory dog meat is sold at $1.60 a pound and cats for $4.00 and up. Do not say, "That can't happen here!" Until last week many people laughed at the idea that American coasts could be bombarded. Rather ask yourself: How can I face the burdens to be imposed by the widening, lengthening war and by the perils of the aftermath? How will I learn to help my brother in the critical changes that may overtake us? Only by knowing Jesus and having the joy of His salvation in our souls!

Missionary Willis R. Hotchkiss tells us that his long search for a word to convey the idea of *Savior* in the unwritten language of a Central African tribe was finally rewarded when one of his men told how a native had been "saved" from an attacking lion. The missionary at once used that term to explain Christ's redemption, and immediately the Negro's face lighted up as he exclaimed: "I understand now! This is what you have been trying to tell us all these moons. Yesu died to save us from sin." Later, recalling the joy which illumined that black man's countenance, Missionary Hotchkiss wrote: "I have dwelt four years practically alone in Africa. I have been thirty times smitten with the fever, three times attacked by lions, several times by rhinoceroses, a number of times ambushed by the natives. For four months I never saw a piece of bread, and I have eaten everything from ants to rhinoceroses. But let me say to you: I would gladly go through the whole thing once more if I could again witness the joy of having the word *Savior* flash out in the darkness that envelopes another tribe in Central Africa." In much the same way, come what may, if you study the Lord's holy eagerness to suffer for you, His spirit of self-giving will be transplanted into your soul and show itself in your willingness to serve, work, pray for the bodily and spiritual help of your fellow men, even your enemies.

II

HE SUFFERED FOR OUR FREEDOM

The Savior's mercy is matchless also because His suffering brings us freedom and salvation. We might think that at His betrayal and before His capture Jesus would be so engrossed in His own pain, so terrified by the thought of His impending crucifixion, that there in the Garden, before being taken captive by the Roman legionaries, His

thoughts would center in His own shattering sorrows.
Some people continually bemoan their aches and pains,
though their troubles are small and sometimes insignificant.
How different Jesus! Here in Gethsemane He forgot His
approaching torture in His deep concern over His disciples.
Unless He intervened, they, too, might be captured; and
if He were sentenced to death, the eleven might have to
share His fate. If these disciples were destroyed, what
would become of the Church? So at the very first clash
with His enemies Jesus voices no appeal for Himself; He
pleads for His followers. In the spirit of the Scriptural
warning *"Touch not Mine anointed, and do My prophets
no harm!"* He faces His persecutors squarely and says,
"If, therefore, ye seek Me, let these go their way!" He is
willing to endure the most excruciating pain that degenerate
men could invent; His disciples, however, must be spared.
Similarly throughout His entire suffering He showed deep
personal anxiety for those who had accepted Him as their
Savior. The whole torture of Gethsemane, Gabbatha, and
Golgotha was in our behalf, to liberate everyone who would
accept His mercy from the tyranny of sin, sorrow, hell,
despair, and death itself.

True, there have been martyrs who lived and died for
their fellow men. "He laid down his life for others" was
the headline of a London paper which recorded the tragic
death of Captain L. Oates, member of the ill-fated Scott
expedition to the Antarctic. He was one of the five who
got through to the South Pole in 1912, but eighteen weeks
later, after constant exposure to snow and ice, he was so
severely frostbitten that he could make only a short distance
each day. His brave comrades refused to desert him, but
Captain Oates knew that food and fuel were becoming
scarcer with every hour and that if his four friends were
kept back by his slow progress, they would all die. So

one day, without warning, he staggered out of the tent, declaring, "I am just going outside, and I may be gone some time." The blizzard howled as he closed the door, and he walked out into the frozen, lifeless Antarctic waste with this one purpose: he would freeze to death and let the snowdrifts cover his body so that his companions, unhindered by his weakness, could be saved. Even this self-sacrifice could not rescue the others. As their diary, discovered later, showed, they struggled on for almost two weeks and died only eleven miles from the depot where a ton of food and quantities of fuel awaited them. But Jesus never fails, He does far more than lead those who trust Him close to the glories of heaven. He brings them, by His mercy and might, into their prepared place.

We can well understand why people love their own family, their friends, those who have helped them; why Christians desire the good, beautiful, clean; yet how can we explain that Jesus loved us when we hated Him, when our sins insulted Him, our unbelief wounded Him, our transgressions sent Him to the cross? The Scriptures tell us, not while we were good, virtuous, pure Christ gave Himself for us, but *"while we were yet sinners, Christ died for us,"* for every transgressor, including especially also those who have dropped to life's lowest levels, who are shunned by polite society or regarded as outcasts even by criminals. It is a miracle of grace that Jesus loved Judas and would have restrained him from his suicidal course. Far greater wonder, however, than His choosing one who afterward became unfaithful, greedy, gold-loving, is the fact that in His glorious grace He chose you and me, that through faith we may point to the Savior and say: "He loved me despite my ingratitude, my unworthiness, my stubborn pride, my carnal mind. He loved me and — oh, mercy without measure! — gave Himself for me."

The Savior who pleaded for His disciples in the Garden went all the way to the cross for them and their salvation. *"Having loved His own, which were in the world, He loved them unto the end,"* the heart-breaking, soul-crushing end at Calvary. His burden might become heavier, the cruelty He endured deeper, the blasphemy more shocking, yet His Savior-love never wavered. Many women who have suffered pain and abuse at the hands of a brutal husband or who have been the victims of repeated unfaithfulness write: "My husband killed something in me. I can't love him any more." But the entire sins of a wicked world could not kill the Savior's devotion to us. Unfaithful, ungrateful though we have been, He shed His blood to prove His divine, unchanging, unending affection.

What radiant reassurance that the Christ of the Garden, now no longer weak and wan from his wrestling with the powers of darkness but glorified in heavenly strength, loves us with the same intensity today! When dangers combine to overwhelm us, He can intervene with His divine authority and power to declare: *"Let these,"* My disciples, *"go!"* If you who are Christ's could only understand from how many dangers He has protected you, your life would be a continuous hymn of praise. Day and night, at home and work, His guardian love has shielded you. It will be of surpassing comfort for you parents who give your Christian sons for the nation's defense, to have the assurance that if your dear ones face death, the same Savior can, if it be His will, divert the bullets, shells, bombs, torpedoes, and say, *"Let these,"* My children, *"go!"* After the war — and, O God, we pray, let it end soon, with a just peace and a victory that will not sow the seeds of even more bloodshed! — the veterans of this second world struggle will cite thousands of instances in which the Savior intervened to push aside what seemed sure, inescapable destruction.

Especially in the spiritual realm do the words Jesus spoke in the Garden find their fullest application. Every time your conscience seeks to accuse you and to whisper into your ears, "You are marked by sin; you have broken God's will; there is no pardon or peace for you!" you can turn to Christ and, believing that His blood *"cleanseth us from all sin,"* find Him standing at your side to repel your doubts and weaknesses, to answer Satan's whispering with the majestic, "Let this child of Mine go!"

Should worries seek to embitter us and we grope about, unable to find a way out of our perplexities, what better can we do than approach the Lord Jesus with the confidence that as He restrained His enemies in the Garden, so He can banish everything which would destroy our happiness and teach us to cast all our cares on Him. This is the promise of His Word, *"He careth for you."* Even when the last, the most destructive of adversaries seems to gloat confidently as death prepares to call us from the land of the living, the triumph of the grave will be only momentary for those who believe in Jesus Christ and the power of His resurrection. They rely on Him, the Lord of life and eternity, who commands the forces of hell and eternal darkness: *"Let these,"* My believers, My faithful, *"go,"* for He promises, *"If a man keep My saying, he shall never see death."*

This matchless mercy is offered freely, without payment or price, without any contribution or credential, only by His unrestricted, unlimited love. Do you really know what Christ's full and unconditional grace means? Think of the debt which our iniquities have heaped up with the Almighty, the sins that started apparently small and insignificant but soon led to complications and tragic developments, the transgressions for which we could never pay were the whole world ours! In this overwhelming indebtedness Jesus comes with His mercy. Unlike the procedure of modern business, His Gospel does not try to make a settlement with us by having us pay so much on the dollar, but He takes the total charges of our indebtedness, marks them, "Paid in full by faith in My atonement"; and, just as in the Oriental world when an account was settled, it was nailed to the debtor's door, proving publicly that the creditor was satisfied, so Jesus nailed the handwriting to the cross to show the world that every sin of every sinner has been fully paid by the only payment which God would accept: the Savior's precious blood.

You see, then, why the grace of Christ is matchless; but you can also realize why this love and its liberty must be proclaimed throughout the land. The supreme task of the Church, amid the multiple projects clamoring for its support, is to help reveal the crucified Christ as the divine Redeemer of our race, the most considerate Friend of the outcast, the highest Example of unfailing, tender mercy.

A few days ago 3,000 school administrators met in San Francisco to consider the nation's needs. One speaker asked our people to stop attending night clubs and ruining their health with late hours and drinking. We heartily endorse this request, but temperance and more sleep alone will not remove this crisis. — A Federal school official at this convention said, "Education must give us the means to defend ourselves against tricksters and tyrants." Nevertheless, it has often been education that has equipped the tricksters and tyrants. A crude, uncultured criminal can start a street brawl or a gang fight, while an intelligent, well-read criminal can throw his country or the whole world into turmoil. We need far more than culture. This war did not start among barbarous, primitive tribes, the Bushmen, Kafirs, Hottentots, Igorrotes, head-hunters of Borneo, the Pygmies or the giant savages of Africa, but among the mechanically, scientifically most advanced peoples. Last week one of the world's leading literary figures and his wife committed suicide. The letters they both left behind showed that they were unwilling to bear the hardships of life; yet true Christians with resigned trust accept whatever God ordains as good. Another speaker at the San Francisco meeting declared, "America needs character education," and claimed that the United States has entered this war with "perhaps the lowest moral standards in its history." But how are we to build character? How, indeed, unless we *"let this mind be in"* us *"which was also in Christ Jesus,"* and, reborn by faith, follow in the Savior's footsteps.

We hear much in these days of the Singapore spirit, the deadly inertia responsible for the quick fall of the $400,000,000 fortification. A former resident of the city gives this explanation: The people continued with their parties and dancing until the very last. The climate, the easy, luxurious life, the laziness of the people, combined to undermine the morale and make Singapore's capture easy. "It was just parties, bridge, dancing," the wife of the previous commander summarized. — Do you know that there is a Singapore mind in the religious life of many American people? They refuse to be aroused by the dangers threatening their souls. They go on straight to the greatest of all disasters — the loss of their salvation, the surrender to the enemies of God.

To avoid that, to be blessed eternally by the Savior's blood-bought redemption, accept the Lord Jesus Christ now as your own individual, personal Savior! Have Him speak the peace of forgiven sin and the promise of new life to your heart, and at the cross you will find a joy that many of you have never known before! Put Christ into your homes! As your tires wear out and gasoline is rationed, bring blessing on your stay-at-home evenings by restoring the old family Bible to its proper place, re-establishing the family altar and the Christian home ideals! Assist in spreading the kingdom of Christ here in our own country! If there is anything we can say or do that would bring you or your home closer to Jesus, let me now in the Savior's name offer you our services or the counsel of thousands of Gospel ministers who, completely united with me in faith, will travel many miles, if necessary, to point you to His marvelous grace. Write me now, while the Spirit moves you! Standing at your side, Jesus will face all the accusations of sin that would keep you from Him, the inner doubts which make you question His grace, the hardships or the temptations pulling you from His outstretched arms, the threats of hell itself. With majestic, victorious power He will command, " 'Let My servant go' — into the blessings of faith now and into the glories of heaven hereafter!" God grant that Christ's matchless mercy will thus bring you to salvation! Amen.

———————

CHRIST'S CHALLENGE TO SEVENTY MILLION AMERICAN UNBELIEVERS

> *"When He had thus spoken, one of the officers which stood by struck Jesus with the palm of his hand, saying, Answerest Thou the high priest so? Jesus answered him, If I have spoken evil, bear witness of the evil: but if well, why smitest thou Me?"* — Saint John 18:22, 23

Jesus, Merciful Savior of Our Souls:

Help us testify to millions that Thou, our heavenly Redeemer, canst cleanse from all impurities everyone who trusts Thee! Give us whatever else Thy mercy may decree; but, O Christ of endless compassion, grant us Thy saving grace! Destroy our pride, our love for self, our indifference toward the suffering of others, our unclean impulses and desires! Lead us to confess our many, repeated transgressions and to cry, "If Thou, Lord, shouldest mark iniquities, O Lord, who shall stand?" Strengthen us also to believe assuredly that, cleansed by faith in Thine atoning blood, we can face our heavenly Father and hear Him speak pardon and peace to our souls! Send the Spirit to stir us into flame and enrich us with an intense eagerness to serve Thee! May we proclaim Thy name courageously and confidently challenge those who attack Thee! Make the masses of this country repentant, so that Thou canst look on us with Thy favor, and soon grant us a blessed, building peace! Be with all the distressed throughout the land and bring many sorrow-laden, grief-stricken sinners and sufferers to Thy comforting, saving, sustaining love! Amen.

"TOO little and too late!" once more is the reason for startling military losses. Yesterday Manila, Singapore, Batavia; tomorrow Rangoon and perhaps other pivotal cities — all lost because of poor preparation, too little planning, and help too late for victory.

"Too little and too late!" also accounts for reverses which many churches suffer: Too little Gospel — too late in applying its power! Whatever the outcome of the war, however long the struggle, whichever degree of victory is ours, this much seems certain: Atheism and unbelief will find in the postwar upheaval fertile fields where the seeds of discontent may be sown freely. Each international conflict has been followed by a period of restlessness and revolt; and the present hostilities, mightiest of all, may be succeeded by the most destructive consequences. After the American Revolution crime and irreligion increased. Colleges surrendered to skepticism and the ridicule of the Christian faith. If 150 years ago the follies of the French Revolution made slow but sure progress across the Atlantic to our country, then in this age of quick communication, radio, cable, clipper, superspeed liners, we can expect the denial of God, now widely spread through Europe, to find its way swiftly into many discontented lives on our shores. We are constantly being warned that the American people must accept a lower standard of living: For civilians, no more automobiles, tires, typewriters, radios, no more unlimited supplies of a thousand other commodities, at least during the war; and at the same time increased taxes, higher prices. Christians — for they love this signally endowed nation — can bear up under these restrictions, and they are willing to forego more than cuffs of their trousers, the pleats on their dresses, and the second spoonful of sugar. There are others, however, who, unwilling to make the real sacrifices required for patient, painstaking rebuilding, will be easily won by the agitators, the Red revolutionists who cry out: "Cancel all debts!" "Make all people financially equal!" "Destroy the right of private property!" "Down with the Church!"

In our present emergency, therefore, when millions look to our Christian faith for spiritual defense, the churches must purify and prepare themselves as never before. We must have houses of God in which the preaching of Heaven's Law and Christ's Gospel are not pushed aside by dances, plays, theatricals, even gambling. Neither is there any hope in congregations that neglect sound doctrine, appeal chiefly to the emotions, agree to disregard differences and join in a union which is outwardly impressive, yet unacceptable to God, since it is built on the denial of divine truth. We must pray for true Christian unity, of course — and I hope you do — asking the Holy Spirit to bless and guide all who acclaim the Bible as God's infallible Word and bring them together in complete doctrinal agreement. The churches which are to be the salt of the earth in a day of spiritual decay should be 100 per cent loyal to Christ and His Word, courageous, outspoken, militant, seeking to please God rather than men; churches that do not ask whether the world offers its applause, but first of all whether the preacher sees eye to eye with the Lord Jesus Christ; pulpits which, while telling all men that without Christ there is no hope for a blessed eternity, warn the sinner of his evil ways and relentlessly attack unbelief.

In this respect Jesus has been a divine Pattern for us. There was nothing evasive or compromising in His words, and He could not be intimidated. As we pledge ourselves anew to follow His example and repel every assault on the Gospel, we employ this third Lenten devotion formally to issue

CHRIST'S CHALLENGE TO SEVENTY MILLION AMERICAN UNBELIEVERS

We find this suggested in the words of Saint John (chapter eighteen, verses twenty-two and twenty-three): *"When He had thus spoken, one of the officers which stood by struck Jesus with the palm of his hand, saying, Answerest Thou the high priest so? Jesus answered him, If I have spoken evil, bear witness of the evil: but if well, why smitest thou Me?"*

I

CHRIST CHALLENGES, "HAVE I EVER 'SPOKEN EVIL'?"

After Jesus had permitted Himself to be taken captive in the Garden, He was bound and led first to Annas, probably the most influential figure in the religious life at Jerusalem. For six or seven years he had been the high priest, the representative of God to His people. When he had been deposed by the Roman governor, five of his sons, his son-in-law Caiaphas, and one of his grandsons were successively installed in that exalted office. He was immensely wealthy and received a large income through the sales at the Temple booths. At the same time he was a Sadducee, who openly denied the resurrection and otherwise paid little attention to doctrine. How he hated Jesus for cleansing the Temple, thus interfering with his revenue! How determined he was to destroy the Savior! — Today, too, the most brutal attack on the Christ of the Scriptures comes from the clergy itself, from Modernists who occupy top positions in their denomination, the twentieth-century Sadducees who under the guise of religion traitorously attack the Savior.

Annas began by cross-examining Jesus in regard to His disciples. If the Savior Himself would reveal the names of those who had followed Him and preached His doctrine, they could be captured and sentenced with Him. Oh, how faithful Jesus' love! Although every disciple had shamefully deserted Him despite the promise of loyalty, He did not forsake them; He refused to answer Annas' question. He could have assumed a friendly, ingratiating attitude to win His liberty; but He spurned every thought of currying favor and even withheld a reply to some of Annas' inquiries. May our heavenly Father give us the courage to follow Christ in defying the foes of our faith! Because God is on their side, Christians dare not be timid, apologetic, servile. There are times when we must be defiant, and for those moments may God infuse us with heroic resistance! We need much more of the courageous spirit that lived, for example, in Polycarp of Smyrna: When told by the Roman governor that unless he denied Christ, he would be banished, the venerable patriarch replied, "You cannot banish me, for I am at home wherever Christ is." The chagrined official continued, "I will take away your property." Polycarp responded, "I have none; if I had, and you took it away, I would still be rich, for I have Christ." His captor warned, "I will take away your good name." That hero of the faith answered, "It is gone already, for I have long since reckoned it a great joy to be counted the offscouring of all things for Christ's sake." "I will put you in prison," the Roman ruler threatened, only to be told, "You may do so if you please, but I shall always be free, for where Christ is, there is perfect liberty." "I shall take away your life," the governor concluded, but Polycarp triumphed, "Then I shall be in heaven, which is the truest life." Ignatius, first-century martyr, cried out: "Come fire, come cross and crowds of wild beasts; come tearing, rending, and breaking of my bones; come the mutilation of my members and the shattering of my whole body and all the torments of the devil! I would rather die for Christ than rule the world."

When Annas continued to examine Jesus concerning His teachings, our Lord once more refused to respond directly, declaring: *"In secret have I said nothing. Why askest thou Me? Ask them which heard Me!"* Had the high priest been a poor, contrite, groping sinner, eagerly seeking the way to God, how carefully, lovingly Jesus would have explained His Gospel, answered every question, outlined the whole plan of salvation; for — let this be your comfort! — no sincere inquirer after divine truth can be too lowly and despised to be welcomed, instructed, strengthened by the patient Redeemer, who loves the humble and the penitent. But let this serve as a warning: No one, not even powerful Annas, the man who ran religious affairs in Jerusalem, can be high and imposing enough to secure Christ's consideration if he is moved merely by curiosity, or, worse, by a desire to destroy His Church.

The Savior's protest, *"In secret have I said nothing,"* shows how open, honest, undisguised His truth is. Millions are attracted to secret organizations and occult creeds with mysterious rites and ceremonies, undercover oaths, passwords and privileges only for the initiated. But Christ's Gospel is as opposed to all this as the brightness of day to the utter darkness of night. Jesus has nothing to conceal but everything to reveal. It is necessary, of course, that our soldiers and sailors guard military and naval secrets. Billboards throughout the nation remind us how dangerous it is even for commonplace information to fall into enemy hands. Yet because the Gospel is dedicated to save men's souls rather than destroy their lives, Jesus wants us who know His grace to proclaim the promise of His love. He still declares, *"Ask them which heard Me!"*

Now comes one of the most brutal scenes in our Savior's entire suffering. One of the Temple servants, turning sharply to Christ and demanding, *"Answerest Thou the high priest so?"* struck Jesus a heavy blow. Henry Martyn, missionary among the Mohammedans, tells us that when he was translating the New Testament into the Persian language a native lad, reading this passage for the first time and inwardly shaken over this blasphemy, asked, "Sir, did not his hand dry up?" We, too, often wonder how the innocent, stainless Son of God could endure such brutal treatment without striking His assailant dead on the spot. Christ, however, had thoughts only of love and life, not of hatred and destruction. Even that soldier, guilty of the most terrifying sins, could have found forgiveness in the Savior's unlimited grace, just as His arms are never closed when you approach Him penitently, however black and blatant your unbelief may have been.

Instead of threatening or cursing the man who struck Him, Jesus looked Him squarely in the face and said, *"If I have spoken evil, bear witness of the evil."* Had that soldier taken time to ask himself: "After all, why have they made this Nazarene a prisoner? What is His offense?" he would have come to the same conclusion — had he been fair and open-minded — which Pilate reached when He pronounced Jesus innocent in the verdict, *"I find in Him no fault at all."*

This challenge *"If I have spoken evil, bear witness of the evil!"* is directed to all unbelievers today and now particularly to the seventy million Christless people within our shores. I deliberately ask any individual or organized group to produce evidence of a single destructive action or teaching in our Lord's life. Since the days when His enemies stooped to perjury and false witness, the opponents of our faith have always used fraud and lies to discredit Christianity. A renowned scientist, seeking to heap ridicule on the Biblical doctrine that man was created by God, actually manufactured spurious evidence for his assault on the Scriptures — only to have his dishonesty and duplicity exposed. From the first century, when Jesus' followers were branded as enemies of the State, Christ's creed has been maliciously attacked, His utterances misquoted, His meaning misinterpreted, His love willfully misunderstood. The New Testament has been fine-combed by hostile critics seeking to accuse our Lord of inaccuracies. Every word He spoke has been examined and cross-examined by experts as no other utterances in history, all in the hope that some flaw or contradiction might be uncovered. Yet with millions of dollars spent in assailing Jesus, long years devoted to discredit His Word, the truth of Scripture has been repeatedly confirmed by archaeological research.

Confident that our Bible is God's own errorless verity, we demand of those who oppose Jesus, "If He has *spoken evil, bear witness of the evil!*" Is there anything wrong with the Savior's teaching that He is the Son of God? In this age of broken promises, who would want to rely on man's word, when Christ as our Lord offers heaven's unbreakable truth? On the day after last Christmas the British public was told by an acclaimed orator, "Sure I am, we are the masters of our fate." But it has well been pointed out that we are not the masters even of our feet, since the Scriptures assert, *"A man's heart deviseth his way: but the Lord directeth his steps."* Particularly during the uncertainties of war, American Christians want the divine Christ in control of their fate, the heavenly Ruler of their destiny.

Is there anything *"evil"* in the Savior's love which led Him from celestial radiance to an earth encrusted with sin, greed, hatred, that He might become one of us, yet without sin, and give His life as the Ransom, the Atonement, the Forgiveness for iniquity?

Is there anything *"evil"* in the glorious Gospel promise that *"God was in Christ reconciling the world unto Himself?"* Does our hate-ridden, strife-burdened age not plead for a compassion like Christ's which offers the inner peace of pardon to all men, including the lowliest and most despised?

Is there anything *"evil"* in the magnificent mercy by which Jesus forgives, without any payment whatever? Think of the startling, constantly growing indebtedness sin heaps up against every one of us! A few days ago, the newspapers reported, a drug clerk claimed that in 1929 when he was discharged, the company owed him $8.96. Now, in 1942, only thirteen years later, this amount, through penalties, unpaid back salaries, compound interest, has become $18,720; and his lawyer is appealing to the courts that this large sum be awarded his client. With the increasing indebtedness of our transgressions unspeakably greater, what objection can you have to a Redeemer who has wiped out all charges against us, whose Word pledges, *"By grace are ye saved, through faith, and that not of yourselves"*?

Is there any *"evil"* in the bounty by which Jesus offers His love and help to those staggering under the burden of care and worry? Do you find fault with our Lord because of the guidance He offers during life's dangerous moments? One of our Lutheran young men who gave up a university career to enter the United States Army Air Corps writes: "Last Monday I took off from the field, and after gaining an altitude of about seventy-five feet, my plane's left wheel came off. For an hour and a half I circled the field, preparing to land. At the same time preparations were made on the ground for a crash. Thanks be to God, I was able to land safely on one wheel, damaging the plane only slightly. During the entire incident I was able to remain calm only through and because of my entire trust in God." Why do you unbelievers want to take away that trust, and what will you give us in place of this divine guidance by Christ? The fatalists claim: Everything happens by luck, good or bad; life is only a series of accidents, men the weak creatures of chance. — You can have this if you want it, but in hours of desperate need, when human power proves its pitiable weakness, you will scream for a divine refuge.

Is there anything *"evil"* in Christ's teaching concerning

the home, business, government? Which of these does the nation need today, the Savior's code of family ethics with husband and wife bound together by undying love and self-sacrificing devotion, with marriage a holy, blessed, life-long union, and children welcomed as the gifts of God's goodness — or the destructive theory that matrimony is only an arrangement of convenience and pleasure, to be broken when these ends are no longer served? What does our country require in this crisis? The Christian idea of business and labor as a service, as an expression of Jesus' Golden Rule, *"As ye would that men should do to you, do ye also to them likewise,"* or capitalists and laborers striving to secure the highest possible prices, income or wages, while millions of young military men risk their lives at hardly ten dollars a week? Do we want the Christian type of patriotism which is wholeheartedly *"subject to the powers that be,"* yet at the same time prays God soon to give the world a real, righteous peace — or the spirit of a St. Louis woman quoted as declaring that she hoped the war would last for years, since both she and her husband were enjoying the highest salaries they had ever received?

Above all, is there *"evil"* in Christ's teaching concerning death and the promise of a glorious resurrection, a life beyond the grave, a radiant existence with fullest compensation for earth's tears, sweat, and blood, its sorrow, pain, and toil, a heaven where the wrongs of earth will be righted? How can anyone except those with a diseased mind kick this crutch of hope from beneath staggering men and women with the claim man dies like a dog and his personality, his thoughts, his being are destroyed forever with his last breath? A few days ago newspapers carried the account of a Memphis man, thirty-six years old, doomed to die of cancer within a few months. Through an Associated Press dispatch he asks for counsel as to how these last weeks of his earthly life should be spent. Probably he will receive hundreds of suggestions, directing him to *"eat, drink, and be merry"* before he is wrapped in the silence and destruction of the grave. I have wired that man and now tell him: "You have one supreme duty as your end approaches. You must prepare to meet your Maker. None of us can see God in our sins, yet by faith in Christ, His Son, the Savior of the world, our transgressions have been completely removed. Accept Jesus now as your Redeemer, and He will help you bear your pain, strengthen you in the hour of your departure and receive you in the heavenly mansions where there will be no more cancer, no more suffering, no more death! Put your whole trust in this Christ, and these last months of your life can be your happiest! Enjoy all the good things God still gives you and do not fear the end! Christ has destroyed death. Your Christian fortitude may help bring others to the Lord. Your Christian endurance can preach powerful sermons. Faithful unto death, you can be assured of the crown of eternal life." I ask you: What can unbelief give this afflicted man that is comparable to the Savior's pledge of eternal life?

Today, as we point to our captive Savior, defying the unbelief of His day, *"If I have done evil, bear witness of the evil!"* we repeat that challenge publicly by asking any unbeliever, Modernist, Christ-denier, atheist, skeptic, scoffer (your letters, particularly the anonymous communications, prove that many of you listen in) to send me a single instance of evil in the words of our Lord, and in turn I will read any real charge or indictment of Christ over this coast-to-coast broadcasting system. At the same time, however, let me enlarge this challenge and ask: If you remove Jesus as the Savior of the world, whom will you follow in His stead? Karl Marx, with his atheistic Communism that stands clearly condemned in its immoral consequences? Voltaire, who was a deceitful, immoral sophisticate? Once when he tried to versify the Fifty-first Psalm, that great penitential outpouring of David's soul, everything went well till the French radical came to the words, *"Create in me a clean heart, O God!"* Then terror seized him, his body shook, his pen refused to move at the dictates of his hand, and his mind was so disturbed that even later he could not recall this incident without a feeling of gnawing uneasiness. What will you substitute for the Savior's mercy and love at a time when the world is bleeding from ten thousand wounds? What will you offer in place of Christ's widespread charity? We have forty-seven hospitals in St. Louis — Lutheran, Baptist, Methodist, Roman Catholic, Episcopal, and others. We have dozens of orphanages, old folks' homes, convalescent sanatoria, and similar institutions erected by the churches or by civic funds which directly or indirectly have come from the impulses of God's Word. But nowhere in the whole city, as far as I know, is there a single charitable institution erected by atheists or agnostics.

II

JESUS CHALLENGES, "WHY SMITEST THOU ME?"

That servant in the palace of Annas could not point to anything evil in Christ's words or in His life, nor could he answer the Savior's further question *"If I have spoken well, why smitest thou Me?"* Probably the misguided soldier struck Jesus in order to secure the high priest's favor, just as some of you have thought you could advance yourselves by turning from Jesus, denying the Lord of your childhood and youth. Like Judas, you have sold your souls for money, or, like Peter, you have become unfaithful because you could not stand the ridicule of unbelievers. Still others have been coaxed from Christ because, swayed by blind infatuation, you married someone in whose heart and life the Savior plays no part. For a dozen different reasons your fists are clenched against Jesus. He condemns sin; you love it. He warns against the lusts of the flesh; you want to follow them. He asks humility, self-denial, self-sacrifice; but you are proud, unbending, selfish. So you try to push His love aside, claiming that Christianity is contrary to reason and spurned by all brilliant minds. Yet some of the world's mightiest intellects have acclaimed the captive, scourged, crucified Christ their Savior. Notable in the history of the sciences is the work of Michael Faraday. On one occasion, after a brilliant lecture on magnetical electricity, he performed an astonishing experiment that brought long, thunderous applause from the distinguished audience. Then the Prince of Wales, later King of England, proposed that official congratulations be extended to Faraday. The motion was seconded and carried as applause again rocked the hall. After the handclapping subsided, the celebrated scientist had vanished. Later it was revealed that he was the elder of a small church which had only twenty members on its roll. The evening on which Faraday gave the remarkable lecture was the time for the midweek service, a meeting he never neglected, and while the applause re-echoed through the crowded hall, he had hastened, unnoticed, to worship his Christ in prayer. If you will take time to meet your Savior, to have His Spirit convince you of sin's great curse yet of Christ's greater grace, you, too, will know the Lord is the highest Wisdom. Go back to the Bible, the divine Word, *"which is able to build you up"*!

Terrifying beyond words are the consequences of denying or striking that innocent Savior. The whole high priesthood in royal Jerusalem was soon wiped out completely. The city which crucified Jesus was visited with such widespread destruction that the Roman conquerors under Titus could not find enough timber on which to nail the rebellious citizens. The whole land of Palestine, blessed as no other spot on earth because Christ taught and preached within its borders, seems to have been blasted by divine wrath, overlaid with a heavy penalty. Similarly, no people has ever permanently prospered that has risen up against the Lord Jesus. We must take note of that truth in our country and counteract every anti-Christian influence arising in our schools, our homes, in the affairs of our Government, and even in our churches. This is the hour for the most striking testimony to Christ this country has ever known.

Even more, now is the time for some of you, enemies of the Savior, to accept Him as your own Deliverer from death. It is His promise that *"Him that cometh to Me I will in no wise cast out."* However destructive and damnable your past sins may have been, however defeated your life, that scourged, crucified, bleeding, dying Redeemer has thoughts of compassion especially for you. With your wartime needs and wants, above all, your sins of unbelief and rejection that place you side by side with the soldier who struck Christ, the Savior of surpassing love asks you to make Him yours in an eternal unity that neither battle's horror nor prosperity's temptation can ever destroy.

Blessed by that Savior, your faith and life should continually bear witness that He *"hath done all things well."* You will know in an exalted confidence that the Lord Jesus Christ, whom we have beheld in His Lenten suffering as the persecuted, beaten Victim of man's hatred, is, in God's own truth, the Savior with matchless mercy, with free forgiveness for every transgression, almighty help in every weakness, divine comfort for life's most crushing sorrows, the unfailing Guide from earth to heaven's hallowed glory. May every hand clenched against Him or lifted to strike Him, now be raised in the oath of loyalty! May you with firm-founded faith declare: O my crucified Savior, accept me, despite all my sins, frailties, selfishness! Wash me, purify me, through the cleansing power of Thy blood! With Thy help I promise to bear witness to the world that Thou art holy and perfect, my Lord, my Redeemer, my King. Amen.

JESUS, SAVIOR, KING OF KINGS

> *"Pilate therefore said unto Him, Art Thou a King then? Jesus answered, Thou sayest that I am a King!"* — Saint John 18:37

Christatom, Our King:

Give us the grace to believe that despite the shame and sorrow Thou didst endure for us under Pontius Pilate and in the agonies of Thy crucifixion Thou art our Lord, the Sovereign of our souls, the heavenly King of power, grace, and glory! Enrich us with a deep-rooted desire to seek first of all Thy kingdom! May we daily come before Thee for pardon of our sins, strength against our weaknesses, courage in our afflictions, believing that Thou didst shed Thy blood for us and die on the cross the death which brings us life! Increase our loyalty, help us withstand the many temptations which would lead us to a Judaslike betrayal of Thy love! In beseeching Thy blessings on us, we also ask Thy benediction on our beloved nation and its armed forces. Particularly do we entreat Thee to protect all Christian young men called to the colors, who daily meet danger as they battle on our behalf! Show them that they fight not only against treacherous enemies from without, but also against ruthless forces from within; and that in a courageous faith they have promise, power, and victory! Abide with us, O divine Redeemer, and remove not Thy mercies from us! Amen.

"THE King is deposed!" "The Czar is murdered!" "The Kaiser is in flight!" "The Emperor will abdicate!" "The Queen goes into exile!" "The Sultan has been dethroned!" — How often have similar cries resounded during the last twenty-five years, the age that saw more thrones topple, more crowns removed, more kingdoms destroyed than any previous quarter century! After the first World War fifteen supreme rulers of as many nations were ousted, and during this second struggle eleven monarchs have already been captured, exiled, or stripped of their power. Excepting the quisling puppets and the native potentates of India and Africa, only England, Sweden, Italy, Japan still acclaim their own sovereigns, and some

[298]

of these may disappear when the conflict is over. Royalty is on the way out.

Who knows what will take its place in the totally new world order before us? If this war keeps on for years and nations are bankrupt, there will be a wide swing toward atheistic Communism, with its massacres and brutality, or toward totalitarianism, with its racial persecution and regimentation. While we ought daily to beseech God for a true and just peace, this generation, if it remains unrepentant and hostile to God, must be prepared for national upheavals, restricted liberties, and increased human suffering. When the masses are hungry, destitute, unemployed; when they see that while a privileged few have profiteered, they have lost their savings, their homes, their sons in battle, they will be ready for the overthrow of any government that has brought such misery to them. They will listen to any agitator who promises food, shelter, clothing, work. If the past twenty-five years have produced startling political changes, must the world, particularly the defeated nations, not expect mob rule, violence, and anarchy?

Yet one kingdom cannot change or suffer defeat by the mightiest armies or navies. One and only one realm will remain universal, all-victorious. That dominion, my fellow redeemed, is the empire of Jesus Christ, Lord of lords, Sovereign of sovereigns. Because He, the almighty, ever-merciful Savior, must reign supreme in your heart if you are to have pardon for your sins, peace for your mind, comfort in darkest sorrows, joy during the bitterest moments, life even in death; because Christ, the Ruler of the universe, alone can offer the true guidance, protection, help, and strength which this battered, baffled age needs, hear Him today, in this fourth Lenten meditation, when in answer to Pilate's question, *"Art Thou a King then?"*

He replies (Saint John, chapter eighteen, verse thirty-seven), *"Thou sayest that I am a King!"* and then, kneeling in spirit before Him as your Lord and your God, acclaim Him

JESUS, SAVIOR, KING OF KINGS!

Ask Him, "Come, Redeemer, reign victorious in our hearts, our homes, our churches, our country! Yes, reign triumphant throughout the world!"

I

JESUS *IS* THE KING OF KINGS

Early on Friday morning, probably between six and seven o'clock, our Savior's countrymen brought Him to the Roman governor, who alone could pronounce the death sentence. What perverted zeal! What satanic eagerness! Jesus had done nothing but good. Throughout the land He had healed the sick, fed the hungry, comforted the sorrowing, raised the dead. Yet the leaders of His people could not rise early enough to destroy Him. What if the Jewish codes of civil laws completely ruled out as illegal every trial by night? What if their court regulations expressly stated that a trial with death as the penalty could not be concluded in a single day? Law or no law, these religious dictators at Jerusalem, already guilty of bribery, perjury, and a brazen disregard of their own criminal procedure, now dragged the Lord Jesus, ridiculed and tortured during a sleepless night of peril, before the Roman governor, telling themselves all the while that they were doing the divine will.

Since that Friday morning men and women have repeatedly sought to justify the most dastardly actions by appealing to the Church for endorsement. During the Crusades misguided masses under fanatical leaders thought they were obeying God's instruction when they ran their sword through a Mohammedan or beheaded a Jew. Nor have we shaken off that spirit entirely. The cloak of religion is still used to cover plain, unmistakable lawbreaking. Even in some smaller issues of modern life, the misdirected notion persists that wrong becomes right when practiced by church groups. City regulations condemn bingo, bunco, and games of chance; but spin roulette wheels in the name of religion, raffle an automobile for the benefit of a parish, and often the police will help protect a public vice as a religious virtue.

What a terrifying spectacle to behold officials of the Old Testament Church, men who were to be guided by the highest standard of righteousness and truth, deliver Jesus, their own Countryman, into the hands of the hated Roman government! This, though, was only the first in a long line of similar tragedies, by which religious bigotry requested the state to kill tens of thousands of innocent victims. Men and women charged only with worshiping the Lord Jesus according to the dictates of their conscience, have been turned over to the civil authorities by malicious, bloodthirsty clergymen who later insisted: "We did not destroy these men! The state killed them!" In this sense it is often claimed that Pilate crucified Jesus, not His own countrymen; but the stain of blood cannot be removed thus easily. God knows that behind the death sentence framed by Pilate were the unprincipled, scheming priests and Temple leaders, just as behind many persecutions we must find the cold, painstaking plotting of those who are called God's representatives. The Almighty give us always a spirit of tolerance and love, so that even if we differ in denominational issues, we may never incite the government to raise the sword of persecution against any religious group!

Despite their eagerness to have Pilate sentence Jesus,

these Jerusalem priests would not even step over the threshold in the governor's palace, for fear that close association with the Roman heathen would make them unclean. What an upside-down conscience they had! Almost mad in their determination to shed innocent blood, they nevertheless shrank from contact with their own governor. Is it not much the same today? Some people lay more stress on forms, rituals, and outward ceremonies than on penitence and personal faith.

From the outset of our Lord's hearing before Pilate, the governor, shrewd, scheming politician that he was, felt convinced of Christ's innocence and even showed a certain admiration for this strange prisoner, just as many of you really have nothing against Christ except that you think Him a harmless idealist or a mistaken reformer. Twice Pilate declared his complete conviction of the Savior's guiltlessness, and three times He proposed to release Him. One charge, however, struck Pilate. Our Lord's accusers had declared, *"We found this fellow perverting the nation and forbidding to give tribute to Caesar, saying that He Himself is Christ, a King."* When Pilate heard the word *King* and the accusation that Jesus had promoted a rebellion against the Roman rule, set Himself up as a rival monarch who would lead His countrymen, He knew that this charge required investigation. Without questioning Jesus concerning His teaching, His promise of salvation, Pilate sweeps all this aside and demands, in the spirit of a practical politician, *"Art Thou a King then?"*

Pilate's words seem to show how personally assured he felt that Jesus was anything except a King. How was it possible, he may have asked himself, that the religious leaders of Jerusalem expected him to regard this gaunt, beaten Jesus of Nazareth as a Sovereign? What was His kingdom? In all Palestine not a single foot of ground was His. Who were His subjects? A few misguided Galilean fisherfolk, and they had deserted Him soon after His arrest! Where were His palace, His throne, His crown, His ermine robes? This Jesus a King? Not even those who accused Christ took this charge of an opposition realm seriously, and the soldiers soon showed how the masses ridiculed the very thought. A king must have a crown; so they arranged a circle of deep-cutting thorns and blasphemously forced it on the Savior's head. A king should have a scepter; so they plucked a reed from a marshy spot near by and put it in our Lord's hand. A king ought to have royal robes; so they rummaged about and found a piece of purple cloth to throw over His shoulders. A king needs subjects; so with satanic scoffing they bowed down before Him to cry, *"Hail, King of the Jews!"*

The same ridicule heaped on Christ the King is directed toward the Savior today. We worship Jesus as our God and Redeemer, but worldly-minded politicians and preachers have only scorn for this basic Bible truth. We plead for Christ-centered education, and they laugh that away as old-fashioned. We ask for prayer in Jesus' name, only to have them sneer at that as superstitious. We say that there is no other cure for sin, no other hope for the sinner but in the cross and the blood; yet they reply, "How can you be so stupid and blind?" We insist: this war-torn age needs Christ above all else, and every program which deliberately rejects His Word is doomed to failure. How have world leaders responded? They have cast Christianity aside, and for the second time in our generation they are fighting on the fields of bloody battle.

This ancient and modern sarcasm does not change the fact that in heaven's own truth Jesus *is* a King. Long before He came into the flesh, prophet and psalmist welcomed Him in advance as Lord and Ruler. They cried out to all believers, *"Behold, thy King cometh!"* When Jesus now stood cross-examined before Pilate to face this question, which involved the salvation of the entire race, *"Art Thou a King then?"* even though this answer would finally help to seal His death warrant, Jesus replied without hesitation or evasion, *"Thou sayest that I am a King."*

If only Pilate had permitted God's Spirit to clarify his vision, he would have realized indeed that Christ, contradicting reason and appearance, was actually a Ruler, in reality the King of kings. And if only you, the uncertain and unconvinced, would likewise take Jesus at His word, you, too, would understand that while the earth has seen mighty monarchs, the proudest of these potentates are but dust and ashes in comparison with Him whom prophets, evangelists, disciples, apostles, angels and archangels, the mighty seraphim and the glorious cherubim, acclaim their Sovereign.

Jesus, first of all, is the King of power. "What power?" you ask, picturing that lonely, persecuted, sorrow-filled Sufferer before Pilate. Let the Scriptures answer, *"For by Him* [Jesus] *were all things created, that are in heaven and that are in earth, visible and invisible, whether they be thrones or dominions or principalities or powers: all things were created by Him and for Him."* We marvel at the might of modern wealth; yet how disappointing some of the world's greatest fortunes are! A few years ago one of the nation's leading power and light companies was offered $700,000,000 for its property and business. The directors held out for $1,000,000,000. Yet recently it was revealed that the whole enterprise, with assets of only $2,000,000, is now bankrupt. But the Lord Jesus Christ can never be bankrupt. The silver and the gold are His. The whole earth is His: the heavens with a sun one third of a million times larger than our globe; with stars, like Sirius, having a force of light 27 times greater than our sun — all these and the many heavenly bodies in the impenetrable expanses of the universe, beyond the reach of the most powerful telescope, belong to Christ the King, who has told us, *"All power is given unto Me in heaven and in earth."* Can you not see, therefore, that if this Savior King is yours, He has unlimited resources at His command? His angels can guard you in every way. You never need worry about family affairs or lie awake at night wondering how you can make ends meet. Christ can provide in overabundance.

We are awed by the size of modern armies, but Christ our King is stronger than the battalions of all nations. He is so powerful that if it but be His will, He can make a quick end of the present struggle. Do you doubt that? Read the twentieth chapter of Second Chronicles, and you will see that in the days of Jehoshaphat, when the superior numbers of their enemies threatened to overwhelm them, God's people took this crisis to Jehovah in penitent prayer. In answer a prophet arose who told the Israelites, *"Ye shall not need to fight in this battle: set yourselves, stand ye still, and see the salvation of the Lord with you."* The people accepted that startling promise. They marched to battle, raising their voices instead of their weapons, singing, *"Praise the Lord, for His mercy endureth for ever."* What happened? The Lord Himself intervened. The powerful enemies were completely destroyed because Israel had faith in God. Christ our King can likewise give peace and victory to an America that sincerely confesses its sins and with trustful prayer bows humbly before Jesus. If, however, masses refuse to crown Him King; if unbelief, worldliness, lust, continue to increase; if churches keep on going farther away from Christ, He can withhold His blessings until the people realize He is the supreme Ruler of the nations.

In the present chaos Jesus may appear to be far from wielding control over human affairs. Modern unbelief would still press the crown of thorns on His brow if He were with us in the flesh. Often it seems that the power of evil is becoming more solidly entrenched, unbelief bolder even in the churches, and atheism more widespread throughout the world. But be sure of this: Rule He will, for rule He must! Pilate was soon deposed. Caiaphas the high priest was likewise thrown out of office. Herod was similarly removed and sent into exile. Judas took his own life. The members of the council who condemned Jesus paid bitterly for their shocking rejection. The people who screamed, *"His blood be on us and on our children!"* brought a horrifying curse upon themselves, for many of them were brutally killed in the siege of Jerusalem. You may be ever so rich, self-confident, and your life crowded with personal triumphs; yet if you refuse homage to Christ, the time will come when your self-assurance will vanish, and God's wrath will make you realize that Christ is King. How is it possible, you ask, that Jesus, weak, wan, friendless, as we behold Him before Pilate, is really a King? To understand the seeming contradiction, you must believe that He is also the Lord of love, the Sovereign of your souls. Today men are asked to suffer and die in behalf of earthly rulers and human governments. But Jesus suffered and died for us, the King for His people, the Lord for His subjects, God for His erring, rebellious children. Russian history tells us that when Catherine II was to pass through an uninhabited section of the Black Sea territory, artificial homes, entire sham villages, even make-believe cities were hurriedly erected along the banks of the river on which the royal barge would travel to disguise the deserted countryside. French history recounts that when Queen Marie Antoinette made an extended tour, the authorities ordered all the maimed, diseased, hungry off the streets along her route in order not to irritate the Queen by disagreeable sights. English history relates that when the Prince of Wales visited the hospitals for World War veterans, the physicians tried to keep the mutilated, shell-shocked, and mentally unbalanced out of his sight. But as New Testament history assures us, Jesus deliberately sought the lowliest, the most destitute and distressed as the objects of His particular love.

Most people are never granted the privilege of approaching their king or president personally and speaking directly with him. Yet our Savior King invites us, *"Come unto Me!"* and promises, *"Him that cometh to Me I will in no wise cast out."* Julia Ward Howe, author of "Mine Eyes Have Seen the Glory of the Coming of the Lord," once wrote a prominent member of the United States Senate to enlist his help for a man who had suffered shocking injustice. The senator replied, "I am taken up so much with plans for the benefit of the race that I have no time for individuals." Jesus, on the contrary, was particularly concerned about individuals. Even at Calvary, amid agonies you and I cannot begin to fathom, He had mercy for a penitent thief and promised him the immediate glories of Paradise. He had compassion on His weeping mother and instructed John to provide for her. He looked on those who nailed Him to the cross, and pleaded, *"Father, forgive them, for they know not what they do!"*

Earthly rulers use force. They maintain armies and navies. They wage war — offensive and defensive. But in His realm of grace our Savior-King reigns with love and mercy. One day in exile on the lonely island of Saint Helena, Napoleon told General Montholon, his attendant,

"Alexander, Caesar, Charlemagne, I myself have established far-flung empires. Upon what did we build our power? We have built upon force and violence. Jesus Christ has built His kingdom upon love." And in this age of hatred and might-makes-right, how sorely we need the mercy of the Savior who died for Adolf Hitler, Benito Mussolini, Hirohito; a Redeemer in whose sight all men — white, black, red, yellow; all classes — capitalists and laborers, underprivileged and overprivileged; all races — the primitive and the advanced, Jews and Gentiles — are held in such heavenly devotion that Christ the King gave His own body, shed His own blood to save them for eternity! Not long ago a cable from Asia revealed that in the heart of ancient Mongolia a silver casket had been found which apparently contained the remains of Genghis Khan. This dispatch was restricted to a short paragraph tucked away with inconsequential news on an inside page. Yet Genghis Khan was perhaps the mightiest militarist of all times. He ruled from China to Europe; in twenty-two years, it is said, he killed fifteen million people. While today Genghis Khan is unknown to most people, millions dedicate their lives to Christ, the Lord of love, the Prince of Peace, who gave Himself for His enemies, for the cruel priests and churchmen, plotters of His destruction, the fanatics screaming for His blood, the Roman soldiers guilty of the most monstrous misdeed in history. He died personally for you and for me, even though our thanklessness and rejection of divine mercy had arrayed us against God and His Anointed. No one else can save us but Christ, and there is no cleansing power besides His blood. The newspapers tell of a Missouri young man who offered to sacrifice a cornea to be grafted onto the eye of an elder brother now facing life-long blindness. The surgeons decreed that the operation would be futile. Now, if men cannot transplant a good eye for a diseased eye, how can they ever hope that one man's sin-stained soul can redeem a brother's? Where human effort fails, Christ our King comes with heaven's mercy to give Himself as the Healing for our sin-sickness, the Atonement for our total depravity. While earthly monarchs require payment for their favors, the mercy of the Lord Jesus Christ is free. Salvation is *yours*, purely by faith!

All other rulers in the changing pageants of history have lived their life span and then disappeared forever. Christ alone is eternal and gives eternity. In the great climax of His conquering love He completely vanquished the last enemy, death. What seems to be the triumph of the grave is really a joyful victory when sinners, saved by grace, are brought to the waiting arms of their Father in the heavenly homeland. In one of the smaller islands of the Philippines there is a street of unusual name and character, "Victory Road," leading to a cemetery. It is the way along which the broken, ravaged bodies of dead lepers from a Christian colony are carried to their final resting place. To them, as to Saint Paul and all heroes of the faith, death is glorious release, the evidence of eternal triumph. When Christ is your King, He will so fortify your courage that you, too, can exult: *"O death, where is thy sting? O grave, where is thy victory? ... Thanks be to God which giveth us the victory through our Lord Jesus Christ!"*

II

WE OUGHT TO SERVE HIM AS THE KING OF KINGS

If, therefore, the Lord Jesus, above our poor powers of comprehension, is the King of life and death, the self-giving Sovereign of your soul, the heavenly Ruler who can provide for every need, protect you in each danger, preserve you against all enemies; if Jesus in His kingdom of power and mercy is the Great Hope of our disconsolate age, you should fall on your knees before Him, accept Him as your Lord and Savior, believe every word He spoke, and trust Him through the perplexity of life into death itself. You belong to Christ since He purchased you with a price, His holy, precious blood. By His suffering and dying He Himself redeemed you from the curse of the Law, hell's horror, and death's eternal doom. Pledge Him your sincere, undying allegiance!

Every Sunday among the vast numbers who worship with us in this mission of the air are many American and Canadian citizens, outwardly respectable people, who may have had too much success — or sorrow — thus to acclaim the Lord Jesus Christ their Sovereign and Redeemer. Yet as every Sunday I use the facilities of this coast-to-coast network to imprint on their souls the truth that they are lost without the Lord Jesus, so today I plead with them to ask themselves where they will be without Christ in the fearsome future before them. Our age more than any other should teach everyone of us that we cannot chart our own ways through these increasing perplexities. We need God in Christ with a constantly growing urgency. If you remain outside His kingdom here on earth, you will be excluded from His kingdom in heaven. Take time, blessed time, therefore, you, the skeptics, you, the burdened, weighted down by increasing agonies, to read and hear the sacred truth of Scripture by which the Holy Spirit leads you into the Savior's realm! Because Christ wants to be your King, He can use that Word of His grace to make you His child, however black and stained your soul, and give you the new birth, new life, new assurance which is yours through trusting reliance on His promises.

Jesus, as the supreme Ruler of our souls, ought to be petitioned for the riches of His grace with even greater confidence than that with which people approach earthly rulers. In this harassed hour the cry to every American which should resound even above the many specialized slogans asks, wherever the American flag may fly, "Keep Them Praying!" We shall be farther along the road to righteous peace if the masses in our country put their trust in the Lord Jesus Christ and constantly commune with Him in His Word and fervent prayer.

Since Jesus is our King, we must be ready to defend Him, not with instruments of war, with bigotry and hate, but with an unquenchable loyalty to His truth, an irrepressible determination not to permit one attack on His holy name to go unchallenged and unrebuked. I hope that all of you will join me in a resolute rejection of every assault on our glorious King. Whenever the newspaper in your community prints a slur against Christ, make the editor take it back! If the children in your schools are forced to use textbooks ridiculing Scripture, see that those textbooks are banned! Should the leaders in your church, which in its charter is committed to the whole Gospel truth, deny Christ, question His Word, and permit infidelity to flourish in a building dedicated to the Savior, get these men out or protest until they put you out!

With Christ as our King, we must be eager to tell others of this glorious Savior and Sovereign. How sorely our country needs such missionary testimony to the Lord Jesus! Not long ago a young mother in Pennsylvania was executed in the electric chair for having taken part in the murder of a State trooper. On the witness stand, however, she declared that not once in her whole life had anyone invited her to attend Sunday school or church in her city, a place crowded with churches. And because we are continually moving toward a pointed crisis in which it will be either "Christ or chaos" — and these are the very words recently used by one of America's leading economists — I plead with those among you who love the Lord Jesus to speak up and let the world know that you worship the King of kings. This mission of the air, as its name, Bringing Christ to the Nations, proclaims, seeks to spread the message of the sovereign Savior to everyone in this country, and many more nations, far beyond the twenty-five in which we now have stations. That is why I am not the least reluctant to appeal for your generous support, since I ask nothing for myself but only means for broadcasting the Gospel throughout a spiritually dying world. How gladly we ought to give to the Lord Jesus! Seven years ago Agha Khan, a Mohammedan potentate, received from his people twice his weight in gold. For his coming diamond anniversary three years hence, his followers propose to present him his weight in diamonds, a staggering sum representing at least $25,000,000. If the subjects of a Moslem leader thus pay lavish tribute to an earthly king, how much more generously should we support the work of Jesus, our divine King!

Sincerely acclaiming Christ the King of power and the King of grace, we also have the assurance that in heaven He will be our King of glory. There the same Jesus of whom Pilate demanded, *"Art Thou a King then?"* will reign supreme in a beauty that eye hath not seen, amid celestial anthems that earthly ears have never heard, and with the marvels of divine magnificence of which the human mind cannot even begin to conceive. My greatest hope, my constant prayer, my pleading with you every Sunday is directed toward the one supreme purpose that on the great day of the resurrection it may be given to me, by our Savior's abounding grace, to present many of you to the Lord Jesus as white-robed saints, cleansed by Christ's blood, saved by that faith in the Cross, resurrected by His power over death, which these broadcasts every week, with the Spirit's guidance, would bring into your hearts.

God direct us all to live loyally as Americans and as Christians, to the end that, by His grace, we may strengthen our beloved nation with exalting righteousness and help extend the kingdom of the Lord Jesus Christ! We ask it in Jesus' precious name. Amen!

———————

FOR CHRIST AND COUNTRY

> "*If thou let this Man go, thou art not Caesar's friend.*" — Saint John 19:12
> "*Render . . . unto Caesar the things which are Caesar's and unto God the things that are God's!*" — Saint Matthew 22:21

Strengthening Spirit of God:

Fill our hearts with deep, sincere loyalty to our Savior and our country's welfare, so that we may gladly serve both Christ's kingdom and the better interests of our beloved land! Keep us humble, penitent, believing, ever mindful of the truth that by following the Lord Jesus in faith and life we can give America that which it most needs — exalting, building righteousness! Look down on this strife-torn world to grant us and all nations a true peace! Because of our multiplied sins we are not worthy of this blessing; yet we approach Thee by faith in the Lord Jesus Christ and, trusting in His blood-bought pardon, beseech victory according to Thy will, peace according to Thy love. Enter the homes throughout the country which have been afflicted with grief, especially the families bereaved by war and its disasters! In every need of body and soul show us the grace, the comfort, the power of the redeeming, sustaining Christ, who lived and died and rose again for us! We ask it in His blessed name. Amen.

DURING the past few days many of you have read newspaper dispatches which told how Japanese troops, landing on New Guinea, were guided on their march across the island by American missionaries. I for one simply do not believe such reports! To start with, these cables were based only on second- and third-hand sources. Besides, no modern invasion army needs missionary guides; long before the war started, the Japanese undoubtedly had accurate maps of this territory. Above all, true ministers of Jesus Christ are uncompromisingly loyal to the government under which they work. They have but one consuming purpose: to serve their fellow men by bringing them the Gospel. They want to keep out of war and follow the pathway of peace. Yet they do not hesitate to withstand enemies when the souls and bodies of their charges are at stake. A Lutheran worker in China, for example, a young man who only a few years ago studied at our theological seminary in St. Louis, had to take charge of our divinity school in Hankow after the Japanese occupied the city. When the victorious Nipponese troops started to man-handle villagers near Hankow, five hundred women and girls fled to the enclosed seminary compound for refuge. By day and by night the wily invaders sought to scale the walls and capture the women. But our young missionary faced enemy bayonets and the threat of bombardment to protect these refugees. By God's blessing and his bravery the five hundred women not only escaped rape and ruin, but during the weeks of siege many of them learned to know the Lord Jesus and were led to accept the Savior in a great ingathering of souls.

Protesting against every slanderous claim that Christians are unpatriotic, that the Gospel is a creed of disloyalty, I want to show you today with the Spirit's help that the Christians' resolution always is:

For Christ and Country!

To this end we shall study the practical, present-day lessons contained in these two passages, Saint John, chapter nineteen, verse twelve: *"If thou let this Man go, thou art not Caesar's friend";* and Saint Matthew, chapter twenty-two, verse twenty-one: *"Render unto Caesar the things which are Caesar's and unto God the things that are God's!"*

I

CHRISTIANS HAVE BEEN LOYAL TO THEIR COUNTRY

Through the trial and conviction of our Lord men who previously had despised each other became friends and dropped their enmity as they united in crucifying Christ.

Herod and Pontius Pilate had long been political rivals; yet on that first Good Friday, as each played his role in condemning Jesus, their mutual dislike vanished. Although two opposing factions, the Pharisees and the Sadducees, clashed in the religious life of Jerusalem, the desire to spill the Savior's blood made them forget their deep-rooted differences. Various cliques could be found in the Sanhedrin, the council of Christ's own countrymen; nevertheless when Caiaphas asked them for their verdict concerning Jesus, without a single dissenting vote they cried, *"He is worthy of death!"*

More than satanic agreement, however, can be found in these actions. After Pilate had repeatedly pronounced Jesus innocent and the Roman governor seemed on the verge of setting the Savior free, the priests' diabolical craftiness became evident. They began to pose as patriots, and knowing Pilate's weakest spot, bluntly warned him, *"If thou let this Man go, thou art not Caesar's friend."* The mention of Caesar, the mighty Tiberius, was a threat that could bring fear into anyone's heart, particularly to the soul of a cheap politician like Pilate. With a record none too clean, he realized that if the citizens of Jerusalem ever formulated charges against him, the days of his official power would probably be at an end. Besides, one of his influential friends at Tiberius' court had just been convicted of treason, and even now the emperor's secret agents might be mingling in disguise among the crowd before Pilate's palace to investigate his loyalty. It was partly to protect himself, then, that against his own conscience, against all the evidence, against his wife's warning, against the Savior's clear statements, Pilate listened attentively to these prearranged charges advanced in sham patriotism by the hypocrite Temple officials with their holy robes but their hellish hatreds.

No fair and honest judge could have found in the suffering Christ a foe of Caesar. Jesus was no one's enemy, He loved those who spurned Him and was ready to do what the most devoted friend, the most unselfish sacrifice, could never accomplish — lay down His life for the heartless mob that was screaming: *"Crucify Him! Crucify Him!"* He was actually to give Himself into death for the leprous souls of those priests, for Pilate, even for Emperor Tiberius, a ruthless wretch, guilty of indescribable debauch. The false testimony, the malicious perjury, the scheming malice had not been able to prove that Jesus was anyone's adversary. On the contrary, Pilate, the rabbis, and the rabble should have recognized Christ as the greatest Benefactor of humanity ever to walk the pathways of Palestine. Hate people? Why, Jesus loved them with an intense devotion which led Him to heal the afflicted, assist the poor, champion the underprivileged, feed hungry bodies and starved souls — in unnumbered other ways to reveal Himself the Guide for the lost, the Hope of the helpless. This Christ an enemy, Caesar's rival, a competitor with the Roman dominion? He did not have enough physical strength left to oppose even a child; for only a few moments before He had been tortured by one of the most terrifying penalties the old, brutal world knew — scourging. The Gospel writers pass hurriedly over the horror of that suffering, a punishment so terrifying that often as the leather lashes, pointed with lead or spikes, lacerated the back, chest, sometimes even the face, the victim collapsed, a bleeding mass of torn flesh. No wonder, Pilate, with open contempt for the Savior's accusers, twice placed the pale, staggering Christ before the sullen, bloodthirsty mob crying, first, *"Behold the Man!"* and then, *"Behold your King!"* He must have felt that His abject misery could soften even their granite hearts with the feeling of compassion that jungle savages sometimes seem to show.

This plea: *"Behold the Man!"* *"Behold your King!"* echoes over the centuries to us with personal invitation to contemplate the Christ of agony. When you see Him, thorn-crowned, crimson-robed, His garments splashed with blood still flowing from His back, His countenance white, not with death's terror, but with the horror of our sins' crushing penalty, does it not require a mind poisoned with hatred and a heart steeped in vileness to loathe Christ as some of you have? A missionary to the Indians tells us of Red Owl, known as a mighty orator among the Lower Sioux. Fearful of losing his influence, he never attended church. One day, however, he came into the schoolroom and, stopping before the picture of the thorn-crowned Savior, asked: "What is that? Why are those thorns on His head?" For the first time he was told the story of the Savior's crucifixion. On one of his next visits to the Indian village, the missionary was surprised to see on the near-by prairie a newly made grave, marked with a plain cross. On inquiry he learned that Red Owl had suddenly taken ill and while dying told the young braves: "The story which the white man has brought to our country is true. I have it in my heart. When I am dead, I wish you would put a cross over my grave, that the Indians may see what is in Red Owl's heart." As *you* behold the thorn-crowned, captive Christ, may the Holy Spirit lead you to acclaim Him your Savior and with a penitent, personal faith trust His immeasurable, atoning love. But do not wait until you lie on your deathbed! Your immortal soul, worth more than all the world, according to Jesus, is too precious to risk on the possibility of an eleventh-hour repentance.

When the Savior's persecutors told Pilate that he could not be a friend of Caesar if he refused to sentence their prisoner to the cross, they implied that Christ was a public enemy of the Roman state. They lied, of course. They knew well enough, these priestly hypocrites, that only three days before they had tried to trap Jesus with the question *"Is it lawful to give tribute unto Caesar?"* and He had answered uncompromisingly, *"Render . . . unto Caesar the things which are Caesar's!"* They lied because they must have recalled how when popular opinion, swollen to high-pitch enthusiasm, sought to crown Christ king, He had declined such honor and immediately escaped this fanatical homage. They lied, since deep in their hearts they were convinced that if His whole life were examined under the microscope of minutest investigation, not one suggestion of rebellion against Caesar's administration, as rotten as it was, could be discovered. So in mock patriotism they screamed out their malicious charges against Jesus, whose record was completely flawless, and almost in the same breath demanded the release of Barabbas, convicted by the courts of open revolt against the authorities.

The same falsehood, in principle, branding Christ and His followers as opponents of the state, has been repeated through the ages. Soon after Saint Paul was beheaded as hostile to the empire, not only the Roman rabble but also the upper classes, men of power, historians and authors, accused the Christians of hating the human race. Nero blamed the first believers in the capital for setting Rome on fire; and although Latin writers express their doubt that the odious Christians were really guilty, although we now surmise that the fire was started by the fiendish ruler himself, yet the despised disciples were covered with pitch or saturated in oil, nailed to pine wood pillars, then lighted and burned alive. Such persecutions continued until the beginning of the fourth century, the rule of Diocletian and his co-regent Galerius, a second Nero. These two tyrants, who called themselves gods and claimed divine honors, tortured and killed aged men, nursing mothers, tender children — all on the false charge that these Christians were enemies of the state. Either reject Christ and worship the emperor or forfeit your Roman citizenship, your property, your life — that was the choice placed before these early believers. To the honor of their faith let it be said that many of them, innocent of every crime against their government, accepted the pains of martyrdom rather than deny their Lord.

Even after the Christian faith was securely enthroned in Europe, the same vicious calumny continued. No more hideous records exist in the annals of the human race than the black chapters dealing with the destruction of the Waldensians and the Albigensians. These peace-loving, industrious, thrifty people in Northern Italy and Southern France were savagely assaulted by heavily armed regiments of soldiers, killed by the thousands. Why? They were accused of treason. On what count? They wanted to read the Bible in their own language and serve Christ in the light of Scripture doctrine. Nor has the human race dropped to deeper depravity than in the massacre of the Huguenots. Their leader, Admiral Coligny, was a man of notable loyalty to France; they themselves were God-fearing, thrifty, industrious people. However, because they insisted on reading the Bible in their own language, worshiping God according to its truth, they were branded as foes of the French king. It was maliciously claimed that in their church services they secretly plotted to overthrow the state. This is a lie, of course, but its falsity did not save tens of thousands from being cut down in one of the cruelest carnages men have ever witnessed.

Not only in bygone generations but also today, when the power and blessing of the Christian faith should be clearly manifest, the same groundless accusation persists that the Old and New Testaments oppose national interests. In Germany Nazi critics of the Church berate the Gospel not merely as weak and effeminate but also as directly contrary to their country's welfare. They continue the blasphemy of Friedrich Nietzsche, who wrote, "I call Christianity the one great curse, . . . the one indelible blot upon the achievement of man." Don't try to laugh away statements like this by claiming that Nietzsche was insane or that the United States is not concerned with him! A Kansas publisher recently reissued the German philosopher's attack on the Church in a cheap fifty-cent edition, glorified as "a great liberating work," and asked the masses in our own country to study it, asserting, "All culture, all scholarship, all progressive thought goes to support the indictment of Christianity which Nietzsche made." And now comes the worst. The books of that publisher are featured in three full pages of advertisement by a large Saint Louis newspaper, which thus permits its columns to champion anti-Christian, anti-moral, anti-American poison.

Similar slander is being taught in certain American colleges and universities. Bertrand Russell, whose lectures are compulsory for some public schoolteachers in New York City, declared, "I say quite deliberately that the Christian religion as organized in its churches has been and still is the principal enemy of moral progress in the world." And in a hundred different ways campus men and women, except in Christian, church-maintained schools, which deserve your special support, are often instructed to regard our faith as an outworn superstition, hostile to the masses, thwarting progress, a menace to democratic development. One shudders to think what the future will bring if tomorrow's leaders, the college men and young women of today, turn these destructive theories into practice.

More dangerous, however, is the unmistakable spread of atheistic Communism. Well known is Karl Marx's slogan "Religion is the opiate of the people." He held that no nation can be really happy until religion has been abolished. Frederick Engels, co-founder of Communism, asserted, "There is no room for either God or a ruler," and he urged a thoroughgoing campaign to root out every creed. Lenin cried: "We must fight religion! . . . Religion must be abolished! The best country is a godless country." Lunatcharsky, educational expert of the Communists, admitted: "We hate Christianity and Christians. Even the best of them must be regarded among our worst enemies." The second woman in the Communist movement warns: "The struggle against the influence of religion among women is one of the most important duties of . . . the state. The Church must entirely disappear from . . . woman's life. She cannot be a faithful disciple of Lenin unless she is 100 per cent godless. . . . I . . . dedicate my life's endeavor to making the women . . . godless." Communism's hatred for the Savior's followers has been written in blood. A conservative scholar estimates that 1,860,000 Christians, regarded as enemies of their government, were slaughtered in a single year, 1918. American church members cannot close their eyes to the growing specter of Communism and collectivism. To my mind it constitutes one of the major menaces of tomorrow; we should use every means at our disposal to counteract its growth within our boundaries.

As the Savior's accusers lied when they told Pilate, *"If thou let this Man go, thou art not Ceasar's friend,"* so Communists lie when they label our faith a national foe. Wherever Christ's Gospel reigns, the power of idolatry and paganism has been broken, tyranny and brutality checked, polygamy and divorce restricted, women and children elevated, the home and family firmly established, slavery and oppression abolished, labor and industry exalted, ignorance and superstition banished, schools and colleges multiplied, the sick and the needy supplied, hospitals and orphanages fostered, and a thousand more blessings otherwise impossible systematically promoted. Without the influence of the Gospel there would be no permanently free nation on the face of the earth today. The French Revolution, with its bestial terrors and tortures, shows the failure of a government founded on atheistic ideals of human freedom and equality but avowedly against Christ. The faith He gave the world is truly *"the salt of the earth,"* a preservative against internal decay.

You do not have to look for proof. Right here in our own country there is a vast demonstration of the building power exercised by faith. The United States was settled, not by Communists, freethinkers, atheists, but by Christians. The charters of our colonies were not sealed in the name of Buddha, Zoroaster, Moses, Lao Tse, but in the name of the Lord Jesus. Each of the thirteen colonies had a Biblical foundation, and each revered the Scriptures as divine authority. The Supreme Court of the United States has officially stated, "This is a Christian nation," not in the sense, of course, that we have an official religion or that the country does not tolerate all creeds, but because, as the highest court explains, the founding fathers, the original charters, the early practices throughout the country were distinctly Christian. Our blessings come from the Bible, from the Savior, from His Gospel. The reverses of the last years stem from the neglect of Christianity and the rejection of its truth.

The loyalty of the Church and its deep-rooted patriotism are not loud and boisterous, but sincere and effective. True pastors do not preach politics or engage in impressive demonstrations to attract public attention. In a quiet, unassuming way they occupy themselves with strengthening men's souls, and thus build our spiritual defenses. The Christian workman who goes about his daily task in a quiet, unnoticed manner, who puts in a full day's honest labor, lives frugally, can mean more for the welfare of the United States than many a lime-light orator who makes his own money by shrewdness and does not care how he spends other people's. A God-fearing mother who sacrifices herself to bring up her sons and daughters *"in the nurture and admonition of the Lord"* gives more to America in God's sight than some of the career women who do not want children, so that they can live public, applauded lives, unrestricted by families. The church member who saves defense stamps until he can buy an $18.75 bond may be a better patriot than the godless millionaire who buys the maximum quota simply for an investment.

Even by measurable standards, however, the Christians' support of their government is outstanding. The largest single group in the present United States Army, Navy, Marine and Air Corps is made up of church members. The first soldier in the AEF to step on European soil was an active Lutheran from Hutchinson, Minnesota. The best, the physically and spiritually strongest young men now engaged in national defense, come from Christian congregations.

This loyalty, of course, is of the highest type because it is not a blind, unconditioned allegiance. Our cry is not, "My country, right or wrong!" (for no follower of the Savior can ever be in favor of anything wrong), but "My country, may she always be right! But if she is ever wrong, God help me make her right!"

II

CHRISTIANS MUST ALSO BE LOYAL TO THEIR GOD

Now, because Jesus can bless, enrich, defend our shores and in this war give us victory with a triumph of truth and righteousness; because no religion except the Gospel, no God other than the Trinity revealed by Christ can help in the emergency before us, we can fulfill our highest responsibility to the nation and ourselves by pledging allegiance to Christ and country. If during the storm and trial of the Civil War, Abraham Lincoln could say, "Intelligence, patriotism, Christianity, and a firm reliance on Him who has never forsaken this favored land are still competent to adjust in the best way all our present difficulty," how eager we should be to follow the Savior's pointed direction, *"Render . . . unto God the things that are God's"* and to accompany devotion to our country with complete dedication to our heavenly Father! Fellow citizens and friends beyond our borders, our greatest need and yours, in Canada, in Mexico, wherever you may be, is the faith which enthrones our Lord in the hearts of the multitudes. Correspondingly, the most serious menace confronting our people is not the possibility of economic depression, but the decay of Christianity. Wherever Christ disappears, forces hostile to true Americanism always rise. When the flowers of Gospel faith are permitted to wilt and die, the poisonous weeds of godlessness and tyranny begin to flourish.

Therefore, my appeal asks first of all that you accept Jesus as the Redeemer of your soul, the Son of God whose atoning death on the cross grants you, without any charge, as without any doubt, the assurance that even your black and scarlet transgressions have been removed forever; the pledge that life after death, heaven's joys after earth's sorrows are granted by His divine promise and power.

Whatever may have kept you from Christ up till this moment, whether it be personal pride, the destructive self-righteousness which makes you thank God you are better than most people; or whether it be love of sin, greed for money, lust of the flesh, the sorrow of life, be fair enough and considerate of your soul to hear what Jesus offers and to ask yourself if there is any real reason why you dare refuse His matchless mercy. If you have to be humbled to gain Christ; if you have to lose money, work, health, home, even the love of some who are as dear as life itself, some blessed day you will thank God for the hand that seemed to strike harshly but really saved your soul.

Now, through Jesus we have not only this complete forgiveness, joy of life instead of depressing worry, spiritual strength to withstand temptation and overcome evil, eagerness to turn from self and serve one's fellow men, power to triumph over all trials, but also — and this is the thought I would emphasize — the power to be a good citizen, to build the moral and spiritual defense of our country, to help increase that righteousness which, God's Book says, exalts any nation.

When the Lord Jesus is securely enthroned within your heart, you will be able to apply the divine power Christian faith offers for helping this country. You will understand why in this emergency the cry must be: "Back to God! Back to Christ! Back to the Bible! Back to the Christian Church!"; why our heavenly Father wants a contrite, repentant, sin-hating people in the United States. You, on your knees in penitence and humility before the Almighty, can invoke Heaven's strength. Do not ever lose sight of the divine mercy that if the Lord was ready to spare even Sodom and Gomorrah, those indescribably vile cities, had there been only ten in their midst who did seek Him, then, if it be His purpose, His favor can be extended to any land in which masses of Christians implore His mercy. Blessed by the Lord Jesus, as a true American citizen, you have the promise of answered prayer for yourself and your penitent nation; but always remember that the Almighty answers our pleas in His own way and at His appointed hour. A Christian America on its knees, subject to God's will, could pray its way out of these difficulties into a quick victory with a just peace and the sparing of many young lives.

Daniel Webster once declared, "If we abide by the principles taught in the Bible, our country will go on prospering and continue to prosper; but if we and our posterity neglect its instructions and authority, no man can tell how sudden a catastrophe may overwhelm and bury our glory in profound obscurity." He is right, and we who love Christ must defend our Bible against seemingly unimportant questioning of its truth. Attacks on Scripture come from unexpected places, as we have been reminded during the past days, when a women's magazine printed a statement from a very high source asserting that the Biblical record of Adam and Eve is wrong and has been "disproved by science." That claim directly contradicts the faith of millions of Protestant and Catholic Christians in the United States, besides rejecting the verdict of outstanding scientists who have bowed reverently before the first three chapters in Genesis. If we deny what Moses wrote concerning Adam and Eve, we must admit that Saint Paul, who refers to the first parents as actual, historical people, was wrong and therefore must be questioned in everything else he has written; we must even assume that our blessed Lord and Savior, who Himself speaks of the Garden of Eden, was mistaken, and we must consequently subject everything He says to the verdict of what some people call science. If these opening chapters of the Bible are allegorical, is the heaven of its closing chapters likewise only an allegory? If Adam and Eve never existed, as the Bible says they did, how about the Savior promised them? Is He fictitious too? You see, my fellow Christians, how disastrous it is to question or deny Scripture truth and how constantly vigilant we must be to defend the Word at all costs and in all places, particularly when vague shadows along the unformed horizon of tomorrow forbode for American Christians increasing assaults on their faith.

Let the worst come, here is the cry for this crisis, the resolution for every American, the pledge for every Christian, the declaration by which the true victory is ours: For Christ and country! God give every one of you in full measure the faith and courage to speak that double dedication to our glorious Savior and our God-blessed homeland! Amen!

ARE YOU A SOLDIER OF THE CROSS?

*"When the centurion saw what was done, he
glorified God, saying, Certainly this was a
righteous Man." —* Saint Luke 23:47
"Truly, this was the Son of God."
Saint Matthew 27:54

Jesus, Our Savior and Our King:

*As once, on the first Palm Sunday, Thou didst enter Jerusalem
amid waving branches and loud acclaim, so come now into our
hearts! Help us welcome Thee as our Redeemer from sin, the divine
Deliverer from death and hell! But grant us the sincerity and stead-
fastness of faith through which, refusing to crucify Thee anew by
unbelief and ungodly living, we remain loyal to Thee! To this
end bless our broadcast, as every message of Thy true Gospel!
Enlighten many, as they behold Thee nailed to the cross, and so
illumine their spiritual vision that they find in Thee their Savior
slain for their sins! Strengthen our young men in the nation's
armed forces with a trusting faith in Thy heavenly mercy! Give
prisoners of war the assurance of Thine abiding Presence with all
who love Thee! In Thy time and manner, O Christ of endless
compassion, grant us true peace with the triumph of right! Hear
us, ever-blessed Atonement, for we pray in Thy name! Amen.*

"CAN my son remain a Christian in the Army?" "Is
it possible for a young man called to the colors from
a God-fearing home to maintain his devotion to the Lord
Jesus?" "Will my boy come back from the Navy with his
faith in the Savior unbroken?" Questions like these are
asked repeatedly by fathers and mothers throughout the
country, voiced in many letters I receive from parents who
daily pray that God will keep their sons now serving with
the nation's armed forces safe in body and sound in soul.
They recognize that the legions of hell are not debating
whether they are to work forty or forty-eight hours a week;
their schedule calls for 168 hours; and these regiments
of moral ruin direct their attacks particularly against young
soldiers away from home, separated from their churches,

brought into constant contact with some who oppose our Lord, daily confronted with the temptation to enjoy life while you can.

Yet Christian faith can triumph over all assaults and enticements. To reassure worrying parents, I say that the spiritual care of our military men has never been as far-reaching as in the present struggle. For the first time large numbers of chapels have been erected by the government in the training camps, and churches are supplying greater quotas of chaplains than ever before.

Some of the mightiest military leaders have been the humblest believers. During the Revolution: George Washington, kneeling in persistent prayer; during the Civil War: in the South, "Stonewall" Jackson, who personally supported the distribution of evangelical tracts among the Confederate soldiers, almost 150,000 of whom are said to have been converted during the four years of that conflict — and in the North, General Howard, who refused to attend an elaborate reception in his honor, even though the President was the sponsor, because the evening chosen was the regular night for his midweek worship; during World War I: men like General Pershing, who told the soldiers, "Hardship will be your lot, but trust in God will give you comfort; temptation will befall you, but the teachings of our Savior will give you strength." These and many other professing Christians renowned for leadership in military tactics and strategy show our soldiers in World War II that with the motto For Christ and Country they need not sacrifice any of their devotion to the Lord.

True, many American soldiers leave for the front without knowing Jesus. Every time you read in the papers that a tanker has been torpedoed or a destroyer sent to the bottom, every time you scan a new list of men killed in action or in air clashes, think not only of the sorrow and the loss their death has caused; think also of the souls which have gone to face their Maker! We dare not permit ourselves to take these death notices complacently. Rather must we ask: Are we doing everything possible to help each soldier, sailor, marine, and airman accept the Lord Jesus? Are we personally concerned about having all our armed youth receive the blessing of Baptism before they go to the front? Plead constantly with God for their salvation and His divine protection of their souls!

Today, however, on Palm Sunday, when we see Jesus enter Jerusalem amid the glad hosannas of the common people and, looking five days further, find Him rejected in the same city, nailed to the accursed cross, we should remember that almost since the beginning of the human race another struggle has been in progress throughout the world — the conflict between our Lord and every anti-Christian force; the battle with sin, hell, death; the crusade against the world, our flesh, our sinful hearts; the attack on disbelief, doubt, and despair. Now, because you are either for Christ or against Him, either allied with other Christians for glorious Gospel victories or mobilized with His enemies for opposition to divine truth, I ask everyone this direct, personal question:

ARE YOU A SOLDIER OF THE CROSS?

May the Holy Spirit help you answer, "Yes"! To this end hear the story of the first soldier convert, who stood beneath Calvary's cross. Of him it is written in our text, Saint Luke, chapter twenty-three, verse forty-seven: *"When the centurion saw what was done, he glorified God, saying, Certainly this was a righteous Man,"* and Saint Matthew, chapter twenty-seven, verse fifty-four: *"Truly this was the Son of God."*

I

TO BATTLE FOR JESUS YOU MUST KNOW AND BELIEVE IN THE CRUCIFIED CHRIST

If you want to answer the appeal "Who is on the Lord's side?" with a clear-cut "I am," study the conversion of this officer. There should be unusual comfort and encouragement for all of us in the fact that the centurion was a Roman. While tradition places his birthplace in several distant countries, this much is sure: he was not a member of the chosen Hebrew race, but a Roman, a representative of the heathen world. At Calvary the barriers which help classify men as Jews and Gentiles disappear. No longer in God's plan of salvation is there a single nation with special, pre-eminent privileges. The children of men, whoever, wherever, whatever they are, stand on the same level. No longer an exclusive priesthood restricted to the members of one family, but a universal priesthood, with every believer in Christ called to proclaim His saving name! No longer a Temple from which foreigners were banned and in which even believers were excluded from the Holy of Holies! Instead, the worship of the Lord Jesus, anywhere, everywhere, that men hear His Word and accept His love! No more sacrifice of passover lambs, no more sprinkling of blood on the Day of Atonement, for Christ by His one perfect sacrifice paid the full price demanded by God's justice for the atonement of humanity's sins! No more food laws, tithe laws, Sabbath laws, ceremonial laws; for Calvary means the precious freedom of faith, the liberty of the Gospel for every man! Therefore, when you see this centurion, a soldier accustomed to war's brutality, a pagan, who had lived in idolatry and false worship, and now find him accepting Jesus, take heart and believe that, whatever your past may have been, your present and future can be glorious with Christ! He is always waiting for you.

Men and women by the hundreds of millions, differing as much as night does from day in intellect, physical appearance, social standing — people of poverty and wealth, some cursed and others blessed — all have been welcomed, pardoned, glorified by our Heaven-sent Redeemer.

This centurion (the term implies "an officer in command of one hundred troops") had probably witnessed much of the Savior's suffering. It seems likely that he had seen Jesus crowned with thorns, mocked and ridiculed by some of the soldiers from his own garrison. Shocking as that scene was, it did not make him behold Christ in His true light. Perhaps it was this centurion who supervised the unspeakable horror of the scourging; but not even the sight of this excruciating agony brought him to his Lord. He saw Pilate arguing the Savior's innocence, pleading for his release; heard the crafty priests, the blood-thirsty mob screaming for Christ's death; yet his heart remained untouched and unconcerned. He led the detachment of troops accompanying our Lord to Golgotha and watched Him collapse under the weight of His cross; but he had to go all the way to Calvary before he knew Jesus. He had to stand under the cross, to hear the Savior's parched lips speak the seven last words; he had to wait until Jesus died and the earth shook in protest against this screaming injustice, before he acclaimed his Lord.

You, too, must go to Calvary if you would know Jesus aright. It takes the cross to make a Christian. Only when you have stood there in spirit, when you have taken time to learn that the Savior's cross is different from every other cross in history; only when the Holy Spirit, working in your sinful heart, pictures to you the crucifixion with its God-forsakenness, its agony of body, yet far deeper anguish of soul, the ridicule of the milling mob, the words of mercy spoken by the divine Martyr, His collapse in cold death, then the rumbling quake of outraged nature, the darkness caused by the sun's hiding its face from that murder, can you discover the heart and center of the saving Gospel. If in the past preachers have told you that Christianity should be pictured in symbols of beautiful flowers, bright bluebirds, sweet melodies, captivating fragrance, balmy sunshine, rippling laughter, then I tell you now in the Savior's name that the climax of His creed makes everyone of us witness at Golgotha the loving Lord's merciful self-giving, but also the most hideous scene in human annals, the most repulsive, rebellious act that puny creatures have ever directed against the holy God. Yet just this spectacle of blood and horror you must see as the centurion beheld it. Everyone of you with irresistible necessity must ask yourself Pilate's question: *"What shall I do, then, with Jesus?"* Real neutrality has been impossible in this war, and it is ten thousand times less possible during the struggle in which I ask you to stand up for Christ. Take time during this week, which brings us the anniversary of His crucifixion, to read, hear, study the record of your Redeemer's death at Calvary! You always risk your soul when you neglect or postpone any invitation to accept His loving-kindness; but in our age the refusal to heed His *"Come unto Me"* is doubly disastrous, with life as uncertain as now. How can you ever face the bar of His justice, before which *"we must all appear,"* if you have never been fair enough to learn who Jesus is and what He has done for you? How can you ever get right with the Almighty if you spurn Him who gives you divine righteousness? As the shadow of Friday's cross looms before us, I tell you in all the earnestness the Holy Spirit puts into my words that there is no *"other name under heaven . . . whereby we must be saved"* but the name of the Crucified; no other mediator between God and men besides Him who hung suspended between heaven and earth; no other plea to save us from hell except the appeal *"Father, forgive them,"* spoken from the accursed tree by Him whose lifeblood sealed that pledge; no other Paradise but that which the agonized Savior promised the penitent thief; no other way to a blessed hereafter than the faith by which the repentant malefactor was immediately transferred to heaven.

If only you will take time for Jesus, by God's grace the glory of the centurion's conversion can be repeated in you. So marvelous is Christ's merciful redemption that it often takes only the study of His Word to bring souls in revolt to humble reverence. Soon after the turn of this century Ivan Pannin, a young man who had left his home in czarist Russia, entered Harvard University. An ardent nihilist, he publicly advocated the assassination of Russian leaders as the remedy for his people's woes. He soon realized, however, that killing rulers would offer no permanent solution to his country's problem. In search for light, he finally turned to the New Testament, which he had previously despised. As he read on, the Holy Spirit convicted him of his sinful rebellion against God. His past life and its destructive, murderous hatreds now loomed before him with all their guilt. He found himself condemned in the Lord's sight; but at last the Spirit brought him down on his knees before Christ. He discovered pardon and peace in his Savior, and the former nihilist who once sought to kill men now devoted his life to saving them through the Gospel.

If up to this moment you have regarded Christ in an indifferent, unconcerned way, read your Testament with a prayer for the Savior's guidance, in the radiance streaming from Calvary! You, too, will find that the darkness of spiritual ignorance vanishes, and in the clear light of faith you will discern the true and blessed Redeemer.

It took the greatest catastrophe in history to make the centurion think of Jesus, and often since it has required sorrows and reverses to turn men's hearts in the direction of the cross. English army records tell of an eminent officer in the East India service, General Poole. Because he reveled in sin's debauch, he hated the Bible and the restraints it placed on his lusts. To increase his ridicule of Scripture, he read it again, and found it even more opposed to his philosophy of life and his reason. He now pronounced God's Word a gross falsehood, a shocking forgery. He went so far as to throw the Bible on the floor and kick it out of his house. But sickness and reverses began to overtake him; his self-confidence failed; the reliance on atheistic friends collapsed, and in his agony he turned to the Book he had desecrated. On its blessed pages, by contemplating the Christ of the cross, he found the assurance of a Savior who could forgive sins even as vile as his. He was rescued by trusting the promises of the Volume he had violently condemned.

Last week a Minnesota woman wrote me that her family had previously given no time or thought to Jesus. Things went prosperously, it seemed, without Him; consequently there was plenty of drinking, cursing, poker playing, flirtation, questionable stories — everything required to be "a good sport and be considered a good fellow." She had never said a prayer, but she had committed the greatest sin of which a mother can be guilty. Then one day her father was brought down to what became his deathbed. Suddenly terrified by thoughts of the hereafter, she called one of our clergymen, and the Word of Christ he spoke to the dying man saved his soul for eternity. At the funeral our pastor did what a true minister of the Lord Jesus should do on such occasions. Instead of indulging in fulsome flattery of the deceased, he spoke in warning, yet in thanks to the Almighty for His eleventh-hour grace. That appeal touched the rest of the family. They are now being instructed for membership in the Church. The mother, her own life completely changed, reports that household devotion takes the place of suggestive, profane talk. Drinking has been banned. Time is now eagerly found for the Savior. All this happened by the direction of God, who in taking the father from that home shook the others into the realization of their utter hopelessness without Christ. Blessed the affliction, the agony, the bereavement, which makes some of you, convinced of your own helplessness, turn to the Crucified!

Note particularly the way in which the centurion came to Jesus. After our Lord had died and the Roman officer reviewed the whole horror of the crucifixion, it dawned on him that the Savior was innocent. The scribes and the Temple crowd might mock, wag their heads, scream their ridicule as bullies taunt a helpless victim, but this Roman officer was unmoved by the politician-priests' rabble-rousing tactics. Though it was dangerous to speak in behalf of the Galilean crucified as a blasphemer, the centurion cried out, so that all could hear, *"Certainly this was a righteous Man!"* He thus became the first witness after the Savior's death who testified to our Lord's guiltlessness. We, too, should have no doubt concerning the fact that Jesus was absolutely holy, entirely sinless and stainless. Every honest investigator has had to repeat this verdict *"Certainly this was a righteous Man!"* Three weeks ago I restated the Savior's own challenge, *"If I have spoken evil, bear witness of the evil,"* and I asked the atheists and unbelievers in our radio audience to bring one real, substantiated indictment against our Redeemer. Since that time we have received between thirty-five and forty thousand letters; but to date not one real, honest accusation against our Lord has come to our attention.

If Christ had to suffer injustice, who are we to believe ourselves free from similar persecution? The world still hates Jesus, and Christians should expect no consideration from it. If equity is cast to the wind as men of the world deal with one another; if selectees risk their lives for $10 a week, while the secretary to the vice-president of a manufacturing concern received a bonus of $39,356 for work performed in the safety of an office; if the income of certain executives has increased 700 per cent, while the salary of many in the Army and the Navy has dropped to one seventh of its peace-time size, how can we expect the world to deal fairly with us who are Christ's?

The centurion, however, was not satisfied to call Jesus innocent. He went far beyond that when, according to Saint Matthew's account, he added, *"Truly this was the Son of God."* "How," you may ask, "could the centurion know that the suffering, bleeding, dying Savior was divine?" The Scriptures do not answer. Probably he heard the crucified Jesus mention His heavenly Father in His first word, *"Father, forgive them,"* as in His last, *"Father, into Thy hands I commend My spirit,"* and he believed that Christ was in truth the Son of the Almighty. Even skeptics, scrutinizing our Lord's death, have expressed their conviction that He must be more than man. His departure from life was altogether different from the final moments of any mortal being. Others, too, have died as victims of screaming injustice. Socrates, the Greek philosopher, was falsely found guilty and sentenced to drink the cup of hemlock poison; yet, when the French philosopher Rousseau, whose loose life betrayed low morality, compared that Greek teacher with the Sufferer on Calvary, he exclaimed, "If the death of Socrates was that of a hero, the death of Christ was like that of a God!" When, however, the Holy Spirit takes possession of a man's heart, as He enlightened the centurion, the scales of human blindness fall from that man's eyes, and Jesus is recognized as God's Son with divine power and majesty.

I hope that everyone of you, beholding the Crucified, can say, "This is *the Son of God*!" If you are to be freed from the curse of sin, of what help can a human Christ be? If you want strength for the weaknesses of life, what power can you find in an earthly counselor? If you want resistance to evil, impulse to good, a new life and being, you require heavenly help which knows the truth, makes no mistake, and never fails in achieving its purpose.

Listen, then, as Good Friday approaches, and intellectual conceit, academic ridicule seek to enshroud Christ's cross with the darkness of denial. While Jesus is called the Model Man, the Perfect One, the Hero, the Pattern, the Example, but never raised high enough to become our God, I warn you in plain language: Don't believe these men who with enticing words, double-meaning phrases seem to sing Christ's praise but in reality refuse to crown Him Lord of all! Don't follow them, because many of them have never seen the true Sufferer on the cross, while the centurion in our text has. He was there when the square nails crushed through the Savior's flesh. He was there when they raised those two timbers from the ground and the Son of God, suspended above the callous crowd, answered cruel scoffing with a plea for their pardon. He was there when the divine Sufferer, about to die, cried aloud, "*It is finished.*" He *knows* who the Crucified is — and what does he say? O fellow sinners and fellow redeemed, hear it again, "*Truly this was the Son of God*"! He is the more reliable witness because he helped crucify

Christ; he saw Him die and refused to raise a hand in the Savior's defense. But when the Spirit entered his heart, he repeated what God the Father Himself declared, the truth that angels had glorified, the majesty which Christ's miracles proved, the assurance foretold by prophets and fulfilled in New Testament records: Christ is *"the Son of God."*

Nor does the centurion's tribute to our Lord end there. Saint Luke tells us that this Roman soldier who now beheld Jesus in an altogether different light, *"glorified God."* What a startling statement! Why did the centurion speak of God's glory at the Savior's death? Various interpretations offer an answer, but I like to think of it in this way: he knew that because Jesus, as God's Son, was just and innocent, everything He had taught was true. If Christ was guiltless and divine, then He could open the gates of Paradise to a penitent murderer, as He had promised; then Jesus was not suffering the penalty of His own sins but was agonized for the transgressions of others. The centurion *"glorified God"* for the only real reason which gives us occasion to praise God when death comes: the saving truth that Christ is also the Redeemer from sin, the Victor over the tomb. If you have not accepted Him as Heaven's Atonement, the grave is always ugly, hideous, repulsive. How unbelievers shun it! How frantically they seek to disguise its terror! But after you have learned Calvary's lesson of divine love and believe, as the centurion did, that our Lord endured the anguish of the cross to pay for all human iniquities, you can be assured that death, *"the wages of sin,"* has been utterly defeated for those who are Christ's; you likewise can glorify God for this great mercy.

This is the holiest truth of our entire faith: The Son of God is the Atonement for our transgressions. It is the message that must be ceaselessly reaffirmed from Christian pulpits. On the last Sunday of his life Thomas Boston, the eighteenth-century preacher who built his congregation largely by bringing Christ into the family, could not gather enough strength to enter his pulpit; so he spoke to his parishioners in the parsonage garden, preaching on the text, *"Behold the Lamb of God, which taketh away the sin of the world!"* In the evening his congregation returned. He chose the same text. After the service when his daughter asked, "Father, why did you not take another text?" the aged man replied: "That is all they need to know. They need only *'behold the Lamb of God, which taketh away the sin of the world.'"* All that any of you must know to be saved is the blessed truth that God's Son died for you. But you must believe it in a personal, individual, soul-deep faith. Jesus wants more than formal lip worship and mouth service. He asks, *"My son, give Me thine heart."* He is not satisfied with a family faith; He wants individual trust. Any kind of religion is not enough; He requires the worship which adores Him as God and Redeemer, Lord and Savior.

The call of Holy Week asks for humble, penitent confession of all our iniquities. We must kneel in spirit before the crucified Redeemer and cry out: "How terrifying the guilt of my transgressions, since I could be pardoned by nothing less than this agony on the cross! How completely I sold myself into sin's slavery since I could be freed only by the blood that dripped from my Savior's wounds! What an eternity in hell my misdeeds heaped up for me since their penalty could be removed by nothing less than the sacrifice of God's Son Himself!" Yet at Calvary the Savior's mercy must loom greater than the wrong abounding in our lives, and we, too, should join the centurion in glorifying God and crying out: "What a compassionate

Redeemer my crucified Lord is, since here He bore all my sins, the unnumbered, unspeakable, ungrateful violations of Heaven's holy Law! What a merciful Savior He is, since He left nothing undone that I must finish and so completely satisfied the justice of His heavenly Father that I need or can pay no amount to secure forgiveness! What a marvelous reconciliation He promises me since His love pledges that everything hard and crushing in life and death is hallowed here at the cross, so that through faith it becomes in reality a blessing! What an assured grace is granted here at Golgotha, where, every doubt removed and contradiction rejected, I can exult with Spirit-filled confidence, '*I am persuaded that neither death nor life nor angels nor principalities nor powers nor things present nor things to come nor height nor depth nor any other creature shall be able to separate us from the love of God which is in Christ Jesus, our Lord!*' "

The centurion had that certainty of faith. Others might quibble, question, or sneer sarcastically, but listen to him once more: "CERTAINLY *this was a righteous Man!*" "TRULY, *this was the Son of God!*" When Isaac Newton, universally recognized as the prince of scientists, lay on his deathbed, he could have recalled many learned accomplishments; but in humble, cross-directed truth he spoke these words: "Two things I have learned in my life: one, that I am a great sinner; the other, that Jesus Christ is a still greater Savior!" If this pre-eminent scientist could thus declare His trust in our Lord to be the outstanding lesson of his career, why should any of you shrug your shoulders at Calvary or put question marks behind the assured promises of its cross? God make you rather twentieth-century centurions, so that with rugged, heroic assurance you, too, can say, " '*Certainly,*' '*truly,*' this Christ is my God and my Savior!"

II

TO BATTLE FOR JESUS YOU MUST PROCLAIM AND DEFEND THE CRUCIFIED CHRIST

With that firmly founded faith you can be — you must be — a soldier of the Cross! While everything required for our salvation is free, once we have accepted Jesus, we must show our gratitude for His complete self-giving by enlisting ourselves, our time, energies, money, for the spread and the protection of His saving truth! As Count Zinzendorf, beholding Stenburg's picture of the crucifixion, under which the words had been inscribed: "All this I did for thee. What hast thou done for Me?" stood riveted before that canvas for hours and then spurned a fortune to lay his treasures and talents at Christ's feet and become a missionary in distant American colonies, so may the Spirit now direct your hearts, that, when the scourged, suffering Jesus, His penetrating eyes fixed on you, asks: "All this I did for thee. What hast thou done for Me?" you may answer, "Precious Savior, I give myself to Thee, now and forever!"

This means that you show your sincerity by a Christ-exalting life. If the unbelieving world could clearly recognize true disciples because they live their faith, the Church would rise to new power and unparalleled blessing. Jesus will not tolerate hypocrisy — saying one thing and doing another — worshiping God on Sunday and adoring gold and sin the rest of the week. The heavy sentence recently placed on spies who worked against our country emphasizes that you cannot remain a citizen of the United States if you co-operate with this nation's enemies; and in an even higher degree you cannot continue in Christ's kingdom if your words and actions show traitorous disloyalty.

If we are to be soldiers of the Cross, we must also be ready to defend its truth. How encouraging the example of the centurion's testimony! He had nothing to gain by declaring the Crucified the Son of God. On the contrary, he might have lost his position, perhaps his Roman citizenship, maybe even his life by speaking in behalf of the dead Savior. Yet he showed no fear. So today we need men who consider neither cost nor consequences, but cry out in protest every time the Savior and His blood-bought redemption are attacked by unbelieving men! Our heavenly Father grant that fires of loyalty will flare high in this age of agnostics and skeptics! The Holy Spirit give us centurions in the pulpits and in the pews who are *"not ashamed of the Gospel of Christ"* but declare to friend and foe alike that it is *"the power of God unto salvation to everyone that believeth"*!

As soldiers of the Cross we must be steeled for hard, long-drawn-out battles. The world, contrary to roseate predictions, is not drawing closer to Jesus. We see no real signs of a nation-wide revival, as blessed as that would be. The churches should now prepare for the inevitable test which must come when the war is over; they should mobilize for a perpetual drive against destructive forces which will seek to transplant to this God-blessed nation the roots of atheism, collectivism, Communism, Fascism, and other suicidal systems of the Old World. Battling for Christ, we can confidently say, "Onward, Christian soldiers!" since we are *"strong in the Lord,"* protected by divine weapons, the armor of divine truth, *"the breastplate of righteousness," "the shield of faith," "the helmet of salvation," "the sword of the Spirit, which is the Word of God."* Even if the howling of hell increases and the threats of atheism multiply, believe that with Christ as the Captain of our salvation, with the faith that implicitly follows Him, the Commander-in-chief, we have

the promise of divine truth *"This is the victory that over-
cometh the world, even our faith!"*

Every young man called to our nation's defense must
take an oath of induction. I have made a few changes
in it so that it may become the pledge of every Christian
warrior. Today, on Palm Sunday — a time commemorated
by many as the day on which they publicly pledged their
faith in the Redeemer and, confirming their baptismal vow,
promised to suffer even the pain of death rather than deny
Him — may we who love the Lord Jesus, and particularly
you who have been indifferent to His mercy, stand now in
spirit at Calvary! When I ask you, "Are you a soldier of
the Cross?" raise your voices in the centurion's spirit to
repeat this pledge of loyalty: "I do solemnly promise that
I will bear true faith and allegiance to the Christian
Church, that I will serve honestly and faithfully against all
enemies; that I will follow both the Gospel of Jesus Christ,
the Head of this Church, the Savior of my soul, and the
guidance of Christian pastors and teachers appointed over
me according to the rules and articles of His holy Word,
the Bible. God help me in this, for the atoning Savior's
sake!" Amen.

THANK GOD FOR THE EASTER VICTORY!

"Now is Christ risen from the dead. . . . In Christ shall all be made alive. . . . Thanks be to God, which giveth us the victory through our Lord Jesus Christ!" — 1 Corinthians 15:20, 22, 57

O Jesus, Victor Over the Grave, Destroyer of Death,
*   Lord of Life Everlasting:*

Endless praise, glory, majesty, adoration by men and angels be to Thee, Thou Son of God and Savior of our souls, that on the first Easter Day Thou didst rise from the sealed sepulcher to prove Thyself the living God, our eternal Redeemer! Bring the radiance of Thy resurrection to many hearts and homes through a firm, joy-filled faith! Show those who have surrendered to doubt or disbelief, that though the wages of unforgiven sin are death and exclusion from heaven, in Thine endless mercy Thou didst die on the cross and then victoriously come forth from the tomb to grant us the full assurance of our redemption and entrance into heaven! Help us, as we stand in spirit before the open grave, to realize that our confidence in Thy resurrection can banish sorrow, worry, doubt, pain of affliction, and fear of death! O Christ, our risen Redeemer, come to us, abide with us, and preserve us for the radiance of the celestial Easter with Thee! We ask these everlasting blessings by Thy triumph over death. Amen.

EASTER, the festival of life in a world of death! What redoubled joy and hope the Savior's rising from the dead should bring multitudes in our country this year! When bullets kill our soldiers on the Bataan Peninsula; when sailors from torpedoed tankers sink into the ocean depths; when aerial bombs blast the bodies of American fliers into bits, where can we find unfailing answers to questions like these: "What happens to those who have died fighting in the nation's defense?" "How can we best equip the young men called to the colors with assurance for the next life?" As plans for military offensives and counteroffensives are proposed, we must be prepared — and

[346]

high authorities have issued this warning — to pay a higher price in human blood before victory is ours. While the casualty lists continue to grow longer, from whom can we learn the truth concerning the eternity beyond the grave?

That perpetual problem, however, disturbs many more than the men in our military forces. It confronts you, the aged, who have advanced far along life's pilgrimage and know that the last milestone must be close; you, the invalids on sickbeds, who wonder what the doctor's verdict or the real result of the operation will be. Where can all of you, even the young, strong, brimful of energy, secure the calm of confidence required to meet the inevitable hour when your breath stops and your features become rigid in death's paralysis? The most serious issues before you, the heaviest burdens on many minds, the steadiest assaults on your peace and happiness are these disturbed demands: "What is my final destiny? What will happen to this body when I am placed in the grave?" Everything else in life, the most crushing sorrow, the hardest blow, is only a trivial disturbance in comparison with what some fear in death. A young woman in Ohio, for example, writes these revealing lines: "I have never seen a person die, and I hope that I never will. I have seen only three corpses in my nineteen years, but I have heard of the death struggle, the death rattle, and how terrible it is for people to die. It all seems so horrible."

Some of you, however, think that the grave need cause you no concern. You have no family lot in the cemetery. Funerals are distasteful to you. Anyway, you conclude, death is far away. But are you sure? Can anyone declare with finality that tomorrow he will still be numbered among the living? Accidents on the highway decrease because of the rubber shortage, but fatalities in the home increase. We conquer old diseases — and thank God that yesterday hope for the cure of infantile paralysis was announced! — yet new scourges arise. The only absolute certainty before everyone of us is the inescapable fact that we *must die;* and where, in this world of decay, can we find the means required to remove the terror of the last hour?

Not in science, for Professor Arthur H. Compton, Nobel Prize winner in physics, declares candidly: "I want to know what happens to me after this hull decays. But to this question science has no straightforward answer to give!" Neither can spiritism, fraud that it is, settle the issue. A few weeks ago in a Chicago park a friend of the late Clarence Darrow again tried to summon the spirit of that departed agnostic. Darrow had promised that after death he would make every effort to return with information concerning the hereafter; but neither he nor anyone else has ever come back. Nor is there help in the religion often miscalled "modern" and proclaimed from many American pulpits; for what possible comfort can a twentieth-century Sadducee bring a mother bereft of her only child, by mumbling some pretty words to the effect that there may be a survival of the ego, a perpetuation of personality — whatever that is?

For a positive pledge concerning the hereafter; for a reassuring reply to the anxious query "What becomes of my body when death's decay sets in?" we must turn not to men, earthly speculation, human guesswork, but to Christ, to His revelation of eternity, and — this is the Easter glory — to His own triumph over the tomb.

Now, to offer everyone of you the full resurrection rejoicing; to show that the anniversary of our Lord's rising from the grave should be welcomed also by war widows, war orphans, and homes saddened through bereavement; to remove the black fear of death from any sin-scarred, sorrow-burdened soul, Easter, the climax of Christian hope, bids us accept the angel's invitation, *"Come, see the place where the Lord lay!"* As we stand in spirit once more before the rock-hewn grave, with Pilate's seal broken, the heavy boulder rolled away, the shrouds torn asunder, the tomb itself empty, may we

THANK GOD FOR THE EASTER VICTORY!

That gratitude is suggested by Saint Paul's doxology in First Corinthians, chapter fifteen, from which our text has been chosen (verses twenty, twenty-two, and fifty-seven): *"Now is Christ risen from the dead. . . . In Christ shall all be made alive. . . . Thanks be to God, which giveth us the victory through our Lord Jesus Christ!"*

I

CHRIST HAS DEFEATED DEATH

The fifteenth chapter of Saint Paul's First Letter to the Corinthians should be emblazoned with imperishable letters of faith on every Christian soul. Despite the distractions of this wartime Easter, the fashion parade, more expensive and extravagant than ever before, the war, more critical than many imagine, take time to read this resurrection chapter carefully! You have heard these words at funerals in the church and at burials in the cemetery; but as God's own truth they are so inexhaustibly rich that 1900 years of restudy and restatement have not been able to plumb their divine depths. As you go through this victory declaration, verse by verse, you will see that Saint Paul loses no time in arguing or debating the fact that Jesus rose from the dead on the third day. Greek philosophers might ridicule this truth, his own countrymen deny it; but here, enshrined in faith which becomes stronger the more violently it is attacked, is the apostle's triumphant conclusion, *"Now is Christ risen from the dead!"*

Neither should we involve ourselves in intricate arguments concerning the Easter reality. To me as a Christian — and I hope to you — the fact that Jesus did not molder in a Palestinian grave but on the first Easter gloriously burst death's bonds is a verity more definitely assured than ten thousand records of past history, since the resurrection record is the revelation of God's unimpeachable, unchangeable Word.

Long before Christ rose from His garden grave, it was foretold that, though He would die, His body would not *"see corruption,"* and whatever Scripture promises it performs exactly. Jesus Himself repeatedly predicted His startling conquest over death; and I defy anyone to prove that Christ does not keep His pledges to the letter. Witnesses, friend and foe alike, singly and in groups of as many as five hundred, in various places, at different times; the four evangelists in separate yet harmonious accounts; even an angel from heaven — all have testified to this climax of our faith, "On the third day He rose again from the dead." Altogether thirty-one New Testament passages repeat the assurance that the grave could not restrain the crucified Christ. One utterance is sufficient when God speaks, but thirty-one statements by the Almighty should convince even the most distrustful mind.

True, atheists and agnostics contradict this testimony, but if they are consistent, they ought to deny every other event in history. For no occurrence of bygone centuries has been more clearly corroborated by trustworthy testimony than the glorious miracle by which your Savior and mine came forth from His tomb. His resurrection revolutionized the Christian calendar. Before Easter, the Sabbath, the last day of the week, was set aside for worship. But in the New Testament liberty with which Christ has made us free the Sabbath is abolished. (Remember Saint

Paul's admonition, *"Let no man . . . judge you . . . in respect of . . . the sabbath days."*) When the early Christians had to select a time on which they would stop working and come together for prayer and praise, they chose the day on which Jesus rose from the dead, Sunday, the first day, and they called it reverently, as we should, "the Lord's Day." Every Sunday therefore is an anniversary proof of Christ's victory; and though fiercely assailed in the past, the Lord's Day has remained a striking memorial to the Savior's marvelous defeat of death. Enemies of God tried to abolish Sunday during the French Revolution, but the leader who planned to make every tenth day a period of atheistic relaxation, was executed by fellow conspirators. The Lord's Day outlived that reign of terror. Communists, in brazen rebellion against Christ have made the fifth day of each week the rest day, but their wickedness will likewise not survive. Under the stress of the present emergency, Sunday labor is helping to decrease attendance at many churches and deprive workers of the Lord's Day's blessings. As far as the seven-day working week is necessary for national defense, Christian workers will bring whatever sacrifices this new order requires. Let churches hold extra services for those necessarily employed on Sunday! The family altar, household prayers and Scripture reading, should be restored and re-emphasized to help meet the emergency. The consequences of encouraging a willful disregard of the Lord's Day, the memorial to Christ's resurrection, can be fatal.

The truth of the apostle's declaration *"Now is Christ risen from the dead"* is proved today by the Savior's transforming power. Godless men torn from dissolute lives become witnesses for the Lord; brazen women turned from lives of shame to careers of consecration; nations led from the darkness of pagan vices to the light of progress; sufferers sustained in agonies which otherwise would drive men to despair or suicide; dying sinners radiating joy in their last hours — such miracles can be explained only when we realize that the crucifixion is not the end, that the Savior's body has not returned to the dust of Judean soil, that the Christ who died for our sins was *"raised again for our justification"*! Have you ever heard of a single person being reborn into a new life of faith, a career of honesty, purity, cleanness, self-sacrifice, unquenchable joy, and the assurance of eternal bliss by following any leader who was defeated by death?

We who love the risen Savior cannot stop evil tongues and blasphemous minds from denying the resurrection victory; but when it is repeatedly and ungratefully charged that men of scientific achievement and scholarly acclaim regard the Easter Gospel as legendary, we protest emphatically. While we accept divine revelation, whether scholars subscribe to it or not, we are gratified to note that in opposition to the denial of second-rate mentalities, many academic authorities have endorsed the literal truth of the Easter story. Dr. Cyrus Northrup, "grand old man" of Minnesota University, was not only a noted educator; he also had the rock-ribbed faith which enabled him to declare, "As long as I stand at the head of Minnesota University, I shall uphold Christianity as the religion which is to save the world." Other college presidents please copy! He issued this deliberate statement concerning the Easter truth: "For myself I should have very little confirmation of immortality from all the arguments . . . or human longings if I did not believe that Jesus rose from the dead, as He said He would rise and as we are told that He did. . . . I recognized in Jesus a Messenger from God who had power to lay down His life and power to take it up again." Cyrus Northrup is but one in a long list of distinguished intellectuals frequently mentioned in these broadcasts who have unhesitatingly subscribed to the truth attested by the empty grave. If ever it seems to you that the resurrection record contradicts reason and you demand proof, remember how the doubt of Thomas was removed. He knelt before Christ to hear Him say, *"Blessed are they that have not seen and yet have believed."* Immeasurable joy will be yours if you also kneel in spirit before the risen Savior, study the Easter Gospel, and hear its promise in the sermon of a true Christian minister. Then, if doubts arise, you can pray, *"Lord, I believe; help Thou mine unbelief!"* and Jesus will mightily strengthen you to overcome doubt.

Easter is also heaven's own proof that our Lord keeps His word. He asserted, *"I am the Resurrection and the Life"*; He pledged, *"Destroy this temple, and in three days I will raise it up!"* and this prophecy became actual history. Some religious leaders tantalize and then disappoint their followers with false, exaggerated promises. But not Christ! His fulfillment — to the letter — of every prediction concerning His resurrection brings us the guarantee we all need for these sorrow-marked days, divine assurance for our own trials, temptations, griefs, bereavements; and these promises can never be broken, though the earth itself collapse and the heavens be dissolved into nothingness. Take heart at the open grave and believe that Jesus fulfills His pledge; that *"all the promises of God"* for your deliverance on earth and your salvation in heaven *"in Him are yea, and in Him amen"*!

Throughout the early Church, Easter was the outstanding Christian holy day, called "the crown and head of all festivals." On this day, a fourth-century writer says, "all labor ceased; all tasks were suspended. The farmer threw down his spade and plow to put on his holiday attire, and the tavern keepers left their gain to be present at the Easter services. The land was free of travelers, the sea of sailors, for all tried to be home on this great day. All Christians assembled together as members of one great family." Emperor Valentinian marked Easter by granting many pardons. When this happy day came, those early believers canceled their debts, freed slaves, suspended lawsuits. We would do well to reestablish those customs. The world is profited little if this resurrection anniversary is merely an occasion for poems and pictures of reawakening nature. Let the children have their joy; but no child in America should be kept in ignorance of the blessed fact that this is the day of Christ's victory, not merely a holiday with bunnies, chickens, baby ducks, pussy-willows, and budding flowers! No home should be too preoccupied with social activities which start after the subdued Lenten season to welcome the risen Lord. No Christian should indulge in such extravagance for food and holiday finery that scant interest is left for the resurrected Savior and only incidental funds for the spread of His message. Recently I saw pictures of the fabulous artificial eggs which each year were given as Easter remembrances in the household of the last Russian czar. Designed by expert craftsmanship, they were made of gold, studded with gems, and filled with intricate mechanical devices, so constructed, for example, that a bejeweled rooster would appear every hour. They could bring no real happiness, however; while the royal family spent a king's ransom for these overdone holiday luxuries, masses of Russian peasants suffered inexpressibly from poverty and cruel oppression. Neither can you, however wealthy and prosperous you may be, find any permanent joy in life, except through personal, penitent, praise-filled worship of the risen Redeemer and through the Easter faith, which rejoices, *"Now is Christ risen from the dead!"* Come, then, cast away all distracting thoughts, suggestions of doubt, heaviness of afflicted hearts, worry over the war, over your family, your health, your business, and believe that, because Jesus lives, He can help you in every need, strengthen you in weakness, direct you in each moment of uncertainty, and finally bring you to share fully with Him the radiance of His resurrection glory!

II

WE TOO SHALL DEFEAT DEATH

Now to the question in many minds, "Well, what difference does it make for me if Christ rose from the grave?" I answer pointedly, "All the difference in the world!" With a firm, personal reliance on the Easter Gospel, you have Heaven's own solution to the mystery of death, the answer to the questions concerning life in the next world. The Savior's repeated promises: *"Because I live, ye shall live also"; "Where I am, there shall also My servant be"; "I am the Resurrection and the Life"; "If a man keep My saying, he shall never see death"* — these and a score of other pledges of a blessed existence beyond the grave have been mightily endorsed by the Easter record. This existence is also the promise of our text: *"In Christ shall all be made alive."* For Jesus conquered sin, the cause of death. The divine Creator made man for an everlasting existence; but disobedience to the heavenly will robbed him of his immortality. If you want to find the cause of death, however it may come, you need not look far: every cemetery, tombstone, grave, is the consequence of human transgression. No matter how unbelief may belittle this basic truth, American pulpits question it, or *"science falsely so called"* oppose it, the verdict of the Scriptures remains unchanged: *"The soul that sinneth, it shall die"; "The wages of sin is death."* Therefore, if endless life is to be restored, the tyranny of our transgressions must be broken, our iniquity completely removed.

How — and this has been the searching question of the ages — can we defeat the superhuman and satanic power of evil? We cannot pay our way out of transgressions. Micah exclaims, *"Wherewith shall I come before the Lord and bow myself before the high God? Shall I come before Him with burnt offerings, with calves of a year old? Will the Lord be pleased with thousands of rams or with ten thousands of rivers of oil? Shall I give my first-born for my transgression, the fruit of my body for the sin of my soul?"* He shows us we need more than fabulous wealth, more even than human life, to cancel our iniquities. We cannot work ourselves out of sin; for though we wear the flesh off our hands and feet, though we toil ceaselessly through long, sleepless nights, we must fall short of earning our redemption. Eternal Truth warns, *"By the deeds of the Law there shall no flesh be justified."* We cannot cheat our way into pardon by declaring that we have no guilt, for the holy God sees into our hearts and uncovers our hidden lusts, private vices, the concealed wrong we may vainly seek to cover. We cannot scheme our way into God's grace. The processes of earthly justice may be thwarted; cunning attorneys may help their clients escape the full penalty, but divine justice never makes a mistake. His truth cannot be outwitted, His punishment never outrun.

Nor can others complete what you fail to accomplish. No chemist has produced an antiseptic to cleanse your soul of a single blot. No friend can take your place before God's life-and-death tribunal. Pious parents, godly pastors, self-denying saints, are all powerless to remove your sin and deliver you from death. Dictators and tyrants may send millions to war and destruction, but earth's mightiest ruler cannot send a solitary soul to peace and life. Angels, sinless and stainless in their celestial holiness, may wipe out armies, but they are unable to destroy a single sin. Even Jesus Himself could not have saved us, had He remained in the grave. Saint Paul's warning still rings true: *"If Christ be not raised, your faith is vain; ye are yet in your sins."*

God be praised, however, because Easter proves that in the plan of divine mercy there is a positive cure for sin, the holy, precious blood of the Lord Jesus! There is a substitute for human wrong, the death of the crucified Savior at Calvary. There is life instead of eternal death, because the resurrection miracle proves that Christ is, as He repeatedly taught, the true Son of God, stronger than the grave.

His victory over sin and decay is sure. Modern minds may seek to contradict the repeated testimony to its truth, but Job declares, *"I know that my Redeemer liveth."* A famous liberal preacher speaks of the Easter hope as "the soul's surmise"; but Saint Paul challenges, *"Who is he that condemneth? It is Christ that died, yea rather, that is risen again, who is even at the right hand of God."*

Christ's offer of heaven and eternity is free. Men pay fabulous sums for trinkets and trivialities, but the greatest gift Heaven itself could bestow and men receive is the pledge of immortality granted by full mercy. The Easter doxology declares, *"Thanks be to God, which giveth us the victory through our Lord Jesus Christ!"* If God *gives,* we need not earn it.

The Easter promise is universal. Race riots may show the depths of hatred that flares up between various social classes; but before our merciful Father and through Christ's compassion all men may receive never-ending blessedness. For here is the Savior's promise: *"God so loved the world, that He gave His only-begotten Son, that whosoever believeth in Him should not perish but have everlasting life."*

This eternity with the Savior is splendor beyond compare. The resurrected body will be reconstructed without blemish or defect. The Bible teaches that our risen bodies are to be like the glorified body of our Savior, perfect, powerful, bright as the sun. What comfort to know not merely that our personalities survive death but that our own forms and features will be restored; that although our bodies may be crippled and diseased, they shall be recreated without injury or loss of members! And what can we say of the celestial beauties and the happy, pain-free existence amid radiance too marvelous for description, forever removed from tears, safeguarded against all departure, so surpassing in its loveliness that the most marvelous of earth's attractions are limp and faded?

Do not sneer at this sacred truth by declaring that when a man dies, he is dead forever, or by claiming that no body decayed in the grave, blown into a thousand bits, or decomposed on the ocean floor, can ever be resurrected! Modern unbelief teaches that men can do almost anything, while God, if indeed there is a God, can do little. People applaud the shipbuilder who makes thousands of tons of iron and steel built into a battleship float in the water; but, they say, God's prophet could not make the axhead float in the Jordan. They honor radio engineers who have shown that the air all over the world is filled with many different sounds, which can be heard when selected by a radio receiver; but emphatically they deny that the God who made the air and the sound waves can be everywhere, that the Spirit can work in the hearts of men thousands of miles apart. Much admiration is showered on a Saint Louis scientist who has made a human heart beat after the body was dead; but skeptics ridicule the idea that the great

God can revive a dead man's spirit. We admire the startling processes of modern industrial chemistry, by which coal tar, distilled and processed, can be changed into attractive crystalline plastics; but why do skeptics refuse to concede that Christ can resurrect our remains and *"change our vile body, that it may be fashioned like unto His glorious body"?* Presidential medals are showered on botanists who develop special seeds that, sown into the ground, decay, yet produce the germ from which beautiful, multicolored flowers emerge. But why do haughty men insist that the omnipotent Creator, who first made man from the dust of the ground, cannot remake him in heavenly radiance?

End all doubt on Easter! Throw off all denials before the open grave, and with the mind of Mary Magdalene, who was the first to meet the risen Christ, greet your resurrected Redeemer today with trusting faith! Learn to welcome death and, in the spirit of Christian martyrs who rejoiced that they would soon behold their Lord, conquer the fear of *"the last enemy"* through the love of Christ! Don't shriek or scream at a funeral as though there were no hope for those who have the Lord Jesus! Don't clench your fist against the Almighty, as though He were heartless in permitting bereavement to enter your home! Defy Satan, hell, and the grave with this powerful cry of triumph: *"O Death, where is thy sting? O Grave, where is thy victory? ... Thanks be to God, which giveth us the victory through our Lord Jesus Christ!"*

Show your thanks by living the faith! The Scriptures remind us that, because we are risen with Christ, we should *"seek those things which are above."* Learn to talk about heaven, pray for it, yearn for it! Have the whole family, father and mother, brothers and sisters, prepare for it, so that in the celestial home they may all be reunited before the throne of the Lamb! Help each member of the household accept the Lord Jesus in personal, penitent faith, and then, whatever the future may hold for you — sorrows in your individual lives, persecution in your churches, long-drawn-out conflict for the nation — beholding the open heaven beyond the open grave, you can exult, *"The sufferings of this present time are not worthy to be compared with the glory which shall be revealed in us,"* when in the eternal Easter we come face to face with Jesus.

Real, sincere thanks for the Savior's resurrection must show itself in an intense desire to spread the message of the living Lord. Therefore I ask you on this Easter day: Have you ever done anything which would help lead others to everlasting life? Have you personally told anyone today of the resurrected Redeemer's grace, His power, and His eternal blessing? Too many Christians, I fear, have not raised their voices in offering friends, acquaintances, fellow workers, neighbors, this glorious truth of the Easter miracle that they have a Savior who not only gave Himself into the agony of the crucifixion but also proved His divine power and grace by breaking forth from the grave and defeating death's tyranny forever. What tens of millions in America and hundreds of millions all over the face of the globe need is complete reliance on the living Christ. Everything else in this world is only of secondary and often of doubtful importance. While we treasure the Gospel light, let us strive and sacrifice to bring it to others over the face of this war-scarred earth! How I thank God that I can now report publicly one of the most startling advances in the spread of our radio work! A few days ago a cable from the Icelandic government informed us that the facilities of the 100,000-watt superstation in their capital, Reykjavik, has been placed at our disposal. Because this station with its tremendous power is regularly heard in England, Ireland, and Scotland, we are enabled to enter Europe for the first time. With the help of God we hope to feature Icelandic messages for the people of the island and broadcasts in English for our soldiers in Iceland as well as for the people of Great Britain.

All this, however, must be only the beginning of our European work. Masses on that war-ridden continent should have the promise of a new life in heaven and a new existence here on earth through faith in Him who died and rose again for them. Stand by us, then, with your prayers, your interest, your gifts, as we publicly pledge to broadcast the promise of the risen Christ, wherever over the face of the earth God thus grants us openings!

At the Church of the Holy Sepulcher in Jerusalem this morning, fire is said to have descended miraculously from heaven and to have lighted the candle held by a high official of the Greek Orthodox Church. Great crowds from many parts of the civilized world pressed forward to light their candles from this supposedly celestial fire and thus to find good luck for the future. While all this is misrepresentation and superstition, everyone of you can find the fire of fervent faith here at the open grave which will bring you not good luck but new light for every day, new courage for every affliction, new hope in every sorrow, new triumphs over the fear of death. As we answer the joyous Easter proclamation *"He is risen!"* with the response of trusting faith "He is risen indeed!" (and once more I ask that this be your Easter greeting today) let our faith declare joyfully in this nation-wide testimony to the risen Savior, *"Thanks be to God, which giveth us the victory,"* triumph over death, darkness, and despair, *"through our Lord Jesus Christ,"* the resurrected and eternal Redeemer! Amen.

LORD OF LIFE, "ABIDE WITH US!"

"They drew nigh unto the village whither they went, and He made as though He would have gone further. But they constrained Him, saying, Abide with us; for it is toward evening, and the day is far spent. And He went in to tarry with them. And it came to pass, as He sat at meat with them, He took bread and blessed it and brake and gave to them. And their eyes were opened, and they knew Him; and He vanished out of their sight. And they said one to another, Did not our heart burn within us while He talked with us by the way and while He opened to us the Scriptures?" — Saint Luke 24:28-32

Jesus, Our Resurrected Redeemer:

"Abide with us!" we, too, pray as the shades of this world's night overshadow us. Unmistakable signs point to Thy quick return during the last hours of this far-spent day. Until Thou dost come again in Thy glory, draw near to us constantly through Thy Gospel! Walk with us along our pathways, as on the first Easter Thou didst accompany Thy two disappointed disciples; but open our eyes to find in Thee our living Savior, whose resurrection is the seal of our own eternal life! As we behold Thy holy radiance, make us keenly mindful of our daily sins and the anguish that follows all unforgiven iniquity! Speak to us through Thy Word, and implant within us a real sorrow over our denials of Thy mercy; yet make "our heart burn within us," too, when we take hold of Thy mercy which can remove sins ten thousand times more numerous and grievous than ours! Dwell in our homes, and during these months of war and woe, give us that sense of inner gratitude which leads us to accept our daily bread and Thy multiplied bounty with thanksgiving! Into Thy fatherly care we place the cause of this nation. Be not distant from us, for danger is near! Bring us constantly closer to Thee, along any road on which Thou wouldst draw us to Thy grace! We know that Thou wilt hear us, for Thou hast often promised to answer those who put their trust in Thee. Therefore, "abide with us," Lord Jesus, our only, but all-powerful Savior! Amen.

LAST week sorrow suddenly changed to joy for the crew of a vessel in the Caribbean Sea. It was carrying a cargo of precious oil, when an enemy submarine suddenly blocked its path and began to rake the decks with shellfire, shrapnel, and pom-poms. A torpedo then struck amidship and tore a gaping hole in her side at water level. The steering apparatus was destroyed; fire broke out; the craft began to list; and the "Abandon Ship!" order was soon given. Only one lifeboat and three rafts were undamaged, and on these most of the crew were able to escape, leaving the gallant captain and eight seamen dead on the flaming decks. By hard rowing the lifeboat and the rafts were brought safely outside the danger zone. A night of darkness and deep anxiety followed. But can you imagine the thrill those prisoners of the waves experienced when, as the sun rose over the eastern horizon, they saw their ship still afloat? The fire had burned itself out, and the safety compartments had prevented the vessel from sinking. The crew hastily rowed back to the tanker, made emergency adjustments, and after several days brought the craft into an American port. The lost vessel was rescued, the valuable cargo saved.

In many other ways this war has produced sudden happiness for those cast down by its crushing sorrow. Airplanes given up as destroyed return to their base; troop transports, long overdue, posted as missing, sail into their harbors; soldiers reported by official war department announcements as killed in action reappear alive and uninjured. But not even parents who have received notifications that their sons, mourned as dead, were in joyful reality living, could have experienced the whole-souled rejoicing which came to two disciples of our Lord on the road to Emmaus, a small village near Jerusalem. Despondent because Jesus had been crucified, they were transported to raptures when the same Christ who had been laid into the grave, unexpectedly appeared on that dusty highway, spoke to them, entered their home, and left them with a blessing.

It is the grace of the resurrected Savior, however, that everyone who accepts His atoning death and His Easter victory over the grave can share in the Emmaus disciples' gladness. And because many of you, through personal reverses or distrust of God's promises, are missing the happiness of a life in faith, let us, lingering for another Sunday in the Easter exultation, make the request of the two disciples our personal plea as, turning to the risen Savior, we ask:

LORD OF LIFE, "ABIDE WITH US!"

For this fortifying of our faith we shall study, under the Spirit's guidance, the words recorded in Saint Luke's Gospel, chapter twenty-four, verses twenty-eight to thirty-two: *"They drew nigh unto the village whither they went; and He made as though He would have gone further. But they constrained Him, saying, Abide with us; for it is toward evening, and the day is far spent. And He went in to tarry with them. And it came to pass, as He sat at meat with them, He took bread and blessed it and brake and gave to them. And their eyes were opened, and they knew Him; and He vanished out of their sight. And they said one to another, Did not our heart burn within us while He talked with us by the way and while He opened to us the Scriptures?"*

I

WE NEED THY PRESENCE ON OUR DARKENED PATHWAYS

We know little definitely about these two disciples. The one is called Cleopas, but this does not identify him for us. The other remains entirely unnamed, although some students of the Scriptures have held that he is Saint Luke himself. Nor can we locate with certainty the village of Emmaus toward which they were hastening on this first Easter in the early afternoon. We do know, however, that their hearts were overburdened with grief such as few of you have endured. The death of a beloved one, as many know from funerals they attended this week, always brings heart-crushing anguish, even though it is the release from pain and the end of a long, troubled life; but these disciples were gripped by inconsolable heartache because they had learned to love the Lord Jesus as a *"prophet mighty in deed and word before God and all the people."* With clinging faith they had trusted that He would redeem Israel, break the Roman rule, and establish God's kingdom on earth. All their hopes, their ideals, their ambitions were centered in Christ, and when the churchmen and the politicians *"delivered Him to be condemned to death and . . . crucified Him,"* that shameful death made their aspirations and yearnings crash in utter ruin. The foundation of their faith had collapsed, and they found nothing on which they could rebuild assurance or regain joy in life. The reports they had heard a few hours before from Mary Magdalene and other women that Christ was risen; the announcement by certain disciples that the grave in which Jesus had been laid was now empty — these claims left the two disconsolate disciples untouched, except perhaps to increase their sorrow, for they regarded such accounts as idle, impossible rumors. Therefore it seemed a cruel, heartless taunt to raise false hopes, which would only cause fresh wounds of anguish. In short, their whole happiness was blasted away, because they definitely believed that Christ was mouldering in the sealed tomb.

With earnest concern for your soul's salvation, a peaceful mind, and a victorious life, remember that you likewise will never know the highest happiness if you reject the fact of our Savior's resurrection. You may be ever so religious, constantly concerned about a moral goodness, daily devoted to the reading of spiritual books and church magazines; you may spend much money for instruction courses in some of the new creeds which pretend to offer divine solution to human problems; you may rigidly follow programs of self-denial, fasting, praying; you may be high officers in fashionable, influential congregations; you may be even a pastor with a string of university degrees behind your name, applauded for your intellect and oratory: but if you believe that Jesus did not rise from the grave; that Christ was only a man, though you admit, the mightiest; that His life was only an example, though the noblest; that His words were only human wisdom, even if the choicest; that His crucifixion and death with all the rankling injustice and fearful agony were only the usual end of man — you are robbing yourself of the one hope of eternal blessing that God Almighty can give you. To lead the life worth living, to find sorrow worth the suffering, to be strengthened for the death worth the glorious dying, you must — there are no exceptions, no exemptions — believe and confess that Jesus Christ is both Son of God and Son of man, that He was both sinless and sin-cursed as He bore all our transgressions in His holy body at Calvary, that He was both slain on the cross and then raised from the garden-grave *"for our justification,"* pardon, and eternal peace.

While the two forlorn followers of our Lord were trudging along the Emmaus road, engrossed in their gloomy, dismal thoughts, they suddenly met a mysterious Stranger, whom we identify as the risen Redeemer, but whom they failed to recognize because, as we read, *"their eyes were holden that they should not know Him."* Have you likewise been unaware of the Lord's presence? He would come close to you each time His name is mentioned, wherever you pass a true church of God, see a Bible, or view a picture presenting a scene from His life — and how happy I was recently to find on public exhibition in one of the nation's largest department stores two immense and impressive canvases portraying our Lord's trial and crucifixion! The risen Savior approaches you personally whenever, as in this message, you are told that Jesus, God's Son and Mary's, laid down His life and then took it up again for you. Yet how many there are who have not identified the inner appeal for repentance and redemption as the voice of Christ and His Spirit! Too often the Word falls on the stony soil of indifference, so that after short-lived enthusiasm your ardor cools and you forget Jesus. You think that it is of little importance whether you believe or disbelieve, take the Gospel or leave it. — When the world-famous Koh-i-noor, one of the most magnificent diamonds in the world, was discovered in India, it was entrusted to a high official for safekeeping. Weighted by the cares of state, he dismissed the precious stone from his mind and even forgot where it had been placed. Six months later Queen Victoria ordered the Koh-i-noor sent to her. After considerable search the small package in which it had been wrapped was found in a trunk. The native servant had thought it merely an interesting piece of glass, and his master had been almost as unconcerned about the immense treasure. I am offering to you now, in this broadcast, through these very sentences, a possession far more precious than ten thousands of Koh-i-noors. What will you do with it? Will you not at least be considerate enough of your soul to take time for the reverent hearing and studying of Christ's invitation and instruction? — The Earl of Chatham, noted British statesman, was once bequeathed a large, attractive estate, but the country lawyer whose duty it was to inform Chatham of this important bequest was at first not admitted to the Earl's residence. The doorkeeper bluntly reminded him, "His lordship does not receive every countryman who comes to town." After several other refusals the attorney's persistence was rewarded. He was ushered into Chatham's presence. But the earl cautioned him, "I am so busy with the affairs of state that I can give you but three minutes." The lawyer began to read the will, but Chatham's mind still lingered on national issues; he heard only a jumble of legal terms like "whereas," "aforesaid," "hereby"; and when the reading was finished, he demanded emphatically, "Well, what has all this to do with me?" Amazedly the attorney replied, "Don't you understand that this whole estate is yours, that this document makes you a wealthy man?" In much the same way some of you have been paying merely half-hearted attention to what I am telling you, reading the Sunday newspaper or washing the dinner dishes and catching only a few phrases of this broadcast. Put the paper away, let the dishes stand a few minutes, while I offer you, in the Savior's name, these spiritual riches and heavenly treasures which *"neither moth nor rust doth corrupt"* — the assurance that Jesus Christ is your Savior; that He is risen from the grave and has now, in the realms of His celestial glory, prepared a place which can be yours if you will but accept His promised grace!

Evidently gloom was written on the faces of the two soul-weary travelers on the Emmaus road, and sorrow expressed itself in the tone of their voices; for as soon as our Lord joined them, He asked the cause of their sadness. That is always Christ's merciful manner; He constantly inquires into the reason for human suffering; and while you may think that He, the great and glorious God, would be too engrossed in momentous world issues to have even a thought for you and your perplexities, believe that His

Word, which has never made an exaggerated or misplaced pledge, includes you in the invitation *"Come unto Me, all ye that labor and are heavy laden, and I will give you rest"*!

It took the disciples only a few moments to outline the reasons for their grief; but it took the Lord Jesus longer, almost all the way into the village, to teach them and us a lesson vital for every spiritual life. In plain language, which seems blunt in the translation, He told His companions that their sorrow came from disbelief. With the patience Jesus always showed disturbed, inquiring souls, He reminded them, *"Ought not Christ to have suffered these things and to enter into His glory?"* and we read, *"Beginning at Moses and all the prophets, He expounded unto them in all the Scriptures the things concerning Himself."* Our Lord referred to the Bible as the one source of absolute authority.

"Back to the Scriptures! Back to fulfilled prophecy!" must be also our motto whenever doubt or disbelief assails our soul. It has always seemed to me that, if skeptical, uncertain minds would only follow Christ's procedure and consider the predictions foretelling His vicarious suffering, His substitutionary death, and His victorious resurrection, all for the salvation of the sinner, they should be convinced of the unique and divine power in our Christian faith. Human predictions, including scientific forecasts, are often false. Two weeks ago today in Baltimore the weather bureau announced in the press, "No precipitation"; yet, while the newspapers were being sold, a record snowfall of twenty-two inches was in progress. At the beginning of the war a United States Senator turned soothsayer and asserted that within six weeks the Japanese would be wiped out; the fall of Bataan Peninsula after four months of bitter struggle makes the end seem farther away than ever and asks every American citizen to pray harder, work longer, give more generously, until victory be ours with a God-pleasing peace. But Christ's prophetic Word has never made a mistake. Aging centuries before He went the way of the cross, only to vanquish death, every major aspect of His crucifixion and resurrection was foretold in clear, startling statements, all of which were fulfilled to the letter. By exactly the same truth and divine power Jesus will keep everyone of His promises to you. When the Bible directs, "Cast *'all your care upon Him, for He careth for you,'* " bring your worries and anxieties to the foot of the cross, and in fulfillment He will take their burden from you. When the Savior pledges, *"Your sorrow shall be turned into joy,"* nothing on earth can be more certain than that through faith your reverses become causes of rejoicing.

Later, when the disciples reviewed their remarkable conversation with the risen Lord, they exclaimed, *"Did not our heart burn within us while He talked with us by the way and while He opened to us the Scriptures?"* The fire of faith can burn also within you if you will only read Christ's Word, hear the truths of Scripture expounded, and believe God's promise in Jesus. You may be ever so world-weary, *blasé,* emotionally cold; you may complain that you have tasted all life's pleasures and have become stolid, hardened, immovable, oversatiated; you may insist that the heavy hand of sorrows has crushed you completely and you no longer react to surprise or disappointment; but I promise you, if you open your heart to the Savior and His Word, *"which is able to build you up,"* you will experience a newness, a verve of faith, an upswing of joy, such as you have never before considered possible.

Back to the Book, then, the whole Book, including the Old Testament, which Jesus here cites as God's literal revelation and which He knowingly calls *"Truth"!* Back,

then, to the Christ of the cross and the open grave! Back
to the Church that preaches His full Gospel! And through
that blessed return the Savior, who promised, *"Lo, I am
with you alway, even unto the end of the world,"* will walk
at your side along the bitterest pathways, as He accompanied the Emmaus disciples, always to inquire concerning
your sadness, to correct your errors, raise your drooping
spirits, and stir the cold embers of dying hope into flames
of fervent faith.

II

WE NEED THY PRESENCE, PARTICULARLY
IN OUR HOMES

When the risen Lord and His disciples all too quickly
came near the outskirts of the village, each step increasing
the wonder of the two men, Jesus *"made as though He
would have gone further."* Possibly He would have passed
through the village had His companions not pleaded
earnestly, *"Abide with us!"* You see, the Savior awaits an
invitation into our homes; He will not force His way into
any family circle which refuses to receive Him. He wants
devoted, thankful, penitent faith. And because those two
faint-hearted followers, still not recognizing Christ, yet
learning to love Him as a fascinating Bible expounder,
a friend with authority and counsel, were not satisfied
merely with extending the invitation, *"Abide with us!"* —
"they constrained Him." They were so eager to keep Him
that they *"constrained Him"* to accept their hospitality.

We, too, should invite Christ with the same constrain-
ing fervor: "Lord of life, *'abide with us'* in our hearts and
in our homes!" For if Jesus is not welcomed into our
household, our families will not be welcomed in the eternal
mansions. According to Scripture and by the verdict of
the Lord Himself, no other pathway leads to that Paradise
than the faith in the blessed Savior who declares un-

reservedly, "*I am the Way, the Truth, and the Life. No man cometh unto the Father but by Me.*" Therefore, first of all, accept Christ as your own grace-bestowing God! Ask Him, above *everything* else, to abide with you! Approach Him penitently, with full and unreserved admission of your own sins, without any excuse or attempt to disguise or reduce the wrong which abounds in your heart, and, clinging only to His promise of mercy, you will find complete pardon, perfect peace, the seal of your salvation. As soon as you have declared yourself for Christ, do not rest until He abides with your whole family; for His presence in the home can give husband and wife, parents and children, the promise of a blessed reunion in heaven.

We should likewise pray, "*Abide with us!*" and constrain Jesus to grace our family circle because the American home, as the unit-basis in the development of the nation, the Church, and the individual, needs the uplifting power which His presence bestows. In consequence of the war normal family life has collapsed throughout vast areas of the world. In Russia juvenile crime has assumed such proportions that only a few years ago a law was passed imposing the death sentence for theft committed by children twelve years old. In Germany strange, vicious theories, which would put the interests of the totalitarian state above the Biblical principles of marriage, have gained acceptance in Nazi circles and have increased youthful immorality. From England social experts send us pointed warning calling attention to war's devastating effects on home life. They report a 50-per-cent increase in youth crimes, a growing wave of disobedience to parents, and a disregard of authority. Because British fathers and mothers are frequently too occupied with the issues of war properly to care for their children, the emergency has broken many families. Teen-age boys and girls working in English war industries receive unprecedented high wages, which many promptly squander in harmful pastimes and for destructive purposes. In our country the family base is being assaulted as never before. The forces of impurity, using printed page, pictures, and public entertainment, ridicule the exalted standards of Christian morality and openly endorse the violation of God's purity commandment. It is considered smart and sophisticated in many quarters to indulge in repeated divorce. A man with six matrimonial ventures is featured, without condemnation, by our newspapers. Perverted opinion still regards willfully childless families as fashionable and socially desirable — although some voices outside the Church are finally raised in commendation of larger families. The questions of discipline and respect for parents are constantly becoming more acute as juvenile delinquency increases and mothers, by necessity or desire for more money, work away from their households.

If the Emmaus disciples pleaded with Jesus, *"Abide with us; for it is toward evening, and the day is far spent!"* how much more should we, upon whom the twilight of history has descended, ask for the Savior's sustaining companionship! All the signs of the last times are being fulfilled before our eyes, and the day of this world is truly *"far spent."* Jesus is coming soon in a majestic return to judge the quick and the dead. Make your peace with God now, in this accepted time, while you still have the chance! *"Set thine house in order!"* More than in any previous age of our nation's existence the American household should repeat the Emmaus prayer, *"Abide with us!"* for Christ, as He steps across our threshold, can bring Heaven's help, together with the faith which will bless the whole family and counteract the forces of lust and hatred.

How reassuring to read that our Lord accepted the

disciples' invitation and entered their dwelling! It was probably only a small, modest house, as most Palestinian homes were in those days, but it was not too humble for Christ. He is the Savior of the meek and lowly. Any family, however poor and unimportant it may be; any home, a one-room cabin on the wide Western plains or a pretentious mansion in the city's most exclusive section; any fathers, whether they are laborers or corporation heads; any mothers, hard-working scrubwomen with only meager schooling or socially prominent college graduates; any children, sons and daughters of the ragged or of the rich — all who in true, trusting faith say to the Savior, *"Abide with us!"* can have the assurance that He will enter their homes to bless them. — He does not come visibly, of course, as He did on that Easter afternoon; but He enters our homes just as effectively through His Word. His promise *"Where two or three are gathered together in My name, there am I in the midst of them"* holds particularly for households in which the reading of God's Word forms an essential part of the day's activities. Let this, then, be the cry that offers promise for better homes, better churches, a better nation: "Bring the Bible back to the American family. Make each home in the United States a Scripture-loving, Scripture-searching house of God!"

When Jesus *"went in to tarry with them"* at Emmaus, He, the Lord of Life, accepted the food prepared for the simple evening meal; but before eating, He asked divine blessing. Wherever His Spirit rules, His holy example will be followed reverently. Yet, while Christians know that the three meals they enjoy each day come from God and that He who gives can also withhold, it is to be regretted that in most American families, including many with church connections, there is no time for even a word of prayer or a hymn of thanksgiving at mealtime. The masses stolidly accept these daily blessings as though they were automatic and their tables had to be filled morning, noon, and night. This year especially, when we contrast the lavish bounty our country enjoys with the specter of famine facing other nations, there should not be a single household from coast to coast in which grateful voices are not raised to the Almighty in Jesus' name.

Where the Redeemer reigns, prayer is regarded as a high privilege; both parents and children set aside appropriate time daily and regularly to commune with God, to plead for His guidance and His strength. If up to this time you have neglected grace at meals, family worship in general, behold Jesus as He speaks the blessing in that Emmaus cottage, and, asking God to forgive your past negligence, resolve today that yours will be a Christ-dedicated home! If you need help in consecrating your household to the Savior and you want instruction as to how your family can serve God, write us! We will gladly assist you in dedicating your dwelling to the Lord.

In the midst of that memorable evening meal Jesus suddenly permitted Himself to be recognized. The eyes of the two disciples *"were opened, and they knew Him."* What indescribable joy theirs must have been! What inexpressible, almost unbelievable exultation surged within them when they knew that Christ had kept His word, and found that the Savior who on the third day previous had been laid into the grave was now victoriously risen! Gone were all their doubts, vanished every shadow of sadness! The Lord whom their unbelief had mourned as dead was now with them in His resurrection radiance.

Jesus will reveal Himself also to you. If your home is overclouded with selfishness, strife, misery, I am sure that you will find the cause for this unhappiness either in your own unwillingness to accept the Savior fully or in the rejection of His mercies by another member of your family. If sorrow, loss, bereavement, have blighted your household and you remain uncomforted, inconsolable, is this not ultimately to be traced to the fact that you do not fully accept the risen Redeemer's sacred pledges nor permit the balm of His love to heal your wounded heart? Give Him the supremacy in your family circle, enthrone Him as the heavenly Head of your home; and as you worship Him humbly, yet confidently, He will reveal Himself in His full glory, and your eyes will be opened to behold Him as the mighty God with unlimited resources for your help; the all-merciful Savior with pardon for every sin; the un-failing Counselor for parents; the faithful Guide for children; the living Christ who even now waits to welcome us into heavenly glory!

God bless American homes with the faith that beseeches Jesus, the risen Redeemer, *"Abide with us"!* God bless everyone of you with the firm, living trust which constantly prays, "Come, Lord Jesus, and be our Guest"! *"Even so, come, Lord Jesus!"* Amen.

AWAY WITH DOUBT! BELIEVE!

"After eight days again His disciples were within and Thomas with them; then came Jesus, the doors being shut, and stood in the midst and said, Peace be unto you! Then saith He to Thomas, Reach hither thy finger, and behold My hands; and reach hither thy hand, and thrust it into My side; and be not faithless but believing. And Thomas answered and said unto Him, My Lord and my God. Jesus saith unto him, Thomas, because thou hast seen Me, thou hast believed; blessed are they that have not seen and yet have believed." — Saint John 20:26-29.

Blessed Lord Jesus:

As we raise our hearts to thank Thee for Thy manifold mercies: the complete remission of our sins, the assured salvation of our souls, the free gift of grace, Thy love and companionship in every hour of joy or need, we also implore Thee, O Christ of endless compassion: send us the Holy Spirit to remove all doubts concerning Thy redeeming death and Thy life-giving resurrection! Constantly strengthen our trust in Thee! Show us daily that without Thy guidance we are hopelessly lost but that with Thee we are more than conquerors of every enemy that assails our faith! Direct us to find our highest joy and deepest satisfaction in a victorious reliance on Thee, a consecrated career of humble service that seeks to avoid sin! Guard our country against all dangers! Protect our military forces and, Christ, our Lord and God, grant us soon, according to Thy will, an equitable, honorable peace! For the perilous days ahead we need the constant power of Thy love. Bless our land with a far greater reverence for Thee! Hear us, merciful Savior, for our help is in Thee alone! Amen.

"THERE are no atheists in 'fox holes,'" Lieutenant Colonel Warren J. Clear told a Washington audience a few days ago, after his return from the bloody battles on Bataan Peninsula. He revealed that our valiant soldiers there, weeks before they had to surrender, were under constant attack and suffered increasingly from undernourishment and overexertion, yet how trust in God was for many

[377]

the one sustaining force throughout the hopeless struggle. During a particularly heavy air attack, Colonel Clear explained, when it seemed that the whole earth would be blasted to pieces and the roar of bursting bombs was enough to split the ear drums, he and a sergeant sought safety in a "fox hole," a hastily dug small trench for a single soldier. There, without apology or hesitation, both prayed aloud to God, pleading for divine protection. During such overwhelming danger, the Colonel related, when every hope of human help collapses, as you seek shelter in a hole and know that the next moment you may be blown into eternity, all self-confidence, pride, denial of God, or doubt of His Word disappears completely. — Nor would scoffing or atheism be found anywhere on the face of this war-racked world if people only understood how much they need the Lord Jesus Christ and how without Him they will be hopelessly lost during the trials and agonies they may be forced to face.

These thoughts of the future suggest themselves for today, which brings us to the final live broadcast in our current ninth season. By the swift flow of time another six months in our radio ministry are drawing to their close. Between this April Sunday and the October Lord's Day when our mission of the air resumes its work, lie momentous weeks filled with possibilities of blessing or disaster for the nation, our churches, homes, and individual lives. By next fall many of you may be working at different occupations, removed to other parts of the country. You soldiers and sailors, for whose support I am deeply grateful, will probably be in distant sections of the globe. Some will have left this earth for another world. Fortunes will be made or lost; health, regained or sacrificed; life, preserved or destroyed. For the salvation of your soul, the peace of your mind, the joy of your spirit, all doubt concerning Christ must be removed; you must have a firm faith in the Lord Jesus as your own Savior.

Therefore, while the forces of unbelief increase and insolently assail our Christian truth; while the menace of atheistic Communism, the inroads of the Nazi philosophy, grow bolder and even churches put question marks behind the assurance *"Thus saith the Lord,"* I plead in Jesus' name, and in the final appeal of this ninth broadcasting season   AWAY WITH DOUBT! BELIEVE!

May today's message, blessed by the Holy Spirit's power, drive every uncertainty from your souls, draw you closer to the Christ of all compassion and to the strengthening comfort of our text (Saint John, chapter twenty, verses twenty-six to twenty-nine): *"After eight days again His disciples were within and Thomas with them; then came Jesus, the doors being shut, and stood in the midst and said, Peace be unto you! Then saith He to Thomas, Reach hither thy finger, and behold My hands; and reach hither thy hand, and thrust it into My side; and be not faithless but believing. And Thomas answered and said unto Him, My Lord and my God. Jesus saith unto him, Thomas, because thou hast seen Me, thou hast believed; blessed are they that have not seen and yet have believed."*

I

JESUS REJECTS THE "PROVE IT" SPIRIT OF UNBELIEF

When the risen Savior first appeared to His followers at their secret meeting place, Thomas was missing. Was he away on business? Had he begun to doubt the power and blessing of fellowship with believers? Was he so completely bowed down by the weight of his Lord's crucifixion that he shunned the company of the other disciples to brood alone over this crushing loss? We find no answer; but we do know that, if Thomas had met with them on that first Easter, he would have had no reason to doubt. He would have seen Jesus Himself on the very day of His resurrection.

Similarly many of you lack the assurance of faith because you keep away from your fellow believers and shun the worship in a true Christian congregation. You may hold a grudge against the Church; you may have listened to some preacher who never even quoted the Bible, left your problems entirely untouched, and made you feel worse after he had finished than you felt before he started. Perhaps someone unknowingly hurt your feelings at a ladies' aid supper. You may have received the impression, with all the costly cathedrals and high-steepled structures, that the churches are against the poor and the working classes. Perhaps you have listened to scoffers who claimed that the churches exist simply to coax money from credulous followers. Whatever the reason is, you no longer attend the house of God regularly; and although you think you can get along without the Church, you are cutting your soul off from a vital source of spiritual strength. Just as Thomas missed Jesus because he was absent, so by your absence from the house of God you have lost powerful, precious opportunities to meet the Savior. Join a Scripturally sound, loyal, Christ-blessed church! Let me help you find one where you can stand shoulder to shoulder with those who love the Lord Jesus in the unity which acknowledges *"one Lord, one faith, one Baptism, one God and Father of all, who is above all and through all and in you all."*

It is the great mercy of Jesus, however, that often He seeks us when we do not seek Him. Thomas missed Christ at the resurrected Redeemer's first appearance among the disciples, but he was to have another chance. Seven days

later the risen Savior returns for one particular purpose —
to find the disciple whom He had previously sought in vain.
Jesus could have said: "Well, Thomas should have been
with the other disciples and learned that what I told them
of My resurrection is true. Now I am through with him;
it is his own fault." But our blessed Savior, as a rule, does
not stop with a single invitation. He has been calling some
of you for years, appealing to you personally through each
of these messages; yet you have not come all the way to
Christ. Don't delay another day! We cannot tell what
might have befallen Thomas had he been absent on that
second Sunday evening when Jesus returned; and neither
can we tell what will happen to you if, as our chain broadcasting stops for the summer months, you still refuse to
accept the Lord as your own personal Deliverer. Who
can give any guarantee that this may not be the last time
in which the promise will be offered you, *"Believe on the
Lord Jesus Christ, and thou shalt be saved, and thy house"*;
the last time you will ever be told that the nail-scarred
hands of the Lord Jesus are raised to welcome you into the
joy of pardon and heavenly peace? How terrifying beyond
all words and understanding if you should spurn this final
plea! There is no excuse in the claim that you never heard
of Jesus, for every sermon I have preached has emphasized
what I now repeat, namely, that a sinner is washed,
cleansed of sin, ransomed, redeemed, saved for eternity
only by faith in the Savior's atoning death and life-giving
resurrection. You cannot say that you were not warned,
for I tell you in this solemn moment, *"He that believeth
not shall be damned"*; and these are the words of Christ,
our God, Himself. Do not repeat what a man told me on
the Pacific Coast last Sunday! He walked over twenty
miles to attend our meeting in the Santa Ana Bowl; and
as the tears rolled down his face, he said that no one had

ever asked him personally to accept the Lord as his Savior. For now I ask all of you individually to receive Jesus, acclaim Him your Savior, crown Him your King, love Him with all your heart, soul, and might. In this broadcast Jesus approaches you, as once after His resurrection He drew near Thomas. God grant that you will come to Him in contrite faith!

When the Savior came to help disappointed Thomas, He found the disciples once more behind locked doors. Although they had seen the risen Savior, they were still gripped by the dread of persecution and, as a measure of safety, kept their doors tightly bolted. Such fear is a destructive, devastating force, as many of you know. Anxiety for health, money, reputation; dread that your sins will be disclosed and you must pay their horrifying consequences — all this is keeping you locked behind your own horrors, the shackled slaves of distrust. Much of the restlessness, nervous breakdowns, lined faces, whitened hair, the hunted, haunted look in many eyes, comes from the tragedy that misguided men shut themselves in with their fears.

Yet in Heaven's glorious truth the same Jesus who time after time greeted His timid disciples with the calm assurance *"Fear not!"* the same Savior who by the miracle of His resurrection body could pass through the closed doors, can help you, burdened as you are by disquieting thoughts. And once Christ, Lord of love, Friend of the friendless, the Helper of the distressed and forsaken, is yours, no bolts or barriers that men have ever made can keep Him away if you ask Him to bless your heart and home with His presence.

Jesus had hardly entered through those closed doors when, over the hush that quickly fell on His amazed followers, He spoke these clear, comforting words, *"Peace be*

unto you!" Oh, how sorely everyone of us needs the benediction of the Savior's peace on his disquieted soul! Too
often people look for rest and relief in money, pleasure,
learning, feverish activity, even alcohol, narcotics, though
this usually tends to increase distress. The one hope men
can have for a tranquil life, untroubled by worry and
gnawing care, is given by the Bible's pledge *"Being justified by faith, we have peace with God through our Lord
Jesus Christ."* That inner peace, as it spreads from heart
to heart and life to life throughout the world, can help
check war and promote concord among nations. If only
the Christ who greeted His awe-stricken followers with the
wish *"Peace be unto you!"* would rule the hearts of those
responsible for this world conflict and stifle every program
of conquest and aggression, the lust for blood and love of
war profits, so that the nations could work together
harmoniously in a world with room and resources enough
for a population several times as large as the present! The
living Savior has the power to break the bow and cut the
spear in sunder; and if it be His will, He can show this
power by making a sudden end to these hostilities and
granting a righteous victory. Oh, turn to Christ now and
learn that, because He has taken away our sins, restored us
to our heavenly Father, *"He is,"* as the Scriptures pledge,
"our Peace," Peace of soul, Peace of mind — our Peace in
a world at war!

Jesus had entered through that shut portal to greet all
the disciples, but He had come especially for Thomas.
The great and good Shepherd of His flock, who leaves the
ninety and nine to go and seek the one stray lamb until
He finds it, was concerned not in the first instance about
those who had met Him a week before. His special love
goes out to that doubting, really disbelieving disciple, just
as this broadcast, while directed to the masses from coast

to coast, from Canada beyond the Rio Grande, wings its way especially to you for whose faith and trust Jesus pleaded again and again. Singling Thomas out of the entire company, our Lord addresses him personally and says, *"Reach hither thy finger and behold My hands, and reach hither thy hand and thrust it into My side."* How those words must have cut into the bewildered disciple's soul. They were the echo of his unbelief, *"Except I see in His hands the print of the nails and put my finger into the print of the nails and thrust my hand into His side, I will not believe."* Suddenly it must have dawned on his questioning mind that Jesus had heard every syllable of his doubt — just as He listens to every word from your lips, knows each unspoken thought. We should learn to say not only, *"Thou, God, seest me,"* but also, *"Thou, God, knowest the thoughts of my heart."*

Particularly, however, should we avoid the proud, haughty spirit by which a man like Thomas sought to dictate the terms on which he would either accept or reject the Lord. What right had he, or what right has any man, to say when, why, how, he will receive his Savior? And how utterly absurd, yet how completely modern, is this spirit of Thomas, whom we called the "doubting disciple" but who in reality was the disbelieving disciple! He demands in effect: "Prove that Christ rose from the dead! Let me see the wounds in His hands and side to be sure they are real! Let me put my fingers into the marks of the nails and the spear!" He would not admit the Easter truth unless he could see and feel; yet even as he spoke, he accepted a hundred mysteries in his own body, in the world about him, on the ground beneath, in the sky above, although he could not see or feel the forces behind them. Mark you, Thomas did not say, for instance, "Unless I see the power that drives the wind, put my hand on its mechanism, I will not believe that there is a wind"; or, "Unless I behold the blood coursing through my members and put my finger on the impulse which circulates this vital fluid, I will not believe that blood is being driven through my body"; or, "Unless I see the elements that make up the water I drink, measure the hydrogen and the oxygen, I will not believe that water is compounded as it is!" He did not say: "Unless I feel the principle of life, I will not believe that there are living beings. Unless I touch the mysterious power that makes a tree spread and enlarge, I will deny that it grows." But, like many of you, he insisted on placing human reason above divine revelation. While you cannot explain or prove the commonplace experiences of the nature surrounding you, the life you live, the world in which you exist, you demand proof positive for the things of the spirit which no human eye can see and no natural intellect understand.

This defiant doubt and proud denial rules much of our world today. It is found in high schools, when teachers deliberately go out of their way in holding up God's Word to derision, and sneer, "Does anyone still believe the Bible?" The same we-don't-believe-it-because-you-can't-prove-it spirit holds sway in many colleges and universities, even — we say this with especial regret — in schools founded by churches. A few days ago a student at a Minnesota college which was established and supported by Christians wrote me: "My biology professor is an atheist and an evolutionist. My English teacher tells us that the Bible is merely a book of old literature, most of it legend. Thank God, I was reared in a Christian home, and my faith cannot be moved. But I have seen students come here in faith and leave for home evolutionists and doubters." If even church schools thus reject divine truth, what can we expect of colleges where Christian influence is ruled out from the very start?

Today parents have a great responsibility and, correspondingly, a decided difficulty in choosing a school for their children where faith in God, in the Bible, in Christ, will not be systematically assaulted. Now that graduation approaches and this issue is put squarely before many of you, I am glad again to offer you my counsel in selecting a college for your son or daughter which will help build faith instead of destroying it.

If you ever feel, as Thomas did, that you want proof before you believe — and moments of doubt can come upon the most firmly rooted in the faith — then remember how unhesitatingly some of the mightiest minds have welcomed Christ in faith, instead of demanding proof. William Kitchen Parker, anatomical authority, asserted: "All through these fifty years the joy of the Lord has been my strength and . . . the four Gospels . . . have been the strength of my life. They have lifted up my mind." Alexander McAllister, physiologist at Cambridge University, declared: "It has been my experience that disbelief in the . . . death and resurrection of our Savior is more prevalent among what I may call the camp followers of science than among those to whom actual scientific work is the business of their lives." Admiral Alfred T. Mahan, American naval expert, stated publicly: "I assure you with the full force of the conviction of a lifetime that to one who has understood the Word of God, even imperfectly, it brings a light, a motive, a strength and support which nothing else does." Dr. Howard A. Kelly, internationally recognized gynecologist, gives this confession of faith: "I believe Jesus Christ to be the Son of God, without human father, conceived by the Holy Spirit, born of the Virgin Mary. I believe that all men, without exception, are lost sinners, alienated from God and thus utterly lost in sin. The Son of God Himself came down from heaven and by shedding His blood on the cross paid the infinite penalty of the guilt of the whole world." Jean Henri Fabre, widely honored French entomologist, daily spoke the prayer of the dying Savior, *"Father, into Thy hands I commend my spirit."* Louis Pasteur, French chemist, to whose life-saving work tribute has been paid by every civilized government in the world, when questioned concerning his creed, did not insist on visible, tangible proof, but admitted: "The more I know, the more does my faith approach that of a Breton peasant. Could I know all, I would have the faith of a Breton peasant woman" — and the Breton peasants were proverbial for their childlike trust. Sir William Dawson, world-renowned geologist, told a questioner: "I know nothing about the origin of a man except what is stated in the Scriptures, that God created him. I do not know anything more than that, and I do not know anyone who does." Sir William Abney, former president of the Royal Astronomical Society, authority on the photography of the heavens, exclaimed: "The doctrine of salvation is not and cannot be learned from science. It is a matter of faith. . . . The mystery of the atonement is no greater mystery than many other matters which we cannot explain." Sir David Brewster, a prominent founder of the British Association for the Advancement of Science, said that he clearly recognized the love of Christ in his own life and added, "It is presumptuous to doubt His Word." — These and scores of other leaders in scientific research accepted the Scriptures without demanding proof. Now, who in this wide audience would venture to say that he knows more than these experts? — God grant, having now heard the living Christ say to Thomas, *"Be not faithless but believing!"* you will feel His displeasure at the skeptical insistence on proof and cry out in faith, "Away with doubt!"

II

JESUS PLEADS FOR THE "BELIEVE IT" SPIRIT OF TRUST

It seems that, after Jesus had rebuked Thomas for his distrust and appealed for full faith, the amazed disciple learned the lesson of complete reliance on the Savior's promise. When he sees Christ, he forgets his skeptical insistence on examination; he does not critically touch each of the Savior's five wounds. Convinced that Jesus has returned to life, he disavows doubt, and all that he can do, with penitent regret for his unbelief, but with marvelous assurance of the Savior's presence, is to gasp, *"My Lord and my God!"*

Only five words; yet what a world of spiritual truth they contain! They proclaim that Jesus is more than a man, more than a great leader, more than an unparalleled preacher, more than a prophet sent from heaven. He is the almighty God who has proved His divine power by defeating death and overcoming the grave. Only God could have heard the familiar words which came from Thomas' lips and marvelously removed all rejection of divine truth. Note, too, that this repentant, convinced disciple calls Jesus not only *"Lord"* and *"God,"* but, *"My Lord and my God!"* There is in his confession of faith a personal, individual, intimate ring which shows how completely Christ has taken possession of Thomas' heart, soul, and mind.

My fellow redeemed, I pause to ask whether you have that faith. Can you say, not only, "We believe, we in our church, we in our Bible class, we in our Sunday school, we in our home," but also, "I myself, convinced of my own sin, yet trusting in the Savior's greater grace for me, believe that Jesus is *'my Lord and my God'* "? Recently in St. Louis a man who thirteen years ago enlisted in the

United States Army only to desert, visited our Soldiers'
and Sailors' Memorial. When he stood in that building
erected to the heroism and the devotion of those who have
laid down their lives in the nation's defense, he was struck
by his own faithlessness and surrendered himself to the
authorities. Some of you who once enlisted your souls
for Christ but who forsook your Lord and joined with
His enemies, have now stood with us under His cross to
hear that He died for you and was raised from the dead
to give you life. May you, as your gaze centers on the
Christ of the pierced hands, the wounded feet, the riven
side, cry out: "Away with doubt! This Jesus is *'my Lord
and my God!'* "

That was a glorious day for Thomas. But believe
Jesus when He promises that your blessing can be even
greater! Before our Lord leaves He tells His repentant, re-
assured disciple, *"Thomas, because thou hast seen Me
thou hast believed; blessed are they that have not seen
and yet have believed."* What a remarkable pledge!
It guarantees that the worst sinners, the poorest, most un-
learned, least noticed, hardest burdened, can receive an
even greater blessing than that showered on Thomas if
with childlike trust they welcome the Lord Jesus Christ as
their God and Savior — even though on earth they never
have the privilege of beholding Him in His glorious
resurrection body. Nothing else in life really counts besides
this spiritual firmness which exults: "Away with doubt!
I believe!"

The Savior declares, *"Blessed are they that have not
seen and yet have believed!"* And who can describe the
rich blessings of unquestioning faith: joy in your soul over
your completed, pledged salvation; happiness in your heart
because you know that you are Christ's and that nothing
can happen to you without His knowledge and His love;

rejoicing in your mind because your place in the celestial mansions has been secured and prepared for you through all eternity by the Savior's grace; contentment in life since you are persuaded that *"all things work together for good to them that love God";* an eagerness to follow in the Savior's footsteps by serving needy men and spreading the message of mercy; divine guidance for the clouded pathways during these turbulent years of war and distress; a calm acceptance of death and an eagerness for heaven — these and many other benedictions are the gifts that Jesus includes when He says, *"Blessed are they that have not seen and yet have believed!"* Come, then, meet Christ in His Word and ordinances, study His Gospel for yourself and with your family, constantly approach Him in prayer, plead with His Spirit for light and understanding, for strength to resist temptation, for wisdom to overcome doubt, for humility instead of haughty insistence on proof; and in His name I promise that, though you will never be entirely free from the onslaughts of unbelief, though hell itself will work with intensified opposition to tear you from the faith, yet, as long as you penitently turn to Jesus and confidently accept His living presence in your life, this conviction will give you blessing, victory and glory!

For such trust in many of your lives I thank God on this last broadcast of our ninth season; because your faith, prayers, interest, gifts, and the prompting love of Christ have not only supported our mission of the air during all these years, but have also helped to make the last season by far the most blessed and spiritually successful of all. It has been the good pleasure of God, to whom we ascribe all glory, that during the past months we have been able to broadcast over almost 350 stations in the United States and twenty-five foreign countries. During the last six months about a quarter of a million people have written us. Your financial support has been more generous than ever, your interest greater, and — above all — the number of souls won for Christ, we pray, much larger. Someone has figured that for every minute of these messages a sinner has been reclaimed for his Savior. There have been difficulties, of course; I have been attacked and slandered, just as our preaching of salvation in Christ alone has been repeatedly opposed. The wonder of it all is that there have not been more assaults and more treachery during this spiritually darkened age. But you have been praying fervently for the broadcast, and your petitions have helped restrain atheism and unbelief. For everything you, my co-workers and my fellow redeemed, have done to help make the past season, under God, such a signal blessing, I say to you in behalf of millions who have worshiped Christ with us every week: "Thank you! God bless you!"

In the fall, God willing, we begin our tenth-anniversary season; and even now we are weighing plans which will make the coming broadcast the mightiest network a radio system has ever employed, with many more stations in the United States and in a far larger number of foreign countries.

But all this is only the beginning. If you believe with us that Jesus Christ is the one Hope of a sin-cursed world; if you want this broadcast, conducted for no personal profit, to take the message of the cross and the open grave even farther into this cold, dark world; if you want this Bringing-Christ-to-the-Nations mission of the air to be an all-year-round testimony to our Savior, stand at our side to hold up our arms through your intercessions, your testimony, your contributions, until our goal is reached!

With a song of thanksgiving in my heart for your love, with the plea that those still without the faith may be brought to Christ and those loyal to Jesus may be preserved in their allegiance, I now commend you in prayer to the grace of our Lord.

O Jesus, watch over every immortal soul in the vast reaches of this radio mission! Call careless sinners to repentance, supplant doubt with faith, comfort the sorrowing, strengthen the weak, receive the dying! But, O Jesus, our Lord and our God, our Savior and our Redeemer, bring us all, of all races, colors, and kindreds, who love Thee as the only Savior, together before Thy throne in eternity! God the Father, who hast created us; God the Son, who didst redeem us with Thy holy blood; God the Holy Spirit, who hast enlightened and sustained us, preserve and keep us! — O Triune God, be with us until we meet again in Thy name, to Thy glory, for the saving of lost souls and the testimony to Thine eternal truth! Amen! *"The grace of our Lord Jesus Christ be with you all!"* Amen!